ROUNDHEAD GENERAL

The Right Valiant and
Expert Commander S.
William Waller K. &c:

W. Riddiard Excudit

A contemporary print showing Sir William Waller at the height of his fame during the
English Civil War.

ROUNDHEAD GENERAL

The Campaigns of
Sir William Waller

John Adair

SUTTON PUBLISHING

First published in 1997 by
Sutton Publishing Limited · Phoenix Mill
Thrupp · Stroud · Gloucestershire · GL5 2BU

British Library Cataloguing in Publication Data

A catalogue record for this book is available from the British Library

ISBN 0 7509 1312 6

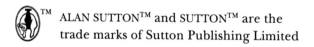

ALAN SUTTON™ and SUTTON™ are the
trade marks of Sutton Publishing Limited

Typeset in 10/13pt New Baskerville.
Typesetting and origination by
Sutton Publishing Limited.
Printed in Great Britain by
Hartnolls, Bodmin, Cornwall.

Contents

Acknowledgements   vi
List of Maps   vii
List of Plates   vii
Preface   ix

Part One: *A Brave Little Spark*

1	Early Life	3
2	My Little World	11
3	This War Without an Enemy	21
4	First Success: The Siege of Portsmouth	31
5	William the Conqueror	38

Part Two: *General of the West*

6	The Night Owl	51
7	Western Successes	57
8	Hereford Taken	67
9	Worcester Attempted	71
10	Preparations for Battle	75
11	Victory at Lansdown	80
12	My Dismal Defeat at Roundway Down	87

Part Three: *London's General*

13	A Warm Welcome	101
14	How the West was Lost	108
15	Raising a New Army	116

Part Four: *General in the South*

16	A Fling at Basing House	127
17	Deliverance at Farnham	137
18	The Storming of Alton	141
19	The Siege of Arundel	147
20	A Great Victory at Cheriton	154

Part Five: *A Fading Star*

21	To Oxford	175
22	A Dance in the Midlands	181
23	My Dishonourable Blow at Cropredy Bridge	189
24	Facing Westwards	201
25	The Second Battle of Newbury	211
26	Missed Opportunities	217
27	Hopeless Employment into the West	223
28	Laid Aside Like a Broken Vessel	234

Part Six: *Triumph of a Moderate*

29	The Road to Exile	241
30	Three Years in Captivity	250
31	So Ensnaring a Time	257
32	The Restoration	262
33	A Clear Evening	267
	Notes and References	275
	Bibliography	298
	Index	307

Acknowledgements

The author would like to thank Dr Ian Roy and Dr John Wroughton for their help in revising the original text and preparing it for this new edition. Grateful thanks also go to Stephen Beck for the use of his line drawings and Mike Komarnyckyj of Aardvark Illustration for the maps that appear in the book.

The author would also like to acknowledge Sarah Bragginton and Jane Crompton at Sutton Publishing and thank them for their help and encouragement throughout.

List of Maps

 1 Southern England at the time of the Civil War   12
 2 Western England at the time of the Civil War   28
 3 The Lansdown campaign   76
 4 The battle of Lansdown, 5 July 1643   82
 5 Central England at the time of the Civil War   88
 6 The battle of Roundway Down, 13 July 1643   92
 7 South-western England at the time of the Civil War   102
 8 The Cheriton campaign   155
 9 The battle of Cheriton, 29 March 1644   162
10 The battle of Cropredy Bridge, 29 June 1644   192
11 The second battle of Newbury, 27 October 1644   214

List of Plates

Between pages 150 and 151

1 Sir William Waller. (National Portrait Gallery)
2 Lady Anne Waller, his second wife. (Courtauld Institute of Art)
3 A contemporary engraving of Sir William Waller when he was at the height of his fame in 1643.
4 Robert, Earl of Essex, Captain-General of the Parliamentary forces. (British Museum)
5 Sir Arthur Heselrige, Waller's Lieutenant-General of Horse, 1643/4. (Lord Hazelrigge's Collection)
6 Colonel Nathaniel Fiennes, Govenor of Bristol. (Lord Saye & Sele)
7 Patrick Ruthven, Earl of Forth. Waller's opponent at Cheriton. (The Bodleian Library, Oxford)
8 Lord Ralph Hopton, King's General in the West and Waller's chief opponent. (Petworth House, The Egremont Collection (The National Trust): photograph, Courtauld Institute of Art)
9 Sir William Waller's letters written to Royalists in June 1643, mainly concerning exchanges of prisoners. The page includes the only draft in his own hand of his famous letter to Lord Ralph Hopton. (The Bodleian Library, Oxford. MS. Clarendon 22, fol. 113r)

Preface

In the midst of the English Civil War, after the capture of Arundel Castle, an anonymous poet in London presented Lady Anne Waller with some laudatory verses on her husband. They concluded on a prophetic note:

> Methinks, I already read that large page
> Of Chronicle, in the ensuing Age,
> Which shall contain his Name, unless that he
> Go on so far, it must a Volume be:
> Then, as I turn the leaves, perhaps, I finde
> Some lofty strain to speak his gallant minde
> And tell our after-nephews part of all
> That made him up a perfect Generall.

In fact, as his later career revealed, Sir William Waller was far from being 'a perfect Generall'. But he was a very good one, probably the best on Parliament's side during the early part of the conflict he would call – in some immortal words – 'this war without an enemy'.

Waller's bold and imaginative exploits as a soldier fill many pages in this book. They won him the respect and sometimes the admiration of his opponents. His ability to choose and shift his ground, for example, are 'great abilities in a soldier', wrote one such Royalist officer. As for his distinctive use of night to cover his swift marches, that earned him among the Cavaliers the nickname of the 'Night Owl'. On the Parliamentarian side, Waller's early string of successes in the first year of the Civil War won him the popular sobriquet 'William the Conqueror'. Gradually he lost that reputation for victory as the war proceeded. But when the forces at Waller's disposal are taken into account, his failures became more explicable. As he himself said, 'Possibly I might have made more bricks if I had more straw.'

Waller's contribution to the political story of the middle years of the seventeenth century is often eclipsed by his brilliant career as a soldier. Yet he was first a Member of Parliament, and only secondly a general of Parliament. Unlike Oliver Cromwell, Sir William never suffered from a confusion of loyalties in that respect. As a soldier, he was distinguished by his vigour in prosecuting the war. But this single-minded enthusiasm in the field was balanced by political moderation. Waller's vision was not of some revolution, but essentially one of restoration: a free parliament, a king who exercised his prerogatives wisely under the law, and a nation with true liberty under God.

In his long struggle against despotism – first King Charles I and then the Army – Sir William would suffer much. We shall see him forced into exile, and then, on his return, imprisoned by Cromwell for three years without trial. Yet it was *his* vision – not Cromwell's – that triumphed in the end. He would live to see history vindicate him. Moreover, as these pages record, Waller did much more than hitherto has been supposed to help history take the course that it did.

The London poet spoke of Waller's 'gallant minde'. I must confess that it was as much Waller's nobility of character, gaiety of spirit, chivalry to women, kindness to all and an unfailing sense of humour – all disproofs of any lingering stereotype of what a Puritan might be – that attracted me to Sir William. It was his character that gives enduring interest to his colourful military and political career. There is more than a touch of romance about him. What other Parliamentarian general in the Civil War received a loving letter from a Cavalier lady in a pause during a battle, begging him to change sides? Who else could reply that 'as I was never traitor to my love, so I would not be to my cause'? I hope that my affection for Sir William as a person, however, has not blinded me to his faults and imperfections as a soldier, politician or as a man. As far as possible, I have let him tell his own story.

What did Waller (his name was most probably pronounced with a long first vowel, as in *wall*) look like? The fine painting of him, reproduced on the cover and later in this book, was probably painted by Robert Walker. It shows him aged between forty-three and forty-five years and dressed in black armour, his white collar tied by a black bow. Thinning brown hair falls almost to his shoulders, and he wears a sparse moustache turning slightly upwards at the corners and a pointed beard. The nose is prominent; his blue-grey eyes and firm well-shaped mouth give him a commanding look. Waller was short in height. One letter-writer in 1644 called him 'a brave little spark' and it is a description that serves him well.

PART ONE
A Brave Little Spark

CHAPTER ONE

Early Life

'In my infancy, when I lay in my cradle, I escaped a great danger, upon the casual discharge of a piece, the shot whereof missed me very narrowly.'[1] Born at Knole House in Kent and baptised on 3 December 1598, William came under fire in this way for the first time five years later at Dover Castle, where his father resided as Deputy Lieutenant. The child owed his first sights and sounds to this martial environment: long grey walls above green fields and white cliffs, garrison musters, the boom of great cannon, and the urgent tapping of the drum.[2]

As a boy William explored this exciting new world to the full. His *Experiences*, written in middle age in praise of Providence, contain two incidents from these days, which suggest an adventurous spirit. One describes a rescue from drowning in a pond, the other a narrow escape from the hooves of his own horse: 'When I was about nine or ten years old I had a great deliverance from a fall from my horse, my foot hanging in the stirrup, I was dragged a great way by him, and struck at several times, and yet the Lord be praised, I had little or no hurt.'[3] No doubt these episodes distilled a certain amount of caution in the boy's reflective mind, but never enough to dampen completely his natural boldness.

In his youth William would have learnt the story of his family. His father, Sir Thomas, could trace descent from Alured de Waller, a twelfth-century knight of Norman origin, whose device of 'three walnut-leaves or between two bandlets argent' adorned the family escutcheon. Early in the fifteenth century the senior branch of his descendants had settled at Groombridge in Kent. One of these Kentish Wallers achieved more than local celebrity by capturing Charles, Duc d'Orléans (father of Louis XII of France) on the field of Agincourt in 1415. This champion, Sir Richard Waller, entertained the royal prisoner, a noted poet, at his seat at Groombridge for several years, and it was said that he largely rebuilt the house from the ransom. The family crest, a shield hanging in a walnut tree with the arms of the Duke (a fleur de lys), and the motto, *Hic fructus virtutis*, commemorated this lucrative success.[4] The walnut tree was a pun on the family name.

The law of primogeniture compelled Richard's younger grandsons to seek their fortunes outside their native country. In William's youth and early manhood the longest established of their progeny could be found at Oldstoke in Hampshire, and the most celebrated of them at Beaconsfield.

The head of the Hampshire Wallers, a namesake of William's, fathered two daughters who later married prominent Royalist opponents of their distant cousin. Edmund Waller, the poet, born at Beaconsfield in 1606, fared worse in the King's cause and would have lost his head had not William pleaded before the House of Commons for him.

William's grandfather died in 1595, leaving Groombridge to his eldest son, Sir George, father of Hardress Waller. But Sir Thomas continued to live in Kent, where he had secured the favour of a gentleman with considerable influence in the county, Lord Henry Howard, later Earl of Northampton. Sir Thomas attended him on several occasions, and received preferment in local government. In 1600, for example, he was a member of a commission appointed to make the Medway navigable beyond Tonbridge. Three years later he became deputy to the Lieutenant of Dover Castle and the Cinque Ports. When the Earl of Northampton became the Lord Warden of the Cinque Ports in 1604 'he replaced (upon hearing and arguing before him) Sir Thomas Fane in the Lieutenancy with Sir Thomas Waller'. Election to Parliament as one of the members for Dover followed shortly afterwards, and Waller's position in the county had become substantial.

Sir Thomas never forgot his debt to Northampton, and in his will he bequeathed to his 'dear and most honoured Lord' a diamond worth £40 on account of 'that great duty and zealous affection I owe his Lordship'.[5]

Northampton may have been instrumental also in securing for Sir Thomas the reversion, after his mother's death, of the grant of 'prisage and butlerage' of all wines, except in Wales, Cornwall or the Palatine Earldom of Chester.[6] In his will Sir Thomas described himself as 'Chief Butler of England and Wales', but he may not have enjoyed the revenues of the grant until 1611. An even greater noble, Thomas Sackville, the first Earl of Dorset and Lord Treasurer of England, probably bartered his influence in this matter. Sir Thomas in his will stipulated that an annuity of 500 marks from the profits of 'prisage' – the ancient duty levied on imported wine – should continue to be paid to the Lord Treasurer for life, and also (presumably on the death of Sir George) he sold him the ancestral home at Groombridge. As the Earl of Dorset died before the will of Sir Thomas could be proved, this life annuity did not burden the Waller family for long.

The scant surviving correspondence and official records of Sir Thomas Waller reveal him as a diligent civil servant, highly esteemed by his colleagues in the local government of Kent. He was not devoid of a sense of humour: in one letter to his close friend, Sir Francis Fane, who held a high position in Northampton's household, he could refer to Dover pier as 'his Lordship's darling and An Ornament of the State'. Even allowing for conventional wording the preamble to Sir Thomas' will suggests that he was a man of religious conviction, charitable enough to leave £20 to the poor of Dover.

Sir Thomas married Margaret, daughter of Sampson Lennard, Esquire, whose family lived in Knole House, at least until the Earl of Dorset bought it in 1604. Lady Margaret bore her husband another son called Walter, a daughter with the odd name of Fenes, and possibly some more children who died in infancy. She lived to a ripe old age much honoured by William.

There was no good school in Dover and William probably received his early education from a tutor. On the day he should have set out from home to enter the University at Oxford, he contracted pleurisy, but he matriculated as a member of Magdalen Hall on 2 December 1612. The Earl of Dorset is reputed to have been at Hart Hall for a short time, and this may be the reason why William transferred there shortly after his matriculation, to remain in that college until the end of his university days.[7]

It may be assumed that William gained no less from Oxford than his contemporaries there, who were mostly sons of the wealthy gentry and the nobility. Although the curriculum still centred on rhetoric, logic and the classical texts, some college fellows were already teaching the humanities to their pupils. Nor would William's intellectual appetite be restricted to a diet of lectures: the Bodleian Library had been reshelved at the end of Elizabeth's reign, and stood open to undergraduates. William's love of reading and reflection remained with him through life. His later writings, especially his *Vindication*, included numerous references to Homer, Plato, Virgil and Tacitus, as well as contemporary writers. William's tutors may have fathered the style and methods of his *Vindication*, written in the years after the Civil War, but it was the university as a whole that gave him that broad social and intellectual education which shaped his mind.

William left Oxford without taking his degree, but this was not unusual for the son of a well-to-do gentleman. No evidence of how he spent his study or leisure hours has survived, although it may be deduced from his later writings that he received a good grounding in the classics. Contemporaries frequently alleged that many undergraduates passed their days in whoring and playing football, idleness and dissipation. Oliver Cromwell, four months younger than William, did not escape such accusations about his time at Sidney Sussex College in Cambridge as a seventeen-year-old undergraduate. William went up to Oxford somewhat younger than the average, being only just fourteen years old when he matriculated, a tender age for some of the illicit pleasures to be found in Oxford even if William inclined towards them, which is unlikely.

In July 1613 Sir Thomas Waller died. In his will he left to his wife the manor of Barnes at Brenchley in Kent, and a third of the 'prisage' rents and profits until William attained his majority. The other two-thirds he allocated for the support of William and the younger children, with the exception of Walter, who received a life annuity of £140. Sir Thomas made careful provision that the total income from 'prisage' reverted to William upon his twenty-first birthday. That third portion allotted to the younger children would lapse to him as soon as each child had received £2,000, a handsome dowry for Fenes. Upon his birthday William would also inherit the office of Chief Butler, which was put in trust for him until that time.

After coming down from Oxford, William succumbed to smallpox, and only the timely arrival of Sir William Paddy, King James I's doctor, 'prevented the administering of some physic to me which in that disease would have proved mortal'. As soon as William had regained his health he left England to travel upon the Continent. A Paris academy taught him the art of fencing and the management of the great war horse, both necessary social accomplishments of a gentleman.[8]

It is a sign of the comparative wealth of Waller's family that they could afford to send him not only to France but to Italy as well, for the cost of an Italian tour for a young gentleman has been estimated at about £1,000 a year. Not always could the money be counted as well spent. Often young men preferred the pursuit of pleasure to serious studies watched over by an attendant tutor, and sometimes they sank into debauchery. Others of a more serious turn of mind, among whom we may safely number William Waller, availed themselves to the full of the opportunity to study the architecture and language of Italy. Venice and Padua were the favourite stopping-places. A visit to Rome was less customary owing to the persistent proselytising of Roman Catholic priests. Indeed, the Roman Catholic Church, no less than the robbers and brigands which infested Italy and the natural hazards of travel, constituted one of the dangers which made a *Giro Italia* such an adventure for a young Protestant Englishman.

These contemporary hazards are well illustrated by incidents recorded by William Waller in his *Experiences*. In Padua, for example, he very narrowly escaped an epidemic of burning fever, while near Gradisca in Friuli an overcrowded boat ferrying him across the River Isonzo began to sink: 'I was fain to leap out, and falling short of the bank, I had been carried away by that swift stream, but that I caught hold of a bough of a tree, which supported me, till I was helped out.' At Bologna, on the way from Venice to Florence, a priest, who had travelled with him in the same party, informed against him to the Inquisition. What remarks stirred the wrath of the priest are not known, but they may have been Protestant sentiments mild enough in England but dangerous in Italy. 'I was searched, my trunk, wherein I had nothing but clothes, was rifled to the bottom, but it pleased God to so order it, that they let alone a box, wherein I had some papers, which might have exposed me to question; when they had it in their hands ready to open it.'[9]

Instead of hurrying home, William entered the service of Venice as a gentleman volunteer. At that time the Republic of Venice stood at war with Archduke Ferdinand of Austria upon her northern borders, and gratefully accepted the assistance of English gentlemen and mercenaries. In 1618, for example, Sir Edward Peyton commanded a regiment of 500 English foot under the Doge's flag, and William may have served under this veteran of the Dutch wars. He saw professional soldiers at work in at least one siege, for he wrote: 'at the leaguer before Rubia, I escaped several very near shot; one grazing at my foot, another lighting between Sir John Vere and me, as we sat close together by the battery, and yet touched neither of us, besides divers others both great and small shot that endangered me.' Sir John, born an illegitimate son, had fought in the Low Countries with some success under the kindly eye of his celebrated uncle, Sir Horace Vere, and could teach much about the profession of arms to his young companion. At this time, the spring of 1617, Vere commanded a company of Dutch soldiers under Count Henry of Nassau.[10]

Waller's visit to Italy and brief spell of soldiering make a considerable impression upon him. He learnt at least some Italian during his stay, and some thirty years later he seriously considered entering the armies of the Doge as a mercenary general. His love of fine furniture may well have been engendered in the elegant interiors of Venetian palazzos. Certainly, William would possess in later life a sense of proportion and a breath of tolerance denied to many a land-locked soul in Stuart England.

William returned to England in time for his coming of age. Apart from the Waller's annuity and several small legacies in his father's will, he now enjoyed the rent of 'prisage' after an annual sum of £500 had been paid to the Crown. The lessee of 'prisage' could take one tun of wine from every imported shipment of ten to twenty tuns, and two from larger cargoes landed at Bristol and the ports in the Bristol Channel. In 1606 Sir Thomas or his mother had sublet the right for thirty-eight years to a syndicate of merchants. From them he received £110 a year, and a tax of £6 or £4 on a barrel taken, depending upon the quality of the wine. As a tun of claret in 1624 could fetch £25 and 'Canary, Madeira, Malaga, Sack, Coniack or Sherant' sold for £14, these 'prisage masters' made a handsome profit, even after they had paid customs duty.[11]

The revenue from 'prisage' would give Waller a handsome annual income which cannot be now calculated with accuracy as the relevant accounts have not survived. Probably it would have fallen somewhere in the bracket between £1,000 and £3,000 a year. A peer's income at this time averaged about £10,000 a year, although a few received twice that amount. The incomes of the gentry varied widely from the few hundred pounds a year of those like the Cromwells of Huntingdonshire, who were little above the level of yeoman farmers, to the makers of fat fortunes either from large estates, such as Sir Arthur Heselrige, or from financial dealing, such as Sir Giles Mompesson, a notorious monopolist in the reign of James I, at the other end of the scale.

In the winter of 1619 one concern became paramount in English Protestant hearts: the fate of Queen Elizabeth of Bohemia, daughter of King James I. As a young and enchanting princess she had married Frederick, Elector Palatine, in 1614. In a bid to break the Habsburg succession to the Imperial throne the Elector had accepted the crown of Bohemia from the leaders of a national revolt. This brave but ingenuous act stands out significantly in the train of events which, in 1618, precipitated Europe into the Thirty Years War, for it fused in one man all the key issues dominating the minds of Continental statesmen. As an elector-prince Frederick could represent 'German Liberties' against Habsburg absolutism; as a Calvinist he became a symbol of resistance to Roman Catholic imperialism. The Palatinate, astride the strategic route from the Spanish recruiting grounds in Northern Italy to the Low Countries, placed him in the centre of the conflict between Spain and the United Provinces, two countries officially at peace with each other only until 1621.

Frederick's potential friends, Bourbon France and the Protestant powers of Holland, Sweden and Denmark, would choose their own time to enter the war, and their hour had not yet come. Consequently, Frederick's rule in Prague rested upon two shaky pillars: Count Mansfeldt's mercenary army and his Bohemian levies. King James I wisely regarded the internal affairs of the Empire as none of England's business, but many of his subjects dissented. While the King's councillors may have seen dangers in the loss of the Palatinate or the subjugation of Bohemia, for the great majority of the politically conscious gentry the issue had become more personal: would Frederick, the Protestant champion, and Elizabeth, daughter of their King, survive in the stormy sea of German politics or not? Mansfeldt's reverse at the battle of Sablat (June 1619) and the impending conquest of both Bohemia and the Palatinate increased the pressures of public opinion upon the King, and in January 1620 he authorised Sir Horace Vere to raise 2,000 soldiers to secure the Elector's principality.

Vere's regiment mustered at Gravesend that summer. Hardened with a core of professionals it was composed mainly of gentlemen volunteers, among whom was William Waller. In these ranks gathered many who would meet on opposite sides over twenty years later in the English Civil War. Robert Devereux, the 29-year-old Earl of Essex, would one day be Captain-General of Parliament's forces, while Ralph Hopton from

Somerset, at twenty-four years of age, nearly three years senior to William, would be the King's general in the West and Waller's chief opponent.

Yet at this time these young men were united in their enthusiasm to serve the Protestant Queen who was herself no more than twenty-two years old. Sir Henry Wotton caught their mood in his poem *Elizabeth of Bohemia*[12] which ended:

> So when my Mistress shall be seen
> In sweetness of her looks and mind,
> By virtue first, then choice, a Queen,
> Tell me, if she were not design'd,
> Th' eclipse and glory of her kind?

Waller echoed these words when he wrote of her thirty years later as 'that queen of women, the Queen of Bohemia, whom I had the honour to serve at Prague in the first breaking out of the German war'.[13]

William had probably met Elizabeth at Court before her marriage, and observed her vivacity and good looks: the loveliness of a young girl joined with the unattainable estate of royalty. It was a heady mixture for a man of William's temperament. In the young Queen he glimpsed the essence of womanhood to which he responded with appreciation, respect and a lifelong devotion.

From their landing points in Holland the English forces marched up the Rhine to the Palatinate, where Vere occupied Frankenthal and Mannheim. In September, Spinola's Spanish army invaded the Palatinate while the forces of the Catholic League, under Count Tilly, renewed the struggle in Bohemia. Vere despatched a troop of mounted gentlemen 300 miles across Europe to act as a Lifeguard to Queen Elizabeth and this party included Waller. In Bohemia he found a dismal scene of confusion as the national forces fell back before the Walloon and Pole, Irish and Cossack mercenaries who fought side by side in Tilly's polyglot army.

As the Imperialist soldiers approached Prague the handful of English cavalry may have been used in the field. 'I had a miraculous escape out of the hands of the Cossacks,' William wrote later, 'when in a skirmish my horse was killed under me, and in the clearing of myself from him, I fell with my foot hanging in the stirrup, in making my way through them, I had several shot made at me, at a close distance, yet it pleased the Lord, none wounded me; only one grazed lightly on the top of my head, and I came off with safety.'[14]

The reign of the 'Winter King' in Prague came to an abrupt end when Tilly inflicted a severe defeat upon the Bohemian army just outside the city (8 November 1620). This battle of the White Mountain compelled the royal couple to flee from their capital, taking with them their infant son, Prince Rupert. The English volunteers escorted the 'Winter Queen' through the falling snow. When deep drifts halted the coaches and baggage waggons Ralph Hopton carried the Queen of Bohemia behind on his horse for 40 miles.[15] On 5 December the Queen, pregnant with the future Prince Maurice, rode into Frankfurt-on-the-Oder, accompanied by her Lifeguard of sixty horse.

After a severe winter, the war in the Palatinate assumed a dreary aspect for many of Vere's gentlemen volunteers cooped up in their Rhine fortresses. In the summer of 1621, led by the Earls of Essex and Oxford, a few of the more wealthy returned to England, and William followed their example before the onset of winter. Adventure, however, had not deserted him, and the ship in which he set sail from Holland almost foundered in a channel storm: 'after much distress, the skippers ran their barque on ground near Queenborough, and I was glad to land there.'[16]

CHAPTER TWO

My Little World

At Wanstead in June 1622 King James knighted William at the age of twenty-four, a seal to the good reputation he had won abroad. Two months later, on 12 August in the parish church of Wolborough in Devon, he married Jane who was the sole daughter and heiress of Sir Richard and Lady Lucy Reynell.

After their marriage, Sir William and his wife lived at Forde House. In the October following Jane's marriage, Sir Richard granted William Waller an annuity of £133 6s 8d, income which was derived from some of the Wolborough lands. He also settled more land upon Jane and William, upon his own and Lucy's death. These included Wolborough Meadow with tithes, the manorial farm of Forde, Kebery Mills, the manors of Langaller and Braunton Abbot. Sir Richard, aged sixty-five years in 1622, probably handed over to his son-in-law the management of his estates in Devon. For the next fourteen years, Sir William lived the life of a country gentleman.[1]

Sir Richard, knighted in the same year as his son-in-law, spent some thirty years as a lawyer, holding an office in the Court of Exchequer. He had acquired great wealth, which had enabled him to purchase Forde House in the parish of Wolborough near Newton Abbot in 1599, as his family roots lay in that part of the country. The Reynells were in fact an ancient Devonshire family, possessed of considerable lands before their expenses during the Hundred Years War had impoverished them. Both Jane and William had ancestors who fought at Agincourt, but hers had not been fortunate enough to capture a French duke. Sir Richard now set about building up the family's estates in the West Country. In the next twenty years he made sixteen land transactions, all but one being purchases.

Sir Richard had married Lucy Brandon, daughter of Robert Brandon, Chancellor of the City of London and a descendant of the Dukes of Suffolk. According to the memoir of her life by her nephew, Edward Reynell, Lucy was steadfast and strong-minded in her Christian faith, given to great generosity, humility and kindness. Her Puritan faith was formed during her girlhood days in London. 'However bred in a place which largely afforded, and too much invited, the extravagancies of youth, yet she set forth timely to seek (yea found) him whom her soul loved, betaking herself to prayer, reading, meditating, working, and such other religious duties as might hinder her from employing her time in

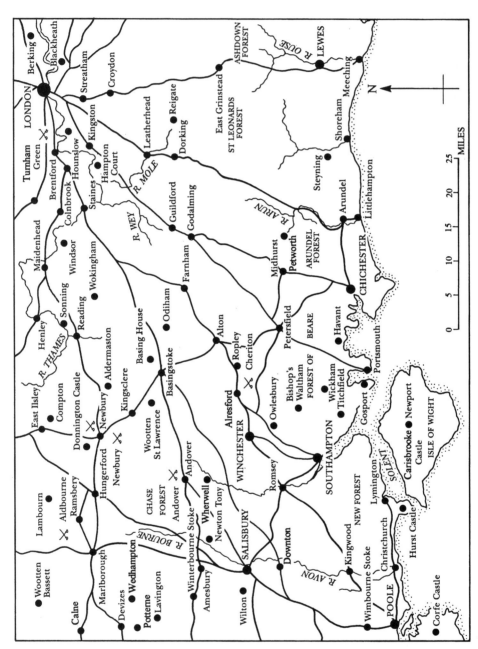

1. *Southern England at the time of the Civil War*

those vanities which many both of her age and sex about her . . . spent in painting, patching and adorning themselves.'

As to forms of religion, Lucy eschewed factions of any kind, which she held to be 'quarried up with too much rubbish and nastiness'. Instead she 'seconded public ordinances [religious observances] with private devotion, and seeking her God in secret'. She 'adhered strictly to Lords-days and times of public (as well as her own private) fasts, and days of humiliation, so far as her health would permit'. Edward Reynell implies that Sir William Waller, and his children in their turn, belonged to the same religious tradition.

Certainly some of William's later attitudes reflect the values of Lucy Reynell, who must have been like a second mother to him. In her religion she was both extremely committed on fundamentals and also most flexible over forms of prayer and such like. 'However willing rather to endanger her own safety rather than betray God's cause,' wrote Edward, 'yet was she not so far made up of one entire bone (without joints) but that, in matters merely indifferent she stood not so strong as in those of absolute necessity.' But 'she hated neutrality in matters of God's worship, and would not make new friends by changing her old religion'.

Lady Lucy was clearly a woman of intelligence, with a love of learning which her daughter Jane inherited. She spent much time in conversation with ministers discussing religion and philosophy. She read a great deal, principally the Bible but also classical and contemporary authors. She also retired for private prayer in 'her weekday temple, a consecrated closet'. Doubtless she also attended the daily morning prayers which Sir Richard or a local minister took for the family and household servants.

Lady Lucy was also extremely fond of needlework, done probably in the porch chamber at Forde House where the light is good. She made herself 'coverings of tapestry and clothing of silk and purple, to look well to the wants of her household and to clothe her family in scarlet, but especially reaching out her hand to the needy, in making all kind of garments for them. So that whensoever any came to visit her, they should find her like a princess in the midst of her maids of honour.'

Lucy's generosity to the poor extended beyond the almshouses which she built and endowed for widows in Newton Abbot. Edward stresses that these were built near to Forde House so that she could give the widows many weekly 'helps' and she hoped that those who came after her might do the same. 'Her charity extended to all (not knowing their hearts) yet she thought it mistaken . . . when it relieved vain and idle people . . . her bounty (especially) reflecting on those that were old and unable to work, or very young and so unfit for it.' The rules of her almshouses reveal a commonsense concern for good order and harmony as much as her own Puritan charitable policy: 'There shall be no gadders, tatlers, talebearers, nor given to reproachful words, not abusers of any. And no man may be lodged in any of the houses; nor any beer, ale or wine be found in any of the said houses . . .' Today her almshouses, known as 'the Widows' Houses', still stand in East Street as her memorial.

If life sounds rather bleak in the almshouses, especially for nature's gossips, it was far from cheerless at Forde House. Lucy Reynell took immense trouble over her guests, knowing that 'a true friendship was not to be maintain'd . . . lean cheeks or a bare discourse'. The demands of constant hospitality were such that 'her soul was almost stifled (as oft times it was) with the frequency of visits, and she feared Courtesy might jostle out Piety'. She was an excellent hostess, 'the beams of her liberality having this way of influence upon every branch and leaf of those that were near her.' When her guests left, she had a habit of looking out at her window 'lest through the servants neglect, some might go away unsatisfied'.

Lady Lucy spoke much of 'the strength and grace of God in her', though grace here (as so often) may only have perfected a natural strength of character. Referring to her loathing for swearing, Edward writes of 'her very presence affrighting the swearer to silence'. She sounds like a rather formidable woman, with powerful emotions. Her nephew mentions 'the great difficulties she met with in her affections (her constitution of body sometimes inclining her to passion, whereof she often complained)'. Living in the same (comparatively small) house as Lady Lucy must have been an education for William. It may have taught him to accommodate himself to strong personalities, masking his own feelings for the sake of harmony. Certainly in his later career this virtue enabled him to live and work with some extremely strong and sometimes discordant characters in pursuit of the cause of Parliament.

Waller did not represent a Devon constituency in the early parliaments of Charles I, nor does he appear to have been one of the deputy lieutenants responsible for the county militia. Between 1620 and 1636 he attended the Quarter Sessions as a Justice of the Peace only twice: Michaelmas 1632 and Epiphany 1633.[2] His friends Ralph Hopton in Somerset, Bevil Grenvile in Cornwall and Robert Harley in Gloucestershire, all sat in the early parliaments of Charles I and played a prominent part in local government. As a newcomer to his county, Waller would not possess their inherited advantages, but even so at this stage of his life he seems devoid of that mixture of personal ambition and burning desire to serve the public which characterised his later career. Perhaps they were there, but repressed.

'They that have been acquainted with the passages of my little world, in the former course of my life,' he wrote in his *Vindication* after the Civil War, 'can bear me witness how little I have affected great things . . . and have desired no greater preferment than to be mine own man. God has blessed me with a competent fortune, and given me a mind (it is his gift) fitted to enjoy that blessing. In that retired way, I enjoyed myself freely, *Nella Signoria di me,* as the Italian says, in the kingdom of mine own mind, without other thoughts than such as might arise from quiet senses, looking upon public affairs, as men use to look upon pictures, as a distance.' Perhaps one can read into these sentiments a reaction against his father's dependence upon the Earl of Northampton.

A man may be often known by his friends, and Waller probably shared to the full the interests of Sir Bevil Grenvile, both as a landlord and as a man. Like Sir Bevil he could show severity on occasion to his tenants, as his later conduct in Hampshire revealed. No doubt Sir William also matched his thrifty oversight with the same kindly charity to the needy and generous hospitality to friends and neighbours which are revealed by Sir Bevil's correspondence with his wife.

Waller, for example, followed Lady Lucy Reynell's good example and endowed a workhouse for the poor in Newton Abbot. In later life he swore that he would increase the hundredth of his income used for 'pious purposes' to one tenth, the Biblical tithe.

In a less disinterested frame of mind, Waller attempted to supplant Mr Gilbert Yarde of Bradley, owner of the manor and borough of Newton Abbot, in possession of the borough's market. It was a lucrative prize, for Newton Abbot was a thriving centre of the wool trade. Yet Yarde was not a man to brook such interference. In the Court of Star Chamber he prosecuted John Reynell, yeoman, George Knight, minister, and others, for cutting down an elm tree, assault, embracery and endeavouring to oust his lessee from the fair in Newton Abbot. Waller took his case to the Court of King's Bench, where he lost. He endured much trouble and expense, a just punishment he recognised later, for acting 'out of a covetous end'.[3]

Although no proof exists that Waller rivalled his Cornish friend in bringing the new scientific spirit to the practice of husbandry he certainly shared his love of learning. Indeed as contemporaries at the university they may have first met there. 'When I was a youth at Oxford,' wrote Grenvile to his undergraduate son, 'I so fell upon the sweet delights of reading Poetry and History in such sort as I troubled no other books and do find myself so infinitely defective by it, when I come to manage any occasions of weight as I would give a limb it were otherwise.' He urged the boy 'to bestow his forenoons' on logic and philosophy, and not to neglect his Greek or Hebrew.[5]

On one occasion Waller took Grenvile's son out to dinner in Oxford, further evidence of the warm friendship between the two men. Indeed, when

Grenvile obtained a three-year-old horse for Sir William, 'the best I can get in all this county,' he would not hear of payment: 'I beseech you name not money between you and me, it is a thing so much beneath my thoughts, and under the respect I owe you, my noblest friend, as it is not considerable with me.' He signed himself 'Your truest honourable and faithfulest servant'.[6]

Grenvile spent much care and time at Stowe on laying out his gardens and orchards, adorning his house with pictures and tapestries. Waller also had developed a love for furniture which doubtless provided Forde House with some beautiful pieces. Grenvile may have found time to admire these furnishings on one of his journeys to London to sit in the Commons as Member for Launceston, for he must have spent many nights at Waller's home.

In March 1625 a more important visitor came to Forde House when King Charles I, on his way to inspect the fleet at Plymouth, stayed a night there. The local gentry entertained him at a sumptuous banquet. Charles, twenty-three years old and King for less than six months, was in a cheerful frame of mind. Next morning, before setting out, he pleased the ladies by kissing some of them and saying 'God give you joy' to the others.

On his return journey in September, the King came once more to Forde, and lingered there for several days. The steward's accounts show that the cost of feasting the King and his retinue upon this occasion came to £55 5s, more than double the first entertainment, but many neighbours rallied around the Reynells with gifts of every kind, which included from Sir Amias Powlet, a buck, from Mr Luff of Torre, a doe, from Dr Clifford, a hunted tagge (a yearling doe), and from Mr Beard, a mutton, killed and dressed. To this were added eight score of mullet, three dozen and a half of whiting, four salmon, seven peels, seven dories, twenty-one plaice, twenty-six sole, forty-eight lobsters, five hundred and fifty pilchards, sixty-nine partridges, six pheasants, twelve pullets, fourteen capons, one hundred and twelve chickens, four ducks, six geese, thirty-seven turkeys, sixty-nine pigeons, ninety-two rabbits, one barnacle [goose?], one heronshaw (young heron), twelve sea larks, eleven curlews, twenty-one and a half dozen larks, one heath pult, two linnets, six sea-pyes (oystercatchers), one stone curlew, four teal, three pea hens and two gulls. And for meat they had six oxen, five mutton, two-and-a-half veal, ribs of beef, chines, tongues, sides of lamb and a Westphalia gammon.

During or after this feast two of Sir Richard's nephews were among those whom the King knighted. On Sunday he graciously accompanied the Reynells and their family to a service in St Mary's Church. With his retinue he then left for London on the following day, no doubt much to the relief of his hosts.[7] It is odd to reflect that when the King next passed this way again, he would be on a homewards march from Cornwall with an army to do battle with Sir William Waller at Newbury.

In the years following the King's visit, the public affairs that William Waller watched at a distance must have given him cause to reflect deeply although he could not have imagined that they were steps on the road to civil war. The ill success of English military expeditions on the Continent and the increase of illegal taxation, billetings and imprisonments rendered the King unpopular and his favourite, the Duke of Buckingham, even more so. In 1629 the House of Commons listed many of these grievances in the *Petition of Right*. The reluctance of the 1629 Parliament either to grant money or to abandon their attack upon the High Church policies of the bishops, whom he favoured, caused the King to dissolve this Parliament and to imprison its foremost spokesman, Sir John Eliot, in the Tower until his death in 1632. For the next eleven years Charles chose to rule as a benevolent and insolvent despot without the benefit of Parliament's advice or criticism.

Waller's occasional visits to London or to his mother's home in Kent may have kept him well informed about this troubled political scene, besides also exposing him to the dangers of travel. England wanted not for desperadoes as the crops of soldiers Buckingham had raised for the Continent had returned home, poorly paid and half starved, to wander about the countryside. In one anecdote Waller conjured up the atmosphere of suspicion and uncertainty which dogged the traveller in the 1620s. 'In Dorsetshire, being benighted upon my journey (as I was travelling into Devonshire where I then lived with my first dear wife) I was near being mischieved by a rogue, for being somewhat wearied and alighting to refresh myself at the descent of an hill and my men staying with the horses a little behind I walked down alone, suspecting nothing when suddenly out of a lower hollow way there crossed upon me a man on foot, with his hat under his arm as covering something with it. I demanded what he was, but he returned only a soft grumbling answer which I heeded not, and so walked on, and he kept on a little way by me: but my men shewing themselves near upon the coming down of the hill, he parted from me into the woods which were close by: but my men, in his passage near them observed he had his sword drawn under his arm with his hat covering the hilt, so that in all probability, if in that instant of time he had not discovered my men, I had been assaulted by him, when I expected nothing else.'[8]

William's only brother, Sir Walter, died in 1625. He had served as a company commander in the same regiment as Lieutenant-Colonel Ralph Hopton under Mansfeldt in 1624, and had taken part in the ill-starred Cadiz expedition in the following year. John Rushworth in his *Historical Collections* printed only 'Sir W. Waller' in his list of Colonel Sir Charles Rich's regiment, thereby misleading later historians into believing that Sir William served under Mansfeldt, but it was his younger brother who had this misfortune. Nominated as captain of a company in Ireland he died there, probably from a disease caught in the King's plague-ridden ships.[9] He left no widow or children, and the duty of perpetuating the family line now rested upon William and his wife. After seven years it began to look as if Jane was barren, but in the summer of 1630 she dispelled all anxiety by becoming pregnant.

Jane's labour began on 12 January 1631. William stayed at his wife's bedside until his growing fears on her behalf drove him from the room. 'I could not but be very apprehensive of the weakness of her condition; and having retired myself to prayer, and earnestly besought God to strengthen her, and being desirous to comfort myself with some portion of God's word, I took the Bible to read, and letting it fall, with some passion, upon the table (but without any particular design at all upon one place more than another) it opened upon the 128 Psalm, in the singing Psalms, *Like a fruitful vine on thy house side, so doth thy wife spring out.*' Two more falls of the Bible convinced William that this was no accident, and in a few hours Jane gave safe birth to a son, Richard.[10]

Two years later Jane presented her husband with a daughter, whom they called Margaret. The new baby was baptised in February 1633, in Exeter Cathedral as her brother had been before her.[11] It is doubtful, however, whether the small-boned, delicate Jane fully recovered from this child-bed, and in the following May she died in Bath. The tragedy of his wife's death finds no place in any of William's writings, but it must have demanded all his resources of patience and fortitude. He had lost in her, so he wrote, 'a virtuous, discreet, loving and beloved wife'.[12]

Waller's grief found a splendid expression. He commissioned the noted Herefordshire sculptor Epiphanius Evesham to erect a tomb for Jane under the great blue, red and yellow stained-glass window in Bath Abbey's north transept. The gift of £5 he made to the abbey library for the purchase of books, may well have been a mark of his gratitude for permission to build the tomb on this site.

Almost at once Evesham set to work, and gradually the black and white monument took shape. By the end of August the sculptor and his assistants laid down their tools and William could inspect the finished tomb. Evesham had created a masterpiece. Beneath a classical cornice, supported by four Corinthian pillars, a recumbent alabaster effigy of Sir William in armour still leans upon one arm and gazes down into the face of Jane, who is looking up into his eyes. Unfortunately, Cavalier soldiers, who occupied Bath in 1643, hacked away their features, but they failed in their purpose, for somehow the sword scars enhance the nobility of the monument. At their head and feet kneel the two children, dressed in the long skirts of childhood. Upon the western panel above their heads Evesham had chiselled in graceful letters an epitaph which suggests the hand of William's cousin, the poet Edmund Waller, praising 'the right virtuous and worthy Lady Jane':

Sole issue of a matchless paire
Both of their state & vertues heyre
In graces great, in stature small,
As full of spirit as voyd of gall,
Cherefully grave, bounteously close
Holy without vain-glorious showes:
Happy and yet from envy free:
Learn'd without pride, witty yet wise.
Reader this riddle read with mee.
Here the good Lady Waller lyes.

William visited Bath several times after his wife's funeral. In 1635, for example, he purchased thirty shillings worth of sugar from the City's Chamberlain.[13] But death snapped more of his ties with the West Country. In 1634, Sir Richard Reynell, at the age of seventy-one, followed his daughter to the grave, and he was buried in a vault beneath an altar tomb in Wolborough Church erected by Lucy. In effigy he lies beside her, finely dressed in half-armour with lace and scarlet ribbons and a jewelled chain about his neck. His head rests on an olive-green cushion with gold cords and tassels and his hands hold a gilded book, presumably his Bible. He has the air of a dignified, wealthy and religious man. Father Time, holding a sand-glass, stands at their feet, while Justice guards their heads, his sword now broken by the passage of centuries. On the side of the tomb there is a fine reclining marble effigy of Jane, while another statue commemorates their little boy John who died in childhood.

Two years later, William's five-year-old son Richard shared his grandfather's fate and was presumably buried in the family vault. His death left his baby sister the wealthy heiress of Forde House, together with extensive family properties and lands in the West Country.

These bereavements came as a train of afflictions, wrote her nephew, to the indomitable Lady Lucy: 'the death of her dear daughter . . . who was a lady of great abilities (sanctified with heavenly wisdom) . . . carrying about her a confluence of all rarities and perfections (learning itself being thought not only useful but necessary by her) . . . needs must the mother be troubled to lose so near a part of herself.' Then followed her husband's death, and then that same frost had nipped 'a tender bud of that spreading tree', her grandchild and Jane's son Richard.

William was now left alone with Lady Lucy and his baby daughter, Margaret. It is not surprising that, after an interval of time, he resolved to marry again, and he departed for London in search of a wife. Margaret was left in her grandmother's care, safely except for one occasion in the Civil War when she was briefly taken prisoner to Exeter by some Cavaliers. For her part, Lucy would not contemplate another husband.

She refused one suitor, and was 'so cold and icy towards any new engagement, as that they seemed to make love to snow that courted her'.

With William gone, Lady Lucy proved to be an able manager of the estate at Forde throughout her long widowhood. She tempered business sense with her religion, wrote her nephew, 'so far was she from wronging a man and his heritage, as that many times she rather suffered herself to be damaged in her estate, than trouble those who wronged her'. Nor did she neglect to share her wealth, to the extent that 'when she received the incomes on her estate, she thought herself burdened therewith until she had lightened her store through a right disposing thereof'. As a result of this good stewardship she was able to hand on to Margaret her inheritance in excellent order. In the house which had resounded with the merriment of King Charles' courtiers, she would one day entertain Sir Thomas Fairfax and Oliver Cromwell in the closing months of the Civil War. She died in 1654 after a long illness, surrounded by her great-grandchildren.

Meanwhile Sir William was searching for a wife. At least one lady turned him down, and he must have rejected many others. For, as he wrote, 'I humbly besought God to provide such a wife for me as might be a help to me in the way of his service, and that I might have a religious woman or none.'[14]

Eventually Providence, as he believed, directed William to Lady Anne Finch, one of the five daughters of Sir Thomas Finch, later first Earl of Winchelsea. No doubt this lady's strong Puritan convictions and her high birth drew him towards her as much as her personality. For her part, the comparative wealth of Sir William must have added to the desirability of the match. Upon Lady Anne's suggestion, the couple spent a day in prayer to seek God's blessing on their marriage.

After the wedding they lived in London until May 1638, when the King granted to Waller the Castle of Winchester with some forest lands in Hampshire as well.[15] One can only speculate that the Lady Anne's near relative, John Finch, who became Lord Keeper in January 1640, had a finger in this pie. Generous as the royal gift was, it does not seem to have created any sense of personal loyalty or obligation to the monarch on the part of either Sir William or his wife.

Meanwhile, the marriage had not yet settled down, although William would later regard this period of discord as the growing pains of unity: 'It pleased the Lord to answer our prayers in as full a measure of comfort, as ever was poured out upon a married couple: and though at first there was some little differences in our natures, and judgements (as to some particulars) yet within a little while, that good God wrought us to that uniformity, that I may say we were but as one soul in two bodies.'[16]

CHAPTER THREE

This War Without an Enemy

The renovation of Winchester Castle occupied much of the attention of
Sir William and his new wife for the first two years of their residence
there. Both Sir William and Lady Anne supervised the workmen taking
down the crumbling medieval walls, and both had narrow escapes from
falling masonry. Into the castle, William moved the fruits of what he
called 'my vanity in furniture'. By chance a list of the 'Goods of Sir
William Waller & other well affected in the Castle of Winton' has survived
in a commissary's account book, dated 6 October 1645, and the furniture
items may include the choice pieces of Sir William's collection including
perhaps some tapestries from the hand of Lady Lucy Reynell:

> Eighteen leather chairs, four chairs and seven stools of Turkey work
> [backstools or armless chairs with hand-tufted floral embroidery
> resembling Turkey carpets], two green chairs and three stools with
> hued [work], fine old Irish-work stools, and one wood stool, one wood
> couch covered with beads, one long Turkey carpet, two pairs of
> hangings, four pieces of dornick hangings [Doornik was the Flemish
> name for Tournai], four pictures [including] Mary Magdalen and an
> old woman. There were also books, mattresses, pots, kettles and
> blankets.[1]

In addition to the castle, Waller's grant gave him the wardenship of the
forest of West Bere and the coppice woods in Parnehold, properties
which had once belonged to his Hampshire namesake before his death in
1616, and then passed to the Earl of Portland. In May 1639 the
inhabitants of Buddlesgate Hundred lodged a complaint before the
King's Council alleging ill treatment by Sir William Waller. Apparently he
had taken out twenty-eight law suits against them for cutting wood from
West Bere forest to repair a beacon on an adjoining hill. The King's
Council ordered Waller to drop his proceedings at once, or give his
reasons in person for not doing so. Perhaps William suffered on this
occasion from bearing a name which signified oppression in the forest,
for his namesake had achieved a remarkable unpopularity.

The prospect of a good bargain always appealed to Waller. In order to
gain a Mr Price's lease near Winchester he laid down £500 'as a claw

upon it by way of a mortgage', but lost both lease and money. A similar 'covetousness' would distinguish or mar his generalship: often the 'good bargain' on the battlefield proved to be as much a mirage as Mr Price's acres. But these early failures made him more wary: he learnt that opportunism did not always yield the desired results. 'I reckon it among my greatest blessings that God would never suffer me to sin prosperously,' he wrote later in his *Experiences*.

By this time Sir William's sister, Fenes, had married Sir John Jackson of Hickleton in Yorkshire. On at least one occasion he took his mother and wife north to visit her, a journey not without incident: 'I reckon it a great deliverance, that when my coach mares, upon the descent of a hill, had broken their reins, and overthrown the coachman from the box and begun to run away, the reins falling down upon the ground . . . one of the mares treading upon them, they checked her bit and gave her a stop, which made the rest stand like-wise.' Sir William seems to have maintained a correspondence with Fenes, and in 1645 he interceded with the Scots commissioners in London to prevent the billeting of Scots soldiers in her house.[2]

Meanwhile, the King's attempt to rule without Parliament was drawing to an end. In 1639 the attempt to impose episcopacy upon Scotland provoked the 'Bishop's War'. The cost of the English army raised for this service induced the King to summon Parliament again in April 1640. In the House of Commons the opponents of the royal policies, now led by John Pym, launched into a long recital of grievances and came to the conclusion that only when the liberties of the House had been secured would they make grants to fill the King's war chest. Even an offer to stop the collection of the unpopular Ship Money tax failed to change their minds, and the King dissolved the 'Short Parliament' early in May.

Without much difficulty a Scottish army invaded the North of England that summer. As only a large sum of money could prevent them marching south, the King had recourse once more to the expedient of summoning Parliament. Known to history as the 'Long Parliament' this assembly gathered for the first time on 3 November 1640, and almost at once Pym and his associates made use of the power that the King's circumstances had given them. Victims of injustice, such as William Prynne, whose ears had been cropped off for writing Puritan pamphlets against the Crown, were released from prison. Into their places went some of the King's ministers, the Earl of Strafford and Archbishop William Laud, while others such as the Secretary of State, Sir Francis Windebanke, and Lord Finch, whose share in the Ship Money trial of John Hampden in 1637 was widely denounced, fled abroad.

In November 1640 one of the two newly elected Members of Parliament for Andover died, and Sir William Waller stood as his successor against a man of court sympathies, Henry Vernon. The right of election in Andover lay with the twenty-four burgesses of the town, and on the appointed day eighteen of these electors appeared before the bailiff and divided their votes evenly between the candidates. The bailiff then declared that three others, one a known Waller supporter, had failed to take their oaths as burgesses, and he gave his casting vote in favour of Vernon. Thus Waller had failed in his first bid to enter the Long Parliament.[3]

The onslaught upon the instruments and methods of the King's 'personal rule' continued in the spring of 1641. In May the Earl of Strafford went to the block on Tower Hill. He had been the chief symbol of the King's unpopular policies, and upon him the Lords and Commons vented their spleen. The first blood had been spilt in the English Revolution, and matters could never be the same again. The summer saw the abolition of the prerogative courts, including Star Chamber, and financial measures such as Ship Money which had enabled Charles to rule without Parliament. Meanwhile the passing of the Triennial Act, which provided for a meeting of Parliament at least every three years, ensured the future of that institution in the political life of the nation.

Many Puritans looked up and saw in these thickening troubles the hand of an angered God heavy over the land. About this time Sir Bevil Grenvile wrote a letter on this theme to his friend Sir William Waller. Perhaps Sir Bevil, his mind essentially Puritan in its severe beliefs, already had some vague and depressing premonition that his own life would be forfeited if these dark political clouds ever broke into a storm. Certainly he could not have had any inkling that the reader of his letter would be so closely bound up with his fate. 'I wonder nothing at what the Divine justice doth threaten the iniquity of the present times with,' wrote Grenvile to Waller, 'but I rather wonder (all things consider'd) that it has not sooner happen'd. Let others look upon secondary causes, I contemplate the original & do believe the evils are deserved; but perchance silence is best.'[4]

When the storm did break, Waller and Grenvile would find themselves arrayed on different sides, narrowly divided in their interpretation of events. What led Waller to oppose his friends, Hopton and Grenvile? At first sight Waller as holder of a lucrative office granted by the Crown and a former Lifeguardsman of the King's sister, might be considered an obvious Royalist. Yet other office-holders sided with Parliament, and in no sense did any of its leaders consider that they made war against the King as a person or against his family. Besides, Elizabeth of Bohemia would also condemn her brother's policies and attempt to recall her sons from their part in the struggle.

Clarendon believed that a personal grudge against the Court lay behind Waller's choice. According to his story Waller quarrelled with one of his first wife's relatives outside Westminster Hall, and 'received such a provocation from the other that he struck him a blow over the face'. It so happened that this relation was a servant of the King, and he found witnesses to swear that the assault had taken place inside the hall itself, which made it a penal offence. Sir William's 'dear ransom' went to his adversary, which left him with a deep sense of injustice, and a vulnerability to any temptation to engage against the Court.[5]

Now it is true that Lady Jane's cousin, Sir Thomas Reynell – knighted when King Charles visited Forde House in 1625 – had been Server-in-Ordinary to his Majesty. After his royal sinecure came to an end, he was given the job of overseeing the granting of wine importing licences in Devon and Cornwall. By the 1640s, Thomas was actively supporting the Royalists and later in 1646 he would be arraigned before the committee at Goldsmith's Hall for 'having adhered unto and assisted the forces raised against the Parliament'. His considerable estate was temporarily confiscated. A pardon was prepared by the Solicitor-General, his 'delinquency' was 'taken off' and his lands returned in return for heavy fines levied by the Lord Commissioners and by the Committee for Wine Licences in Devon and Cornwall, sitting at Exeter. The Exeter committee took £680 from him, a prodigious sum at that time, even though it was payable over a number of years.

There is no other evidence to corroborate Clarendon's story. If there was such a dispute it was probably more likely to have been about wine licences than politics. Nothing in Waller's character suggests that he would allow such a personal quarrel to determine one of the key decisions of his life.

Waller himself explained that he took up arms against the King to preserve the 'natural' order. 'All the ends I had in the carrying on of that service,' he wrote after the war, 'were but to bring things to a fair and peaceable issue; that there might have been a general payment of all duties. That God might have had his fear; the King his honour; the Houses of Parliament their privileges; the people of the kingdom their liberties and properties; and nothing might have remained upon the score among us, but that debt which must be ever paying, and ever owing, love.'[6]

Waller's last sentence succinctly sums up his reasons. Religion stands first on the list. Like a great many English Protestants of his day Sir William would have good grounds for suspecting that the King's ecclesiastical proclivities, as revealed over the past twelve years, might rob God of the fear due to him. Despite an assertion that he stood for the Protestant faith, the King had shown more than once that he favoured Papists, and his policies had brought the Church of England into disrepute with many of his Puritan subjects.[7]

Like Sir Bevil Grenvile, and many others on both sides of the Civil War, Waller's Puritanism consisted in a resolute God-centredness, distinguished by personal godliness, family piety, a generous charity to those in need and a zeal for promoting the cause of God. Such Puritans saw God's hand in the affairs of the nation, and their own daily lives, both chastising sins and revealing unmerited mercies. Thus Waller – like Cromwell – would be profoundly exalted by his military successes, or cast into despair by his failures, interpreting them as signs of God's gracious favour or righteous anger.

If Waller did not support an overthrow of Church order, neither could he be described as a political republican or social revolutionary. Rather he was a constitutional monarchist who believed that the traditional order needed restoring rather than abolishing. Above all, the privileges of Parliament, the representative and safeguard of the liberty and property of the public, stood in need of protection against the King whose numerous infringements of his subjects' liberties had slowly exhausted trust in his concept and exercise of kingship.

Lady Anne Waller's political views strengthened those of her husband, but the later Royalist allegations that she dictated them must be entertained with caution. Yet it is possible, however, that Lady Anne's influence first brought him into the orbit of John Pym and his associates.

This opinion may be supported by juxtaposing two pieces of evidence. First, in 1640, Lady Anne was reported to be seeking to assist the celebrated Puritan divine, John Dury.[8] Son of a Scots Presbyterian minister, Dury attracted wide support both for his ecumenical labours towards Protestant unity and also for his progressive views on education, the advance of scientific knowledge and its technical applications. Secondly, the name of Sir William Waller appears in a list of those who favoured Dury. Besides John Pym it included many who would be leaders of the opposition in the Long Parliament, such as the Earls of Essex and Warwick, Oliver St John, Sir Thomas Barrington, Sir Nathaniel Rich, Sir John Clotworthy and John Seldon.[9] Whether Lady Anne's interest in Dury preceded her husband's or followed it cannot now be determined. Certainly support for the schemes of John Dury and his fellow reformers had brought Waller, before his election of the House of Commons, into close contact with Pym.

The outbreak of the Irish Rebellion in October 1641 created a new problem for Pym and his associates. They feared that the army which would have to be raised to suppress it might be employed first against Parliament. But to challenge the King's right to appoint his military commanders would be to summon the very citadel of the royal prerogative, and many members of the House of Commons hesitated. The Grand Remonstrance, Pym's attempt to establish the King's fundamental unreliability, passed the House by only eleven votes (22 November). Yet two weeks later, one of Pym's chief lieutenants, Sir Arthur Heselrige, placed the explosive issue on the table by introducing a Militia Bill designed to secure for Parliament a check upon all military appointments.

While matters stood thus the King confirmed the worst fears of Pym's supporters by his personal attempt to arrest the Five Members (4 January 1642). This abortive *coup d'état* 'was interpreted as such a horrid violation of privilege,' Waller declared, 'that although his Majesty was pleased to withdraw the prosecuting of it and to promise a more tender respect for the time to come, yet nevertheless this spark (as his Majesty terms it) kindled such flames of discontent as gave occasion first to the raising of guards and afterwards to the levying of an army.'[10]

Parliament's action in issuing the Militia Bill as an ordinance (19 March) made the breach an accomplished fact. Asked by a peer if he would cede control of the militia to Parliament for a while, Charles replied, 'By God, not for an hour!'[11] Nor would he permit any tampering with the institution of episcopacy in the Established Church by those Puritan reformers who had enlisted spokesmen for their programmes in the House of Commons. The King's obstinacy now became a virtue, swinging the conservative pendulum in his favour. By June he had found that his party had swollen in numbers; by August he could raise an army.

Not until a late hour in the quarrel between King and Parliament did Waller enter the House of Commons as a member. Encouraged no doubt by those who opposed the court, Waller had submitted a petition to the Lower House on 30 April 1641, claiming Vernon's seat. Not until a year and four days later, however, did the House divide on a motion that Waller should be declared the rightful second member for Andover. The voting represented the partisan fracture of the Commons, for the tellers for the Yeas and Noes were respectively supporters of Pym and the Court. The Yeas won the motion by the narrow margin of 107 votes to 102. On 12 May the Bailiff of Andover received a summons to attend the House so that his records could be officially amended, and Waller took his seat within the next few days, conscious that his 'weakness and inexperience must often expose me to disadvantages in so great a Council'.[12]

On 16 May Waller's name appeared on the list of 'the Committee of Adventurers' in the House, who received directions to confer with 'the Committee of Adventurers of London' to consider what moneys could be raised for Ireland. The 'Sea Adventure to Ireland' was a scheme for financing twelve ships, six pinnaces and a small land force to prevent supplies reaching the Irish rebels. Waller made generous contributions, including £1,000 in 1643, to this expedition, which was later swallowed up in Parliament's much larger military effort in Ireland. Within a week or two he had also been selected for a committee appointed to examine the wording of the Scots Treaty. Still in his maiden days in the House, Waller clearly enjoyed the trust of the Parliamentarian leaders.[13]

His enthusiasm soon found another outlet. On 9 June Parliament issued an ordinance to secure the loan of money, men and horses for an army. Waller was among the first to respond by making available 'four bay horses with stars on their foreheads, their riders, John Chamber, James Hosier, Thomas Ward and Thomas Cooper, armed with carabiners, pistols, buffcoats and swords, each horse and Arms valued one with another at £26 a piece, and making in all £104'. On this list he was described as 'Sir William Waller of the Charterhouse', the first mention of his town house, one of those built on the site of the old monastery and fronting on to the west side of Aldersgate Street.[14]

In July Waller resolved to venture more than his coachmen. 'My passion to the Parliament imbolden'd me to offer my service as far as to the raising of first a troop (when there were but six appointed in all and it was something to find gentlemen that would engage), and after of a regiment of horse.'[15] His recollection may have been at fault here, for Parliament lacked regimental rather than troop commanders, and Waller's name appeared upon the printed army list in August as one of the six colonels of horse. Yet Waller's statement is significant for revealing that the appointment of the Earl of Essex as captain-general (15 July) did not bring any immediate accession of the more wealthy gentry to the Parliamentarian army, as some have believed.

At first sight Robert Devereux, son of Queen Elizabeth's favoured Earl of Essex, had much to commend him as general of all the Parliamentary forces. Besides great social status and considerable wealth, he enjoyed a reputation as a soldier gained in the Low Countries where he had served the Dutch as a colonel of foot – always his favourite arm. He had also been Vice-Admiral of the mismanaged Cadiz expedition (1625). No strategist, he proved to be better as a tactician and as a battlefield leader, fighting on foot in the head of his well-schooled infantry.

Although not untouched by Puritan influence Essex ranged himself against the King for constitutional reasons. In person he was stout, with a fleshy, double-chinned face, half-hooded eyes, moustaches brushed upwards and a short beard. He looked rather lethargic. He dressed plainly and was given to smoking a soldier's white clay pipe. His contemporaries in the summer of 1642 may be forgiven if they mistook 'Old Robin', as the soldiers nicknamed him, for a simple man.[16]

On 4 July, the House of Commons set up a new committee composed of the following members: Denzil Holles, Henry Marten, Sir Philip Stapleton, Sir John Merrick, Nathaniel Fiennes, John Hampden, William Pierrepoint, John Glynn, John Pym and Sir William Waller. They were to

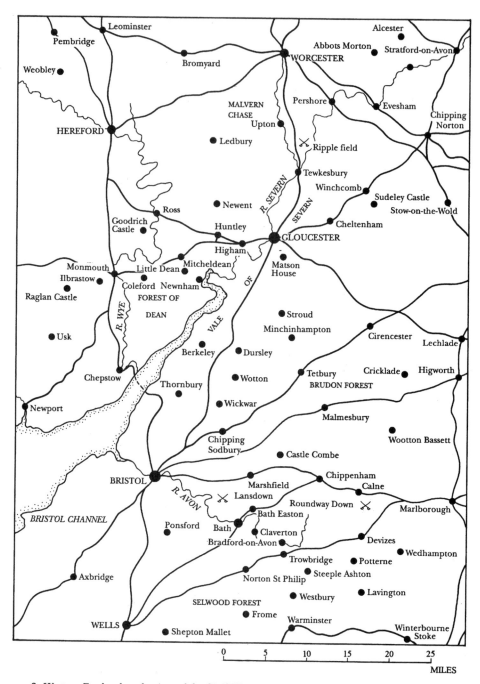

2. *Western England at the time of the Civil War*

join with a like number from the House of Lords in order 'to take into consideration whatsoever may concern the Safety of the Kingdom'.[17] Parliament delegated to the Committee of Safety, as it came to be called, the day-to-day control of military supplies; it also served as a link between the Captain-General, who held command over all the land forces, and the House of Commons. Although legally the direction of strategy rested with Parliament still, in practice Essex assumed it to be his responsibility, a fact which at that time the House of Commons accepted without demur in 1642. Waller's election to the Committee of Safety, however, after only eight weeks as a Member of Parliament, illustrated his progress in the esteem of the Lower House, although it may have been at least partly inspired by an exaggerated contemporary notion of his military experience.[18]

In their early meetings the newly elected committee no doubt took careful stock of the military resources in the hands of Parliament. In July the three largest arsenals in the country, the Tower of London, Hull and Portsmouth, were held by their officers. Sussex iron foundries and forges, the Wealden cannon works, and Surrey powder mills could be relied upon in due course to replenish the vaults of the Tower as they were all in Parliamentarian areas. The London Militia and the Fleet both supported Parliament. Although a majority of the English officers who had seen active service on the Continent entered the King's Army, a number of professional Scots veterans who enlisted under the Earl of Essex to some extent redressed this balance.

The territorial frontiers between each side remained ill-defined throughout most of the war, but initially they were determined by the outcome of struggles in the counties for control of the militia. In the summer of 1642 the rival protagonists of Parliament's Militia Ordinance and the King's Commission of Array fought for mastery in the seats of county government. In some counties, however, there was hardly any contest. Puritan East Anglia, the South-East and the parts of the Midlands nearest London, appeared to have been secured for Parliament by the end of July. An important factor in the West was the spontaneous uprising staged in the Mendip hills by the local community on behalf of Parliament, for it thereby gained control of the Somerset trained bands.

For his part the King held virtually undisputed sway over certain other regions, notably the Cornish peninsula, South Wales and much of the North. In the main, these were lands dominated by great Royalist nobles, such as the Earl of Newcastle and the Marquess of Worcester. By dint of generous loans from the wealthy and much hard labour from his veteran officers, the King swiftly achieved a parity of military strength with Parliament. Initially, before foreign armies could be introduced into the country, or Parliament realise her full war potential, all would depend upon the skill of commanders and the courage of soldiers.[19]

In spite of his enthusiasm for the Parliamentary cause and willingness to fight for it, Waller did not take up arms with the alacrity of a soldier of fortune. 'The war I abhorred, though I acted in it, as upon the defensive (which I thought justifiable), but it was ever with a wish . . . that the difference might end rather in a peace than a conquest; that . . . the one party might not have the worse nor the other the better.'[20] As a political statement this was true, and it led him to show every civility to his opponents 'so our differences might be kept in a reconcilable condition, and we might live to be friends'.[21] He also voted in the House of Commons for such peace proposals as promised 'a fair closure' with the King without the forfeiture of his own principles. But Waller may be distinguished at once from scores of other moderates on both sides, by his wholeheartedness in the field. For some, like Viscount Falkland, the decision to fight was made in perplexity and executed in despair. Waller escaped this paralysis of the sword arm because he saw clearly the need for a significant measure of victory in the field before the King could be brought to the conference table in earnest. With these purposes in mind, Waller plunged into the conflict which he would later sadly describe as 'this war without an enemy'.

CHAPTER FOUR

First Success: The Siege of Portsmouth

By the last week of July 1642, King Charles, repulsed before Hull, had retired with his army to York. Here he received some news no less good because it had been expected. The Parliamentarian Governor of Portsmouth, Colonel George Goring, who had been appointed Lieutenant General of Horse in the Parliamentarian Army, had sent 'a jolly letter' to the Earl of Manchester excusing his protracted absence from this post by declaring that he had received command of Portsmouth from the King and dared not absent himself without the royal leave. Those who had witnessed the political antics of Goring over the past year could have expressed no surprise at this act of betrayal.

Parliament had now lost a great arsenal, said to contain 100 cannon and 1,400 barrels of powder, and a port which the Venetian Ambassador could describe as 'the most capacious and most convenient in England'.[1] He may have had in mind the Queen's intention to recruit soldiers in France when he penned these words, for the Isle of Wight and Portsmouth would give the Royalists a suitable bridgehead for an invasion from the Continent should their ships be able to elude the Fleet, which had declared for Parliament. Moreover, rumours circulated in the capital that Bristol, Plymouth and Dover would shortly fall prey to similar Royalist *coups de main*. For these reasons, Parliament felt it necessary to recover Portsmouth with all speed.

Standing upon an island connected to the mainland by a single narrow causeway, Portsmouth possessed an initial strength to which military engineers had made significant additions over the years. The Tudors had erected an earthwork *enceinte* about the town, and studded the coast half a mile below it with Southsea Castle, an artillery fort commanding the sea lanes into the haven. In his three years of governorship Goring had wheedled large sums of money out of the government for modernising the fortifications. A system of flooding the low-lying fields around the town betrayed the influence of the Dutch military school and further justified Portsmouth's reputation as 'the strongest and best fortified town then in the kingdom'.[2]

On 2 August Goring could muster for the King some 500 professional soldiers and a number of officers without commands, gentlemen volunteers and their servants. From the latter Goring formed a cavalry troop, which he placed under Lord Wentworth. Money supplied by the Queen in ample quantities made up for any initial lack of enthusiasm on the part of the common soldiers, and Goring's ability as a leader could not be questioned.

Even Clarendon, who did not gloss over George Goring's faults, admitted in full the personal charm of the man. He was an archetypal Cavalier, as deft with bottle and cards as with sword and pistols. When he walked he dragged behind him a foot scarred with an old wound, an outward reminder to all of his service in the Low Countries. Courage and gaiety he possessed in plenty, but also a derisive contempt for those he considered inferiors, and a genial laziness sometimes found in such born soldiers. Yet Goring's qualities and the fortifications of Portsmouth soon led public opinion in London to hold that 'unless the loyalty and steadfastness of the garrison fail him, the efforts of Parliament to compel him to surrender will prove vain'.[3]

With the King concentrating an army in the North to march on London, the Lord General did not care at first to despatch any of his foot regiments to the siege of Portsmouth. The Hampshire Committee of Deputy-Lieutenants, which controlled the 4,000-strong county militia for Parliament, appeared more than willing to take this particular burden off his shoulders.

On the Thursday after Goring's declaration the Hampshire trained bands, perhaps 4,000 strong, had begun to assemble upon Portdown, a low ridge on the mainland. Within the next two days these levies imposed an effective land blockade on Portsea island, preventing small groups of Royalist sympathisers – such as the cathedral clergy of Winchester – from passing supplies through to the town.

In order to maintain this valuable blockade the trained bands had to be paid, an extraordinary expense which the Hampshire Committee could not immediately meet. Therefore the Committee of Safety ordered Sir Gilbert Gerrard, the Lord General's treasurer, to make ready the sum of £1,000, for the siege. This money needed to be escorted to the headquarters of the Hampshire forces, and the troops of Colonel Sir William Waller and Captain John Urry were chosen for this service.[4]

In addition, Waller apparently received orders to take command of the besiegers if necessary. Besides his local standing in the county, Waller's somewhat rusty military experience may have commended him for this role, for in the words of the proverb, 'In the country of the blind, the one-eyed man is king.' Waller's regiment of horse was still being raised, and he may have chosen Urry to act as his major. This Scots professional later ended his career as a double turncoat on the gallows, a sinister compliment to his value as an officer. With these two troops of horse and 'some twenty firelocks that look like desperate soldiers' guarding the money, Waller arrived at Portdown on 5 August.[5]

Goring had erected a half-moon fortification and a battery of five guns to cover the bridge onto Portsea island. The company of musketeers he had installed in these works could hold the bridge with ease against the six or seven hundred Hampshire levies on Portdown. Behind this shield the Royalists seized their opportunity to provision the town from the island farms. Two thousand acres of corn awaited harvest, but it is doubtful whether Goring's troopers troubled themselves with scythe or sickle. Barns and granaries were robbed of their contents and livestock driven off. When the town's storehouses could hold no more, the surplus cattle and sheep were left to graze in the dry moat. The misery of the inhabitants eased only with the arrival of seven Parliamentarian warships off Portsmouth (8 August). The Lord Admiral, the Earl of Warwick, sent a flotilla of boats to evacuate the islanders, but such animals as could be rounded up in time had to swim the straits to Hayling island.

On Friday 12 August Goring withdrew his musketeers and guns from Portbridge, leaving only eight soldiers to dismantle its timberwork. At 6.00 p.m., however, Waller and Urry led twenty volunteers at a gallop over the passage and fell upon the Royalist rearguard. They captured one or two prisoners before fleeing back to Portsmouth. The two officers then chose a 'forlorn hope' of forty troopers and rode up to Portsmouth to show their colours. [The phrase derives from the Dutch *een Verlorene Hoop*, literally a lost troop or squadron. Picked up in the Low Countries by English professional soldiers, it meant an advance patrol or decoy often sent forwards ahead of the main body.] Goring's cannon opened fire upon them, and the Cavalier horse made a brief sally.

Next day a cavalry skirmish centred around a gun from the Portbridge battery which had been abandoned with a broken axle near the town. Goring's troopers, accompanied by two field pieces loaded with musket balls, drew the gun into the town, but not before one of Waller's dragoons, firing from the saddle, had shot a gunner dead. On the same day the Hampshire militia and some local troops of horse under command of Colonel Richard Norton marched against a water-mill 'fast by the Town Mount, whereon their Ordnance was planted'. The garrison depended upon this mill 'that only goeth at the ebbing of the sea' to grind their corn, and the common soldiers repulsed the Parliamentarians with spirit.

Skirmishing continued for the next few days. On one occasion a brave Scots trooper followed the Cavaliers into the town and continued to fight when the gates had been shut. He yielded his sword only when three gashes in the head had almost blinded him. Characteristically, Goring had his wounds bound up, gave the man three pieces of gold and exchanged him for one of the Portbridge prisoners. In another incident

Captain Browne Bushell and a party of mariners seized the Royalist pinnace *Henrietta Maria* by night from beneath the cannon of Portsmouth and brought her safely out to sea. Waller used four of the ship's guns to guard Portbridge against any surprise counter-attack from the garrison.

Although the King confidently expected that Portsmouth could hold out unaided for three or four months, Goring knew that he must hasten the reinforcements he had gambled upon. Warwick's squadron prevented any succour from the Royalists in the Isle of Wight, or upon the Continent, and the disorganised supporters among the Hampshire and West Sussex gentry were powerless to help him. Consequently Goring redoubled his attempts to smuggle messages through the blockade to the King or his nearest general, the Marquess of Hertford, in Somerset. His methods were ingenious: the Parliamentarians found letters concealed in false heels, coat-linings and even the head of a dummy baby.

Such stratagems served, however, only to inform Waller and the Hampshire Committee that Goring expected the arrival of Hertford with 1,000 Horse and Foot on 18 August, and in response to their appeal, the Lord General sent eight companies of Sir John Merrick's regiment of Greycoats together with another troop of horse to stiffen the besiegers. With them came a second sum of £1,000 and a new commander for 'all the foot forces that lie before Portsmouth', Sir John Meldrum. This Scots veteran specialised in military engineering, and his skill had been proved already in early July when he took part in the defence of Hull against the King.

Meldrum divided his 130 pioneers and set one half to work on two batteries at Gosport, and the other half digging trenches on Portsea island. The Hampshire levies did not care to assault the town, and they were content to let the pioneers dig their way forward like moles. Goring and Wentworth, however, could not afford to wait and together they led a night attack against the Parliamentarian 'Court of Guard', near Waller's farmhouse headquarters a mile and a half from the town. On this occasion, as so often later, Waller did not allow himself to be surprised. After a brief fight in which they lost three men, the Royalist commanders withdrew, taking with them six prisoners. One of the captured Royalists, Mr Winter, an alderman of Portsmouth and the Lieutenant of Southsea Castle, asked if his son might bring him fresh linen from the town. Waller agreed, but indulged his sense of humour by sending the boy back to Portsmouth with a tale that the King was at Romsey and would shortly be brought back as a captive to Colonel Richard Norton's house on Portdown.

In the late evening of 18 August Goring's guns opened fire on the Gosport pioneers. Undeterred, Meldrum's men continued work on their two batteries, one, for two guns, behind a screen of faggots on the beach, and another for ten pieces in the lee of a barn. The smaller battery returned the fire across the water against the Mount where Goring had placed many of the thirty guns he had allocated to the west side of Portsmouth. One or two accurate shots induced Goring and Wentworth to work a whole night, with all who could be spared from other duties, to dig a trench along the top of the Mount so that the gunners could take cover when they spotted the orange flashes of the Parliamentarian guns on Gosport beach.

Both sides gained minor artillery successes. The Parliamentarians blew the leg off a Frenchman on the Mount, and the Royalists blasted away forty rounds or more at a very drunk soldier who wandered over from Waller's lines one night with a lighted lantern in his hand to capture the town single-handed. It says little for Goring's gunners that this Don Quixote survived their artillery fire, only to be 'laid asleep with a musket shot' near the walls.

'The dogs (so we call the guns) bark all day and night', wrote one Parliamentarian soldier on Portsea island, but at a distance the staccato crack of gunfire blended and echoed over the water, so that an officer aboard the *Paragon* could claim that 'our greatest harmony is the thundering of Cannons'.

For the most part the artillery on both sides concentrated upon military targets. Goring threatened to run his sword through one gunner who would not sight his piece on Gosport, but most of the cannon balls aimed at that town crashed harmlessly through the house roofs, for good neighbours could not afford to alienate each other. In similar fashion Meldrum's two guns fired only at the Mount and the smaller batteries next to it outside the walls of Portsmouth. The Parliamentarians, however, did shoot at a church tower in the town which the garrison had been using as an observation post, ringing the bells to signal any new arrivals of enemy ships or troops of horse. Even so, from the Gosport beach battery the tower would be visible only above the Mount, and it may have been some lucky over shots which brought down one of the offending bells and bounced off the stonework through the roof. 'Aim high' seems to have been the unwritten order of the day on both sides.

The morale of Goring's motley garrison sank lower as each day passed without sign of relief. Every night four or five deserters slipped over the walls, bringing Waller tales of disaffection and shortages, especially of salt and corn. The water-mill had been hit several times, making it dangerous for the townspeople to grind what grain they could keep from the soldiers. By the third week of the siege the officers and gentlemen in Portsmouth found that they were spending as much of their time watching their subordinates within the walls as the enemy without. Yet at a parley on 27 August Goring threatened to hold out to the bitter end, which could mean that he intended to blow up the arsenal. Clearly Waller had to find a way of breaking the garrison's will to resist without pounding Portsmouth into submission. If he ordered the gunners to do so, a stray shot exploding the magazine and devastating the town would soil the Parliamentarian cause with an atrocity.

On Saturday evening, 3 September, a council of war assembled in Waller's headquarters to discuss the situation. After a long debate the colonels and captains agreed to make ready two troops of horse, 400 Foot, and 20 scaling ladders that night in order to storm Southsea Castle, half a mile beyond Portsmouth. Waller's and Urry's troops and three companies of Greycoats were chosen for the assault party, and at 10.00 p.m. they set out towards their objective. Within an hour the sentries on Goring's redoubts had seen or heard them, and at least thirty guns fired in their direction. Waller and his fellow officers ordered the men to halt, and they did not resume their march until past midnight when the guns had fallen silent.

At 2.00 a.m. the soldiers paused once more, two bowshots from the castle, to await a diversionary attack on Portsmouth. As soon as he heard the noise of battle from the town Waller sent forward Captain Browne Bushell and a trumpeter to demand the surrender of the castle. After a parley had been sounded several times, the acting Lieutenant, a suspected Roman Catholic named Captain Challender, came out onto the drawbridge and heard the terms offered, but 'being something in drink and newly arrived out of a deep sleep' he desired Waller's messengers to return in the morning, when he would discuss the matter. Bushell then told him that Waller, Norton and Urry were not far off and awaited his surrender. The befuddled Challender kept talking, in the belief that he was passing the time away until morning.

Meanwhile, Waller had despatched a company of Greycoats around the south side of the castle towards the sea. Once on the beach their officers led them in the shadows until they had come abreast of the castle. The men then clambered up the slight sandy cliff. Several broke limbs crossing the dry moat, which was 12 feet deep and 15 feet wide, but their fellows scaled the walls, edged through empty gun embrasures and rushed down upon the garrison of a dozen startled soldiers, who flung down their arms in dismay. Captain Challender accepted this *fait accompli* with alcoholic cheerfulness, only beseeching the Parliamentarians to discharge one or two of his twelve-pounder guns, all mounted upon the landward side of the castle. But far from suggesting to Goring that Challender had struggled hard against overwhelming odds, these courtesy shots signalled the fall of the castle of Portsmouth, and thirty guns opened fire upon it, their flashes illuminating the grey dawn. Within a very few minutes the Parliamentarian captains decided to withdraw, leaving behind a garrison of eighty soldiers.

By the light of the morning, Sunday 4 September, Goring appraised the situation. Through his perspective glass he could see that Meldrum's larger battery had been completed. With Southsea Castle in enemy hands

Portsmouth was now exposed to fire from three directions. No more than sixty men in the town would still fight, and these were officers, gentlemen and servants, many of whom lacked the skill to traverse the great guns, or even to handle a musket. The experienced eye of the Governor saw that the capture of Southsea Castle had checkmated him; the mutinous carriage of his men left him no option but to sue for terms.[6]

As it was the sabbath the Parliamentarian council of war postponed the parley until Monday. At 10.00 a.m. that morning, after the customary exchange of hostages, the delegates sat down to hammer out the surrender articles, which were not ratified until 7.00 p.m. in the evening. Goring had driven a hard bargain. In exchange for the lives of himself and all his men, with liberty to go where they pleased, he agreed to hand over the town and magazine intact. Still, with such a prize before them, the Parliamentarian leaders prudently observed the old maxim, 'If your enemy will flee, make him a golden bridge.'

Goring and his friends spent Tuesday packing their belongings and putting their affairs in order. The Parliamentarians do not appear to have occupied the town that day, but under the terms of the treaty they sent in three officers to secure the stores and magazines. A Royalist source named Waller as one of these military observers, and it is not unlikely that this would have been the case. If so, it is a matter of regret that the young diarist John Evelyn, who had ridden over to Portsmouth to bid farewell to the Governor, left no pen portrait of Sir William.

That evening Goring set sail for Holland in a pinnace, dropping the town key into the harbour as a last gesture of defiance and vowing that the Royalists would take Portsmouth again before Christmas. At 6.00 a.m. Meldrum marched into the town at the head of two troops of horse and two companies of foot. Waller's only recorded act at the time of the occupation was to reinstate the former garrison chaplain. Shortly after the appointment of Sir William Lewis as Governor of Portsmouth (8 September) Waller and Urry left Hampshire to rejoin the Lord General's Army at Northampton.

The captures of Southsea Castle and Portsmouth head Waller's list of 'several prosperous successes' in his *Experiences*. It may be said that in these actions he had revealed a natural aptitude for military command. In particular the night raid on Southsea bore the hallmark of his soldier-craft: a bold plan, the use of surprise, caution in the approach and an eye for the tactical lie of the land. In the early phase of the siege one writer had noted that Waller and Urry 'behave themselves bravely', some evidence that Waller did not lack that cardinal military virtue, courage. A more likely candidate for high command could scarcely be found in the ranks of Parliament.

CHAPTER FIVE

William the Conqueror

On 9 September the Earl of Essex left London to take the field against the King. From Northampton he marched northwards with an army of 20,000 which now included Waller's regiment. Meanwhile the King, who had raised his standard at Nottingham on 22 August, strove to complete his own army. So successful was he in this work that he left Shrewsbury on 12 October with an army hardly inferior to the Lord General's.

The Royalist cavalry under Prince Rupert gained the first blood. On the eve of Essex's entry into Worcester they scattered ten troops of Parliamentarian Horse at Powick Bridge (25 September). Hesitancy now invaded the counsels of both armies. When the King left Shrewsbury he could not make up his mind whether to give battle or continue his march on London. Although a week of manoeuvring left him at Edgcote, nearer to the capital than the Parliamentarian commander at Kineton, he turned a deaf ear to a proposal that he should unleash his cavalry southwards. Instead, the King ordered his generals to take up a position on the steep escarpment of Edgehill and offer a trial of arms to the rebels.

Owing to poor intelligence work Essex could only muster 14,500 soldiers from his scattered quarters in the surrounding countryside for the battle. On the morning of 23 October he drew these up with his Foot in the centre, and Horse upon both flanks. Essex placed Waller's regiment in his left wing, which consisted in all of twenty-four troops of horse, commanded by a highly respected Scots professional, Commissary-General Sir James Ramsey. Ten of Ramsey's troops were those who had been broken at Powick Bridge. Waller's regiment may not have been complete, for a captain of the Irish service, Sir Faithful Fortescue, acted as major to him on that day in place of Horatio Carey, who had received his commission for that post as early as 6 August.[1]

Before a subsequent committee of enquiry Ramsey averred that he formed up his cavalry upon a slight ridge in front of the village of Kineton facing Edgehill. His troopers, he claimed, were ready for defensive or offensive action. He had 'interlined the squadrons with convenient numbers of musketeers', a device which suggests the influence of Gustavus Adolphus. Three hundred dismounted dragoons stood along a hedge behind his extreme left flank. Ramsey crowned these careful preparations by addressing some Scots oratory at his men, and then he turned to watch the Royalist advance.

Spilling down the slopes of Edgehill the King's dragoons rode forward to clear the hedgerows. After some sharp skirmishing they had achieved their object and the entire Royalist army marched forward in their wake. Prince Rupert rode at the head of the Cavaliers on the right wing, and as soon as the level fields were reached he ordered his regiments to extend into two lines. The sun shone down from a blue sky upon the prancing, glittering horsemen as they trotted ever nearer to Ramsey's waiting troops. As if they could bear the tension no longer Sir Faithful Fortescue and his men spurred forward from Waller's regiment to meet them, but to the consternation of the Parliamentarian army they discharged their pistols into the ground, pulled off their orange scarves and deserted *en masse* to the enemy. At once Rupert broke into a gallop and the Cavaliers swept forward behind him in a shooting charge. The demoralised Parliamentarian Horse could not absorb the impact: they broke and fled.

Ramsey's own mount carried him at least two miles in the rout, leaping hedge and ditch in the middle of an enemy squadron pursuing his own men, but he escaped with his life. Waller enjoyed a similar good fortune. 'At the battle of Edgehill,' he wrote, 'I had my horse shot under me, but I was preserved from any hurt.'[2] Although the Parliamentarian right wing troops held their ground, it was the stubborn gallantry of the Lord General's infantry which preserved him from a defeat. Essex soon abandoned any attempt to control the battle and fought at their head with a pike. Although these hedgehogs of pikemen and musketeers enabled him to claim a dubious tactical victory at the day's end, the Royalists could still march on London. Therefore the strategic honours of Edgehill lay undoubtedly with the King.[3]

The battle may have taught Essex to place an undue trust in his infantry. Many of his cavalry commanders learnt the converse lesson, that drastic improvements would have to be made in the recruitment and use of the Parliamentarian Horse, and Waller may be confidently placed among them. He had already selected experienced troopers when he could find them and his wealth may have attracted a better type of recruit to his colours than those 'decayed serving men and tapsters' who, according to Oliver Cromwell, filled the ranks of the Parliamentarian Horse. Waller would later concentrate on building up and training a body of Horse which could rival the Cavaliers.

Moreover, Edgehill seems to have convinced him of the weakness of a passive defence against a cavalry onslaught. Ramsey's wing might have proved more solid if he had copied the methods of Gustavus Adolphus more accurately and placed clumps of pikemen with the musketeers between his troops. Waller avoided the difficulty altogether when he became a general by ensuring that his Horse never stood still to receive a Cavalier charge, but spurred forward to take it at the trot. Fortunately, he escaped paying with ransom, blood, or even reputation for this invaluable hour under the tutelage of Prince Rupert.

The King and his army marched at a leisurely pace towards London by way of Oxford. In early November they approached the embattled capital from the west, causing considerable alarm among the citizens. Waller attended a meeting of the Committee of Safety on 11 November, but there is no evidence that he took any part with his regiment in the hot skirmishing around Brentford and the western suburbs which occurred at this time.

The high tide of the King's advance washed away some of the invisible walls which held in check the Royalist gentlemen in Surrey, Hampshire and Sussex. Perhaps emboldened by the King's brief residence at the palace of Oatlands in Surrey, the poet-courtier Sir John Denham (who had been appointed High Sheriff of the county), together with a party of gentlemen and their servants, seized Farnham Castle. This medieval fortress stood upon a hill overlooking the town and commanded the London–Winchester road. It also guarded the more obvious route for a Royalist invasion of Kent.

Captain George Wither, who had held the castle for Parliament until ordered back to London, declared that there were not more than six gentlemen in the four hundreds adjacent to Farnham who were well affected to his cause, and so Denham could rely upon considerable local support.

The Surrey trained bands may have mustered for that siege but they were few in number and lacked leaders as forward in Parliament's service as Horton, Lewis or Jervoise in Hampshire, and for this reason Waller was sent from London with his regiment to infuse vigour into the proceedings. Waller reached Farnham on 26 November and immediately summoned the castle. Denham, however, perceived that Waller had brought no artillery and he refused to surrender. The 100 soldiers under his command possessed plenty of weapons and ammunition, and food and drink. The low stone bastions around the shell keep and the dwelling house could be easily held by a garrison of that size.

A general attack lasting three hours yielded no results. Then Waller's petardier affixed his bomb onto the gate and blew it down. The Parliamentarians rushed forward and kicked down a high barricade of stacked logs. Sword in hand, Waller led the assault into the castle, escaping a 'very near shot from one of mine own men, as he followed me into a narrow passage after I was entered'. Colonel Fane, a Parliamentarian officer, fell dead with a bullet through his cheek. Soon the Royalist soldiers threw down their arms and cried for quarter. To this they had no right, having refused the summons, but by Waller's order all were spared and sent to London as prisoners.[4]

Sir John Denham was soon released. When George Wither was shortly after this brought prisoner to Oxford, and was in some jeopardy, having been taken in arms against the King, Sir John begged King Charles not to execute him, for 'while Wither lives, Denham will not be the worst poet in England'. This good-natured epigram contributed to the saving of Wither's life, which at least proves that King Charles was not without a sense of humour!

In early December the Royalist army began to settle down for the winter in the towns and villages around the King's headquarters in Oxford. On 3 December Lord Grandison with four troops of horse and 600 dragoons occupied Marlborough, a town in Wiltshire from which he could play havoc with the trade between London and Bristol. Hardly had Waller returned to the Lord General's camp at Aylesbury when he received fresh orders to take four regiments of horse and two of dragoons and chase Grandison out of Marlborough. These regiments were not complete and amounted to no more than two or three thousand men, but they formed Waller's largest command to date. Of their commanders, the Scotsman John Urry had served with Waller at Portsmouth. Arthur Goodwin, a Buckinghamshire Member of Parliament, and Sir Arthur Heselrige commanded the other two regiments of horse, each of perhaps two or three troops. A nineteen-year-old Scot, John Middleton, and a London wood merchant, Sir Richard Browne, accompanied Waller as colonels of dragoons.

Waller's cavalcade passed through Windsor to Newbury, leaving behind it a 6-mile-wide path of plundered vicarages. Near Marlborough he learnt that Grandison had ridden with a weak force of horse and dragoons to Basingstoke, where he had driven off some Hampshire levies besieging the Marquess of Winchester's well-fortified castle and then demanded from the townsfolk 2,000 cloths and 500 yards of linen. When the clothiers delayed, Grandison's troopers ransacked their shops. 'If you see Master Lamy,' wrote the town's apothecary to a friend in London, 'tell him he saved his purse in going away but they made bold with his house, he may come down safely now and see what is done. Pray God send peace, or else I see what will come to this land quickly.' On Friday 9 December Grandison departed from the town in the direction of Marlborough, but hearing that Waller marched thither he turned south at Andover and rode to Winchester, a city which had been recently seized for the King by a handful of Royalist gentlemen.

On the Sunday Sir William Ogle, the King's governor, told Grandison that six regiments had come to Andover in pursuit of him. Ogle, incidentally, was married to one of Waller's Hampshire cousins. Grandison, who only had four troops of horse and 600 dragoons with him, dutifully promised to retire into Sussex in order to spare the city a siege.[5] Next morning, however, while dressing in his quarters, Grandison informed the cautious governor that the reported enemy regiments were no more than 'loose parties of horse' and that he had sent out Sir Richard Willis and Sir John Smith to surprise them at Wherwell, a village three miles from Andover.

In the fields five miles west of Winchester Waller's regiments encountered these Royalist troops. One eyewitness described how the Parliamentarians 'came up most bravely and resolutely to them, and gave them the first charge with their horse, and so there began to be a very hot skirmish,' but after half an hour the outnumbered Cavaliers turned rein and fled, protected by the courageous rearguard action of the two knights and eighteen troopers.

A lone horseman galloped through the West Gate at Winchester with the first tidings. Ogle and Grandison stood talking in the High Street when he appeared and they stopped him. 'My Lord asked him, "What news?" The fellow answers, "I am wounded, but we beat up a quarter and took two colours." He made haste to be gone, but Sir William Ogle desired my Lord to make him stay, and demanded where all the soldiers and officers were. He said they were routed and that the enemy did fiercely prosecute them and many regiments were coming to the town with all speed.'

Instead of mustering the city's militia Grandison resolved to hold the walls with his own forces, an impossible task for so few soldiers. On Tuesday at noon Waller put in his first attack by sending Colonel Browne's dismounted dragoons to a place where the medieval town wall had partially collapsed. An officer who led the party up to the breach recounted the difficulty in climbing 'the exceeding high and steep passage to it, so steep that we had no other way to get up but to creep upon our hands and knees, from the bottom to the top as high as most houses, the enemy all the while playing with their musketeers upon us, but slew but three men in our getting up and one of our Captain's that followed me as he was entering the breach after I had led in some twenty men. The bullets all this while flew thick about us, yet I, bless God I had not the least hurt.'[6]

As soon as the Parliamentarians had gained a section of the walls Grandison retired with his soldiers into Waller's old home, Winchester Castle. Waller ringed the castle with troopers and dragoons but part of his force began looting in the city, 'especially some Papists' houses there, and the sweet Cathedralists, in whose houses and studies they found great store of Popish books, pictures and crucifixes, which the soldiers carried up and down the streets and market place in triumph to make themselves merry'.

During the night the Parliamentarians outside the castle prepared bundles of faggots soaked with pitch, intending to burn the castle gate down. At daybreak Grandison asked a second time for a parley and agreed to surrender the castle in exchange for the lives of himself and his soldiers. Forty-two officers and men of note, and some 600 soldiers from Grandison's Horse and Colonel Edward Carey's dragoons passed into captivity, losing weapons, money and mounts. To the disgust of their own officers, many of the Parliamentarian troopers clustered around the richly clad Royalist gentlemen, 'four or five pulling at one cloak, like hounds at the leg of a dead horse'.

The soldiers clamoured for permission to sack the city, on the grounds that the townsmen had joined with the forces of Grandison in resisting them. The Mayor admitted a measure of guilt by compounding for £1,000 to save the city, but in spite of this arrangement, in the heat of the moment, Waller granted the wishes of his unruly soldiers. He lived to regret the decision. 'It was just with God,' he wrote, 'for the punishment of my giving way to the plunder of the City of Winchester, (whereof I was a freeman and sworn to maintain and preserve the good thereof as far as I could) to permit the demolition of my house at Winchester.'[7]

It must be said in Waller's defence that except for his own troops the forces under his command had not been raised by him, and the officers may not have been men that he himself would have chosen. Nor did he have powers of martial law over these regiments. Still, the plunder of the city and the 'many other dishonourable passages' at the castle caused him to omit the taking of Winchester from his catalogue of victories.

Grandison and several other officers escaped from their guards on the road to Portsmouth. Colonel John Urry, who commanded the escort, fell under suspicion of connivance, and the Lord Mayor ordered his London house to be sacked as a reprisal, but the Scot established his innocence and recouped his loss from the fund which had been raised for the relief of Puritan ministers accidentally robbed by the Parliamentarians on their way to Marlborough. Yet the remaining prisoners reached London as a tangible advertisement of a victory which the news-sheets had much magnified by exaggerating the size of Grandison's defeated forces. Bells rang throughout the city, the churches held public thanksgiving services and a small deputation of Members of Parliament – the older Sir Henry Vane, Sir Philip Stapleton and John Hampden – waited upon the Earl of Essex with the thanks of the House of Commons for his 'care and vigilancy' concerning Winchester. Essex was always good at taking the credit, but it would be a different matter when it came to accepting some blame.

Waller marched south from the newly captured city to the coast with the intention of shipping the common soldier prisoners from Portsmouth to London. His men lacked wages, and Parliament directed the citizens of Southampton to provide him with £2,000.

Scarcely had this money been collected and paid out when orders came to march on Chichester. This city had initially declared for Parliament but on 15 November the Royalist gentlemen in West Sussex secured it by a stratagem. On pretext of helping the city authorities to keep order, a bold party surprised the armoury and magazine by night, disarmed the town militia and opened the gates next morning to Sir Edward Ford, the High Sheriff of Sussex, and their fellow Sussex Royalists.

Ford had already summoned the county trained bands by a Commission of Array and dismissed those militiamen whom he considered unreliable. With the weapons he took from them and those which he found in the town, Ford could arm all his supporters. With 100 horsemen he even forayed into East Sussex, but after a sharp reverse near Lewes he withdrew behind the circular medieval wall of Chichester. With his garrison of perhaps 1,000 men stiffened by Lord Crawford's dragoon regiment, and many big guns which had been issued to Chichester in the previous two months from the Portsmouth arsenal, Ford posed a far more serious problem to Sir William Waller than Grandison had done in Winchester. Although not such a dashing soldier as Grandison, the High Sheriff possessed a superior talent for organisation.

'We are at Havant in Hampshire,' wrote a dragoon officer on 17 December, 'whither Sir William Waller and Colonel Ramsey are come with two thousand men, from whence we go against Chichester, which I believe will be a good service if they do not run away before we come.' The cold winter weather had not damped the morale of Waller's forces, although 'we want no hardship, neither by day nor night, for we meet with nothing else . . .'

Hardly had the ink dried upon the paper when the writer heard that his regiment, with those of Goodwin, Urry and Middleton, had been ordered to rejoin the Lord General's army in Buckinghamshire. These regiments, however, marched with Waller as far as Chichester, enabling him to appear before the city with as impressive an army as possible.

On the way to Chichester Waller despatched two troops to capture Arundel Castle, which had been occupied by 100 Royalists. The troopers repeated the successful formula of the assault on Farnham. While some rampaged through the town and others kept the defenders' heads down behind the castle ramparts, a hand-picked party of thirty-six soldiers stormed the gate. After the petardier had blown it down they rushed into the courtyard and secured the Royalists, their horses and booty. Training, speed and surprise had once more robbed the King of a key fortress.

Meanwhile on 21 December Waller's force came within range of the guns on the Chichester walls. They opened fire with a boisterous salute. 'I was nearly indangered by a great shot when I first drew up before the Town,' he wrote in his *Experiences*. Fortunately Waller's own account of the siege in a despatch addressed to the Earl of Essex, by far the fullest on either side, has been preserved.[8]

'The first day we came before it the enemy sallied forth to give us a welcome, but was immediately driven into the Port [Gate], one of their men being slain and another taken prisoner, without losses or hurt of any man on our side, only one horse was shot from the Port. With our troops and three troops of horse and two companies of dragoon (which met us the night before the conduct of Colonel Morley and Sir Michael Livesy) we took up our quarters upon a down called the *Broils*, the only commanding ground about the town.

'That day was employed in mounting our pieces of battery, on which interim the ordnance from the town played liberally among us. Before our battery began, with the assent of Sir Arthur Heslerig and the other officers, I summoned the town by a trumpet, signifying unto them my desire to save effusion of blood if they would hearken to seasonable treaty. Upon which it was agreed that I should send two gentlemen into the town with some propositions, they delivering the like number of hostages for them. The persons I sent were Major Horatio Carey and Captain Carr; the hostages from them were Colonel Lindsey and Lieutenant-Colonel Porter. The terms I offered were these:

1. An absolute surrender of the Town.
2. A delivery of the Sheriff, and other Delinquents voted in Parliament, and all Papists.
3. A permission to the common soldiers to pass out without any arms, to the officers to ride out with their swords, and one horse apiece to be allowed them for their journey.
4. An oath to be taken by them never to serve against the Parliament.

'After a long expectation the answer was [that] the terms were so strict that no men of honour could accept them, and therefore they denied them all but the giving up of the Papists, if they could be found.

'Whereupon the next day our battery played, but our cannoneers overshot the town extremely. On Thursday our battery continued fiercely playing upon the town, when as towards night we received a letter from your Excellency concerning Prince Rupert's approach towards us: whereupon we sent our scouts on all sides to discover.

'The next day, or the day after, we drew our cannon nearer unto the town, and then we attempted the West Gate suburbs, and at last possessed ourselves of it; but the enemy with wild-fire burnt some of the houses; whereupon our men retried out of it again; and upon this the enemy, to prevent our neighbourhood, burned down divers houses at the East Gate also, but we got possession of the Alms-Houses, within half musket-shot of the North Port [Gate], and then planted our ordnance very advantageously which played through the Gate up into the very marketplace of the City.

'That night also we quartered two companies of foot and two troops of horse, that came to us from Arundel under the conduct of Lieutenant Colonel Roberts, at the South Gate, but not without a warm skirmish; for there we were resolutely opposed, but in vain, for our men fought now most courageously and maugre [in spite of] all the enemies opposing them took possession of the East Gate suburbs also, and then from a Church there we galled the enemy extremely, insomuch that they durst hardly any of them appear upon the wall.

'Upon the Monday night following we drew down our whole culverin against the East Gate, even within pistol shot of it, with a resolution to batter down that Port, and at the same time to fire the West Gate, and also to petard a back gate that issued out of the Deanery through the town wall into the fields, and was walled up a single brick thick.

'But whilst we in our quarter were debating about the order of our falling on, there came a Trumpet to me about ten of the clock, with a letter, desiring that to save further expense of blood I would admit of a treaty the next morning by nine of the clock, they to send two commissioners to me, and I to returne two hostages for them.

'Whereupon I presently [immediately] returned an answer according to their desire, and the next morning there came to me Sir William Balnidine and Captain Wolfe, with propositions both for themselves and all of their party in the town, as high as the soldiers could draw them. But I denied them all but one which was touching a cessation of arms during the treaty. They then pressed me for my demands. I told them I had but one offer to make to them, which was quarter, and with it honourable usage. This was refused, and that not without hot indignation; and so we parted, they with a protestation rather to sell their lives than to yield to so low a condition, and we with a resolution to proceed roundly and speedily with them, in the very same way we had agreed upon the night before, namely to storm the town.

'Which [purpose] they within easily perceived by our hasty preparation thereunto, and therefore before I could execute anything I could hear a Trumpet coming out to me, who brought those propositions to me, which I had offered them at first; but I kept (now) close to my last, and returned their messenger with that resolution. Within half an hour after, I received a letter from them, desiring respite till seven of the clock in the morning, and then I should have a full answer: and accordingly I received it, with a full submission to whatever I had demanded.

'But that very afternoon, when I was ready to enter the town, some of the Scottish officers of my Lord Crawford's troop grew into a rage at the strictness of the Article concerning the yielding of the horse and arms, and they vowed rather to die than to submit to it. But they seeing our troops ready to receive them without, upon a second thought, yielded quietly.

'Whereupon we took possession of the town with our whole army, the gates being open for us, and then made fast again. Then the first thing we did was to release and fully set at liberty all the honest men of the town whom they had imprisoned, who being then enlarged we employed in places of trust in the City.

'But in the evening I discovered a train laid to some barrells of gunpowder not far from my lodging. Whereupon search being diligently made, I apprehended the gunner that was suspected, but he would confess nothing, and all the gentlemen being questioned about it, utterly disclaimed it. And thus we were fully and peaceably masters of the City of Chichester, praised be the Lord for it.'

While the High Sheriff, over sixty officers, four hundred 'excellent Dragoneers' and as many foot soldiers set out towards a prison life in London, Waller's triumphant troopers once more turned their thoughts to the prospect of loot. William Cawley, Member of Parliament for Chichester and a prominent local Parliamentarian, collected plate and coin from Royalists in the town and gave Waller a 'donative' of one month's pay for every officer and soldier in his force. The fine on known Royalists did not produce enough money, therefore £900 worth of the Earl of Thanet's plate was added, while £950 worth of plate, previously sent to Portsmouth from Chichester by the Parliamentarian Committee, was brought back and divided among Waller's officers.[9]

As the city had surrendered on terms, the plunder of Winchester was not repeated, but on Tuesday 6 January, after a solemn thanksgiving in the cathedral, the iconoclasts in Waller's forces ran amok through the ancient church. That 'wary man' Sir William Waller, the enraged Dean noted, stood with sword drawn as if to secure himself. The same ecclesiastic recorded the discovery five or six days later of the large cache of cathedral plate by Heselrige's troopers. As the soldiers hacked away at the oak panels in the chapter house, Sir Arthur, beside himself with excitement, is said to have capered and danced around the floor crying out, 'There boys, there boys, it rattles, it rattles'.[10]

Waller could not share Heselrige's delight for he had gone to London, leaving his regiment in winter quarters near Chichester. In the first six months of the war he had captured three towns, two castles and taken over 2,000 prisoners; he had led his regiment with distinction in the Edgehill campaign and served ably on the Committee of Safety. By his sword the Sussex iron foundries and the Surrey powder mills had been secured for Parliament, and the designs of the Hampshire Royalists frustrated. On 15 January he received public thanks in the House of

Commons for his 'valour and fidelity' at Portsmouth, Farnham, Chichester and other places.[11] No other colonel in the Parliamentarian service could boast of such a record of achievement, and it is not surprising that the Londoners gave him such a warm welcome when he rode through their streets, hailing him as 'William the Conqueror'.

PART TWO

General of the West

CHAPTER SIX

The Night Owl

A mild February encouraged an early renewal of hostilities in the spring of 1643. As part of a defensive perimeter around Oxford, the Royalists had occupied Reading, a town well situated to be a base for operations against the south-eastern counties. Foreseeing the danger, Parliament resolved on 21 January that the forces of Kent, Surrey, Sussex and Hampshire 'should be drawn into a body'.[1]

Paradoxically this proposal held least appeal for the leaders of the two more threatened counties. In particular Sir Richard Onslow, foremost member of the Surrey Committee, strongly opposed the idea of an association. Some voices suggested compulsion, but Parliament could ill afford to tamper with the local foundations supporting it, and accepted instead an assurance that the county would provide for its own defence. Only Prince Rupert's raid on Alton induced Hampshire to agree to the scheme in late February.[2]

Had the projected army of 3,000 Foot and 300 Horse been promptly raised, Waller would almost certainly have received command over it, but events in Cornwall and Devon led the Lord General and Parliament to ordain otherwise. On 11 February the Earl of Essex signed a commission appointing Sir William Waller as Major-General in the West.[3]

The Parliamentarian fortunes in that region had not prospered. On the Cornish field of Braddock Down (19 January) Waller's old friend, Sir Ralph Hopton, had inflicted a sharp defeat upon the Devonshire Parliamentarians, leaving Essex with no alternative but to order his general in the West, the Earl of Stamford, to march south to stem the advance of the victorious 'Hoptonians'. This move, however, opened the back door of the West to the Cavaliers. On 2 February Prince Rupert captured Cirencester, thereby bringing the Royalist sword to the eastern edge of the Cotswolds.

Beyond those hills lay the Severn Valley, a prosperous wedge of land between the Oxford region and loyal South Wales. Besides easing communications with the Welsh recruiting grounds, the conquest of this valley would give the King the great port of Bristol, where regiments from Ireland could be landed to swell his armies. With Gloucestershire money in their pockets, Wiltshire cloth on their backs, and Bristol weapons in their hands, such new arrivals might well tilt the balance of war in the King's favour. No doubt Parliament appreciated these strategic factors when it placed the forces of Worcestershire, Somersetshire, Gloucestershire, Wiltshire and Shropshire under Sir William Waller.

The ordinance established the forces of the new command at five regiments of horse and five of foot. Waller planned to take with him a nucleus for this brigade: two regiments of horse, several companies of dragoons and a train of six field pieces. He expanded his own regiment to a cadre of ten weak troops; common soldiers he could find in the West, but not experienced officers or non-commissioned officers. The Lord General belatedly sent him the dragoons, several companies strong, and as soon as they reached his headquarters at Farnham Castle, Waller appointed one of their captains, Archibald Strachan, to be his Quartermaster-General.[4] Meanwhile, Sir Arthur Heselrige busied himself raising the second regiment of horse for Waller's brigade in London. Waller also mustered several hundred foot soldiers as well, but he intended to mount them as dragoons before advancing into the West.

Prince Rupert sallied out of Oxford on 24 February with 1,500 Horse and dragoons to intercept four guns and seven ammunition wagons on their way westwards from Farnham Castle. But spies informed Waller, and he sent gallopers to recall this advance guard from Winchester and to stay the small train of artillery in Surrey. Thus Prince Rupert arrived at Basing House, the Royalist *point d'appui* in Hampshire, only to learn that his quarry had evaded him. Hearing that Waller needed dragoon mounts, the Prince ordered his men to round up and drive off any horses suitable for this purpose. Then a scout brought him word that a party of 200 Parliamentarian troopers had off-saddled at Alton after a long and weary reconnaissance of the Wiltshire roads. With seven times their strength the Prince swooped down upon them. At first Waller's troopers asked for quarter, but when this was refused they prepared to sell their lives dearly. Loading a light field gun with grapeshot, they blasted two successive Cavalier charges. Night closed the unequal struggle and in the darkness the troopers slipped away. After this fruitless skirmish Rupert returned to Oxford.[5]

Waller reached Winchester with his small force on Friday 3 March. Next day he pressed on into Wiltshire, leaving Major Carey behind in the city to levy £600. The Royalist weekly journal *Mercurius Aulicus* claimed that Carey brought one citizen suspected of hiding his horses to Sir William, who in turn handed him over to his Provost Marshal for interrogation. With a halter around his neck the man was led to the stable of the George Inn, where a rack had been prepared. But neither this psychological intimidation nor kicks and blows could loose the citizen's tongue, and the Parliamentarians gave up. Although this tale may have been greatly exaggerated it illustrates Waller's determination to horse his few foot soldiers in order to move as fast as possible into the West.

From Winchester the small force marched to Romsey, where some of the troopers could not resist 'purifying' the ancient monastery church. While a 'zealous brother of the ministry' encouraged them for two hours from the pulpit they hacked, shot and pulled at the 'Popish' ornaments in the nave. Although it is fashionable to label these acts as vandalism it should be remembered that aestheticism – the advocacy of artistic and aesthetic autonomy – had not yet advanced very far, and religious objects, however beautiful, could not yet be severed from their primary religious significance. Waller neither encouraged iconoclasm nor attempted to restrain it. He may have accepted it as a lesser evil than the spoliation of private property, but as a man who delighted in furniture and had commissioned a fine church monument for himself and his first wife he can scarcely have enjoyed such scenes of wild destruction.[6]

On Sunday 9 March Waller entered Salisbury, whence he sent out warrants for money, arms and horses. According to one source he acquired many of the latter by a stratagem. Using the name of Prince Rupert he summoned the forces of Wiltshire to a muster. When the unsuspecting Royalist gentry gathered at the rendezvous, Waller's troopers unhorsed and disarmed them. To their complaints Sir William made the good-humoured reply that 'in regard they had hitherto done nothing for the Parliament, they might very well afford them the use of their horses which should be restored to them again, or else they should be paid for them when the war was happily concluded'.[7]

The Parliamentarian Committee of Deputy Lieutenants controlled the whole of Wiltshire except for Marlborough and Malmesbury, the latter town having been abandoned after the fall of Cirencester. But the service of Parliament had taken second place while two of the leading committee members, Sir Edward Hungerford and Sir Edward Baynton, fought like stags to control the county. After each had imprisoned the other, Parliament intervened in favour of Hungerford. In the place of his former rival he became sole commander of the forces the county had been ordered to raise: two regiments of horse and four troops apiece, and a regiment of 1,000 dragoons. With some of these he occupied Devizes, but withdrew after a few days, complaining that Baynton had constructed the works around the town 'so great and large that he had not enough men to make them good'. He reached Salisbury in time to meet Waller and apprise him of the military situation in the western parts of the county.[8]

Sir Arthur Heselrige and his regiment caught up Waller on the road into Dorset. Heselrige henceforth occupied a unique place in Waller's army. He was more than a lieutenant-general of horse, but less than a co-commander. He owed this position to his political standing. From the early days of the Long Parliament he had been a staunch opponent of the royal prerogative, and had achieved celebrity as one of the Five Members. But the House of Commons had not voted him on to the Committee of Safety, and it may be surmised that some of the more moderate members did not altogether trust his personality or his politics.

Edmund Ludlow, who once served in Heselrige's regiment and knew him well, described Sir Arthur as a man of 'disobliging carriage, sour and morose of temper, liable to be transported with passion, and to whom liberality seemed to be a vice',[9] while Clarendon called him simply 'an absurd, bold man'.[10] One critic from his county was later sent to the Tower for calling him 'but a flash' with 'more will than wit'. But these judgements seem too harsh. Fireworks of anger and excitement could indeed light up his naturally sullen temperament, giving him a reputation as a 'furious' and 'choleric' man,[11] but he was also thought to be sincere, upright and capable.[12]

Politically, Heselrige's connections lay with that extreme wing of the House of Commons, distinguishable from the majority by their suspicion of all peace negotiations and militant desire to win the war. Heselrige exemplified this latter characteristic by his extravagance in outfitting the troops, his bloodthirsty conversation and his studied martial appearance. Neither Waller nor Heselrige recorded their impressions of each other; they appear to have been less friends than political colleagues, bound together by fervour in a military partnership dedicated to victory. Later Heselrige played a prominent part in the affairs of the Commonwealth. At the Restoration he was committed to the Tower of London where he died a prisoner.

Waller marched through Dorset by way of Shaftesbury and Sherborne. Sir Walter Erle, the commander of the Parliamentary forces in Dorset, held sway over almost the whole county from his headquarters in Dorchester. Sherborne had been seized by a party of Royalist gentlemen under Sir John Strangeways, but the approach of Waller speedily put him 'and all his malignant crew' to flight in the direction of Oxford.[13]

Again Waller despatched troops of horse to disarm known Royalist sympathisers, thereby anticipating the Committee of Safety's wishes, for in a letter dated 'Westminster, the 14th March', John Pym had penned these instructions to Waller:

Noble Sir,

We shall be very glad to hear where you are upon all opportunities, that we may dispose of all accidents that may have any relation to you accordingly. We hope you will find Bristol well assured, and Gloucester without any great difficulty to be relieved. If in your passage you can suppress the malignants of Dorset and Somersetshire, and put the weekly assessment in a way of being settled, you shall therein do very good service. Prince Rupert is returned to Oxford, and upon notice thereof, my Lord General did recall that party of his army which was advanced as far as Thame, towards Oxford, and they say put them in some confusion. Our articles for the cessation [are] as far from determining as ever. I believe the King's forces will hardly wander so far from home as they have done. This is all you can for the present receive from me besides the affectionate well-wishes of, Sir,

Your very humble servant,

John Pym.[14]

Yet, despite the interception of this letter by Prince Rupert's scouts, *Mercurius Aulicus* could accuse the Parliamentarians of plundering Dorset for their own profit, claiming that 'Waller got near £30,000 for his own share'.[15]

Waller's reputation went before him into Somersetshire, and weakened resistance to the collection of the weekly assessment. Like its neighbour this county had been secured for Parliament in the autumn of 1642, and to some extent it could be regarded as a buttress of the Severn Valley against the war-torn South-West. The military commander of the Somerset forces, a former naval captain named Sir Edward Popham, could be safely left to support the Earl of Stamford against Sir Ralph Hopton.

Waller marched north from Wells to Bath and thence to Bristol, travelling by night to conceal his weakness. By this time his forces had increased to over 2,000 men, and with these he entered the city on 15 March. The speed and stealth of his night marches no less than his successful handling of the dissident Royalist gentry had won general admiration: 'he is most highly (and that most deservedly) applauded and approved for his wisedom, providence and alacrity in all his actions, like a most renowned patriot,' wrote the Parliamentarian pamphleteer John Vicars.

In 1642 the Lord General had entrusted Bristol to Colonel Thomas Essex, but the appointment proved an unfortunate one. Besides falling under suspicion of corresponding with certain Royalist gentlemen, the governor forfeited respect by his drunken revelry. On one such occasion he shot a Parliamentarian soldier dead with his pistol. Eventually he exhausted the patience of the Lord General, and Colonel Nathaniel Fiennes was ordered to replace him. Fiennes arrested Essex on 27 February, and scotched a plot among the citizens – the Yeoman's Plot, as it was known – to open the gates to Prince Rupert who waited hopefully before the city in the second week of March. Waller's advance from Somersetshire had finally induced these Cavaliers to withdraw back over the Cotswolds.[16]

Member of the Committee of Safety and second son of Lord Saye and Sele, Lord Lieutenant of Gloucestershire, Nathaniel Fiennes became Governor of Bristol for political and social reasons rather than for intrinsic military merit. Bristol was distinctly neutral by inclination, and Fiennes soon realised the precariousness of his situation. But to hold the city he had the foot regiments of Thomas Essex and Alexander Popham, each about 600 strong, his own cavalry regiment and three other troops of horse.[17]

Meanwhile the victorious Cornish Royalists in the south-western peninsula had concluded a month's truce with their adversaries, a pact which the Earl of Stamford justified to Waller on the grounds that he needed time to build up his forces in Devon and Somerset. On 17 March the commissioners agreed to extend the truce for another ten days, and much as Waller disliked such cessations, he accepted it and turned his attention to the remaining enemy in the Severn Valley region.

The King's strategy had envisaged simultaneous attacks on Gloucester from the west of the Severn by Lord Herbert's South Wales levies and from Cirencester by the forces of Prince Maurice, supported if necessary by the Oxford Horse. But the Bristol scheme had diverted Rupert and Maurice, and Herbert's army of 1,500 Welshmen lingered on week after week in their fortified camp around Highnam House, two miles from Gloucester, with two troops of horse and his own regiment of Bluecoats under their 23-year-old lieutenant-colonel, Edward Massey, whom he had appointed military governor. Waller's first task would be to safeguard Gloucester.

Sending Captain John Fiennes – Nathaniel's younger brother – with 200 horse to reinforce Massey, Waller made ready to strike at the nearest Royalist bases. Part of the Oxford army had conveniently moved against Aylesbury, a fact 'whereof you may be sure he had good intelligence', commented the Royalist newspaper *Mercurius Aulicus*.[18] To his three regiments and the Wiltshire forces of Sir Edward Hungerford, Waller added the foot of Colonel Essex, having assured the anxious governor that he would march back and defend Bristol if the need arose.[19] On the evening of Monday 23 March Waller led his brigade into the darkness towards the nearest objective – Malmesbury.

CHAPTER SEVEN

Western Successes

Waller arrived at Malmesbury after a rapid night march on 24 March. 'I sat down before the place yesterday a little before noon,' he wrote in his despatch the following day. 'At my first coming their horse shewed themselves in a bravado under the side of a wood about a quarter of a mile from the town, but upon the first proffer of a charge they retired hastily towards Cirencester-way before we could come up to them. Whereupon we fell to work with the town which is the strongest in land-situation that I ever saw. In the skirts of the outer town there were gardens walled in with dry stone wall, from whence the enemy played upon us as we came on, but within half an hour we beat them out of those strengths, and entered the outer or lower town with our horse and foot, and kept possession of it, the enemy withdrawing into the upper where they had been at cost to fortify.

'We fell on upon the West Port [Gate], in which they had cast up a breastwork and planted a piece of ordnance. The street so narrow at the upper end next the work that not above four could march in breast, this business cost hot water. As we fell on we advanced two drakes [light cannon], and under that favour our musketeers possessed themselves of some houses near the Port from whence we galled the enemy very much. If our men had come out roundly we had then carried it, but the falling of some cooled the rest. And so the first assault failed, after a fight of near half an hour.

'Whilst we were preparing to renew the assault the enemy shewed himself near the town with seven or (as some say) ten troops of horse. Whereupon Sir Arthur Hazelrig fell out upon them with eight troops, but upon his approach they retired speedily. In the meantime before his return we gave on again upon the town and had a very hot fight, which after an hour's continuance at the least we were fain to give over for want of ammunition, the main part whereof was unluckily stayed behind by a mischance of the carriage and could not come up till the next morning. I was in such want of powder, and especially ball, that if the enemy had fallen out upon me I could have maintained a very small fight, and I had no notice thereof from the officer until I was reduced to this straight.

'Whereupon I thought fit to draw off the drakes that night, or rather morning, for it was near two of the clock. The better to effect this and to prevent the hazard of the enemy's sally I caused all the drums to beat and trumpets to sound, drawing both horse and foot out into the streets, as in preparation to an assault, with all the strength I had. Which gave the enemy such apprehension that immediately they sent out a Drum and craved a parley. They yielded upon quarter, and gave me entrance about seven or eight of the clock that morning. They were about three hundred foot and a troop of horse, but the horse I related formerly shifted for themselves upon our first coming.[1]

In Malmesbury Waller captured all the officers and about 300 Foot under Lieutenant-Colonel Herbert Lunsford. These prisoners and the town itself he entrusted to Sir Edward Hungerford, leaving him the Wiltshire forces and 200 muskets with which to arm local supporters.

Waller resolved to march next against Cirencester, the chief staging post for the Oxford Royalists, where he believed there were some 300 Horse and 700 Foot. Towards Wednesday evening, however, his scouts brought him word that Prince Rupert had marched from Oxford to secure Cirencester, and Waller decided swiftly upon a second plan. While Massey diverted the attention of the Welsh armies he would fall upon their rear. At once 'by a sudden night march (in which he was very dextrous and successful)'[2] Sir William set out for the Severn. Massey cooperated wholeheartedly with Waller. At the Framilode passage over the Severn the Parliamentarians found thirty boats which had been floated down from Gloucester awaiting them. The Welsh had neglected to place a guard on this ancient ferrying point and the soldiers crossed the pontoon bridge in the early hours of Thursday morning with hindrance.

Guided by Sir Robert Cooke, the owner of Highnam House, Waller's brigade marched to Huntley and Mitcheldean, villages lying astride the supply and communication lines of the Welsh army. The 'uphills and downhills' had wearied the men and Waller ordered a day's rest on Friday 26 March.

In Newnham that evening two of Waller's troops out foraging met and skirmished with some Royalist scouts, taking four prisoners. On their way home they also arrested a messenger bearing a letter from Lord John Somerset, Lord Herbert's brother and the commander of his 500 Horse, to a certain Mr Mosse, concerning a sum of £910 he should have gathered for the maintenance of the Welsh army. According to one Parliamentarian scout, Waller rode himself to Mosse's house, posing as a Cavalier officer. Hearing that £100 had been already collected, Sir William demanded it, saying 'the Round-headed Waller was coming that way who might misemploy it'. Without demur Mosse handed over the money, only to learn then the true identity of his interrogator.[3]

Early on Saturday morning Waller moved down the road towards Highnam House, where he found Colonel Jerome Brett in command of 1,500 Welsh infantry, two troops of horse and five guns securely entrenched behind an imposing ring of earthworks. In a hard fight against Massey on Friday Brett had lost nine or ten men in exchange for three or four Bluecoats killed and as many taken prisoner. According to one of the Lord General's scouts, Waller arrived at an opportune time, for 'that very morning our horse which lay quartered in Sir Robert's park were put into some disorder by the enemy and in that disorder Captain Edward Cooke was shot in the arm below the elbow with a logget [a wooden missile] which was cut out above but they hope in no danger. The very same time also they sallied out upon the cannon and sorely endangered it but was very well defended by a few.

'By this time Sir William Waller having placed his cannon and shot one shot through the top of the house which made the Welsh look about them and seeing Sir William Waller's body marching towards them thought them to be some of their friends coming to relieve them whereat they much rejoiced and made a declaration that they neither would give nor take quarter. But after this Sir William Waller sending a Trumpet to demand two of our soldiers that were supposed to have been executed much amazed them, returned to Sir William Waller, presently [immediately] after they sent back another Trumpet to him and excused the soldiers carriage to his messenger, assuring him that the Bluecoats he demanded were alive and safe.

'Thereupon he sent a second time to demand the possession of Sir Robert Cooke's house to be delivered unto him and forthwith to lay down their arms or otherwise he would have no more mercy on them than he would have on the devil. They then began to hang out a white flag and desired a treaty and at the same time Lieutenant-Colonel Wigmore came to Sir William and offered to leave the house so that he would give them free quarter, and suffer them to march away with their arms to which he would not yield (for by this time his soldiers had made themselves masters of one of their sconces. So after a little further parley they yielded themselves to his mercy.'[4]

By his own count Waller took over 150 officers or men of quality and 1,444 common soldiers, besides a store of arms and ammunition. The next two days were spent in conveying the prisoners and the spoil into Gloucester, where accommodation became so scarce that Waller and Heselrige moved into the same house. Although Lord Herbert's 'mushroom army' (as Clarendon called it) had existed for such a short time that Oxford scarcely noticed the loss, it had cost the peer's wealthy father, the Marquess of Worcester, the best part of £60,000, a vast sum in those days. The King could ill afford such great expenditure for so little result.

While Major Robert Burghill and a party of horse pursued the Welsh troopers into the Forest of Dean, Waller sent Captain John Fiennes (the eldest son of Bristol's Governor) with a small force to occupy Tewkesbury, according to rumour vacated by the enemy. Fiennes waited near the town while a 'forlorn hope' accompanied by a trumpeter rode into it. But the Royalist garrison met them with superior numbers and chased them out of the town, taking two prisoners and forcing the trumpeter and a few others to swim the river. Fiennes retreated back to Gloucester, having proved that Waller's intelligence service, usually so good, possessed its flaws.

Waller tarried in Gloucester for ten days so that his men could refresh themselves while he attended to the urgent administrative work of his command. Here he received news that on 22 March Prince Rupert's Cavaliers had reoccupied Malmesbury, a feat which underlined one of Waller's dilemmas. If Parliament wished him to keep the field with a marching army he could not at the same time garrison towns. But for this service he must rely upon local commanders such as Sir Edward Hungerford who possessed more social status than aptitude for military leadership, a problem common to both sides in the Civil War.[5] Hungerford's subsequently published *Vindication* constitutes a lame apology for his conduct at Malmesbury. It illustrated more eloquently than the other document the weakness of such amateur soldiers:

'I was appointed to take charge of that town and accordingly expected to have it left with all things for defence, but much business happened, and Sir William Waller hastening out of the town upon his design towards Gloucester, before any consultation could be had concerning the settlement thereof.

'Upon Thursday I went out of Malmesbury towards Tetbury with Sir William Waller. At that time the town was left with more prisoners than soldiers, and by the way mentioning to Sir William Waller the dangerous condition of that town if he left not there a considerable party, especially if he removed to any remote place without forcing the enemy first from Cirencester. . . . Whereupon Sir William Waller did that evening at Tetbury order 3 barrels of powder to be presently sent unto Malmesbury, and appointed Major Clifton to repair thither to join with Major Trayle in the ordering of the forces there, that Captain Talbot with his troop should presently go thither to guard the prisoners from thence the next day to Bath, and Captain Walden with his parcel of dragoons, near upon 20, to remain at Malmesbury.

'I conceiving that the said Major Clifton . . . was a commander able and fit to give direction and secure the town I left all my forces with him at Malmesbury and went myself to Bath attended only with my own servants speedily to send more ammunition, men and horse, whereof there was not at Malmesbury a sufficient number for scouts, as also to get money for the payment of the garrison . . .'

While Hungerford collected two companies, horses and ammunition in Bath news reached the city that Malmesbury had been abandoned on Saturday 25 March and entered by Prince Rupert's Cavaliers on the following morning. Here, claimed *Mercurius Aulicus*, Rupert took eleven colours, eight cannon and much ammunition as well as two officers and four or five soldiers.

Hungerford blamed the garrison he had left behind, listing the reasons why this force, 'not exceeding 120 soldiers' had deserted their post without a blow being struck. Waller had clearly expected Hungerford to stay in the town himself and use his 'power in the country' to supplement the garrison, but, as we have seen, the new governor had departed to Bath without seriously attempting to collect men or money locally. He had displayed poor leadership and a lack of responsibility which should have disqualified him from military command.

Indeed the vagaries of people on his own side caused Waller more trouble than the Royalists at the end of March, for the Parliamentarians in Devon agreed to prolong the 'pacification' with Cornwall for a further ten days and then again until 22 April. Waller courteously acknowledged a letter from the commissioners informing him of the second extension, and then declared: 'I am still of the same opinion, that besides the distaste given thereby to Parliament, there can be nothing more destructive both to the Kingdom and to your own County than these treaties. The Kingdom will loose by this neutrality that strength which might have been derived from your County, and in this way, whilst this and that County shall sit down and think to save their own stakes, leaving the burden of the war upon a few shoulders, his Majesty will with the more ease subdue our party in the field, and that done (being master of the field) march with ease through every corner of the Kingdom, and then all the privilege those poor countries shall obtain that sat down first, will be to be devoured last.

'I am most confident the Cornish party has no real intention to embrace a peace, and I have received some informations that give me an assurance of it. I presume not to write any thing by way of advice; I know very well your judgements and my own weakness; I only represent my own apprehensions, which I humbly submit to you. The happiness I have enjoyed in your country, and the extreme obligation I have received from it, bind me to desire and endeavour the welfare thereof.' The truce, which had brought military action to a standstill in Somerset and Dorset as well as in Devon, was not renewed.[6]

Early in April Waller decided to exploit his victory at Highnam by reducing Monmouthshire. On Tuesday the 4th he marched with 14 troops of horse, the dragoon regiment, Colonel Essex's Foot and four guns against Monmouth, a town which Lord Herbert had garrisoned with some newly raised levies. At Waller's approach these withdrew to Raglan Castle and the Parliamentarian army passed unmolested through unfinished earthworks into the streets.[7] Next day Waller rode south to Usk, which he found also emptied of Royalists.

Apart from releasing a few prisoners he had so far achieved nothing, for the county folk in those parts owed a quasi-feudal allegiance to their landlords, especially the Marquess of Worcester, and these peers and gentry solidly supported the King. Moreover the sums of money which could be extracted by force from that barren sheepfarming country would hardly compensate for the dangers and inconvenience of the collection.

From Usk, Waller turned towards the Severn and led his army through 10 miles of rough country to the fortified town of Chepstow, which he entered on Thursday 'very weary of the Welsh ways over the mountains'. Here he captured the *Dragon of Bristol* in the harbour, his first major prize of the campaign. An undated letter from Waller to Nathaniel Fiennes, beginning 'I beseech you take care of this ship', possibly referred to this prize.

Meanwhile Lord Herbert, appointed on 6 April as the King's Lieutenant-General in South Wales, had concentrated the garrisons of Newnham, Ross-on-Wye, Monmouth and Chepstow into a field army and threatened the Parliamentarians from the west. Also on Thursday Waller learnt from Massey's messengers that Prince Maurice had joined Lord Grandison at Tewkesbury, crossed the Severn on a pontoon bridge above the town and marched south to cut him off from his 'starting hole' at Gloucester.

The Prince's strength, amounted to no more than 2,000 Horse, Foot and dragoons, which he foolishly divided up in the villages south-west of Gloucester. Clarendon declared that the 22-year-old Maurice 'understood very little more of the war than to fight very stoutly when there was occasion'. A courageous man and an able colonel of horse, the Prince lacked his brother's strategic sense. Instead of pressing on south as hard as he could to combine with Lord Herbert's forces, he clung to the passages over the Severn near Gloucester and passively allowed Waller to retain the initiative.

Waller and Heselrige debated the feasibility of striking at the concentrated garrisons to the west, but 'not being able to overtake the Lord Herbert's forces without hazard of the rocks we resolved for Gloucester through Prince Maurice's army. And upon Monday at night, being the tenth of this instant, having sent away our ordnance and baggage with our foot to guard it over [the] Wye to Aust and so on to the far side of the river [Severn] for Gloucester, we, marched from Chepstow all night for Prince Maurice's Quarters with our horses and dragoons.'[8]

Following the Roman road along the west bank of the Severn the columns of horsemen rode into the Forest of Dean, where the dense woods blanketed the clink of harness and the clatter of hooves on the track. In the dark forest it also became difficult to hear or see the troop in front, with dangerous consequences. 'It happened through the sleepiness of an officer,' wrote Waller, 'that the main body was separated a great distance from the fore troop (with which I marched) so I was fain to make a halt for above half an hour within little more than a mile of the Prince's headquarters in broad daylight, the alarm taken and not one hundred horse with me.'[9] As soon as he heard of the commotion at Newnham, Prince Maurice gave orders for his forces to concentrate at Little Dean. Having lost the element of surprise by arriving too late to beat up the enemy's quarters Waller advanced warily with his reunited force towards that village.

Prince Maurice's army consisted of not less than two regiments of horse and one each of dragoons and foot, the latter composed of commanded men, that is, soldiers selected from other regiments. The Foot he drew up in battle order in the southern outskirts of the village, while his Horse occupied a hill to the north of it. Upon Waller's appearance the Royalist Foot stepped forward, discharged a volley and withdrew towards their Horse, closely pursued by the Parliamentarian dragoons. On the further side of the village the dragoons paused and lined the dry walls with their muskets pointing up towards the hill. Waller's Horse formed to support them, and together the Parliamentarians awaited the Royalists. We 'stood about three hours expecting their charge,' wrote Waller, 'the report being they had vow'd we should never return.'

On the hill consternation reigned as the Cavaliers appointed to the 'forlorn hope' weighed up their chances of surviving an onslaught upon the village. 'The charge was seemingly as desperate as any I was ever in,' wrote Richard Atkyns, a captain in Prince Maurice's regiment of horse, 'it being to beat the enemy from a wall which was a strong breastwork, with a gate in the middle, possessed by above 200 musketeers, besides horse. We were to charge down a steep hill of above 12 score yards in length, as good a mark as they could wish. Our party consisting of between two and three hundred horse, not a man of them would follow us, so the officers, about 10 or 12 of us, agreed to gallop down in as good order as we could and make a desperate charge upon them.'

Yet before the first stones of their avalanche could descend, the main Parliamentarian forces had already slipped away. 'Our design at this time was only to make our way through their army, so leaving a forlorn hope of horse and dragoons to keep the passage in the town, we marched in their sight towards Gloucester. When they saw us gone they came down from the hill and fell hotly on our forlorn hope, and some few they killed and some they took. We conceive their loss was as great, that they lost as many men, and two of very good quality.'[10]

Atkyn's account of the much-delayed charge against the Parliamentarians 'forlorn hope' in the village confirmed in detail Waller's outline. According to Atkyns a fusillade from the Parliamentarian dragoons emptied one captain's saddle in the first onset, and the remaining officers intermingled in confusion with the Royalist 'forlorn hope' which had at last elected to follow them into the village.

As a result, Atkyns recalled 'they were so wedged together that they routed themselves, so that there was no passage for a long time. All this while the enemy were upon me, cutting my coat upon my armour in several places and discharging pistols as they got up to me, being the outermost men . . . but when they pursued us to the town, Major Leighton had made good a stone house, and so prepared for them with musketeers that one volley of shot made them retreat. They were so near to me that a musket ball from one of my own men took off one of the bars of the cap I charged with, and went through my hair and did me no hurt. But this was only a forlorn party of their army to face us, whilst the rest of their army marched to Gloucester.'

After they returned to their rendezvous the Royalist commanders held a council of war to decide whether to camp in the field that night or march back to Tewkesbury, which had been left with only a meagre garrison. As they were debating, Waller made a safe and honourable retreat to Gloucester. Divining that the Royalists would resolve upon Tewkesbury he ordered Massey to march with part of the Gloucester garrison to seize that town while his own weary soldiers rested for a day.

Massey's force went up river in boats and occupied Tewkesbury next morning, Wednesday 12 April. Here they broke up a Royalist pontoon bridge over the Severn, watched at a distance by an advance guard of Prince Maurice's regiment, which had arrived too late to secure it.

With some justification Waller could now believe that he had turned the tables on Prince Maurice. Before setting out on Wednesday with his cavalry to join Massey he wrote in a buoyant humorous mood to the Speaker: 'There were eight commanders taken [at Tewkesbury] but we missed Colonel Slater [the Royalist Governor], he being gone last night to give information at Oxford that all Sir William Waller's forces were routed. We doubt not that you will hear strange reports. Believe this, God has been good unto us beyond our thoughts. The taking and keeping of Tewkesbury is of great consequence to these parts. Prince Maurice's design of taking us in the Forest is now spoiled, and too we have the bridge he passed over, but he makes haste. We fear he will find another before we can give a stop. If not, we hope he may taste a little of Wales as well as we have done. We wrote you a letter for some arms and ammunition. We earnestly beg they may be sent, and two hundred horsemens' swords of Kennet's making at Hounslow. [P.S.] We are now marching towards Tewkesbury'[11]

Waller reached Tewkesbury late that night with his three regiments of horse and dragoons. Now the Royalist army could not only cross the Severn below Worcester at Upton, 6 miles north-west of Tewkesbury. That same night, Prince Maurice's horse reached this bridge first, drove off Waller's advance guard and held it in force until the main part of the army arrived early next morning.

Soon after dawn on Thursday 13 April, while the Royalists trooped over the bridge, Waller's brigade marched north from Tewkesbury along the Roman road towards Upton. After 3½ miles the Parliamentarians rode through the village of Ripple, and halted some 400 yards beyond it to take up a defensive position upon a slight ridge running east and west, known later as Ordnance or Old Nan's Hill. The western end of this rising ground curved gently to the south, hiding from Prince Maurice the chequered gardens and paddocks of the village. The hill fell steeply on the north side down to an expanse of flat ground intersected by one or two hedges – Ripple Field.

Besides his cavalry Waller had with him only a part of Lieutenant-Colonel Massey's own company of Bluecoats, perhaps 100 soldiers, and a few field guns taken probably from the walls of Tewkesbury, a force sufficient to hold Upton bridge but hardly to fight a battle in the open. At the other end of Ripple Field, Prince Maurice and Grandison drew up their army in the traditional three bodies. No accurate estimates of the size of either army has survived, but Waller's forces may have amounted to 1,300 men, and the Royalists not many more, perhaps 2,000. With the sun shining into their eyes and the wind in their faces, the Parliamentarian troopers could hardly have been pleased with their position.

The fight opened with some intermittent thunder from the field guns. After a few rounds had been fired, both sides realised that the Parliamentarian gunners lacked either skill or the right ammunition. Waller despatched some officers to investigate, who found in the battery 'neither bullet nor any convenient shot but all things at random'. They reported back to their general, and earnestly advised him either to advance himself or to expect the enemy in that place unchecked by artillery fire. Waller signalled a 'forlorn hope' of Horse to ride forward beyond his own skirmishing line of dragoons, but the Royalist musketeers in the hedgerows soon drove them back. No doubt because he could see so few enemy infantry, Prince Maurice suspected an ambuscade on the reverse slope of Waller's position, and he ordered his Horse not to pursue the retreating Parliamentarian party.

At this point in the fight, Waller decided to fall back to Tewkesbury. He himself may have suffered a fall from his horse in the charges. Seeing the troops of Waller's and Heselrige's regiments disappearing one after the other over the skyline of the crest, Prince Maurice advanced with his main forces towards them. A long track led from Ordnance Hill to the village, fenced on each side by tall hedges, and Waller placed his rearguard of dragoons before the mouth of this leafy lane, with two clumps of Bluecoats like the turrets of a gateway in the hedges on either side of the entrance. But the weight of the Cavalier charges soon scattered his dragoons, and in a mad scramble for safety they broke down the hedges at the field corners, throwing the waiting Bluecoats into disorder. The Royalists killed four or five and had taken as many prisoners before Heselrige's troop hastened back up the lane to cover their withdrawal into Tewkesbury.

Prince Maurice's men rode hard upon the heels of Waller's Foot and dragoons. John Corbet, Massey's chaplain, who must have heard it all from the Bluecoat officers present on the day, has left a vivid description of the hard-fought withdrawal. 'When they came to the next open place our men had the advantage of a ditch to stay the pursuit, and in the heat of the chase one foot soldier, at the command of the Governor, turned upon the enemy a gate then cast [it] off the hinges, which barred their entrance and enabled our men to draw up for a charge. Here for a while they stood in a maze, but on a sudden faced about [and] ran flock-meal, the enemy upon their backs. And the close of this action was like to be miserable, but at the entrance [of] a strait passage near the Myth Hill a supply of foot from the town opportunely met them [and] galled the enemy whilst the Governor charged the leader of the forlorn hope hand-to-hand, and was rescued by the gallantry of some officers when of our's only a small party of horse remained in the field. Yet the escape might equal a victory, and the saving of the forces pass for clear gain.'[12]

Corbet's last sentence accurately assessed the fight at Ripple Field. Waller may have lost two or three score men killed or prisoners and the Royalists only a fraction of that number, but the well-conducted retreat had preserved the Parliamentarian field army and secured Tewkesbury, solid advantages not worth risking for the pleasure of chasing Prince Maurice to the gates of Worcester.

Although Waller's temperamental inclination to be over-confident had marred its closing skirmish, his Welsh campaign had altered the strategic position in the West in the favour of Parliament. Two days after Ripple Field the Earl of Essex sealed these successes in the West by laying siege to Reading. As a result the King called in the garrisons of Cirencester, Malmesbury and several smaller West Country towns to augment his relief army, leaving Waller – at least for the time being – the undisputed master of the Severn Valley.

CHAPTER EIGHT

Hereford Taken

Back in Gloucester after this wearisome campaign, Sir William Waller resumed his endeavours to build up the forces of the Western Association by maintaining, paying and recruiting the old regiments and raising new ones. The old problem of a chronic shortage of money hindered these efforts.

There are glimpses in the surviving accounts of Captain Thomas Blayney, his treasurer, of the artwork of Waller's staff.[1] For example, David Craddock, his secretary, often drew money for the General's troop and became a friend of Blayney. James Buckner, 'my chirurgeon', had also accompanied Waller into the West. John Haynes served as Commissary-General in the army with responsibility for procuring or buying provisions. The train reproduced on a miniature scale the artillery organisation in the Lord General's army. Indeed, Captain Robert Bower who was both Comptroller and a gentleman of the ordnance, had held the latter post in the main Parliamentary army, and it is therefore likely that the Lord General had supplied Waller with at least a nucleus of experienced officers for his train. Soon after Ripple Field, Heselrige rode up to London with twenty officers and non-commissioned officers in order to raise more Horse for the Western army, and the Royalist spies in the capital seem to have mistaken this cadre for the remnants of Sir Arthur's own troop. As a result of his speech setting forth the needs of Waller's brigade, the House of Commons passed an ordinance on 25 April promising to repay all who contributed towards reinforcements for Waller.[2]

Meanwhile, at Gloucester, Waller issued commissions to five new colonels. The foot regiments of Henry Stephens and Sir Robert Cooke were essentially Gloucester regiments, although Waller used the latter to garrison Tewkesbury. But he intended Robert Burghill's Horse, Arthur Forbes' dragoons and Horatio Carey's Foot, when complete, to march with the field army. These officers possessed considerable experience, and Burghill in particular – a veteran of the siege of Chichester – had distinguished himself as an independent commander against a Royalist troop near the Wiltshire village of Sherston in March, and again a few days later in the Forest of Dean.

At Bristol, Colonel Fiennes professed himself utterly discouraged. He had received no money from London to replace the £2,000 Waller took away from the city a month before, money he needed to raise another foot regiment in addition to his own, which was now almost complete. The citizens of Bristol, who for the most part secretly favoured the King's cause, gave only grudgingly towards the wages of his soldiers and the cost of constructing fortifications around the city.

Not all heard the grumbles of Fiennes with sympathy. On 26 April his messenger, John Fiennes, secured an interview with the Lord General, the Earl of Essex himself, at Reading and reported their conversation in a letter to the Governor. 'I made a relation to him of the work about the town and of the vast charges you was at. He replied he was very glad of your care for the preservation of the town, but for your wants he thought no body would pity you, being confident you might get moneys in that place.

'I told him again how Sir William Waller had had what he could get, and how the malignants had conveyed their moneys away, and that unless you would plunder you could not obtain it. Then I moved him for an order for my captain's troop to come to you. He said with all his heart, if you would find another in the room. I replied it was rather your desire to send three troops of your regiment to his Excellency's Army than one to Sir William Waller in regard they was not paid and so likely to come to nothing. And so business came in so fast I could speak with him no longer.'

For his part Waller did all he could to cooperate with the Governor. In a letter addressed to 'my noble friend Colonel Fiennes' and dated 20 April, Waller recommended to him a Captain Bowen for a company 'if you have any to spare'. But he expected one of the governor's officers, who had treated a warrant of his with contempt and allowed his men to speak 'in a slighting way of me', to receive some punishment. His opening sentence in this letter concisely summed up his intentions to the governor: 'I shall ever be tender in trenching upon your right, but I must likewise be careful to preserve my own.' Fiennes failed in his attempt to establish Bristol as an independent command, with a 'circuit' of rate-paying territory supporting a large established garrison, and Waller retained a measure of control over the forces in the city.

At the beginning of the third week in April spies informed Waller that Hereford would fall to a surprise attack. With 1,500 Horse and dragoons Waller made a night march to the city and arrived before it on the morning of Tuesday 24 April.[3] Nathaniel Wharton, who had visited Hereford the previous year with Essex's army, described it as 'environed with a strong wall, better than any I have seen before, with five gates and a strong stone bridge, surpassing Worcester'. The Royalist governor, Colonel Sir Richard Cave, could muster only his own weak foot regiment and a few gentlemen volunteers as a garrison, insufficient numbers to hold the walls effectively.

Waller faced Bicester Gate first, which the Royalists had blocked with earth. He then moved to the Widemarsh Gate with his main forces, while several parties made ready to put in feint attacks against other gates and vulnerable sections of the wall. As they marched into position Waller's gunners opened fire with two sakers upon the Widemarsh Gate: one of their opening shots passed clean through the woodwork and decapitated an unfortunate Royalist officer standing behind it. Shortly afterwards Colonel Cave requested a parley; Waller agreed, and sent Colonel Carey and Captain Edward Cooke to treat with the Royalist delegates. The conference lasted into the night, allowing most of the Royalist infantry to slip over the walls in the darkness and evade capture next morning when Colonel Cave surrendered the city. Consequently, the Parliamentarians took few prisoners for their pains, although the Mayor made haste to promise Waller £3,000 if he would restrain the plundering instinct of his soldiers.[4]

On the same day that Hereford surrendered, the Lord General's army checked at Caversham Bridge the King's move to raise the siege of Reading. The Earl of Essex had previously sent orders to Waller to join him before Reading, but either his messengers had not arrived in time, or his subordinate had decided to turn a deaf ear to the summons, for the Lord General complained on 24 April that 'Sir William Waller does not come to me according to my expectations and order, though Prince Maurice be come from him and turned upon me so that I now have all the Kings forces to deal with both without and within the town without the assistance I had reason to look for'. One may trace here the first seeds of misunderstanding between the two generals. Doubtless Essex sensed that Waller was beginning to think and act above his station as a subordinate commander.

Without Waller's assistance, the Lord General took Reading on 27 April. Meanwhile in the South-West the truce had expired on 22 April and three days later Major James Chudleigh, the 25-year-old son of Sir George, inflicted a sharp defeat on the Cornish Royalists at the battle of Sourton Down. A popular jingle commemorated this run of Parliamentarian successes:

> Reading yielded is,
> Hereford taken is,
> Hopton beaten is,
> Malignants grieve I wis.

Waller stayed at Hereford for a few days while the Royalist gentlemen in the neighbourhood brought in their fines or ransoms. Yet in common with most of the country folk in the border counties the inhabitants of Herefordshire could be described as 'a people naturally malignant, that were dashed at present but did flourish again in the reverse of the King's army'. Only a decisive victory against the Royalists in the field could secure these regions for Parliament. Short of such an event, the cause of Parliament in the Severn Valley had reached its zenith. Bristol, Gloucester, Tewkesbury, Cirencester, Malmesbury, all contained Parliamentarian garrisons. In the West, Sir William had indeed become 'a commander in chief upon whom the hearts of the people could fasten'.[5]

Many Royalist opponents now admired him as the 'Night Owl', a sobriquet which aptly conjured up watchful scouts, swift nocturnal marches and swooping attacks. But the supporters of Parliament who had followed his successes in the West in the news journals, still hailed him with ever mounting enthusiasm as 'William the Conqueror'.

CHAPTER NINE

Worcester Attempted

On 16 May 1643 Sir Ralph Hopton transformed the military situation in the West by defeating Stamford's Parliamentarian army at Stratton. The Earl of Stamford lost no less than 300 men killed, 1,700 taken prisoner, 13 brass cannon and all his baggage. Within the next few days the Cornish Royalist army advanced into Devon, and all the county, except for the beleaguered towns of Plymouth, Exeter, Bideford and Barnstaple, passed into their hands.

Meanwhile the King, knowing that Hopton lacked cavalry, despatched the Marquess of Hertford, his Lieutenant-General in the West, with Prince Maurice and a strong body of Cavaliers, towards him. Consequently, while the Somerset Parliamentarians awaited the Cornishmen with alarm, Sir Walter Erle posted to Gloucester and assured Waller that if he did not intercept Hertford at Salisbury the whole of Dorset would be lost. Believing that he had convinced Waller, Sir Walter returned to Dorchester.[1]

Waller worked hard to affect a concentration of Western Association forces at Bath on 22 May. On his way from Gloucester he paused at Bristol where he asked the Governor for six companies of Colonel Alexander Popham's Foot, and these were duly sent to the rendezvous. On the 24th Popham and his officers wrote to Nathaniel Fiennes informing him that a considerable body of enemy Horse had entered Shaftesbury the previous night, and that Hungerford and his Wiltshire cavalry had retreated about midnight towards Dorchester. Waller, they said, had gone to Gloucester in order to draw his brigade towards Bath, leaving them to ask the Governor for their remaining companies, the Governor's own regiment of horse, Captain Cole's troop and the company of dragoons. Also they wanted money to pay the Horse, and more powder, match and bullet.[2]

On 26 May the regiment of Nathaniel Fiennes reached Bath. Captain John Fiennes reported to his brother that Colonel Alexander Popham had sent all his foot to Frome and gone after them, his design being to surprise three enemy troops of horse there and then to return to Bath. Although Popham promised the Bristol horsemen 20s a man to ride with him, they protested about the short notice and would at first not stir from their new quarters. Only the Governor's own troop would immediately accompany him in return for £120 of arrears.

Soon after their departure Sir Edward Hungerford with his horse and dragoons had ridden into Bath. 'I perceive Sir William Waller's design is something altered,' continued Captain Fiennes, 'he would have Colonel Popham with your horse and Sir Edward Hungerford's and the rest of the horse in Somersetshire to march straight towards Bridgewater together with Colonel Popham's foot; and himself will either come after or march an other way, but it will be some time ere he will be ready to march . . . they have sent a post to Sir William Waller and the answer will be here tomorrow.'[3]

The messenger found Waller preparing to march north towards the last remaining Royalist stronghold in the vicinity – Worcester. In a letter to the Speaker, dated 2 June, Sir Robert Cooke gave Waller's reasons for this change of plan: 'Sir William, finding a necessity for drawing his forces from this part, was desirous to leave in as good condition as he might this country, affected on the one side with the Worcester garrison, and the rather because it was impossible for him to march away with a convenient strength unless he withdrew the garrison from Tewkesbury, consisting, with officers, near 1,000 horse and foot. In this regard he held it both necessary for the country and of great consequence to the main to attempt the taking in of Worcester, that as the works being slighted it might not remain a strength for the Parliament's enemies, and give assurance to their chief body of retreat upon occasion of disaster.'[4]

In fact, Worcester looked to Waller like a good bargain. Later it would be argued that he should have obeyed the Lord General's directions and marched against one or other of the two Royalist armies in order to prevent them joining. For Essex had written to Waller on 21 May: 'Prince Maurice and the Marquess are advancing so rapidly that it is necessary you should join battle with them.'[5] He seems to have allowed local opinion, which much valued the safeguarding of Tewkesbury, to outweigh this strategic necessity – a serious error of judgment. On 20 May Waller set out towards Worcester with his brigade and several companies of Bluecoats. After a night march of 26 miles, the Parliamentarians arrived within sight of the city at dawn.

Colonel William Sandys, the garrison commander, peremptorily ordered Waller's trumpeter to tell his master 'that he was not at Hereford now', a message which the soldier refused to bear as being too uncivil. 'Be off!' retorted Sandys, and walked away, but the trumpeter stood his ground. After some time had elapsed a perplexed Royalist sentry informed Sandys of this fact. During a second interview the Parliamentarian emissary, reflecting the self-confidence but not the courtesy of his general, made an insulting reply to Sandys, and without more ado a Royalist soldier shot him dead in his saddle.

Soon afterward Waller's field guns opened fire, but the heavier pieces on the earthworks proved more than a match for them. The Royalists repulsed an assault upon Friary Gate, yet Waller's soldiers captured a house just outside the walls. 'The defence was obstinate,' wrote Cooke, 'yet within less than four hours we had beaten the enemy out of all their outworks, and had gained the suburbs, and had lodged our musketeers at the very ports, and were in so fair a way in so short a time of gaining the town as could be.' The Royalist foot counter-attacked, took the house, and burnt it. Supported by cavalry sorties from St Martin's Gate they then cleared the enemy musketeers from the eastern suburbs and drove back Waller's light field pieces to a safer distance. Towards evening the Parliamentarian besiegers returned wearily to Waller's main position on Green Hill, having lost perhaps sixty men taken prisoner or killed.

That night five despatches arrived from the South-West containing emphatic opinions that all would be lost there if Waller came not at once. Besides, Sir William Brereton, Parliament's commander in the upper Severn region, had failed to join the siege as expected; instead, reports arrived that a large brigade of horse had left Oxford to cut off Waller from his base.

For these reasons Waller resolved to abandon the siege and march back to Gloucester, 'leaving orders with me,' wrote Cooke on 2 June, 'to throw down as much of the works as the convenience of my time would afford, which I believe is so done that they are made unuseful, though not fully slighted, and to withdraw the force from Tewkesbury to Gloucester, from whence he had sooner departed had not the impossibility of either marching without money or getting it without the employment of his troops to collect it, a little hindered his speed. The country is much troubled at his departure, and unless my Lord General's motions shall divert the other force they fear the worst.'

While barges ferried the wounded downstream, Waller's army trudged down the Roman road, reaching Gloucester on 30 May. Another week passed while the soldiers waited for the county collectors to bring in money for their wages. Without such money Waller could not march to prevent the union of the two Royalist armies, now nearing each other. As Sir Robert Cooke, Colonel Burghill and others of the Committee of Gloucester informed the Speaker (in a letter dated 3 June) they desired to 'interfere', but 'our men are not only too few to encounter theirs, but which is worse, too many to be paid by us; and the want of money has bred such mutinous dispositions in the soldiers that no arguments will make them stir'. They asked the Speaker to advise the Lord General to supply them with forces proportionate to those that had marched from Oxford into the West.[6]

Waller spent much of his time signing pay warrants, food bills and fodder accounts. As a part of his personal preparations for the coming campaign he sent his own brace of pistols to be restocked and cleaned. But there was not nearly enough money in the treasury, and when Waller marched south to Bristol on 6 June, he had to leave behind four or five troops of horse with instructions to follow as soon as they had received their pay.[7]

While Waller had lingered impatiently in Gloucester, the two Royalist armies had joined forces at Chard in Somerset on 4 June. The Marquess of Hertford and Prince Maurice brought with them 1,500 Horse and 1,000 newly levied Foot, whereas Hopton provided 3,000 veteran Cornish infantry, 500 Horse and 300 dragoons; a grand total of 4,000 Foot, 2,000 Horse and 300 dragoons, and a train of 16 field pieces. Hertford and Maurice occupied the two senior posts in the combined armies, while Hopton appears to have become the field marshal. Clarendon shrewdly described Hopton as 'an excellent officer in an army for any command but the supreme to which he was not equal'. Hopton may well have realised this limitation himself, for he accepted the subordinate role assigned him with good grace, and induced his officers to follow his example.[8]

This impressive Royalist army moved first on Taunton, an important town which the Somerset, Wiltshire and Bristol Horse, and Alexander Popham's Foot abandoned without a fight. While Hertford remained in Taunton to establish Royalist civil and military control over the county, Prince Maurice led the army after the Parliamentarians. There were several cavalry skirmishes south of Wells, but Colonel Edward Popham only faced about with his rearguard at Glastonbury and again on Mendip Hill, in order to allow his foot and baggage to withdraw into safety, decamping before the Prince could bring up his main forces.

On 8 June Waller entered Bath with his brigade, and a day later he sent eight troops of horse and a regiment of dragoons to cover Popham's retreat. These arrived at an opportune time, for an hour after sunrise the Earl of Carnarvon's regiment of horse fell on the Parliamentarian rearguard south of Chewton and scattered it.

In the morning mist Waller's regiments met and chased the Cavaliers beyond Chewton, where they found the bulk of Prince Maurice's regiment of horse drawn up on the heath south of the village. The Prince led his men in a charge which scattered half the Parliamentarian Horse as they were arraying themselves, but the remaining troops wheeled and closed in upon the rear of the enemy regiment. In the mêlée the Prince received 'two hurts in his head with a sword and was beaten off his horse'.

For some hours the Parliamentarians unknowingly held the Prince a prisoner, but towards evening a mixed party of Cavaliers led by Carnarvon rescued him after several hard charges. In the darkness both sides retired to their respective quarters in Wells and Bath. In so far as there had been 'a stop put' to the pursuit of Colonel Edward Popham, Waller counted this heavy skirmish at Chewton as a victory.[9]

CHAPTER TEN

Preparations for Battle

At Bath Waller spent the next three weeks enlarging his army. With the Western Association horse and his own original brigade Waller's cavalry now numbered about 2,500 strong, but these regiments could not be used effectively in the small fields and narrow lanes south of Bath. Therefore, Waller needed money to keep them together until the Royalists gave him opportunity to employ them in more open country.

On 22 June Waller and Heselrige reported as much to the Speaker: 'We as your servants cannot but acquaint you with our condition. We have a body of horse by God's blessing able to do the Kingdom good service. The enemy lies still at Wells. That part of the country is altogether unfit for horse. It grieves our souls we dare not attempt what we desire. We must not hazard your trust like fools, neither can we stay here and starve. We have long and often supplicated you for money. Find us but a way to live without it, or else we humbly beg a present supply, if not this horse will certainly disband, which thought makes our hearts to bleed.'[1]

Not long after this letter six troops of Sir Arthur Heselrige's new regiment of horse arrived from London, escorting some chests of money. On 26 June Waller thanked the House of Commons for 'these poor troops which came very seasonably to keep life in us when we were in a gasping condition'. By contrast, two Dorset troops and Colonel Norton's Hampshire Horse, ordered to march towards Waller by 30 June, did not arrive in time for the campaign.

Heselrige's new regiment of horse could hardly be described as 'poor'. According to Clarendon, they 'were so prodigiously armed that they were called by the other side *the regiment of lobsters*, because of their bright iron shells, with which they were covered, being perfect cuirassiers; and were the first seen so armed on either side, and the first that made any impression upon the King's horse, who, being unarmed, were not able to bear a shock with them; besides that they were secure from hurts of the sword, which were almost the only weapons the others were furnished with.'[2]

The differences between cuirassiers and the more common harquebusiers included one of social status, for the former were expected to be gentlemen.[3] Heselrige's accounts mentioned 'three troopers, gentlemen reformadoes who with others submitted themselves with horse and arms at their own charge', while Captain Okey had fifty of such

Marshfield
4 July

TOG HILL

FREEZING   HILL

5 July

St Catherine

● North Stoke

LANSDOWN

● Swainswick   Box ●

Batheaston

4 July   Charlcombe

● Kelston   *4 July*

● Weston   Bathampton

Monkton Farleigh
●

BATHAMPTON DOWN

● Newton St Loe   ● Twerton   BATH   *3 July*

2–3 July   Claverton   *3 July*

CLAVERTON DOWN

ODD DOWN

2 July

Bradford-on-Avon

● Combe Hay   Freshford ●   *River Avon*

Royalist   ▭   ◨▶

Parliamentarian   ▰   ▶

3. The Lansdown campaign

reformado troopers under his command. Reformadoes were officers without a command and volunteers serving without a commission but with the rank of an officer. With their green colours flying at the head of each troop, the Lobsters made a gallant sight as they clattered into Bath.

Waller's real deficiency now was in infantry. The sudden desertion of the former major in his own regiment of horse, who had a commission to raise a new regiment of foot, did not help matters. Colonel Horatio Carey, who bore on his troop's standard the device of a bent bow with its arrow aimed at a winged heart, above the words 'Charles, thus Peace flies to thee', had himself fled to the Royalist camp just before the fight at Chewton, leaving behind his incompleted companies.

Nor was the rest of the foot in good condition. The Royalist cavalry had mauled Popham's six companies near Wells, and many of them had lost their weapons. Colonel Strode's Foot and the remnants of Thomas Essex's regiment had never been strong in the first place, and the addition of soldiers from Stamford's dispersed army probably did not more than maintain their numbers. Thus Waller directed Captain Cooke to ask the governor of Bristol to mount and send him 500 commanded men from the garrison, or as many as he could provide.[4]

On 1 July, five days later, Waller and Heselrige wrote to John Ashe, a local Member of Parliament who was in Bristol, begging him to hasten the forces out of the city. 'Good Sir, Sure you think we have both a lame and patient enemy, that will be knocked and stay till we be ready to answer his return.' Having expected Colonel Fiennes' regiment that day the two commanders had been disappointed to learn that the governor would not send it until Sir John Seymour's men came to Bristol on 4 July. 'What good will this regiment do Bristol if we perish?' they asked Ashe. 'It is a wonder to me,' Waller added, 'to see our friends delay help when they're in safety; and I am confident, Honour is wrapped up in our success. It is said your captains have not yet cast lots who shall come forth; I thought they would have petitioned for employment.

'We shall be happy in Colonel Popham's regiment and Colonel Fiennes also, surely a small guard will keep under malignants. Let not the west of England be lost for a little monies, neither send your supplies too late. There is a time which wise men will not let slip.'[5] Despite this clarion call to arms it is virtually certain that Fiennes spared Waller no more than 500 soldiers, drawn out mainly from his own regiment. Consequently, in early July, Waller could muster no more than 1,500 Foot at the most, compared to a Royalist total of 4,000. Despite his brilliance as a general in covering up this deficiency, Waller's weakness in infantry proved to be a critical factor in the forthcoming campaign.

❖ ❖ ❖

During this period messengers passed freely between the rival headquarters. Lord Arundel sought the return of his children, who had been captured at Wardour Castle, but Waller could only reply: 'it is my unhappiness that I am not capable of performing your command, they being by order from the Parliament directed to Sir Edward Hungerford removed to London. I was a mere stranger both to their taking and removal and therefore [accountable for neither]. I presume your nobleness will impute nothing to me in either . . .'[6] Waller had scored out in his draft the words placed here in parentheses, but they indicate a theme in his correspondence at this time. Without in any way wishing to fall under suspicion of unduly favouring the Royalist leaders, Waller did not want to forfeit his good name with them. It needed delicate steps to walk this tightrope and the deletions and rewriting in Waller's draft book bear witness to his carefulness. Fulsome phrases are crossed out and others substituted, but nowhere does the underlying courtesy falter.

There are four other letters from Waller about such matters, dated this same time, to Hertford, Prince Maurice and Hopton. For example, Waller notified Hertford that having heard that Captain Keighley, badly wounded at Chewton, was still alive, he had sent his servant to attend him, writing: 'it is no more than I have permitted to those gentlemen that are prisoners with me, unto whom I shall not be wanting to express all the civility I can.'

There was some trading of prisoners. For Lieutenant-Colonel Herbert Lunsford, 'a noble gallant gentlemen', Waller obtained James Carr, a Scots professional employed by the Gloucestershire Committee, who had been taken at Cirencester on 2 February. Carr could hardly be described as a Puritan in his dress. At this capture he claimed to have lost, among other items: 'one suit of Spanish cloth, layed with silver lace, a long riding coat of the same, a Dutch coat, lined with foxes, and a scarlet mantire [montero: iron skullcap] lay'd with a silver lace'. Clearly some Parliamentarian officers were as fashionably arranged as their Cavalier counterparts! Carr possessed a considerable reputation as a soldier, and Waller immediately appointed him Sergeant-Major-General of the Foot and dragoons, with the rank of full colonel.[7]

Probably in order to discuss this exchange of prisoners, Hopton wrote a letter to Waller suggesting a meeting between them. No doubt Sir Ralph hoped that his former comrade-in-arms and old friend might follow Carey's example and change sides, but Waller replied to the overture with a letter which had become justly famous:

To my noble friend Sir Ralph Hopton at Wells.

Sir

The experience I have had of your worth, and the happiness I have enjoyed in your friendship are wounding considerations when I look upon this present distance between us. Certainly my affections to you are so unchangeable, that hostility itself cannot violate my friendship to your person, but I must be true to the cause wherein I serve. The old limitation *usque ad aras* holds still, and where my conscience is interested, all other obligations are swallowed up.

I should most gladly wait on you according to your desire but that I look upon you as you are engaged in that party, beyond a possibility of retreat and consequently uncapable of being wrought upon by any persuasion. And I know the conference could never be so close between us, but that it would take wind and receive a construction to my dishonour.

That great God, which is the searcher of my heart, knows with what a sad sense I go upon this service, and with what a perfect hatred I detest this war without any enemy, but I look upon it as *Opus Domini*, which is enough to silence all passion in me. The God of peace in his good time send us peace, and in the mean time fit us to receive it. We are both upon the stage and must act those parts assigned us in this tragedy. Let us do it in a way of honour, and without personal animosities, whatsoever the issue be, I shall never willingly relinquish the dear title of

Your most affectionated friend

and faithful servant,

William Waller

Bath, 16 June 1643.[8]

79

CHAPTER ELEVEN

Victory at Lansdown

Towards the end of June the Royalist commanders impatiently advanced to Frome, where Sir James Hamilton, Major-General of Horse, and two regiments of horse and dragoons joined them. Contrary to Hopton's advice, Hamilton billeted his men in villages between Frome and Bath outside the ring of guards. Informed of this fact by his scouts, Waller sent the veteran French major of his regiment, Francis Dowett (or Duet) with 250 troopers to beat up Hamilton's quarters.

After the party had left, Waller received a firm report that the enemy in fact lay at Stoke Lane and he sent a messenger after Dowett with this information, but Dowett's guides did not know the whereabouts of the new objective and after wandering about the countryside in the dark they only found it by the light of dawn. Under cover of a morning mist the Parliamentarians stormed into the village, throwing grenades into the crowded houses and capturing the troopers of Hamilton's regiment of horse as they tumbled out of doors. With 15 officers, 97 soldiers, 140 horses and 60 case of pistols – all taken at Stoke Lane – Dowett returned to Waller's headquarters and presented the chief captives to his general. Quite apart from the prisoners, the episode had raised the morale of Waller's army – perhaps the main reward of a small success at the start of a campaign.[1]

On Sunday 2 July the King's army marched to Bradford-upon-Avon and secured the key bridge over the river. The Royalists could now march towards Oxford, or advance on either side of the Avon towards Bath, 5 miles away. Waller countered by leading out his army to Claverton Down, 2 miles west of the city, and poised himself to respond to whatever the Royalist generals chose to do.

Later that day Waller heard that the enemy had turned towards Bath, an drawing up his army in battle order on the down he sent Colonel Burghill with his regiment of horse and some commanded Foot north across the Avon beneath Claverton House, where he had previously constructed a bridge beside the ford and a redoubt on the north bank to defend both. That night Burghill occupied the high ground at Monkton Farleigh and laid an ambush in the woods at the foot of the hill.

Early next morning (Monday 3 July), like wasps stinging a sleeping lion, some troops of Burghill's Horse attacked the outguards of the Royalist army. Thus aroused, the Royalists advanced in good order towards

Monkton Farleigh. That morning, after 'a very hot dispute', the Cornish foot cleared the Parliamentarians out of the woods and gained the top of the hill. Having lost perhaps forty soldiers and two light 'murdering' pieces, Burghill made a fighting withdrawal towards the river. The Cavaliers in pursuit soon came up to the fortified crossing point and espied the bulk of Waller's army 2 miles away on Claverton Down.

A pause ensued while Prince Maurice rode up to assess the situation. Then he directed the Cornish infantry to assault the passage, which Burghill's men, with reinforcements, defended bravely.[2] But in the darkness the stout Cornishmen found their way over the river and entered the redoubt, only to find that Burghill's force had slipped away to Waller's main camp. 'Thus had the shifting Rebel deluded us one day with a party, hoping to make us weary with dancing about him, or else to fight where he pleas'd,' wrote the Royalist Lieutenant-Colonel Slingsby, not without admiration.[3]

The failure to hold the passage over the Avon compelled Waller to retreat into Bath, and by midnight the whole army had gained the city. Meanwhile, the Royalist forces became scattered in the dark as they advanced beyond the river, and one body of horse and foot found themselves in the fields near Lansdown, a long kidney-shaped hill dominating the surrounding countryside north of Bath. Hopton, Carnarvon and the other chief officers considered whether or not to ascend the steep slopes without delay, but the dispersed main Royalist forces could not be drawn up to Lansdown that night and rather than expose themselves to an attack from Waller's Horse, the leaders ordered a withdrawal to Bath Easton bridge. At the same time they advised the Marquis to quarter the rest of the army for the night and to try next morning to reach the Lansdown ridge in strength before the Parliamentarians bestirred themselves in Bath.

Before dawn on Tuesday 4 July the advance guard of the Royalist army with cannon and baggage noisily approached the southern flanks of the massive dark hill. As they drew near the foot the growing light revealed the whole Parliamentarian army waiting silently above them on the crest. Waller had divined the intentions of the Royalist generals and led his tired soldiers out of Bath in the small hours of the morning in order to occupy the high ground first. 'Indeed the General of the Rebels was the best shifter and chooser of ground when he was not master of the field that I ever saw, which are great abilities in a soldier,' commented Slingsby, who had remained for the night in the shadow of Lansdown with Lord Mohun's regiment of foot when the Horse withdrew to Bath Easton.

The Parliamentarians now enjoyed a grandstand view of their enemy's discomfiture as the teamsters strove to turn the baggage waggons, the cart-horses bucking and plunging as Waller's cannon banged away above them. Meanwhile, the main Royalist army halted on Banner Hill, a lower

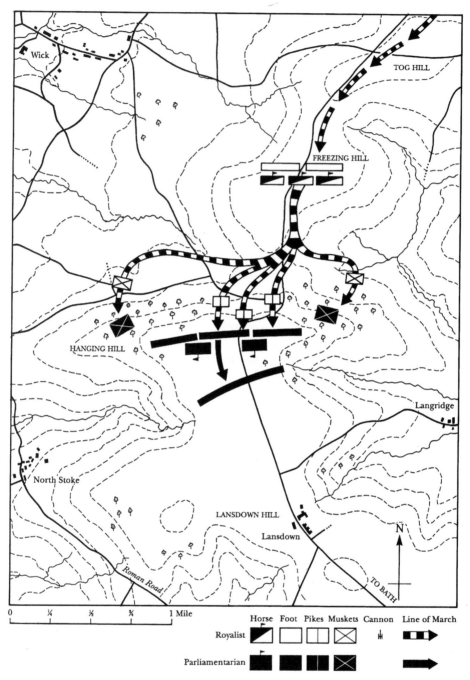

Wick

TOG HILL

FREEZING HILL

HANGING HILL

Langridge

North Stoke

LANSDOWN HILL

Lansdown

Roman Road

TO BATH

N

	Horse	Foot	Pikes	Muskets	Cannon	Line of March
Royalist						
Parliamentarian						

4. *The battle of Lansdown, 5 July 1643*

eminence within sight of Lansdown, where the forces from the valley eventually found them. Both Hopton and Slingsby, it should be noted, place the whole Royalist army in the valley beneath Lansdown. The Parliamentarian sources agree, however, in placing the main enemy body upon a hill at this point in the manoeuvring before the coming battle.

At about 1.00 p.m., after both armies had spent the morning watching each other, the Royalist generals resolved to retreat to Marshfield, four miles to the north-west. Under Hopton's professional eye, the army made a phased withdrawal along two narrow lanes leading to the town. In the same fashion as Waller at Ripple, he guarded the mouths of these lanes with 1,000 musketeers who easily beat off a Parliamentarian 'forlorn hope', and then retired with impunity behind a strong rearguard of their own horse to Marshfield.

Early next morning, Wednesday 5 July, Waller advanced up the old Roman road to the other end of Lansdown, a cross-ridge known at its western end as Hanging Hill, an apt name for the precipitous north face of the escarpment. Upon the highest point astride the highway the Parliamentarians began to throw up a breastwork of stones and timber cut from the nearby ash and beech woods. Meanwhile, the Royalist army had moved westwards from Marshfield and taken up a position upon the 700 feet Tog Hill, some 50 feet lower than Hanging Hill a mile and a half away.

Dragoons from each side began to dispute the hedgerows in the valley and on the plateau of Freezing Hill. After four or five hours of these skirmishes the Parliamentarian dragoons, supported by Captain John Butler's troop of Lobsters, had beaten their rivals back to the large cornfield at the foot of Tog Hill, and rather than waste more of their dwindling stocks of ammunition, the Royalist generals ordered a second withdrawal to Marshfield.

On Lansdown Waller read the minds of his adversaries. Seeing his opportunity he unleashed Major Dowett with 200 Horse, followed by a further 200 dragoons under Colonel Carr. The Royalist Captain Atkyns, present at the battle, declared 'this was the boldest thing that I ever saw the enemy do; for a party of less than 1,000 to charge an army of 6,000 horse, foot and cannon, in their own ground, at least a mile and a half from their body'.[4]

The Parliamentarian Horse and dragoons came on fast. While the Royalist troops masking the retreating infantry wheeled off one by one, they endured a galling fire from Waller's dragoons gathered along the nearest hedgerows, and soon their panic-stricken mounts spread disorder through the foot regiments. Seizing this advantage the Parliamentarian regiment of horse gallantly charged two enemy bodies of cavalry in the rearguard and scattered all but some Cornish foot protecting their flanks.

With pike and musket the Cornish held their ground until Carnarvon's regiment rode up to succour them with a charge. Meanwhile, Sir

Nicholas Slanning with 300 Royalist musketeers attacked a reserve of dragoons under Colonel Carr in the hedges by the lane to Freezing Hill. Gradually more Royalist forces turned back to join in the struggle, and their field guns opened fire to clear the skirts of Tog Hill. Before long Dowett and Carr had no option but to fall back towards Lansdown.

Seeing their plight, Waller ordered Burghill's regiment to advance and fall upon Carnarvon's horse in the flank if they pursued too far. A fierce and confused battle of charge and counter-charge raged between the cavalry forces, as dismounted dragoons and musketeers intermingled with the troopers and clustered behind hedges. Both commanders received wounds: one ball hit Burghill in the arm and another entered Carnarvon's leg. Eventually the Parliamentarians disengaged and made their way up to the brow of Lansdown, having recaptured the two cannon lost on the previous Monday. The fight had lasted two hours and it was now about 5.00 p.m.

'The enemy to encourage us to prosecute this success, gave all the symptoms of a flying army; as blowing up of powder, horse and foot running distractedly upon the edge of the hill, for we could see no further,' wrote Captain Atkyns. One Royalist officer, misled by these signs, begged Prince Maurice for a party to chase after them, but when he came up the hill and saw Waller's regiments still in battle order he thought better of it.

Meanwhile, the Royalist infantry on Freezing Hill, under fire from Waller's guns, shouted for an advance, crying out 'Let us fetch those cannon!' Their generals then gave orders for an attempt upon Lansdown, with a frontal assault up the highway and two flanking attacks on the east and west slopes. But Waller had posted strong parties of horse and foot in the thick woods on either side of his main position, and the slopes before him were almost inaccessible: 'thus fortified stood the fox gazing at us,' wrote Lieutenant-Colonel Slingsby.

Undaunted, the Cornish pikemen under Colonel Sir Bevil Grenvile marched forward, and supported by musketeers on their left and some Horse on the right where the ground was less broken, they reached the lee of the hill. On the steep ascent they were in deadground for much of the time, while a maze of hedges, dry walls and ridges beside the winding road protected them from small arms fire. But once the pikemen breasted the hill they were greeted with blasts of case-shot and some crackling volleys of musketry from the breastwork which halted them in their tracks.

Heselrige's regiment then gave them three shock charges. At the third of these Grenvile collapsed mortally wounded, while his captain-lieutenant fell dead beside him with an enemy colour wrapped around his arm. For their part, many of the Lobsters received pike wounds in their thighs, but the mounts suffered more than the heavily armoured cuirassiers.

Waller himself led four charges through a hail of shot, and his regiment took part in two. As more Cavaliers gained the hill, the 'charges grew so hot on both sides, as the like was never seen in England. Yea, some old soldiers did say, "That the furious fights in France were but a play in comparison of this."[5]

Captain Atkyns wrote: 'As I went up the hill, which was very steep and hollow, I met several dead and wounded officers brought off; besides several running away, that I had much ado to get up by them. When I came to the top of the hill I saw Sir Bevil Grenvile's stand of pikes, which certainly preserved our army from a total rout, with the loss of his most precious life. They stood as upon the eaves of an house for steepness, but as unmoveable as a rock; on which side of this stand of pikes our horse were, I could not discover; for the air was so darkened by the smoke of the powder, that for a quarter of an hour together (I dare say) there was no light seen, but what the fire of the volleys of shot gave; and 'twas the greatest storm that ever I saw, in which though I knew not whither to go, nor what to do. My horse had two or three musket bullets in him presently, which made him tremble under me at that rate and I could hardly with spurs keep him from lying down, but he did me the service to carry me off to a led horse and then died.'

At length the growing strength of the Royalist forces on the lip of the hill, and the opening shots from some light field pieces dragged up to support them, compelled Waller to withdraw his foot from the breastwork to a stone wall that ran across the down some hundred yards to the rear. At once the Royalist generals consolidated their regiments behind the abandoned defences, where they were joined by the musketeers who had at last penetrated the woods on either flank. Waller lined the wall with his own musketeers, and knocked down broad breaches in it so that his Horse could pass freely to and fro, guarding them carefully with pikemen and cannon.

When Atkyns reached the top of the escarpment a second time, at about 8.30 p.m., he found 'the heat of the battle was over, and the sun set, but still pelting at one another half musket shot off. The enemy had a huge advantage of ground upon our men, for their foot were in a large sheepcot, which had a stone wall about it, as good a defence against anything but cannon as could be, and ours upon the edge of a hill so steep that they could hardly draw up. 'Tis true there were shelves near the place like Romish works, where we quartered that night, but so shallow that my horse had a bullet in his neck.'

As darkness descended the crack and whine of bullets died away. Another eyewitness on the hill that night, Colonel Slingsby, described how, 'our right wing of shot [musketeers] got much nearer their army, lodging themselves amongst the many little pits betwixt the wall and the wood from whence we galled them cruelly. About 11 of the clock we receiv'd a very great volley of small shot but not mixed with cannon, by which some of us judg'd that he was retreating and gave this at his expiring. But the general apprehension through our army was that the enemy had intention to try to push in the night for their ground, which they had so dishonourably lost; for we were then seated like a heavy stone upon the very brow of the hill, which with one lusty charge might well have bin roll'd to the bottom.

'It was not long before we knew certainly that they were gone. At their departures they left all their light match upon the wall and whole bodies of pikes standing upright in order within the wall as if men had held them.' Alas, Waller could not know that the Royalist council of war had resolved that in the event of a night attack every man would be told to shift for himself, and accordingly had drawn off their cannon and most of the horse to Tog Hill.

'We had a weary and dangerous days fight the night parting us and so well did we knock each other than in the night we both retreated,' wrote Waller in his despatch to the Speaker. 'Many of their chief commanders and officers were slayne or hurt we lost only one sergeant major of the dragoons and two cornets and not twenty common soldiers. We had the advantage of the ground but the Cornish hedgers beat us from it, though they bought it at a dear rate when our foot left it we maintained it with our horse, and those Sir Arthur Heselrige brought from London did most excellent service.'[6]

Waller counted Lansdown among his victories.[7] He had fought the battle at long range as long as he could, like a boxer leading with long left jabs against a stocky and more powerful opponent. By moving at night and using the reverse slope of Lansdown he had hidden his deficiency of foot from the enemy. His men had equalled the Royalists in valour and inflicted heavier casualties upon them. He had captured 5 officers, 97 common soldiers and 140 horses.[8] Finally, he had made a skilful withdrawal to Bath, leaving burning match and pikes to simulate a watchful army. Although he had left the field to the enemy, the strategic advantage after the day lay with him. Despite the counter-claims of contemporary Royalists and many modern historians, Waller had a rather better right to claim Lansdown as a victory than had his opponents. Yet if this round may be awarded to him on points, the bout as a whole had yet to be decided.

CHAPTER TWELVE

My Dismal Defeat at Roundway Down

The Royalists spent an hour or two after dawn on Thursday 6 July combing the field of Lansdown for discarded weapons and burying the dead. The sun rose into a clear blue sky and, warmed by its rays, the Cavalier army moved back to the rendezvous on Tog Hill, which now became the scene of a remarkable accident.

Sir Ralph Hopton had ridden over to view the prisoners, some of whom were being carried on an ammunition waggon. They had been given burning match to light their tobacco, and a spark from one fell and ignited the gunpowder, blowing them all up. Captain Atkyns found Hopton 'miserably burnt, his horse sing'd like parch'd leather'.[1] Eight barrels of precious powder had gone up in smoke and Hopton, already wounded in the right arm, was badly shocked. The discouraged army marched off to Marshfield, with Hopton travelling on a bed in the Marquess's coach.

In Bath the noise of the loud explosion elated the Parliamentarians for they knew the enemy's lack of ammunition. That day their own wagons were replenished with sixty barrels of powder from Bristol. All Thursday and Friday morning the army refreshed itself in the city. During this time Waller interviewed some of the Royalist prisoners, including the lieutenant of Captain Atkyns' troop, who had been captured unhurt but then cruelly shot twice with pistols by a Scot. He later informed Atkyns that 'Sir William Waller . . . seemed exceedingly angry at the inhumane action that befel him, and sent for his own chirurgeon immediately, and saw him dressed before he went away. He gave the innkeeper charge that he should have whatever he called for, and he would see him paid; that whateover woman he sent for to attend him, should be admitted, and lent him ten broad pieces for his own private expenses.'[2] This Samaritan compassion clearly made a profound impression on the young man. Few incidents reveal so clearly Waller's essential humanity.

Hearing from his scouts that Hertford had begun to move out of Marshfield towards Devizes, Waller determined 'to attend him, not doubting but his bulk of plunder would something retard his journey'. A vaunting sense of confidence now possessed him. He bade a servant of

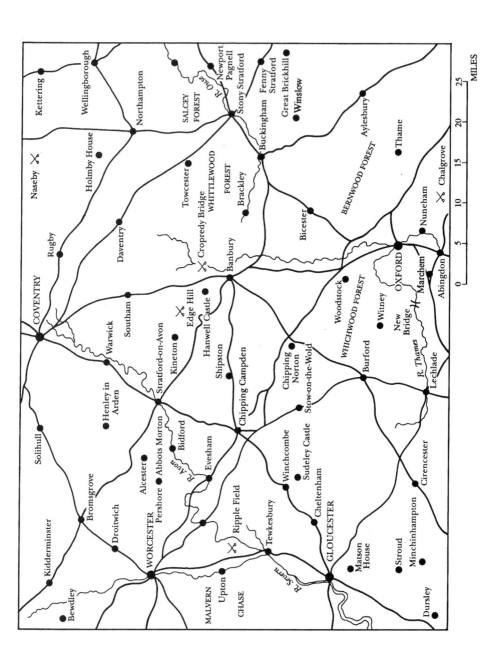

5. *Central England at the time of the Civil War*

Lady Beauchamp 'to remember his service towards her and to tell her that within five days he hoped to set all their hearts at quiet'.³ His letter to the House of Commons, dated 7 July, asked only for money and reinforcements to prosecute his success.⁴ In Bath Lady Waller sent servants to the crowds outside their house to 'bid the good people go home for the work was done already'.⁵ With high spirits the Parliamentarian army marched out of the city on Friday evening to deliver the *coup de grâce.*

On Saturday 8 July, at about 4.00 p.m., Waller's scouts reported that the enemy could be found in Chippenham, some 3 miles away. Expecting to fight a battle west of the town, Waller drew up his army on a plain facing it. The Royalists, deprived of food and intelligence as the country folk transferred their sympathies to the more promising army, marched wearily out to confront him on a moor close to the town suburbs. Parties of Horse bickered together that evening, but they precipitated no general engagement. After a night in the fields the Royalist regiments stood until noon on Sunday, while the generals exchanged some prisoners with Waller.

One of the returned prisoners brought a message from the Marquess desiring that 'there might be good quarter betwixt our Armies, and that we might fight no more in holes, but in the champagne [open and flat ground]'. In answer to this, Sir William sent a trumpeter with a characteristically humorous letter to say 'that he would meet his lordship that afternoon about Sherston-in-the-Plain; and if his lordship wanted powder . . . he would lend him some for the Fight'.⁶ As Sherston lay 8 miles to the north, 'a place I know not where out of the way' wrote one Royalist,⁷ Waller's offer may be taken as light-hearted jest. About noon Hertford replied by hastening back over Chippenham bridge towards Devizes, taking the trumpeter with him for 2 or 3 miles.

Waller's advance guard entered Chippenham on the heels of the retreating Royalists and scattered there one of their troops of horse. On the road to Devizes many deserters turned back to the pursuers, laying down their arms, including muskets ready charged and bandoliers full of powder. Three miles from Devizes Waller ordered his cavalry to attack. 'We fell upon there rear and having little & little beaten their ambuscades they began to start. We killed many & took many prisoners . . .'⁸ Lord Mohun's regiment of foot stiffened the Cavalier rearguard at a ford just north of Rowde Hamlet, making a stand in the open, but when the regiment marched off it left forty dead beside the brook and carried away seventeen wounded. But the blood of these gallant soldiers purchased time for their comrades to reach Devizes, where dusk hindered any further action. Even so, the Royalists had been well and truly beaten into the town.

That night Waller sent three troops to secure a dominating hill some 2 miles north of the town – Roundway Down. Next morning he concentrated the whole army on this dominating feature while the Royalist Horse paraded in battle order on a hill east of the town. Waller commanded three regiments of horse to fall upon them, but the Cavaliers retreated into Devizes before they could come to grips. Here they were comparatively safe behind the town ditches on the north and east, while steep slopes protected the south and west approaches. These defences had been strengthened by some unfinished earthworks begun by Sir Edward Baynton some months earlier, and now Hertford's foot soldiers set to work to complete them. Meanwhile, a body of Parliamentarian musketeers came close and played upon them with their shot until nightfall put an end to their work.

In the gathering dusk Waller had a narrow escape. 'Having been out to visit the guards, and returning to a farm house (at the foot of Roundway Down) where I have given order to my cook, that my supper should be ready against I came in, and finding the meat but newly laid to the fire; in a sudden impatience I resolved not to sup at all, and so took horse again and rode up to the top of the Down, where the body of my horse lay. I was not gone above a musket shot but some of the enemy (knowing the avenues thereabout which I did not; and rationally supposing I might quarter in that place; in regard of the convenient situation of it, between my horse and my foot) came into the house and inquired and made a search for me, and if I had stayed there (as at first I intended) in all probability they might have suddenly dispatched me, and retired in the darkness of night with safety enough.

'Some days after whilst I lay before the town, I rode with a small party about the quarters, particularly to see how the dragoons were laid on the further side of the town; and being about to return back, it pleased God to put it suddenly into my mind, to go another way than that I came, with some of the party, and some of mine own servants (who stayed a little behind) not observing, but taking the former way, they were almost taken by the enemy. I came back in safety.'[9] According to a tavern keeper, Waller rode to Potterne, 2 miles south of Devizes, on one occasion and requisitioned £12 worth of brandy, beer and sack from him. But this man was possibly either mistaken as to the identity of the Parliamentarian 'commissary' or used Sir William's name deliberately to strengthen his case for recovering his money.[10]

Meanwhile, the Royalist generals in Devizes had agreed upon a bold plan. At a council of war held at Hopton's lodgings on Monday evening (10 July) they resolved that the horse under Hertford and Prince Maurice would break out eastwards and ride hard for Oxford while Hopton stayed with the Foot in the town. Then the Prince would return from Oxford with reinforcements and fall upon Waller's army.

Accordingly, the horse mustered in the market place at midnight and galloped away clear of the town without meeting any enemy. 'Over Salisbury plain,' wrote Waller, 'they rid very fast yet all cried "halt halt" but no man stood.'[11] That is except Captain Atkyns, who dropped out of the 40 mile ride when his horse cast two shoes and reeled into Faringdon so exhausted that people thought he was dead drunk.[12]

Next evening Waller's scouts brought him word that 600 Royalist Horse convoying some ammunition wagons from Oxford were approaching from the north-east. Waller sent out an interception party chosen from his own regiment of horse. The two parties clashed in a valley and milled around in the dark firing at friend and foe alike. Major Dowett, however, rallied two troops on the hillside, and charged the enemy in the valley. Already struck by panic, the Earl of Crawford's and Colonel James Long's regiments abandoned five wagons and fled back towards Marlborough. Beside the ammunition and a few prisoners, the Parliamentarians took eight colours. Shortly afterwards another party of Waller's Horse dispersed a Royalist regiment of horse brought from Oxford by Lord Wilmot.[13]

Waller had already sent several urgent despatches to the Earl of Essex imploring him to prevent the King from sending reinforcements to the beleaguered Royalist army.[14] Confident that this would be done, he brought his whole army to Devizes in preparation for a storm, only to receive a trumpeter from Hopton with a request for a truce. 'Being desirous, as he professed, to prevent blood spilling we lost that day by not agreeing,' Waller reported. The corpse of his friend, Sir Bevil Grenvile, was carried through the Parliamentarian lines on its journey to Cornwall, but nothing else resulted from the truce except that Hopton gained a day's respite for his men. That morning, upon hearing that only 150 pounds of match remained in store, the resourceful Royalist general ordered a captain to go from house to house collecting all the bedcords of the town. Beaten and boiled, these cords provided his men with 15 hundredweight of serviceable match.

By this time the Cornish musketeers could use plenty of match, for Waller's soldiers followed up the preliminary overtures of Tuesday evening with a full-scale assault on Wednesday morning, and a battery well-sited upon Coatefield, a hill near the town, poured shot of all sizes onto the streets. The Royalists resisted stoutly. 'We so barricaded the avenues,' Slingsby recollected, 'that their horse could not charge in upon us, neither durst their foot attempt us, we being almost twice their number, and better foot.' In these circumstances the Parliamentarian infantry did well to take some of the outworks. Apart from edging forward to within musket range of the defenders and firing off their pieces they could do little else.

In spite of the failures of his soldiers before Hopton's timber barricades and the steady downpour of rain Waller's spirits soared. In a letter dated 'Roundaway this 12 July, 1643', he wrote to the Speaker: 'We hope God will . . . not destroy this mighty army of the West. He has wrought wonders for us and we hope the Lord will keep us from that great strength they expect from Oxford. . . . We have had such experience

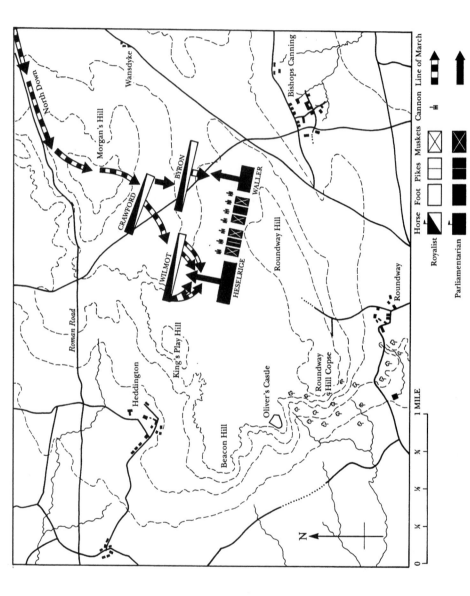

6. *The battle of Roundway Down, 13 July 1643*

Morgan's Hill

North Down

Wansdyke

CRAWFORD

BYRON

WALLER

WILMOT

HESELRIGE

Roundway Hill

Bishops Canning

Roman Road

Heddington

King's Play Hill

Beacon Hill

Oliver's Castle

Roundway Hill Copse

Roundway

N

0 ¼ ½ ¾ 1 MILE

Horse Foot Pikes Muskets Cannon Line of March

Royalist

Parliamentarian

of God that we doubt not to give you a good account of Sir Ralph Hopton, for the present he is miserably burned with powder. We will faithfully labour in your service so long as lives, Sir, your servants. . . . We have taken at least 200 prisoners and divers officers and one Mr Parsons.' (The latter, an 'intelligencer' or spy, was taken with Crawford's troopers.) On the other hand, the long summer days in the field had taxed the stamina of both men and horses. 'This last fortnight we have had scarce leisure to eat or sleep and never more troubled then at this time,' Waller added, to excuse the brevity of his account.[15]

Later in his life, Waller referred to this letter in his *Experiences*: 'so sure was I of victory that I wrote to Parliament to bid them be at rest, for that I would shortly send them an account of the numbers taken and the numbers slain.' Such was his mood of confidence and spiritual elation.

Trouble increased tenfold next morning with the news that a great body of enemy Horse had been sighted in the direction of Marlborough. Due to his good intelligence, Waller had time to draw off all his soldiers from the outskirts of Devizes to a new position on Roundway Down facing northwards. The plateau on top of the down lay like the bottom of a broad and shallow bowl, bounded upon its rim by high ground: King's Play Hill and Morgan's Hill on the north and Roundway Hill, which sloped up to 795 feet at its eastern end. Waller arrayed his army on the northern slopes of this hill, with his foot together in two bodies in the centre, protected by field guns and flanked by two wings of Horse – Heselrige's brigade on the left and his own on the right. Towards 2.00 p.m. on Thursday 13 July these waiting soldiers caught their first sight of a dense column of Cavalier Horse less than 2 miles away on Morgan's Hill.

With remarkable speed Prince Maurice had returned with three brigades of horse – Lord Wilmot's, Sir John Byron's and Crawford's – a total strength of between 1,800 and 2,000 troopers.

Trotting down the straight Roman road from Marlborough over the back of North Down they had turned south onto the 800-ft eminence, Morgan's Hill, where they halted for an hour in sight of Waller's army. Here two light guns were fired, the prearranged signal for the Foot in Devizes to march out with colours flying and fall upon the backs of the Parliamentary army. Although the Royalist gunners lodged in the old castle answered with their pieces, and Hopton urged an advance, a majority of the chief officers at a hastily summoned council of war voted against such a move, fearing that this might be merely a fox-like stratagem to tempt them into open country. Consequently, Waller's reputation enabled him to face the Oxford Horse without being attacked in the rear.[16]

Meanwhile, Lord Wilmot, the Royalist commander, had deployed his regiments. He placed his own brigade on the right, in extended order three ranks deep. On the left and some distance behind, Byron's regiments spread out in a similar formation, while Crawford's smaller brigade, not yet recovered from the upset on Monday night, stood in reserve. On Roundway Hill young Captain Edward Harley, waiting at the head of his troop in Waller's regiment, estimated their strength as 'forty or fifty colours of horse besides dragoons'.[17] At about 3.00 p.m. the trumpeters sounded the advance and the long lines of troops descended into the plain.[18]

As they drew nearer, a Parliamentarian 'forlorn hope' rode out to harass them, but fell back before a Cavalier advance guard of 300 commanded men. With or without orders from Waller, Heselrige then led his regiment of Lobsters forward to support the fleeing troopers. Having formed up his troops in thick clumps six deep and in close order, he doubtless hoped to punch a hole through the extended brigade of Wilmot, but at a full trot the Cavalier regiments caught the Lobsters as in a well-thrown net. Captain Atkyns, who charged in the right centre with Prince Maurice's regiment, graphically compared the scene to an old chart of the English fleet overlapping the Spanish Armada at both ends. The cannoneers in front of Heselrige failed to fire their guns and 'the impenetrable regiment' gave ground.[19] Heselrige rallied them once for a charge and recovered four pieces but, seeing the second Cavalier brigade ready to support Wilmot and already out-numbered by perhaps four to one, his cuirassiers broke away and galloped off the field in wild confusion westwards towards Bath.

Captain Atkyns chased Heselrige at a gallop down one steep slope of Roundway Down: 'in six score yards I came up to him, and discharged the other pistol at him, and I'm sure I hit his head, for I touched it before I gave fire, and it amazed him at that present, but he was too well armed all over for a pistol bullet to do him any hurt, having a coat of mail over his arms and a headpiece (I am confident) musket proof, his sword had two edges and a ridge in the middle, and mine a strong tuck. After I had slackened my pace a little, he was gone twenty yards from me. Riding three quarters speed and down the side of a hill, his posture was waving his sword on the right and left hand of his horse, not looking back [to see] whether he were pursued or not, (as I conceive) to daunt any horse that should come up to him. About six score yards more I came up to him again . . . and stuck by him a good while, and tried him from head to saddle, and could not penetrate him from head to saddle . . .' Eventually, while Heselrige fumbled with the cord attaching his sword to his wrist so that he could hand the weapon to Atkyns, two of his troopers turned back, rescued their colonel with a charge and led him thrice-wounded to safety.

Later, upon hearing this story, presumably from the lips of Richard Atkyns himself, King Charles aptly jested that had Heselrige been 'victualled as well as fortified he could have endured a siege for seven years'.[20]

After the flight of Heselrige's regiment, Waller advanced down the hill with his own brigade of horse flanking the two bodies of foot in battle order. Byron made ready to charge them while Wilmot rallied his horse ready to second him if occasions arose. As the Cavaliers walked their mounts forward, two field guns in front of Waller's horse fired ineffectually at them. On the left some of Waller's dragoons made brisk practice on them and a regiment of horse watched for an opportunity to fall on them in rear or flank, only to have their attention diverted by Crawford's reserve.

Sir John Byron wrote: 'By this time, we were come very near to Waller's Brigade, and the command I gave my men was, that not a man should discharge a pistol till the enemy had spent all his shot, which was punctually observed, So that first they gave us a volley of their carbines, then of their pistols, and then we fell in with them and gave them ours in their teeth.

'Yet they would not quit their ground but stood pushing for it a pretty space, till is pleased God, (I think) to put new spirit into our tir'd horse as well as into our men, so that though it were up the hill, and that a steep one, we overbore them, and with that violence that we forced them to fall fowl upon other reserves of horse that stood behind to second them, and so swept their whole body of horse out of the field, and left their foot naked, and pursued them near three miles over the downs in Bristol way till they came to a precipice, where their fear made them so valiant that they gallop'd down as if it had been plain ground, and many of them broke their own and their horses necks. In my return from the chase, I took two pieces of their cannon, and divers waggons laden with ammunition, and then rallied together our scattered troops, which were as much broken as the enemy by reason of their hot pursuit . . .'[21]

In his memoirs, the Royalist Lieutenant-Colonel Slingsby alleged that Waller fled with the horse. On 5 August Sir Simonds D'Ewes, an Earl of Essex supporter, referred in a speech in the House of Commons to Waller as a 'man who departed away with his horse whilst his foot were fighting'. According to Clarendon, Essex later reproached Waller with having 'deserted his foot and cannon without engaging his own person in one charge against the enemy'. But Sir John Byron may be safely followed on this point. It was reported to him that Waller was among those who stayed on the battlefield. Certainly the two large bodies of Parliamentarian musketeers and pikemen, each probably 600 strong, stood their ground bravely on the very top of Roundway Down for an hour or more, beating off Lord Wilmot's charges and waiting in vain for a return of their Horse. Their brave conduct suggests the presence of good leaders, and Waller was ever one to share the dangers and hardships of his men. Then, a mile below them, the beleaguered and weary Parliamentarian clumps of pikemen and musketeers saw the fresh

Cornish Foot marching up the road from Devizes, itching to join the battle. The appearance of these infantry and the growing weight of the Cavalier charges as more troops returned from the pursuit caused Waller and Popham to order a retreat eastwards.

At first the bristling squares of Foot began 'gently to march off, their officers marching before them amongst which (as I have been told since) Sir William Waller himself was, and Popham,' wrote Byron. 'With that I advanc'd toward them with those troops I had rallied, and shot at them with the cannon I had formerly taken. Their officers thought it not fit to stay any longer, but such as had horses rid away as fast as they could, and too fast for us to overtake them, and the rest blew up their powder, and threw down their arms and betook themselves to their heels.'

While Sir William and his officers rode off towards Bristol, the Foot, who did not cry for quarter, ran hard for the wooded east slopes. The Cavaliers cut many down in the open and others died in an area known today as 'Bloody Ditch' at the foot of the hillside. They claimed to have killed 600 of them and taken 800 prisoners, but these figures may well have been double the actual ones. Thirty-six colours were seized from the survivors or picked up on the field.

'We have not lost many men considering what a miserable rout we were in,' wrote Captain Harley. At Lansdown against pikes he had lost ten mounts and two men; at Roundway, in a cavalry action, five or six more men.[22] His troop may be taken as an index for the cavalry losses at Roundway: perhaps fifty troopers slain and as many badly wounded. Seven brass cannon, all the baggage and ammunition had been lost. Many regiments, scattered over the countryside, could never be reformed as the soldiers had made off homewards. The morale of those who could be gathered at Bath and Bristol had cracked like a broken bell. Only after the regiments had been melted down and recast would the army as a whole ever ring true again. 'Such,' wrote Waller, 'was my dismal defeat at Roundway Down.'[23]

Waller rode back to Bath in deep despair, for the disaster that afternoon had mortally wounded his hopes that he might become the general of a new army. In London some of the more militant Members of Parliament, displeased with the Lord General's conduct of affairs and suspicious of his peace overtures to the King, had secretly planned to raise their own army and pay it well – the first suggestion of a 'new model'.

Waller knew of this design and concluded that his rout at Roundway would kill the possibility that he might be chosen as general over their projected forces. 'This was the most heavy stroke of any that did ever befall me; General Essex had thought fit to persuade the Parliament to compromise with the King; which so inflamed the zealous that they moved that the command of their army might be bestow'd upon me; but the news of this defeat arrived whilst they were deliberating on my advancement, and it was to me a double defeat. I had nearly sunk under the affliction, but that I had a dear and sweet comforter; and I did at that time prove according to Ecclesiasticus, chap xxvi. *A virtuous woman rejoiceth her husband . . . . As the sun when it ariseth in the high heaven, so is the beauty of a good wife.*'[24] In these circumstances it is not surprising that Waller's friends saw in the Lord General's failure to prevent the Oxford cavalry marching to Devizes a thinly disguised plot to discredit him utterly.

The disaster at Roundway Down also caused great consternation in London and indeed throughout the Parliamentarian camp, for it crowned a summer of misfortune. On 18 June Prince Rupert's Cavaliers on a sally from Oxford had slain John Hampden on Chalgrove Field (18 June). Such was Hampden's stature that Parliament had suffered a grievous blow. Moreover, Pym had lost in him perhaps his most valuable link with Essex. It must be added that Hampden, Cromwell's first cousin, had shown himself to be a brave and capable commander, and he had been suggested as a possible replacement for the Earl of Essex as Parliament's Commander-in-Chief. Thus his chance death at Chalgrove, as far as Waller was concerned, removed from the stage a possible rival.

In the North the Earl of Newcastle had totally beaten the Fairfaxes on the Yorkshire field of Adwalton Moor (30 June), while in the Midlands the Queen had arrived at Oxford safely with a great train of arms and ammunition and reinforcements. Had Newcastle exploited his success by marching swiftly south, Parliament's situation could have been desperate.

On 16 July Waller drew out his cavalry from Bristol onto the nearby Durdham Down. After the review, Waller held a council of war, attended by Nathaniel Fiennes, Heselrige, Alexander Popham, William Carr (major of the Lobsters), Edward Cooke and Vandruske. It was a common practice in those times for a general to hold a council of war, even if they had already made up their minds what to do. For it could be held against them that they had not listened to advice in such critical situations if they were ever brought to trial for incompetence later.

Apparently, Fiennes asked Waller for the Bristol Horse and the surviving Foot. Sir William hesitated, saying that he might yet take the field and would need some infantry. Next morning, after a further meeting of the council of war, Waller decided to march off to Gloucester, and there to form a relief army to harry the Royalists if they besieged Bristol.

Before Waller departed with 'fifteen weak troops that did not contain 600 men',[25] he asked Fiennes to sign a declaration approving his decision to withdraw in this manner. Fiennes did so, remarking in a subsequent pamphlet: 'I am still of the same judgement under the favour of this great soldier, especially if Sir William Waller's words were true concerning his horse, that they were such rascals as he could never rule them.' Against this testimony, however, must be set the evidence of Edward Cooke at the subsequent court martial trial of Fiennes, that it was Fiennes who had first suggested that Waller should leave Bristol.[26]

The day after Waller's night march to Gloucester, Prince Rupert marched westwards with a large army to join the victors of Roundway Down, for an attempt upon Bristol. The King urged his nephew to disperse Waller's forces before moving against Bristol but the Prince wisely followed his own counsel and resolved to storm Bristol first.

Waller paused in Gloucester to inspect Colonel Edward Massey's preparations for a siege. Leaving him 200 troopers he then set out for Warwick. 'As I was fording the Severn, at a place near Gloucester, where on either hand of the passage (which was a narrow bank of sand) the water was of a great depth, my horse fell into a disorder and plunged into the deep water with me (being then in my arms) where I was likely to have perished, if with the blessing of God, he had not swum through with me.'[27]

Ironically, when Waller rode into Warwick with 400 men the townsfolk, who had not heard the news of 'Runaway Down', still hailed him as 'William the Conqueror'.[28] Better informed contemporaries would no longer employ that proud sobriquet. The Royalist poet Sir John Denham, who had once suffered defeat at Waller's hands, expressed this fact triumphantly in his lines:

> Great William the Con
> So fast did he run
> That he left half his name behind him.[29]

Colonel Oliver Cromwell wrote in a letter, 'Sir William Waller whom some called *William the Conqueror* has been beaten all to pieces'.[30]

Thus to many, Royalists and Parliamentarians alike, it seemed that Waller's career, like a meteor, had spent itself and fallen into darkness. As he rode towards London Sir William braced himself to eat the bitter fruits of defeat, but a kind Providence and new political patrons had prepared a different banquet for him.

PART THREE

London's General

CHAPTER THIRTEEN

A Warm Welcome

'This town is all mad for raising a new Army for Sir William Waller who, they say, the City will have as their general,' wrote Thomas Knyvett from London in the third week of July 1643.[1] Behind this enthusiasm may be glimpsed the emergence of a 'vehement' or 'violent' party, anxious to block the peace overtures made by the Earl of Essex earlier that month, and a 'moderate' party who supported Essex.[2]

The nucleus of the 'vehement' party – the 'zealous' or 'godly' – stood ultimately for radical changes in the civil and ecclesiastical polity, but this agenda was hidden at first behind a more general enthusiasm for prosecuting the war, until victory in the field was secured. 'Before they quartered any distinction they were not visible,' wrote Waller some five or six years later, with the advantage of hindsight, 'but went in the crowd among those honest men that stood for the interest of religion and liberty; only they were marked for their extraordinary diligence and activity to advance and promote the service, which knit my heart to them.'[3]

At this time the core of this party in the House of Commons numbered about thirty Members of Parliament, stronger than that wing of the moderate party which inclined most towards the peace settlement. The true power in the Lower House still lay with the much larger middle group of moderates, who wanted peace only on their own terms, and under Pym's leadership these members veered in late July towards a policy of fighting on and seeking the aid of the Scots to provide the overwhelming strength necessary for a clear victory. Among the fluid and inchoate factions in the House the relatively small but cohesive group of Independents – as they later came to be labelled – acted as both spark and priming powder for a new explosion of fervour for the cause.[4]

The Independents could count on much support in the City of London, where the Lord Mayor, Isaac Pennington, headed an active 'vehement' party. The disaster in the West had awoken the City to the need for action. As a London citizen, John Greene, had recorded in his diary, the news of Roundway Down 'struck terror generally and men were much disheartened with it that were for the Parliament . . . the City being much troubled'.[5]

The promotion of generals other than Essex, whom these more militant leaders in particular looked upon, in Clarendon's words, 'as a man that would not keep them company to the end of their journey',[6]

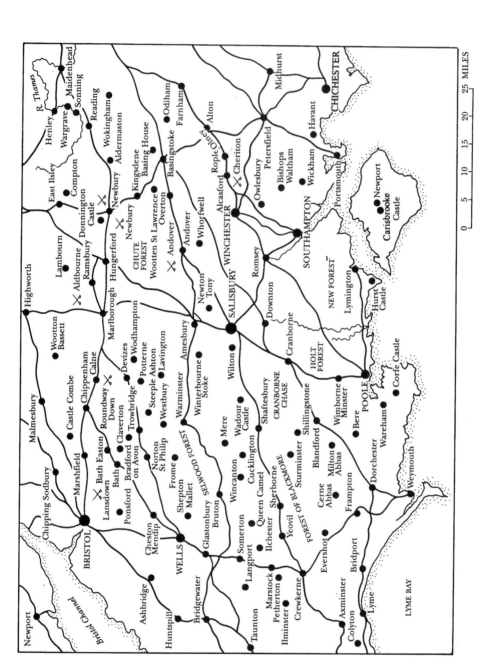

7. *South-western England at the time of the Civil War*

now became the main aim of the 'vehements'. The command of 'a moving body'; of 6,500 Horse and dragoons, voted on 18 July as a direct result of Waller's defeat at Roundway Down (which reached the House of Commons two days earlier) for the defence of Parliament, City, counties adjacent and the whole Kingdom, went to the Earl of Manchester.[7]

Edward Montague, Earl of Manchester, who was forty-one years old, had emerged as a Puritan leader in the House of Lords. He had the distinction of being named along with the Five Members. He raised a regiment of foot and fought under Essex at Edgehill. His personal courage was not in doubt, but his regiment quit the field of Edgehill with indecent speed and was disbanded in November 1642. In August, a few weeks after the vote on 18 July, Manchester was appointed by Essex to be Sergeant-Major-General of forces to be raised by the six counties in the Eastern Association. As a person he was modest, 'a sweet meek man' as his chaplain Simeon Ashe described him. But he lacked the necessary self-confidence to be a Commander-in-Chief, and he 'often professed unto the chief commanders, that because he himself was no experienced soldier, therefore he would rather be guided, than guide'. Politically, Manchester belonged to the more moderate wing of the Parliamentarians, and, as events would reveal, this stance made him less than fully committed to outright victory. Not a suitable general for the new army envisioned in London in July 1643, but better – men might argue – than the Earl of Essex.

Immediately after the vote on 18 July a number of London aldermen and common councillors successfully petitioned the House that all forces raised in the City (in this case 1,500 of the total) should be under the sole command of the Committee of Militia, subject to the direction of Parliament.[8] These cavalry forces, however, would only be the trained troops from London and the surrounding counties, mustered as a show of strength to deter the Royalists from brushing aside the weak army of Essex and marching on the capital.

Two days later (20 July) the militants presented their own petition. 'Divers inhabitants of the City of London and other gentlemen' gave the Lower House the names of those members in both Houses whom they wished to be given power to enlist 10,000 soldiers into regiments 'not only thereby to be siding to the Lord General the Earl of Essex by way of diversion, but to be a distinct Army to fall on the enemy, and to be assisting to the seven thousand horse aforesaid'.

With Royalist forces based on Reading menacing Surrey and Sussex, rumours of an insurrection in Kent, and Prince Rupert at the gates of Bristol, the Lower House resolved to overlook the breach of privilege occasioned by the petitioners nominating the members of the proposed committee, holding that the urgent necessities of the time and the good intentions of the petitioners sufficiently covered this irregularity. Thirteen

Members of Parliament were appointed to the committee under the leadership of Colonel Henry Marten,[9] a fiery militant, to raise, pay and equip the new army and to make recommendation to the House of a fit person to command the forces by an authority to be sought from the Lord General.[10] Without further delay they held their first meeting that Saturday afternoon (22 July) in the Merchant Taylors' Hall. The temper of the new committee may in part be gauged by its choice of chairman, Marten was a convinced republican and later a regicide. Being, in Aubrey's words, 'a lover of pretty girls' (he certainly preferred his mistress to his wife), he would one day live to offend his Puritan associates such as Pym and Cromwell, even those who shared his desire to extirpate the monarchy. At the Restoration he was imprisoned for life and died in Chepstow Castle.

Three days later, on Tuesday 25 July, Waller rode into London accompanied by a cavalcade of a hundred or more of his officers. The City gave them a tumultuous welcome. Cannon roared and bells pealed joyously as the trained bands escorted Sir William through the cheering crowds in the streets. Once in London 'his person, being a man known to be of much honour and courage, silenced invectives against him'.[11]

Parliament greeted him with equal warmth (Sir Simonds D'Ewes, for example, referred in his journal that week to Waller as 'a man of extraordinary valour and integrity'[12]) and soon showed that it still esteemed his advice. On Wednesday 26 July, a day of solemn fast, the Houses called Pym and Waller from church in the middle of the sermon to confer about an unfounded report that the Royalists had entered Sussex. The disastrous defeat at Roundway Down had at least brought Waller back to the centre of power.

Those Puritans intent on winning the war courted Sir William Waller above all others. 'Upon my return to London I found (contrary to my expectation) a multitude of friends (so called) . . . in the Independent party that appeared for me. In that heat (as the sun is ever hottest after a cloud) I had an offer of a very considerable army to be raised and put under my command, with a constant maintenance of it.'[13] The Merchant Taylors' Hall committee proposed, and the Commons accepted, Waller as the Commander-in-Chief of the forces to be raised in London for 'a Flying Army'. The House promised Waller a full and large commission (yet still subordinate to the Lord General), hoping that thus armed he would be able to march as soon as possible to the relief of the West.[14]

Thursday afternoon (27 July) saw an impressive scene in the thronged Merchant Taylors' Hall. In a 'brief but most pertinent' speech Waller addressed the citizens who had assembled to make loans or to list themselves in the new regiments, declaring 'that since through their approbation the Parliament had appointed him their Commander-in-Chief, and that they were willing to hazard their lives in this cause, he would go along, and spend his blood with them, in the defence of their Religion, Laws and Liberties.'[15]

After these stirring words the coins cascaded onto the receivers' tables, backed by promises of a substantial weekly contribution for the new 'flying army'. On Saturday 29 July the Common Council of the City of London also voted Sir William Waller as general of the projected forces, a necessary step as it would be largely raised in the capital. Thus within five days of his arrival at the capital Waller found himself elected and partially confirmed as the head of a proposed handsome army of 10,000 men. Not bad for a general who had suffered a grievous defeat sixteen days earlier.

Parliament had nominated him and the City had approved him, but there remained the third estate in the trinity of military power – the Lord General. Paradoxically, the House of Commons now found itself confronted with an authority bestowed upon one man by Parliament – not unlike the royal prerogative in its effect if not in origin – which could be used to gainsay them. For the Lord General could be as tardy in granting the commissions proposed in the Lower House as the King had been in signing their bills.

'It is reported that Lord Essex is much incensed with the City for Saturday's business, for making Sir William Waller a general, and for their neglect and slight of him. He sent Sir Philip Stapleton the last night to the Houses with a letter, showing how much he is undervalued and abused, together with some propositions to them, and some resolutions of his own,' wrote a Royalist in a newsletter that week. 'Some of the lords are also discontented: if not prevented, they are likely to be of the Earl of Essex's opinion, and be ready to side with him in that course he intends ere long. God direct him and them!'[16]

Essex presented his case in the House of Lords on Friday 28 July. He told the peers that his soldiers were deserting from their regiments for the 'entertainment' money and better wages of Waller's new army, and that he could now muster no more than 2,500 Horse and 3,000 Foot. In his propositions he asked for arrears of pay, 400 pressed horsemen immediately, and a further 200 every month. He also sought satisfaction from those citizens who had scandalously disparaged him for his conduct of the war. In order to silence these critics and remove a major reason for the decline in the numbers of recruits coming forward, Essex suggested an inquest into the causes of the loss of the West.[17] Doubtless he hoped that its findings would prove to be the political ruin of Sir William Waller and his new-found friends.

The Lords sent the Lord General's proposal to a joint committee of peers and commoners. After their discussions Pym reported to the Lower

House on Monday 31 July, and the members voted that 4,000 recruits should be sent to the Lord General.[18] But it was too late to discuss the Lord General's proposal for an inquiry into the Western disasters, and the House deferred the matter until the next morning.

By this time the news of the fall of Bristol (28 July) had reached the City, followed closely by appeals for help from Colonel Edward Massey at Gloucester, now threatened by the Royalist victors. The plight of Gloucester altered the whole political climate in London. It was Parliament's last redoubt in the West, and its fall would send shock waves throughout the Kingdom. Sensing a turning point, Parliament resolved that Gloucester must be saved. But Waller's new 'flying army' still lay wingless in its nest. Suddenly the logic of the strategic situation demanded an alliance between the two forces which actually existed – Essex's army and London's trained bands – despite the political chasm that had opened up between Pennington and his colleagues on the one hand, and the Lord General and his supporters on the other hand. These realities were revealed in the decisions of the next few days, decisions which also reflected the new political power that the threat to Gloucester now gave to Essex.

On Tuesday 1 August Waller attended the House. There he took the Solemn League and Covenant, the oaths that the Scots had demanded as part of the mutual engagement of both nations. The Covenant was not merely a declaration of belief in the Presbyterian system of church government, but a solemn bond binding its adherents to impose their views on society. The Assembly of Divines who met at Westminster that summer had approved it, but the Scots would be disappointed in their hope that it signalled a new ecclesiastical order in England. After swearing to the Covenant, Waller received a direction to march as soon as possible to the relief of Gloucester.

Not until Wednesday 2 August did the House return to the Lord General's request, and then it was decided by 51 to 30 votes not to inquire into the reasons for the loss of the West. The House also resolved that the only way now to preserve the West was to send the Lord General, with his army recruited by the fresh 4,000 Foot and 500 Horse. As for Waller, he was to command the reserve army to be raised for the defence of the City and would consequently be subordinate to the Lord Mayor and Militia Committee.[19]

Later that same day the House nominated Waller as a member of a new council of war, ostensibly to advise about the raising and use of the 6,500 Horse, but also 'to take the whole state of the war into consideration, so far as shall concern the consultative part; and to propound to the Houses, the Lord General, the governor of towns or forts, and other commanders-in-chief, such things as they shall conceive will conduce to the service of the kingdom'.[20]

Owing to the influence of the militant party in both the City and the Commons, Parliament had made its first steps to win for itself a greater share in the direction of the war. Despite his new-found political power, the Lord General could hardly be pleased with this undercurrent which threatened to erode his sovereign authority over Parliament's forces. Moreover, few believed that he would ever see his promised recruits.[21]

CHAPTER FOURTEEN

How the West was Lost

Although the Lower House had blocked an official investigation into the loss of the West, neither private speculation nor public discussion could be stifled. Over two related issues, the defeat at Roundway Down and the fall of Bristol, the protagonists of Essex and Waller fought their verbal duels throughout August, a debate which should be understood as an important aspect of that political struggle between 'vehements' and 'moderates' surging to and from beneath a façade of Parliamentarian uniformity throughout the summer.

At his trial for surrendering Bristol, Colonel Nathaniel Fiennes played the political card for all that it was worth. He asserted that a court martial would not have befallen him 'but for that constant affection and service which he and his family had always showed to his Excellency and his Army, for which Sir William Waller and his party did malign him'.[1]

Waller's case for laying the blame for 'Runaway Down' at the Lord General's door rested largely upon the circumstantial evidence that Essex's army had quartered within 10 miles of Oxford, that he had been informed by several posts that the Marquess of Hertford would seek a decisive reinforcement from the King, and that in spite of these letters Wilmot's Cavaliers had ridden unmolested towards Devizes.[2]

Taking together, these facts suggested that the Lord General's heart, if not his army, had drawn nearer to Oxford. 'It is the common report in the west country that the Lord General had undone them all,' reported one of Luke's scouts on 18 July, while Lady Waller proclaimed the same rumours from the housetops.[3] 'The wife of this esteemed and beloved commander,' wrote the Venetian ambassador, 'accuses General Essex to Parliament, who when asked by three messages to approach Oxford to secure Waller against attack there by a diversion, would never listen. The suspicions against Essex are thus constantly gaining ground. Although some think that this is due to envy of his high rank, the majority are persuaded he has secret relations with the King.'[4]

In London the crescendo of criticism mounted as the days passed, and the Lord General, 'abused in pictures, censured in pulpits, dishonoured in the table talk of the common folk',[5] endured his unpopularity with ill-disguised resentment.

The official remonstrance vindicating the Lord General's conduct was not published until 16 October,[6] but its main points appeared in *The Parliament Scout* in the middle of July.[7] The *Remonstrance*, as the fullest statement of the Essex viewpoint, deserves analysis. It begins by asserting, probably with justice, that Waller disobeyed the Lord General's order to prevent the joining of the armies of Hopton and Hertford. A council of war debated the possibility of sending some cavalry after Hertford's forces but rejected it in favour of a move by the whole army towards Oxford, believing that Waller had marched south as he had been commanded.

At Thame, 11 miles from Oxford, disease struck the Parliamentarian army, 'hundreds in a day falling desperately ill', while ceaseless rain turned the flat clay ground into a quagmire, and even if they had advanced, the river in spate east of the city could not be crossed. Having attempted unsuccessfully to intercept Prince Rupert at Buckingham on his march to meet Queen Henrietta Maria, who was coming down from the north with reinforcements and a convoy of ammunition, the Lord General moved his army to Great Brickhill. Rupert had made his rendezvous with the Queen at Stratford-on-Avon on 11 July and escorted her into Oxford on the 14th.

The village of Great Brickhill commanded Watling Street, the natural route for a combined advance on London by Rupert and the Queen, and Essex felt that he could rendezvous here with the Eastern Association army if this proved necessary. Here he received news of the victory at Lansdown, the pursuit to Devizes, the dispersal of Crawford's force and the retreat towards Oxford of Wilmot's regiment.

At this time Essex wrote to Waller telling him to engage Hertford's army in battle, 'otherwise if the King send any supply of force to the Enemy there (if I have notice thereof) I shall take all possible care to supply you accordingly'. According to the writer no such information was received, except one letter from Heselrige, dated Monday 10 July at noon, and another on Wednesday (the eve of the battle of Roundway Down), desiring him to take care of the forces at Oxford. Within two days of the Lord General's receipt of his last letter from Waller, the disaster had taken place. Without the slightest hindrance from Essex's cavalry, Sir John Byron had been allowed to depart for Devizes on the 12th, and joined up with Wilmot's Horse who had fallen back from Marlborough with Crawford's scattered regiments.[8]

What governed the motions of the Lord General's army? Political duplicity may be dismissed. So can 'those heart burnings and jealousies' which Waller read into Essex's apparent decision to let through the enemy's Horse. More probably the fault lay in poor intelligence work: the Lord General lacked the eyes and ears of a good scouting system.[9] His Scout-Master, Sir Samuel Luke, had no military experience prior to the war and he may have had no conception of the kind of information required, or how to collate reports into a picture which could be verified and acted upon. But the fault lay ultimately with the Lord General, who failed either to brief Luke adequately or to replace him. This, in turn, may have been due to the Earl's own attitude. His apparent reliance upon letters from Waller rather than his own patrols for news of the movements of the Oxford Horse can only be described as absurd.

The march to Great Brickhill, 29 miles from Oxford, a clumsy defensive manoeuvre, could easily have been delayed until his scouts brought in certain tidings of the Queen's movements, and this would have left him at Thame near enough to make a diversion on the city. Then the King would doubtless have hesitated before allowing his generals to draw out such a large body of horse.

Essentially a pedestrian general, Essex failed to appreciate the values of speed and surprise in warfare. He used Luke's troopers to keep him *au fait* with the broad military situation, not as a tactical intelligence service, making possible swift and appropriate responses.

For his part, Waller too easily assumed that others would place the same high premium as he did upon obtaining accurate information for themselves, and acting upon it promptly. Moreover, he unwittingly encouraged the Lord General's failure to set up an adequate system of surveillance around Oxford, or to stay within striking distance of the city, by sending a series of over-confident letters conveying a false impression of the true strategic position in the West.

The *Remonstrance* made no mention of the pressures brought to bear upon Essex by the House of Commons in favour of a diversion on Oxford. Some time before Wednesday 12 July, the Speaker had written to him desiring such a move. Essex replied that Prince Rupert had now returned to Oxford and 'as soon as the army is paid, which will be tomorrow night, I shall advance, God willing, at farthest on Friday'. Essex may have felt that his political enemies had kept him on short commons, and they must reap the consequences.

With heavy sarcasm the Lord General suggested that the 'vehement' younger Sir Henry Vane, as 'an intimate friend of mine', should be sent to accompany the army, and then, 'if he pleases I shall go hand in hand with him to the walls of Oxford'.[10] As Vane had criticised the Lord General's peace propositions during the previous week, the House of Commons rightly perceived this suggestion to be 'little better than a jeer'.[11] When the letter was read aloud in the House, Sir Simonds D'Ewes observed that Vane's father 'looked very blank' and recorded that as soon as his son entered the chamber the House prudently turned to other business.[12] In the long run this kicking against the Parliamentary pricks by the Earl of Essex worked in Waller's favour, for it fed the growing desire of the 'vehements' for a general whom they could call their own.

As an effective supplement to Essex's self-defence many of his friends attributed the disaster at Roundway Down to Sir Arthur Heselrige's part in the battle. This shrewd attack not only absolved the Lord General, but also fastened the blame upon the chief Independent in Waller's army.

Colonel Denzil Holles, a leading moderate and a strong supporter of Essex who had commanded his regiment of foot without distinction at Edgehill and Brentford, later wrote in vitriolic language of the 'violent party that it had pleased God to give them that check in the West, when their Army there was beaten through Sir Arthur Heselrige's default, one of their invincible champions. First, by his ignorant fool-hardiness; and afterwards by his baseness and cowardice; who then found himself to be mortal. For, before, he thought himself invincible, and absolutely stick-free and shot-free, having had the good fortune to be in a gallant regiment under Sir William Balfour, at Kenton-Field [Edgehill], and so not to run-away, but, (as himself did afterwards relate it) to wink and strike, and bear-down all before him. This made him so absolute a soldier that he thought Christendom had not his fellow; and therefore he would not be governed by his Commander-in-Chief, in that Western Brigade, (a gallant and discreet gentleman), but would charge contrary to order, without sense or reason; and, finding that resistance which he did not expect, ran-away as basely with all the horse, leaving the foot engaged.'[13]

Like all good slanders, the story contained more than a grain of truth. According to one contemporary writer, once the cuirassiers of Heselrige had been broken they 'became the ruin of the infantry'.[14] Although not present at the action, Captain Edmund Ludlow, Governor of Wardour Castle, who may be ranked as a 'vehement' and later served as major in Heselrige's regiment, conceded that 'the over-forwardness of some of our party to charge the enemy upon disvantageous ground was the principal cause of their defeat'.[15] Waller himself kept silence on the matter, perhaps in accordance with his principle of accepting full responsibility for mistakes of his officers. In his *Experiences* he referred only to 'a panic of my horse at Roundway Down'.

The second major issue – the loss of the West and of Bristol in particular – caused no less of a public stir. The *Remonstrance* accused Waller of leaving the West to take care of itself and retreating without orders to Warwick. In spite of the sickness of his soldiers and their want of pay, the Lord General had been willing to proceed at once towards Bristol, only to find that Waller had marched in the wrong direction to Northampton.

Far from the 'might' Waller had claimed to have at Warwick, the writer continued, he later wrote to say that he had only 400 Horse and that he desired to lay down his commission before going to London. Next day Waller had met Essex and told him that his Horse had so dwindled away 'that a corporal with an ordinary squadron of horse would rout them', and desired that he might ride to London, where he heard new forces and money would be immediately raised to set him forth again. According to the writer of the *Remonstrance*, this news quashed any possibility of the Lord General and his army marching to the aid of Bristol.

Colonel Nathaniel Fiennes also attempted to shift the responsibility for the fall of Bristol onto Waller's shoulders by claiming that he had denuded Bristol of the better part of its garrison.[16] In a reply written by Clement Walker, a prominent lawyer, to Fiennes' published Commons speech, Waller's officers denied this charge and gave their estimate of the forces which Waller had drawn out of the city, and the strength remaining when he departed after Roundway Down.[17] Walker, together with crop-eared William Prynne, were the prosecutors at the former Governor's trial.

Waller probably agreed with the contents of Walker's pamphlet, for Fiennes alleged 'that Sir William Waller was his enemy, and by confederacy with the prosecutors had been his chiefest instrument of prosecuting this impeachment against him; to which end he produced one Major Dowett a Frenchman (whom Sir William Waller had displaced and so disgusted) to attest that Master Walker's *Reply to Colonel Fiennes' Relation* was showed to Sir William and his Lady before it was printed, and that Sir William had spoken to his officers to acquaint Mr Walker with all such passages as they knew concerning Colonel Fiennes, touching the siege and surrender of Bristol.' Prynne conceded that Waller had read the pamphlet, but denied that he had promoted the case against Fiennes. Dowett subsequently gave evidence hostile to Fiennes.

Much rests on how many soldiers had been commanded out in late June and early July. Most historians have accepted Fiennes' figure of 1,200, but Waller's officers asserted that this was not so, although they had all asked for that number. From their calculations this figure probably represented the total of Bristol Foot in service under Waller from April onwards, a significant difference. According to them Fiennes could muster at least 2,000 Foot for the siege including some 400 soldiers from the foot regiments of the Western Brigade, besides 300 Horse. In the light of such evidence, the court martial at St Albans in December 1643 subsequently sentenced Colonel Fiennes to death for the surrender of Bristol, but the Lord General's intervention saved him from this extreme penalty.

These debates could not undo the main effect of Roundway Down upon Waller's career. It destroyed his chances of succeeding Essex as Commander-in-Chief. Both Houses intended now to retain the services of the Lord General.[18] Only upon this condition would a majority in the House back the 'vehements' in their demand for the new army. But this important decision meant that until Essex had sent a commission to Waller he could not in turn issue commissions to officers for the raising of regiments, troops and companies. Essex realised this fact and played for time.

On 3 August Henry Marten reported in the Lower House that the business of raising the army went forward slowly because Essex had not yet despatched a commission to Waller. According to D'Ewes, no more than 300 men had listed themselves in the new regiments by 4 August. In his eagerness to obtain recruits, it was reported, Waller did not disdain to go himself among the butchers of Newgate Market.[19]

Having established that Anthony Nicholl – Pym's nephew and a frequent correspondent with the army on his behalf – had written for one, the House then appointed Pym and a small deputation – all 'very violent spirits' – to go to the Lord General at Uxbridge and fetch it.[20] Although some moved that Waller's power should be made subordinate to the Lord Mayor or Militia Committee, according to the vote of the preceding day, the House now declined this limitation.

Two days later, on Saturday 5 August, 'Sir William Waller himself and divers other men eminent for religion and piety' voted with the moderates that some of the peace propositions in the House of Lords should be taken into consideration, but not immediately. The 'violent spirits' countered by stirring up the City with pamphlets distributed on the following day, stating that the 'well-affected party' had been outvoted and that the King was bringing 20,000 Irish soldiers into the land. Preachers took up the tale in many London pulpits and joined in summoning all the 'well-affected' to gather at Westminster. Therefore, when the Lower House reassembled on Monday, many members had pushed their way across a crowded palace yard to take their seats. In the debate which took place that day, Sir William was among those Members of Parliament who changed their opinions and voted against joining the House of Lords in their petition to the King. By a narrow majority of 88 to 81, this proposal was now rejected, a notable victory for the militants.[21]

The same day (Monday 7 August) a commission for Waller arrived from the Earl of Essex, but only bestowing upon him the command of the London militia. It was received and read at a conference of both Houses.[22] The Lord General accompanied it with a request that Major-General Philip Skippon, whom he had appointed to command the same militia the year before, should thereby receive no diminution, for he was a gallant man.[23] But Marten and other members who had gone to the London halls seeking money for the new army reported that this commission did not remove all obstructions. Consequently, on the following day the House resolved to get another commission for Sir William which would enable him to lead the forces to be raised, twenty regiments, ten each of Horse and Foot, to any part of the Kingdom. According to D'Ewes, Marten and his committee thereby planned to make Waller an 'independent General', with authority to compel all those not willing to go with him.

Wednesday 9 August, saw the continuation of a remarkable peace demonstration in the capital. A mob of women with white ribbons in their hats gathered for the second day in the Palace of Westminster yard and clamoured for peace. After presenting a petition, they hammered on the door of the House of Commons and called for Pym and the leaders of the 'violent' party, intending to cast them into the Thames. When the guards failed to disperse them with a volley or two of powder they added bullets to their charges and shot two men who were inciting the crowd, but this still did not clear the yard.

Then a troop of Waller's Horse arrived and began to lay about them with the flat of their swords, trampling and wounding a few of the women who even attempted to tear the ribbons from the hats of 'Waller's dogs', as they called them. Eventually the soldiers scattered the crowd, but at the cost of one innocent bystander's life. The trooper responsible for the accidental death was tried by court martial and claimed that his pistol went off by mistake.[24]

For seven days no answer to the request of the Commons came from the Lord General. On 9 August, however, Essex wrote affirming his willingness to hazard his life in person for the relief of Gloucester if his arrears were paid.[25] On 15 August the Lower House sent Pym, John Glynn and the older Sir Henry Vane to Essex's headquarters at Kingston, ostensibly to advise him whether to move his army to Gloucester, Oxford or Exeter, but probably to persuade him to grant Waller's commission.[26] Ten days later (Friday 25 August) Anthony Nicholl reported to the Commons that Essex would grant a commission to Waller, but he desired to know the names of the proposed colonels 'because he had some exceptions to take to some of them'.

The fact that Essex had apparently sent this message by word of mouth caused much debate. At first Nicholl said he had only taken short notes to help his memory, but being pressed, he admitted that he had desired the Lord General to set it all down. He then produced and read the letter which was 'better than Nicholl had delivered it'. As a result the House resolved that Pym and Glynn should go to Essex at Colnbrook and ask him to send away the commission instantly.[27]

Next day Pym delivered the document to the House, but Essex had left a blank space for the recipient's name. 'For naming the gentleman they recommended, it is in their power to place it upon whom they please,' Essex wrote in his letter accompanying the commission. 'I am confident the gentleman is full of courage, and affected to the cause, and for his late services the House may think him fit for this charge, but for some reasons to my own particular [which] I have no great reason to confide, in part is well known to many of the Committee of Safety of both Houses, but I shall never value my own particular [?opinion] when the safety of the House of Commons and City is in question.'[28]

Then 'Sir William Waller having heard the Lord General's letter read in the House and hearing himself there described but not named, took notice of it and said, he conceived that it was he that was intended in that letter, but that he knew not wherein he had ever given any cause to the Lord General to take any the least exception to him: yet if the house would command him, he would die at his feet.'[29] But D'Ewes recorded that the House rested satisfied and the debate soon came to an end on that particular.[30] By a unanimous vote the Commons ordered their clerk to insert Waller's name into the blank space. The Speaker then presented him with the document. As a means of appointing a military commander in the Civil War this ceremony was without precedent, and it conferred upon Waller a unique status among Parliamentarian generals.[31]

Apart from the discords already chronicled, there can be little doubt that Essex resented the emergence of a rival to his high office. Clarendon wrote of him: 'his pride supplied his want of ambition, for he was angry to see any other man more respected than himself, because he thought he deserved it more, and did better requite it.' His sensitive vanity had been wounded not so much by Waller's successes as by his popularity in defeat. Essex responded to the threat with a mixture of lordly indifference and sarcasm. To one correspondent he claimed that a troop destined for his army had been carried to Sir William Waller, and he added a typically sarcastic comment, which he later scored through, 'who is in such favour that I forbear to disturb him'.[32]

Essex had gained time and used it well. As it became clear that he not only intended to remain loyal but also to lead his army to the relief of Gloucester, his supporters in both Houses had no difficulty in securing money and recruits for him. Towards the end of August the Lord General had assembled some 4,000 Horse and 18 regiments of Foot, including five from the London militia. Indeed, in his letter to the House with Waller's commission, he could end triumphantly by declaring: 'I am tomorrow, God willing, beginning my march, and if the army be as willing to march as I shall be to lead them (and the town hold out until we can relieve them) I shall endeavour it, or perish in the act.' Even the Independents could not grumble at such a sentiment.

CHAPTER FIFTEEN

Raising a New Army

While the Lord General marched westwards with 15,000 men, and the prayers of all Parliamentarians, Waller issued a spate of commissions for the new army. From extant claims for arrears of pay it is evident that most of these were granted on 29 August, illustrating the effectiveness of the Lord General's delaying tactics. Yet Waller had clearly planned the army as far as he could, and a number of commissions had been prepared for his signature against the hour when the Lord General should cede him the necessary authority.

In essence the new army represented an expansion of the Western brigade. The regiments of horse of Waller and Heselrige, and the regiment of dragoons formed its core. Other old regiments continued with only small changes. Burghill retired after being wounded at Lansdown and the command of his weak regiment passed to his major, Jonas Vandruske. Majors Francis Dowett and William Carr, both trusted officers in the West, became colonels empowered to raise regiments of horse.

Similarly, four of the colonels of foot – Alexander Popham, James Carr, Edward Cooke and Robert Harley – were men of note in the West, the last two named having the advantage of being the sons of influential and wealthy men. Waller entrusted his own new regiment of foot to Lieutenant-Colonel Ramsey, with the Western veteran John Hillersdon as his major. On the other hand, none of the known officers commissioned into Heselrige's Foot had served in the West, although its commanding officer Lieutenant-Colonel John Birch came from Bristol. Nor did Colonel Andrew Potley's Foot or the train of artillery, to be commanded by a former Master Gunner of England, Colonel James Wemyss, have any traceable connection with the old Western Brigade.

Scots professionals commanded five of the eleven known regiments and the train of artillery in Waller's army, while many of the majors and company commanders also came from over the border.[1] 'I acknowledge that I have, and ever have had, a particular respect and value for that nation,' Waller wrote in his *Vindication* after the war, 'I love their constancy to their covenant, their steadiness in their counsels, their gallantry in the field. Some of them I have had the honour to command, and braver men I am confident, no man could command.' The Scots evidently reciprocated this affection, for (in December 1645) their commissioners in London could refer to Sir William as 'our noble and worthy friend'.[2]

It was the selection of such officers as the Scots professionals that first strained Waller's relations with his sponsors. They wanted 'their General' to entertain none but godly men of their own persuasion whom they would recommend to him, whereas Waller's experience made him reluctant to accept such a condition. He reminded his sponsors that much as he desired zealous men about him, 'there went more to the making up of an officer than single honesty . . . a good man might make a good soldier, but there must go the good man and the good soldier to the composition of a good officer.' He told them also that he would be answerable with life and honour for the service of the army, and 'that it would be a poor plea for me to say it was the officer's fault, when it might justly be retorted upon me as my fault that I took such officers.'

Eventually they accepted a compromise assurance from Waller that officers with both piety and ability would be preferred before all others, but if sufficient numbers of such men did not present themselves, he would be free to commission experienced officers, 'although they were not otherwise so refined men as I could wish'. This policy, it must be added, was not all that different from that adopted by Oliver Cromwell in the Eastern Association, although he may have been more swayed by a man's religion than his social status or professional experience than Waller. Although such a selection policy may have produced benefits in terms of commitment and morale, in the long term it proved injurious to both the army and the state. Waller was right to set his face against it.

Only gradually, however, did the true end behind the Independents' concern for this matter manifest itself: 'I appointed a council of war, whereof Sir Arthur Heselrige was president, to examine the merits of every man that should stand to bear any office in that army, with power to cross all such out of the list as should be judged unfit or unworthy to be employed. But this did not satisfy; and I then found they had it in their design to model and form an army, that should be all of their own party, and devoted to their own ends. Upon this we differed. I trusted not them, nor they me, and so we agreed. From that time forward I may date the expiration of their friendship.'

As evidence of this element of naïvety on the part of the Independents when it came to officer selection, the earliest biographer of John Milton writes that the poet was proposed to the committee in 1644 for the office of Adjutant-General in Waller's army.[3] Milton was a zealous Puritan and a poet of genius, but he was no soldier. It is true that he practised his sword-drill every day and he may well have aspired to a life of action – literary men often do – but he completely lacked the experience necessary to be a senior staff officer. He would have found a niche as Waller's secretary, no more. No, Milton was better employed as a literary champion, firing his printed broadsides against the common foe.

Waller wrote about these events in prison, probably in 1649 or 1650, and it is possible that he read back the intentions of the political and religious radicals of that period into the sponsors of the abortive New Model Army, whom he called Independents. Yet, in the summer of 1643, the group who rallied around the issue of creating a new army with Waller as their general included a wider group of 'vehements' than the Independents as such, let alone such later radicals as Henry Marten and the younger Sir Henry Vane. Oliver St John, John Crewe and Pym himself, for example, must be distinguished from the later republicans and regicides. Certainly the appointment of the board's chairman, Sir Arthur Heselrige, later a republican and die-hard political Independent, ought to have allowed for an interpretation of 'unfit or unworthy' which would have been acceptable to the most Puritan-minded member of the Merchant Taylors' Hall committee, whatever form of Church government they subscribed to.

Unlike Cromwell in his relation to the Earl of Manchester, Waller was not prepared to sever his links with the Lord General and his supporters, or even to bring into the open the misunderstandings between them. In the last resort, both men were political moderates, and both supported a Presbyterian system. Their differences were more temperamental and strategic in nature. Moreover, with the recovery of Essex's prestige and political power the influence of the more hot-headed 'vehements' waned. That autumn the House of Commons sent Henry Marten to the Tower for suggesting 'that it were better one family should be destroyed than many', admitting that he had the family of King Charles in mind. In these circumstances Waller may well have decided to strengthen his ties with Essex, or at least accept the run of events with good grace.

The emergence of the two broad labels of Independents and Presbyterians – broad because men divided more on particular issues rather than anything approaching modern party lines – was related to the divisions in the Assembly of Divines which began its meetings in Westminster Abbey that summer. On Friday 1 September, for example, *Mercurius Aulicus* reported that the proposed new Covenant, to be taken by both the Kingdoms of England and Scotland, 'raised so great a heat between the Presbyterians and the Independents, each standing stiffly in defence of their own cause, that there is little hope amongst their best friends, of any good accord to be had between them'.

The Westminster Assembly had been convoked by Parliament to advise on conditions of the Church, as 'many things in its liturgy, discipline and government required further and more perfect reformation'. The majority of the assembly – about sixty of its lay and clerical members – were inclined to changes towards the Presbyterian system, a tendency much strengthened by the developing alliance with Scotland, and also by the absence or withdrawal of those advocating the traditional episcopalian model. But the Independents, like their forerunners the Brownists, objected alike to the Presbyterian form of Church government and to episcopacy. They favoured the gathering of Christians together in strictly voluntary and self-governing congregations or churches.

While the lawyers and divines debated daily together in the Jerusalem Chamber of Westminster Abbey – they continued until the summer of 1647 until their discussions petered out – there was still a war to be won. A worse time for raising regiments in and around London could hardly have been chosen. Even before the Lord General marched westwards, the hot enthusiasm of the citizens had evaporated. Donations for the new army tailed off, and without money, recruits would not come forward.

On 14 September the House of Commons declared that it would 'take effectual course for the future subsisting of Sir William Waller, and his Army' and appointed Speaker Lenthall to remind them of their promise. Meanwhile, they directed Waller to apply for money to John Trenchard, Member of Parliament for Wareham in Dorset, who would inform the House regularly of his needs. Trenchard's 'Committee of Accounts for Waller's Army' had been nominated the day before and remained responsible for his finances for the rest of the war. Owing to the cooling affections of the Independents, Waller estimated that from this committee between 'the time of my setting forth unto my disbanding, I never received full one hundred thousand pounds (an inconsiderable sum compared to what others had); and yet of that stock I was fain to play the good husband and to be at the charge to pay for part of my arms and ammunition'.[4]

The establishment of this committee reflected growing fears for the Parliamentarian field army. On 8 September the Lord General entered Gloucester, and a week later surprised Cirencester, but he still had to make his way back to London past the King's army which had marched to interpose itself between him and the capital. Parliament therefore attended to Waller's neglected regiments with a diligence born out of anxiety, for they formed a line of defence if Essex suffered defeat in the impending encounter.

On 13 September the Commons ordered Pym to write to the Earl of Manchester, requesting that of the 6,500 Horse and dragoons voted on 18 July, all those raised in London and the counties south of the Thames should be placed under Waller, a transfer which would yield 3,400 men.[5] The day before, the House directed that 5,000 Foot should be raised for Waller by impressment in the same area. As an inducement to volunteers, such apprentices as enlisted in Waller's army would be able to count their military service as part of indentured time, and similar carrots were held out to the Thames watermen. In spite of these expedients to attract volunteers, the Venetian Secretary noted in a letter on 18 September that Waller's regiments 'had more officers than soldiers so far'.[6]

One reason for the shortage of Foot lay in the fact that Trenchard's committee at Grocers' Hall tended to pick and choose among warrants which they received from Waller, favouring captains of their own political persuasion and putting on one side the claims of others. It appears that this practice harmed the infantry in particular, for Waller wrote to Sir Robert Harley on 23 September asking him 'to move the House of Commons that such moneys as have been collected for the raising and payment of forces under my command may not be reserved for the payment of some private troops only, but for the levying of these foot regiments yet not raised; and that the Committee of the Militia do repay to Grocers' Hall such moneys as have been borrowed of them, all to be disposed according to my warrants for the use of the whole.'[7]

In the second and third weeks of September Waller transferred his army from the London suburbs to Staines and Windsor, whence he could more conveniently march out to meet Essex if the need arose. The Committee of Militia sent him Colonel Richard Turner's regiment of horse, eight troops strong,[8] bringing the total of his cavalry up to perhaps thirty troops.[9] Waller's regiment of dragoons, under the command of the Scotsman Major Archibald Strachan, remained in London until 26 September, when a Royalist saw them at a muster of City-trained bands and auxiliaries.

Three regiments of London foot had already been ordered to join Waller, for without a strong body of infantry he could not march. The Yellow Regiment and the Green Auxiliaries, selected by lot on 7 September, and the 'Red and White Regiments of Youths' had all received warning orders. Nor did the staff of the artillery train neglect their preparation. On 20 September Commissary John Frowke signed for a hundred barrels of powder which were ferried down the river to Windsor. As far as possible Waller had made ready his incomplete army for the field.[10]

The Lord General, however, fared well without him. On the 20 September he fought the first battle of Newbury, a strategic victory in so far as it cleared his road to London. Marching by way of Reading, Essex reached Windsor four days later. He quartered the bulk of his army in that already crowded town and rode to the capital, where he made a triumphal entry on the 28th. Basking in the warmth of public acclamation, Essex now felt politically strong enough to reach out his hand for the commission he had been compelled to grant Waller a month earlier.

On 3 October he made his opening move in the Lords, where he could expect a more than favourable hearing. 'The Lord General offered to the consideration of this House the great inconvenience that is by the quartering of Sir William Waller's forces within his army; and that unless the forces of Sir William Waller be under his command, he doubts some inconvenience will soon happen. All which he desired this House to take into their speedy consideration, and give direction herein.'[11] His fellow peers docilely resolved that Waller should be placed once more under the Lord General who alone should have power to grant commissions, and entrusted to the Committee of Safety the task of working out how this decision could be effected.

Waller's political backers, the supporters of the Independent party in the Commons and the City, opposed this bid to take over *their* army, but on 7 October the Lord General goaded Parliament with a threat to resign and go beyond the seas if Waller retained his present authority. By this date Essex no longer advanced merely practical objections, but roundly declared that Waller's commission was intrinsically inconsistent with his own. The Lower House heeled to the wind and voted that the commission given to Waller by the Speaker should be understood as placing him under the Lord General's command.

Sir William, present at the debate, declared 'he ever has been, is, and will be ready to receive and obey his Excellency's commands'.[12] On the following Monday, 9 October, 'upon Mr Pym's affirmation that he was confident the Lord General would grant him another commission to be Sergeant-Major-General in the West in as ample manner as ever any commission was granted to a commander by any General',[13] he voluntarily surrendered his commission to the Speaker. The House then sent four members to inform the Lord General of Waller's act.[14] For the time being the Independents had been outmanoeuvred.

Essex received back the commission from Stapleton, replying graciously that 'he would ever respect Sir William Waller as a person of much honour and special trust in the service of the State'.[15] A limited reconciliation seems to have taken place between the two generals and some contemporaries commented on a new accord between them, but this may have been wishful thinking.[16] It promised a stronger unity in the Parliamentarian camp as a whole, although it failed to deliver it. The failure of negotiations with the King and the internal threats posed by such turncoats as Edmund Waller, had rallied many of the peace party to the sterner and less compromising policy advocated by the 'vehements'. The Solemn League and Covenant with Scotland, the Excise ordinance and the mighty exertion to save Gloucester stemmed from this common will to win. The much desired *rapprochement* between Essex and Waller – probably more formal than real at this stage – coincided with this decisive shift of moderate opinion and completed the closing of the ranks for a second winter of war.

The Independents had buried their hatchet for the Lord General, but not too deep. They would continue to patronise Waller. Perhaps with hindsight, Sir William wrote later of their support: 'I could plainly perceive it was but in the nature of a stale, in opposition to that noble Lord the Earl of Essex, whom they feared and therefore hated implacably; and they were willing enough to ferment those differences between his Lordship and me (to the prejudice of the public service), that they might make their ends upon us both, and gain the better pretence to bring on their new model.'[17]

With what money he could collect, Waller continued his efforts to raise most of the projected regiments to recruit the Western brigade. There still remained the task of reconquering the West, now in enemy hands except for the strongholds of Gloucester, Plymouth, Lyme and Poole. 'We hear nothing of Sir William Waller, but hope our supply is cared for,' Massey had written to Essex on 6 October.[18] Although some advocated an immediate advance on Oxford by the combined forces of Essex and Waller, considering this to be the best way of finishing the war, the soldiers, apprehensive of warfare in cold weather, were known to be against such a move.[19] Consequently, most Londoners expected that Waller's regiments would be employed in a short time for the recovery of the West.

Besides lack of funds due to the waning enthusiasm of the Independents and loss of the western subsidy-producing counties, Waller's appointment of professional officers as colonels may have created further difficulties for him. The standing of a colonel counted much towards the number of recruits he could attract. Londoners entertained warm feelings for Waller and looked upon him as one of themselves. Heselrige, a national figure and a prominent Independent, possessed a popularity of his own. Both were known as men who had spent large sums out of their own pockets towards the expense of outfitting their regiments. On the other hand, the remaining colonels were either professional soldiers, including a Frenchman and a Dutchman, or West Country gentlemen whose names might have raised regiments in Gloucestershire, but could hardly muster a company in London or the Home Counties. No doubt the officers nominated by the Independents would have filled their own ranks with ease, but Waller wanted no 'new model' but a Western Army.

Cavalry regiments required a considerable outlay of money, and neither William Carr nor Francis Dowett could complete their regiments. Carr subsequently quarrelled violently with Heselrige and was sent to the Compter prison in Southwark. Towards the end of October fourteen deserters from the latter's command had reached Oxford with this encouraging news.[21] Yet the old regiments of Waller, Heselrige and

Vandruske were brought more or less up to strength. Colonel Turner's London Horse, however, left Windsor in October with the Lord General when he marched to take Newport Pagnell. Waller's fine regiment of 500 dragoons completed the cavalry of the Western brigade.

The colonels of foot made slow headway with their regiments. On 29 August Waller granted at least one commission for a company in Alexander Popham's foot, but the captain discharged his forty soldiers three months later 'for want of further employment', having received no wages during that period.[22] Presumably the other officers in this regiment followed suit.

The trials encountered by the remaining five colonels may be illustrated by the correspondence and accounts relating to Robert Harley's regiment, which should have contained 800 musketeers and 400 pikemen. Captain Francis Hakluyt, enlisting a company in Essex, wrote to Harley on 22 October thanking him for £10 and adding simply, 'If you intend to raise any more men or to lend those I have raised to any rendezvous you must send me more money.' By 15 November the pay arrears of those men Harley had mustered amounted to £404 6s 8d. On that day the colonel estimated that the sum necessary to complete his regiment, supply it with a month's wages, provide drums, colours, halberds and a surgeon's chest would be £1,707.

The county of Essex belonged to the new Eastern Association, and the Earl of Manchester multiplied Harley's problems by ordering the deputy lieutenants to take Hakluyt's soldiers as recruits into his own army. Nor would he allow any more men to be enlisted in regiments other than those belonging to the association.

In spite of the willingness of the Essex Committee to comply with Manchester's direction, Hakluyt succeeded in keeping his men together. A county trained band then stole their winter quarters. Want of pay and privation turned them into deserters or marauders, twin scourges driving the country folk close to mutiny. Harley seems to have cared little for his regiment or the sufferings of the soldiers, but even so he was not wholly accountable for their misery.[23]

Sir Arthur Heselrige seems to have shared Waller's principles of choosing officers. His position as a great Leicestershire landowner and the fact that he was brother-in-law to Lord Robert Brooke, a leading Puritan and Parliamentarian killed at Lichfield earlier in the year, explained many of his own appointments. At least five officers who had formerly served under Lord Brooke received commissions in Heselrige's two regiments.[24] Although Lord Brooke's second captain had been none other than 'Freeborne John' Lilburne, there is no reason to suppose that this regiment had been a particular hotbed of religious fervour.

Lieutenant-Colonel John Birch, who commanded Heselrige's Foot, probably passed the selection board with flying colours but he owed his place as much to military merit as his political and religions opinions. In truth, Sir Arthur, the only key the Independents possessed to the heart of Waller's army, was both too grand and too shallow a man to play the Cromwell to Waller's Manchester. The Lobsters never became the Ironsides of the Western brigade, infecting other regiments with their Puritan spirit and radical political opinions. Yet there is some evidence that radical Puritans felt more at home in Waller's regiments than in Essex's army. The Royalist editor of *Mercurius Aulicus* noted on several occasions the pretence of Brownists in Waller's army. (The Brownists were adherents of the system of Church government advocated by the Puritan minister Robert Brown who died *c.* 1633. They were later adopted by the Independents.) In June 1643, for example, he referred to Waller's soldiers as 'a rabble of such keen rebellious Brownists, that they usually call his Excellency's followers *Malignants* and *Cavaliers*'.

Waller's act of handing back his commission to the Speaker on 9 October marked the end of his flirtation with the Independents. Yet with their financial help he had re-recreated the horse of the Western brigade and laid the keel for a new body of infantry and a much larger artillery train. Independent political support had cushioned him from the shock waves of the Western disaster, but only more victories could restore his reputation and establish him once more as a potential co-general and even successor to the Earl of Essex.

With none of his foot regiments completed and the short dark autumn days at hand Waller could not advance into the West, but he may well have wished that the King would send a Royalist army against him so that he could retrieve the precious honour lost at Roundway Down. If so, his hopes would not be disappointed.

PART FOUR

General in the South

CHAPTER SIXTEEN

A Fling at Basing House

On 29 September Lord Hopton of Stratton, for so he had become, attended a meeting of Royalist notables at Oriel College Oxford. Here he received the King's direction 'that being reasonably well recovered of his hurts, he should draw into the field for the clearing of Dorsetshire, Wiltshire, and Hampshire, and so point forward as far as he could go towards London'.[1] A new army would be created for him, amounting to 1,580 Horse and dragoons, and 2,000 Foot.[2] Hopton returned to Bristol and set about gathering the regiments which had been assigned to him. In spite of money shortages, he was able to take the field with the Horse and part of the Foot by mid-October.

The Royalist general intended to capture Wardour Castle, a key Parliamentarian stronghold in Wiltshire guarding the main road from Salisbury into the West Country. Then he planned to fall on Lyme and blockade Poole. The first design was thwarted as much by the over-eagerness of the Hampshire Royalists as by the stubborn courage of the Wardour garrison. Under Sir William Ogle's leadership they secured Winchester and advertised their success to the King, who sent Colonel Charles Gerrard with a strong cavalry brigade to support them until Hotpon's army could come up from Wiltshire. Messages conveyed to Hopton the King's wish for an immediate advance to Winchester. Obediently, Hopton prepared a holding force for Wiltshire, and named Amesbury as the rendezvous for the rest of his army.

In the face of the threatening possibility that the Oxford army and the 'Hoptonians' would join together, Parliament became understandably anxious that the forces of Essex and Waller should take the field. While Essex marched northwards from Windsor towards Newport Pagnell and the environs of Oxford, Waller appointed a rendezvous for his regiments on 1 November at Farnham Castle.

By a chance of history, the battle of Newbury, which had played such a large part in the revocation of Waller's independent commission, now enabled him to take the field with a new brigade of infantry. The London trained bands had done such good service on that day that a decision had been reached by mid-October to repeat the experiment and send away three more regiments to Waller's army at Windsor. None of those regiments assigned to him had seen active service before, yet the largest of the three, the Westminster Liberty Regiment, more commonly known as the Red Regiment from its red flag spangled with silver stars, contained 1,084 musketeers, 854 pikemen and 80 officers, while the Green Auxiliaries of London and the Yellow Auxiliaries could muster 1,200 and 1,000 men respectively, and so this recruit was not to be despised.[3] A wealthy London merchant, Colonel Sir James Harrington of the Red Regiment, commanded this brigade of citizens and apprentices. Complete with their own historian, Lieutenant Elias Archer, the Londoners reached Windsor on 25 October and were quartered in the surrounding villages until orders came to march to the rendezvous.[4]

'Monday 30 October we marched to a green about a mile from Windsor, where we made halt and rallied our men, each regiment drawing into regimental forms, where likewise our trains of artillery and wagons of war came to us, and so we marched towards Farnham through Windsor Forest where in the afternoon we met some of Sir William Waller's troops of horse, his own regiment of foot, and one company of Bluecoats with snaphance-muskets, which guard the trains of artillery only; all these marched with us.'[5] Early on Tuesday the tired Londoners halted in Farnham and broke ranks to rest before the muster on the following day.

The Committee of Safety had shown wise foresight in strengthening Farnham Castle as a bastion of the South-East and as a counterweight to Basing House. The Lord General had given a commission to Colonel Samuel Jones on 5 July 1643 'to repair into the county of Surrey and there to take a view of the powder mills and to erect, build and make such works and fortifications at ye Bridge [Weybridge – the main gunpowder magazine in Surrey] and elsewhere for the defence and safety of the said mills and bridges as you think fit.' He also received power to give warrants to constables for labourers and also to beat up his drums in Surrey for the completing of his regiment of Greencoats.[6] Soon afterwards, Colonel Jones had become the Governor of Farnham Castle, with his regiment as a garrison, paid and fed by the Committee of Surrey at Kingston.[7] On 4 August the Committee of Safety sent him two demi-culverins, three sacres, two 'murtherers', 400 'Swedes feathers' [sharpened stakes] and a quantity of ammunition. Next month he received two demi-cannon and 100 hand grenades of various sizes.[8] The pocket notebook of Lieutenant-Colonel Jeremy Baines, second-in-command of the garrison regiment, contains a list of measurements for various sections of the fortifications and mentions 'Castle battery', 'Mid-Demi-battery' and 'High battery'.[9] Farnham Castle, now a stronghold of strategic importance, became Waller's base for the rest of the war.

Beneath the castle batteries lay Farnham Park, and here Waller reviewed his army on the appointed day. Although the Green Auxiliaries had not marched over from their quarters 2 miles away, Lieutenant Archer counted twenty-nine colours of Foot in the park. Besides the white standards of four companies of Colonel Samuel Jones' Greencoats and the blue standards of Waller's own 300 Foot,[10] the remainder stirred at the head of city companies. The cavalry mustered sixteen troops, all Western Horse. Only the regiments of Waller and Vandruske may be identified, but there were one or two old Lobster troops with them. Eight companies of dragoons, all in Waller's own regiment, were drawn up nearby.[11] The train of artillery consisted of ten field pieces and six 'cases of small drakes'. The latter were probably enclosed 'wagons of war' with guns protruding from their loopholes, a primitive form of armoured car making its debut in the Civil War.[12] The Bluecoats carried snaphance-muskets because no gunner could feel secure with musketeers handling lighted match near barrels of powder. The muster also served as an occasion for some exemplary punishment, for that day a court martial met to pass sentence on a clerk in Waller's own foot regiment for mutiny. He was hanged from a tree in the park as a gruesome warning to the rest of the army.

On 2 November the House of Commons appointed three Members of Parliament to point out to the Lord General 'in what dangerous condition Sir Wm. Waller is in at this present, and to acquaint his Excellency that the enemy has drawn his main force towards Sir Wm. Waller.' Essex replied two days later that as eight or ten Royalist regiments of horse and 3,000 Foot quartered near him at Towcester he could not spare reinforcements for Waller.[13]

Realising that the four counties of Kent, Hampshire, Sussex and Surrey would have to allocate or raise regiments for service under Waller, the Lords approved on 4 November an ordinance associating them together. They also agreed to a motion of the Lower House calling upon the Lord General to give a major-general's commission for the command of the Association's forces to Waller.[14]

Although one news-sheet optimistically reported that 4,000 Horse and Foot would soon be made ready in the now revived 'Southern Associated Counties',[15] several weeks would pass before Waller received any soldiers from these counties. Although usually known as the 'four associated counties', they may be conveniently called the Southern Association, as happened in the cases of the Eastern, Western and Northern Associations.[16]

Waller resolved to move towards Winchester. On Friday 3 November the army, perhaps 8,000 strong, marched to Alton and stopped there for the night. Saturday dawned chill and wet: the regiments mustered to resume the advance, but the rain turned into a snow blizzard and Waller dismissed the men back to their quarters. On Sunday the army reached Alresford, 8 miles from the city. Here Waller learnt that a strong body from Oxford had moved south to take him in the rear. In fact Hopton had met the cavalry brigade of Colonel Charles Gerrard at Andover that day and marched at once with his Horse and dragoons towards Winchester with great speed.[17]

Believing that Hopton's army lay before and the Oxford Cavaliers behind, Waller may well have feared a repetition of Roundway Down. Caution therefore prevailed. 'I altered my resolution,' he wrote, 'and marched to Basing, upon the ground that if the intelligence were true I should either fight with them singly – before any other party should join with them – or if I found myself too weak, make a safe retreat to Farnham, but a few miles distance from thence. If it were false, I might either make an assay upon that house – which by all men was represented to me to be but a slight place, and if I could carry it, it would have been a great encouragement to the soldiers – or otherwise I might advance towards Winchester, which was but two days' march, and the most direct way from Alton thither was no less.'[18]

The London brigade slept that night in the open fields west of Alresford. 'This was a very cold night and very tedious to many of our men which never were accustomed to such lodging,' reported Lieutenant Archer of the Yellow Auxiliaries. One hour before dawn the army marched towards Basing and arrived before noon within sight of the house. Here Waller received an assurance that danger no longer threatened him, for Gerrard's brigade had returned to Oxford and Hopton needed time to put Winchester in a posture of defence and to draw in more infantry regiments from the West. Consequently, Waller resolved to attempt Basing House.

'As for Basing house, it is absolutely the strongest place in England, and requires a summer's siege.'[19] This writer, a lieutenant in Waller's army, may have been guilty of overstatement, but the place certainly presented formidable problems to a besieger. In reality there were two houses standing near to each other: an old shell keep on a mound with an attendant medieval gatehouse, and a lofty Tudor mansion built around a pentagonal courtyard.

The entrance to the New House by an even more imposing gatehouse lay on the east side of the ancient castle's outer bailey, a perimeter marked by a dry moat. A stone wall encompassed the houses, and on the north, where the ground sloped down to the River Loddon, a second wall set with dovecote towers enclosed a terraced vegetable garden. The plateau of Basing Park to the south presented the one open approach to the castle, and here great earthworks faced with red brick had been erected to secure it.[20] Within the defended areas of some 15 acres there were no less than sixteen courts, both great and small.

Colonel Marmaduke Rawdon acted as military governor under the Marquess of Winchester. Besides his own and Winchester's regiments of foot, perhaps no more than 500 men in all, Rawdon's garrison included a hundred or more mounted gentlemen volunteers, many of them Papists, with a leavening of experienced officers. Victuals they had in plenty, enough to last for three weeks, and a good store of ordnance, muskets and ammunition.

'I was first guided to the north side of the house,' Waller narrated, 'which was most commanded and fittest to batter, but upon trial I found that the enemy had fortified most strongly on that side, with diverse retrenchments under the command of another.'[21] While 500 commanded musketeers, later relieved by the regiment of dragoons, kept up a brisk fire from the groves near the western redoubt, Waller moved his army onto Cowdrey Down, a high feature north-west of the house.

As soon as his heavy demi-cannon were in position at about 4.00 p.m. Waller gave the order for a dozen rounds to be fired. After the last discharge he sent a second trumpeter to summon the Marquess to surrender. Owing to the accidental discharge of two Parliamentarian pieces on Cowdrey Down, the Marquess detained this man and despatched his own drummer back to Waller with his refusal. Waller returned him with an apology for 'the rudeness of his disorderly guns',[22] and offered all women and children a free pass through his lines.

The trumpeter, who had been directed by kind Royalists in Basing to return by a way which would entail only 'a small leap for his horse over part of a little brook',[23] arrived back in Waller's camp covered in mud, having tried to jump the Loddon in the dark. He had left his horse stuck in the mire, but brought back a courteous message from the Marchioness declining Waller's offer. After a cannonade of thirty shot in reply had echoed over the fields and woods, Colonel Wemyss put his labourers to work improving the gun platform and throwing up a protective mound in front of it.

At daybreak on Tuesday 7 November the assault began in earnest. Two demi-cannons hurled their balls through the grey dawn towards the house, while five smaller pieces added to the noise and weight of the bombardment. Meanwhile, Waller drew up his regiments in battle order on Cowdrey Down. Below them, divided from the terrace garden wall of Basing House by a road, they could see the Grange farm, and a half-moon sited to command the lane which led up from it to their position. The occupation of the Grange red-brick barn and the farm outhouses formed a logical first step towards the capture of Basing House itself, and Waller selected a 'forlorn hope' of 500 commanded musketeers for this difficult task.

By an unfortunate mistake one section of the 'forlorn hope' wandered down the lane into the arcs of fire of two drakes mounted on the half-moon: several blasts of case-shot, tins stuffed with musket balls, sent the

Parliamentarians diving for the hedgerows. Waller at once ordered a diversion to be made against the New House: the Royalists withdrew from both earthwork and farm and their 'noisome guests' moved in and took possession of them.

While the more unruly soldiers ate and drank their way through Royalist provisions which they found in the Grange, or stuffed brass and pewter into their knapsacks, their fellows exchanged a steady fire with the enemy behind the loopholed garden wall, but the volleys which greeted one or two forward rushes induced the officers in command of the 'forlorn hope' to abandon any plans for setting ladders to the wall, or fixing a petard onto the outer gate.

For their part the Royalists decided upon a counter-attack to dislodge the enemy from the farm. The garrison massed behind the garden wall to ply the enemy with shot of all kinds, covering the brave handful of volunteers who sallied out to fire the grain in the outhouses. Soon two or three buildings broke into flames, and the crackle of burning timber and the roar of blazing thatch could be heard above the thunder of the great guns. The Grange barn stood out like a citadel in the dense black smoke, and unless this could be fired, it might harbour two or three hundred Parliamentarians for the night.

A Royalist lieutenant colonel led twenty-five men carrying grenadoes into the farmyard, but Captain Clinton of Waller's regiment met them with a party of musketeers. Swords flashed and pistols barked in the smoke-filled yard as the shouting men slithered in the mud. The Royalists had the best of this hand-to-hand fighting. One blade inflicted a mortal wound on Clinton, and some grenadoes hurled into the great double gateway of the barn ignited a pile of hay much to the discomfort of the wounded soldiers who lay about the floor. With all the farm stables and barns on fire, and the Grange barn soon full of choking, coughing men, the commanders of the 'forlorn hope' judged it expedient to retreat back to Cowdrey Down under cover of darkness. This manoeuvre they successfully performed, leaving twelve or thirteen dead behind them and carrying off as many wounded.

The London brigade had spent the day on Cowdrey Down watching the struggle below them and waiting for orders to advance. For young soldiers unaccustomed to the tactical moves of war the withdrawal of the 'forlorn hope' seemed a serious defeat. 'This and the coldness of the night with foul weather was great discouragement to the London regiments who were not used to this hardness,' commented Waller. Two deputations, one of senior and one of junior officers, surprised him next morning with the news that their men were clamouring to return home and they advised him to abandon the siege for a few days. Waller made them write down this request, a possible document for court martial proceedings. Then he retired the army into Basingstoke for an unearned holiday.

The Royalists had intercepted and published in *Mercurius Aulicus* a letter from the wife of one of the soldiers of the London regiments which vividly illustrates the family pressures on these breadwinners to return home.

Most clear and loving husband, my kind love –
Remember unto you, hoping that you are in good health, as I am at the writing hereof. My little Willie has been sick this fortnight. I pray you to come home, if you can come safely.

I do marvel that I cannot hear from you as well other neighbours do. I do desire to hear from you as soon as you can. I pray you to send me word when you do think you shall return. You do not consider I am a lone woman. I thought you would never leave me thus [so] long together, so I rest ever praying for your savest return.

Your loving wife,
Susan Rodway.

Ever praying for you till death I depart.

The letter was addressed 'To my very loving husband, Robert Rodway, a train-soldier in the Red Regiment, under the command of Captain Warren. Deliver this with speed, I pray you.'

As Captain Warren had led the 'forlorn hope' of the Red Regiment in one of the fiercest assaults on Basing House, perhaps the epistolary silence of Susan's husband meant that he had already found a soldier's grave and 'little Willie' was but one more orphan in this cruel civil war.

While the citizen soldiers refreshed themselves, Waller put the rest of his army to good use. One party occupied The Vyne, a splendid house four miles north of Basingstoke, which Waller thought might serve 'as a bridle' on Basing. Captain Samuel Gardiner's troop captured Lord Salter, a Royalist ambassador returning from the French court, whose baggage contained a sum of money variously estimated between £300 and £6,000.[24] On Saturday 11 November Waller resolved, as he put it, 'to have another fling at Basing'.

Upon information he received from two deserters from the garrison, one of whom had taken service in the King's army after being taken at Roundway Down, Waller planned to make his main assault from the east, from the direction of Basing village, with two diversionary attacks on the south and west, both in Basing Park. The turncoats told him that a section of the curtain wall on the eastern side of the New House courtyard could be blown down by a well-placed petard.

Around 11.00 a.m. on Sunday 12 November, the Parliamentarian Horse 'begirt the House round, braving and calling to the garrison, "Where's your Hopton? Prince Rupert has but three men"'.[25] Meanwhile, the Foot trudged back towards Basing. 'I have intended to have fallen on before day,' wrote Waller, 'but the sluggishness of the soldiers was such that it was afternoon a good while before I could come up.'

After his guns had pounded the defences at close range for an hour or more, Waller gave the orders for the simultaneous attacks to be made. He himself joined the 2,000 Foot massing in the woods between the house and village. 'At this last place I set up my rest [i.e. ventured a final stake or reserve, hazarded all] where Major Strachan – a gallant brave gentleman as draws a sword – fell on with his dragoons, seconded by mine own regiment, and the four companies of Colonel Jones and the petardier with them.

'This was performed with as much courage and resolution as could be done by men. The enemy had quitted one of their works, our men gained the rampart, and the petardier applied his petard, but unluckily mistook the place. For whereas he should have applied to a place in the old wall which was but a brick and a half thick, he set it against a door that was bricked up and lined with earth, so it took no effect.'

In the meantime 500 soldiers of the Red Regiment had advanced to storm a redoubt which jutted out like the prow of a ship towards the south-east, thereby flanking the main Parliamentarian body of foot assailing the New House. Here only six Royalist musketeers and a small piece loaded with case-shot confronted the Londoners, but the gunner ploughed a furrow of death in their ranks with his first discharge. The Red Regiment stumbled to an uncertain halt well out of musket range, fired one ragged volley and then took to its heels. Much encouraged, the Royalists rushed back into the New House half-moon and drove out the Parliamentarians.

A renewal of the onslaught met with a similar lack of success. 'Waller again forces on his men and on they must or die (such order was given to the commanders) but were served as before.' On this occasion women joined their menfolk on the parapet, hurling down brickbats and bidding the soldiers 'Come up Roundheads if you dare!' A wily German engineer knocked a loophole through the side of a building towards the north end which completely enfiladed the outside of the wall. After three or four men had been killed by his accurate sniper fire all enthusiasm vanished in the Parliamentarian ranks, and although Waller rode out ahead of the reserve companies of Londoners they would not come up as far as the front of his horse.

By this time the third attack from the south-west had also foundered. A Royalist party of thirty musketeers sallied into a lane beneath a half-moon, gave fire upon the flank of the Londonders, and as suddenly ducked back to the cover of a winding hedge. This manoeuvre threw the trained bands into confusion. 'Their front fired before it was possible they could do any execution, and for want of intervals to turn away speedily the second and third ranks fired upon them, and so consequently the rear fired upon their own front, and slew and wounded many of their own men.' The half-moon defenders contributed to this 'lamentable spectacle' by firing a drake or two among them with deadly effect. The Londoners lost sixty or seventy dead and wounded in this manner, and withdrew in haste out of range.[26]

The fighting had lasted no more than an hour or two, yet on every quarter the Parliamentarians had fallen back. The steady patter of rain in the chilly and leafless woods now replaced the thunder of guns. The soldiers clustered together in disconsolate huddles, grumbling and complaining as the short November afternoon merged into a cold, wet night.

At 10.00 p.m. some of the Green Auxiliaries bestirred themselves and recovered two abandoned field guns, some petards and an ensign which had been left planted forlornly in the rampart of the New House half-moon. In recognition of this brave deed, Waller promoted Captain Webb to the rank of major, while his lieutenant, Everet, was promised a captaincy 'upon the next opportunity'.

Waller himself must have been exhausted. He laid himself down upon a straw bed among the London trained soldiers in Basing Park, just as Hannibal had once wrapped himself in his red cloak and slept among his men. But this good example of leadership could not still an underswell of discontent in the city brigade. As the wind rose and the rain lashed down, their officers could no longer keep the men upon their guards. Early next morning Waller felt compelled to move the army back into Basingstoke. 'I lost in this service thirty men upon the place and near upon one hundred hurt,' concluded Waller in his account of the siege. If the casualties of the attack on the Grange are taken into account this estimate tallied well with Archer's figure of about 300 dead and wounded – mostly Waller's own regiment of foot and Red Regiment men – for the whole siege.

Operations against Basing House could not be resumed again, for reasons which Waller himself explained in his despatch. 'The next morning early my scouts came in and gave me advertisement that Sir Ralph Hopton with his whole strength was upon his march within six miles of me. And by a party which I had sent out towards Reading I was informed that Sir Jacob Astly had drawn a considerable body of horse and foot out of Reading and the parts thereabouts, and was not far from me. Whereupon I speedily drew the army into the field, and sent out fresh parties on all sides to discover what way the enemy held. For by some prisoners which my men fetch'd in I was informed that Sir Ralph struck out of the road towards me and marched Newbury way towards Kingsclere, which was to join with Reading forces.'

From his scout reports and the interrogation of prisoners, Waller had indeed constructed an accurate picture of the enemy's movements. At Kingsclere, 8 miles north-west of Basingstoke, Sir Jacob Astly met Hopton with 900 Foot from the Reading garrison and other forces, and together they turned towards Waller with 'a very handsome little army of near

3,000 foot and dragoons, about 2,000 horse and a good train of artillery'. Waller continued: 'When the regiments were drawn out as I was riding about to give orders, I was saluted with a mutinous cry among the city regiments of "Home, Home", so that I was forced to threaten to pistol any of them that should use that base language, and an enemy in the field so near. With this they were all very well acquitted.

'I then sent for all the field officers to take advice with them concerning my proceeding. There were three propositions moved. The first, to march up to the enemy and fight with him; the second, to march to Winchester and seize upon that; the third to retire to Farnham and to preserve the country from thence until further supplies came to strengthen us. The first was carried clear, and the officers dismissed to their several charges. But they were no longer returned to their regiments, but the mutiny broke out again, with a protestation those of the city would not march one foot further. Upon this I was enforced to retire to Farnham where I now am.'

CHAPTER SEVENTEEN

Deliverance at Farnham

The army reached Farnham on the afternoon of Wednesday 15 November and mustered in the park while the names of deserters were listed. Then the soldiers began erecting earthworks around the town, labours which the Londoners performed with ill grace, promising themselves that they would march off to London ere long.

In his full letter to the Speaker, written on Thursday, Waller asked the House to hasten his Western brigade regiments and also the forces he had already requested from the Southern Association counties. In the meantime, 'what I can do with my horse and a handful of foot I will, God willing, perform with my uttermost endeavours. It grieves my soul that I can do no more.'

Waller tactfully suggested that his account of the actions of the London brigade might not be construed as 'a reflection of dishonour either upon the city unto which I owe all service and respect and particular obligations or upon all regiments, for there be many worthy gallant men amongst them'. He produced an ingenious explanation for their failures: 'But the truth is, amongst the hirelings which were promiscuously taken up, I have reason to suspect there were malignants that put themselves upon this service only to overthrow it, and that they are the men that have blown these coals.' He wanted the runaways to be caught and punished. In conclusion, Waller begged Parliament 'to pardon my many failings in this service which are not my fault but my punishment'.

This letter revealed a chastened Waller who feared that worse would befall him. At Odiham, only 7 miles to the west, Hopton's regiments hovered like vultures waiting for the strength of their victim to ebb before pouncing.

Upon the receipt of his despatch the House of Commons voted £5,000 for Waller, but this would not suffice. In a letter dated 23 November, he sought a further grant, pointing out that, 'Want of money and want of clothes have produced want of obedience and want of health, I had almost said want of heart in this army, working like a malignant fever upon the spirits of our men and dulling the edge of our swords, though I am confident the metal is unaltered.

'I cannot but take notice with humble thankfulness of £5,000 voted for our supply, but I beseech you to give me leave to tell you it is impossible for this

137

sum or less than double the proportion of this sum to stop the clamorous wants of our soldiers, for the last payment was so small that it would not enable them to buy themselves so many necessaries as they wanted for this winter service and their hopes being fixed upon this supply, if this should fall short, it would instead of a satisfaction prove an irritation to them. God knows, I write this with a sad sense, but I have reason to doubt what command I shall be able to retain upon those, whom I can neither reward or punish. I humbly desire there may be some present course taken to supply the army.

'I have presumed to send some parties to Godalming and Midhurst to take up some coarse cloths, linen, shoes, boots and stockings for the soldiers, and if there may be any assurance given to pay for their commodities, I am confident it would be best for the soldiers and the country.'[1]

Upon reading this letter and an independent report from William Cawley corroborating it in substance, the House of Commons duly doubled its original vote of £5,000 from the excise money and took steps to send reinforcements to Waller. The injection of money into the veins of the army had a tonic effect. Above all, the spirits of the Londoners revived, and they remained at Farnham. Nicholas Cowling, Waller's Commissary-General, kept them well provided with beef, pork, mutton, bread, cheese and beer, a diet which they supplemented with venison poached from the neighbouring parks.[2]

That week the fiery and irascible Sir Michael Livesey reached Farnham with 'a very fair regiment of horse and a company of dragoons consisting of 120 out of Kent', and this reinforcement may have heightened the morale of the city brigade.[3] In any case the Londoners could hardly risk a march back to London without an escort of Horse when a hostile enemy lay 7 miles away. Meanwhile, 'a reasonable good party of horse and dragoons' and about 1,000 Foot under Sir John Berkeley had joined Hopton at Odiham. With these the Royalist general resolved to march towards Farnham Castle 'to see the countenance of the enemy'.[4]

Early on Monday 27 November Waller's scouts brought him word of this advance, but the Londoners, who had stood to arms in the park for twenty-four hours only a few days previously, may have suspected another false alarm and they made no great haste to tumble out of their beds and march to Farnham. But the God who Waller believed had humbled him at Roundway Down and punished him yet again at Basing House now relented. 'At Farnham God appeared wonderfully for me when the Lord Hopton drew up his whole army within demi-culverin shot of me, being (with the forces of Sir Jacob Astly, who was then joined with him) at the least eight thousand horse and foot; and (through the mistake or neglect of my Adjutant-General

[Captain John Fleming] and the slackness of my men in drawing to the rendezvous) I was not able to face him with two thousand. In that extremity the Lord took opportunity to shew himself for me, by sending a mist all the morning, that by reason thereof the enemy durst not give on.'[5]

As the mist cleared the Parliamentarian army under the guns of the castle caught sight of the 'Hoptonians' in battle order on a heath overlooking the park not more than a mile away. As bait to tempt Waller into the open, Hopton sent forward 1,000 musketeers and some Horse, but as soon as these came within range the Farnham Castle gunners began to fire and scored several fortunate hits. Lieutenant Archer overheard a report to Sir William that the first three shots had slain no less than fifteen men and seventeen horses.

As the Royalists had brought with them only two small pieces of artillery which could make no effective reply and as it became clear that Waller would not be lured out, Hopton wisely decided to retreat back to Odiham. Despite the fact that he had made his usual careful preparations for a withdrawal, Hopton could not prevent his rearguard from being 'very smartly entertain'd by the enemy'. In his memoirs the Royalist general paid Waller a rare compliment for this pursuit, which he described as 'very soldier-like'.

Always after gaining a victory, albeit a moral one, Waller's mind turned to the problem of how best to exploit it. For any considerable move he needed more soldiers, and he begged Parliament to make sure that the London brigade stayed with him at least 'till some other strength come up to me, otherwise I am left at sixes and sevens, neither able to follow the enemy or defend myself, and my old friend is so gallant an enemy that he will quickly take advantage of it to my destruction.'

In spite of these cautious sentiments Waller harried the Royalist army with cavalry raids. On the night of 28 November, for example, Colonel Vandruske beat up Sir Edward Stowell's regiment in Long Sutton and captured its major.[6] Stowell's horse counter-charged the Parliamentarians, and drove them off. Vandruske carried away two pistol balls in his shoulder and had to retire from the army to London for a time. Waller publicly cashiered a whole troop of horse next morning for refusing orders to second the attack in which this Dutchman, one of his most favoured officers, had spilled his blood for the cause. According to *Mercurius Britanicus*, Vandruske was brought wounded to London 'to the great grief of Sir Wm. Waller, who had rather lost his right hand'.

Upon the advice of his council of war Hopton gave orders for his army to go into winter quarters. These he chose with two ends in view: first, to shield Winchester from the Parliamentarian army about Farnham, and secondly to outflank Waller by securing the Sussex passages into Kent. Three brigades, each of Horse and Foot, he placed in Winchester, Alresford and Alton, while a fourth occupied Petersfield. A local Parliamentarian force, however, secured Cowdray House, which stood near an important road into Kent.[7]

Taking advantage of an exceedingly hard frost, 'which made his march more easy through those deep dirty ways than better weather would have done', Hopton gave support to a detachment from Petersfield which had already besieged Arundel and captured this strong castle. Leaving in it an ample garrison the Royalist general then rode back to Winchester well pleased with his work. He then moved to strengthen his hold on Romsey, which he regarded as a stepping-stone to the eventual capture of Southampton.

CHAPTER EIGHTEEN

The Storming of Alton

On Saturday 2 December 1643, the day Arundel fell into Royalist hands, Waller journeyed to London. 'The necessities of those poor men that are engaged with me in your service drew me to the Town to represent their condition to you,' he wrote to the Speaker from Bedford House the following evening, 'and to desire they may be [taken] in consideration of their future maintaining as part of my Lord General's army. But coming to wait upon his Excellency I received signification from him that his Majesty is come to Basing or expected there this night. Whereupon I thought it my duty to repair immediately to my charge.'

The Royalist newspaper received a report that at their meeting Essex commanded Waller to return at once to Farnham, or face a court martial, and that Waller had departed, leaving a letter for House of Commons.[1] Although probably untrue, the report does reveal yet again that the Royalists were fully aware of the ill feeling that existed, albeit now in a suppressed form, between the two Parliamentarian commanders. Possibly Royalist high command took this factor into account when formulating their strategy for the coming spring campaign.

'Since I cannot attend the House,' continued Waller in his letter, 'I must with all humbleness leave these lines to tell it, that those poor forces under my command may be so provided for, that they may have a subsistence to do you service. I shall likewise beg that Colonel Harley's regiment, and all such companies as are at present raised, may be completed and armed and dispatched forthwith to me with such other forces as may be added to them.

'As I was writing this,' he added, 'I received advertisement from Farnham from Major-General Potley that his Majesty is come to Basing with two thousand horse and that there are more forces to follow him. I humbly leave the consequence of it to your judgement, and rest, your most humble servant, William Waller.'[2]

The Royalist advance into Sussex, culminating in the capture of Arundel and an unsuccessful dash to seize the crossing over the River Adur at Bramber Castle next day, together with the King's reported move to Basing House, thoroughly alarmed both Parliament and the capital, for it 'looked like a land-flood that might roll they knew not how far'.[3] Some began to wonder whether the Lord General would leave Waller to drown in this new high tide as he had apparently done at the time of Roundway Down. 'The main chance is about good and valiant Sir William Waller,' reported the Scotsman Robert Baillie writing from London on 7 December. 'The grandees would see, they say, that poor man perish.'[4]

As more reinforcements reached Waller at Farnham this fate became less likely. Five companies of Heselrige's foot entered the park on 27 November in time to witness Hopton's withdrawal. Some companies of Andrew Potley's regiment may have arrived with their colonel soon after this event, and Waller appointed the old Scots veteran, who had served for thirty years at a salary of £500 a year with much distinction under King Gustavus Adolphus of Sweden, to be Major-General of Foot in the Western brigade.

Waller did not, however, neglect the former occupant of that post. In this despatch of 28 November Waller drew the Speaker's attention to the imminent disbandment of 200 soldiers of Colonel James Carr, who had been turned out of their quarters, probably because they could not pay for them. Apparently Carr's captains had raised their companies at their own expense and received no pay for them. 'I desire that I may not be deprived of his service, for he is an honest man and a brave old soldier,' wrote Waller. As some compensation for Carr's missing regiment, five companies of Sir William Springate's foot, the Whitecoats of Kent, marched into Farnham in the first week of December. Their young colonel, however, was still recovering from a wound caused by a spent bullet at the battle of Newbury and could not join them until a week or two later.

Once he knew that the King had resupplied Basing House and then returned to Oxford, Waller made plans for an attack upon the Royalist brigade in Alton. He maintained complete security by confiding only in a few senior officers. For a week or more his scouts found their way on to the hills overlooking the small town and studied the fortifications erected by the 900 'excellent foot' from Reading and the troopers of the Earl of Crawford's regiment. Indeed, Lieutenant-Colonel Birch's secretary could recollect for him that 'though you were never at Alton, yet when you had made all ready, you did as well know where their trench was deep and where shallow, and where to enter as if yourself had ordered the work'.[5]

In order to achieve surprise Waller knew that he would have to become a night owl again and march across country under cover of darkness, thus avoiding the main roads upon which the enemy kept a close watch. Yet the train of artillery could not be dragged through slippery plough lanes and over densely wooded hills. Colonel James Wemyss solved this problem for Waller. *The True Informer* reported on 9 December: 'That renowned and unmatchable engineer, Colonel Wemyss, Lieutenant General of the

Ordinance and Train unto Sir William Waller . . . went down from London on Tuesday night last, Dec. 5th, with wagons laden with leather pieces of ordnance, and much other ammunition, and is by this time at Farnham with Sir William Waller. These leather pieces are of very great use, and very easy and light of carriage. One horse may draw a piece, which will carry a bullet of a pound and a half weight, and do execution very far. This is the said Colonel's particular invention, and will be of very great service unto Sir William's army, especially for this winter season.'

Made of toughened leather bound with iron hoops, the light guns could fire seven or eight times, and one horse could pull a piece or pack it over the roughest track. Although the Swedes had made use of them some years before, Wemyss had taken out the English patent. Appropriately it was the 'Night Owl' who employed leather guns for the first time in the Civil War. Some of them were preserved at Wemyss Castle in Scotland and can be seen to this day in the national museum at Edinburgh.

For the design on Alton, Waller needed the services of the London regiments and the task of securing their aid he left until last, no doubt to reduce the risk that any 'malignants' in the ranks might slip away to apprise Crawford of the plan.

Late on Tuesday 12 December the brigade mustered in Farnham Park, and at 10.30 p.m. Waller rode to the head of each regiment and made an appeal direct to the man. Lieutenant Archer, who heard the speeches, recorded in one long sentence both the substance of the address and the response. 'He gave us many thanks for our service past, and told us that according to his promise and our expectation we were to be discharged, and march homewards on the morrow, and said he would not detain us (if we were so bent homewards that we would stay no longer) but withal he told us that yet we could not return with much honours in respect of the bad successes we had in our chiefest service, certifying us withal, that at the present there was an opportunity which might avail the States, and bring honour both to God and ourselves, if we would but lend him our assistance til the Monday following, engaging himself upon his honour and credit, that we should be no longer detained, which we considering gave our full consent to stay, for which he gave us many thanks, in a very joyful expression advising us presently [immediately] to prepare for the service because delays are dangerous.'

After the soldiers had refreshed themselves in Farnham they mustered at about midnight and marched out for 2 miles along the Basing road, a stratagem to throw any Royalist scouts off the scent. The army then wheeled south towards Alton. Hopton afterwards wrote that 'Sir William Waller had very politicly and soldier-like taken advantage the woodiness of that country, and drawn his men and his light leather-guns into the woods and, with pioneers, made his way through them without coming into any of the highways.'

Alton lay at the end of a valley opening south towards Winchester. Crawford posted sentries in the wooded hills north of the town, and although Lieutenant-Colonel Birch took six of them prisoner, one eluded capture and raised the alarm in Alton shortly before dawn. Crawford made a swift decision to ride with his regiment of horse to Winchester in order to bring back a relief force. 'Our horse perceiving that, pursued them, whilst our foot made the woods ring with a shout. There were three or four of them slain in their flight, and being in narrow lanes after half a miles pursuit, our men retreated again, having taken about thirty horse, and some prisoners. In the meanwhiles the foot were not idle, nor Sir William, whose rare exploits in this service may be registered with the rest of his valiant and honourable actions.'

Gradually Waller's plan of attack unfolded. At the north-west end of the town stood the parish church on gently rising ground, with several stone houses, brick barns and wooden outhouses overlooking its expanse of graveyard. Colonel Richard Boles, commander of the Royalist Foot in Alton, concentrated most of his soldiers in this area. While the Parliamentarian Horse chased Crawford's Cavaliers, the regiments of Waller and Heselrige, supported by the Whitecoats, lined the hedges nearest to the church and poured shot at the Royalist musketeers who were firing back at them out of every available window. As the leather guns came into action, the enemy evacuated the more exposed buildings and fell back towards the church.

By this time the London brigade and the Greencoats had assembled on the hillsides west of Alton and marched to take the main enemy forces in the rear. Volleys from a Royalist half-moon and breastwork temporarily checked the Red Regiment, but the soldiers improvised a smoke screen by setting fire to a thatched house up-wind from these works and resumed their advance.

Meanwhile, the Green Auxiliaries had moved south to outflank the half-moon, and they entered the main street of Alton. In considerable haste the Royalist Foot abandoned both the half-moon and the breastwork and fled up towards the church. Leaving a commanded party to occupy them, the London brigade reformed in the market-place and marched steadily up the gradual incline of the main street, their colours flying in the breeze.

For two hours the Cavaliers held the churchyard and a great earthwork to the north of it. Eventually the weight of musket fire from the Londoners in the surrounding houses compelled them to abandon the south-eastern part of the church wall. One or two intrepid sergeants then led parties of City musketeers into the churchyard. As some chased the Cavaliers into the porch, others encountered enemy soldiers falling back to the church from the earthwork: 'Coming in a disorderly manner to the south-west corner of the church, with their pikes in the rear who furiously charged on, in as disorderly a manner as the rest led them, their front was forced back on their own pikes, which hurt and wounded many of the men, and broke the pikes in pieces.

'By this time the church-yard was full of our men, laying about them stoutly with halberds, swords and musket-stocks, While some threw hand-grenades in at the church windows, others attempting to enter the church being led on by Major Shambrooke, (a man whose worth and valour envy cannot stain) who in the entrance received a shot in the thigh (whereof he is very ill). Nevertheless our men vigorously entered, and slew Colonel Boles their chief commander at the present; who not long before swore, *God damn his soul* if he did not run his sword through the heart of him, which first called for quarter.'

After their commander had fallen, only a few Royalists chose to fight on to the death, the rest threw down their arms and cried for quarter. Today, the visitor to Alton church will find memorials to this fierce fight: bullet and pike scars on the oak door, and tell-tale pitmarks lined with musket-ball lead in the white walls of the nave.

Seven hundred surrendered in the church, 100 in a brick barn close by and another 100 in the fields. Waller set some of them to work dragging out the dead horses which had served as breastworks within the church, and dismantling the scaffolded firing platforms under the windows, while others buried their fifty or sixty slain comrades in a pit beside the north wall of the building.

The Parliamentarians had lost no more than eight or nine soldiers dead, and a score or more wounded, mostly, like Birch, from 'dry blows with the musket stocks'. Five hundred common soldiers would subsequently take the Covenant and serve Parliament, but for the present they marched off with the others towards captivity in Farnham, tied two-by-two with match. Many of them rested that night in Farnham church, 'where they may hear better doctrine than they have heard at Oxford, or amongst the Irish Rebels'.[6]

'Great was my exultation,' declared Waller when he later recalled the victory at Alton.[7] Hopton experienced a corresponding depression. 'This is the first evident ill success I have had,' he admitted in a letter to Waller from Winchester on 16 December. 'I must acknowledge that I have lost many brave and gallant men. I desire you, if Colonel Boles be alive, to propound a fit exchange; if dead, that you will send me his corpse. I pray you send me a list of such prisoners as you have, that such choice men as they are may not continue long unredeemed. God give a sudden stop to this issue of English blood which is the desire, Sir, of your faithful friend to serve you, Ralph Hopton.'[8]

The vanquished Earl of Crawford addressed him in more buoyant tones. Previously he had sent a message to Waller offering to exchange some beef and mutton for a barrel of good wine. Although he had no need of the meat, Waller's sense of humour prevailed, and he duly despatched a 'loving complement' of half a hogshead. After the capture of Alton, some soldiers looting the Earl's quarter found not only his cloak and gloves, but the full hogshead of wine.

'Sir, I hope your gaining of Alton cost you dear,' wrote the Earl. 'It was your lot to drink your own sack, which I never intended to have left for you. I pray you favour me so much as to send my owne chirurgeon, and upon my honour I will send you a person suitable to his exchange. Sir, your servant, Crawford.'[8]

The attack on Alton must be ranked as one of the finest operations of its kind in the Civil War. Clarendon had it specifically in mind when he wrote of Waller: 'beating up quarters was his masterpiece'. It had an immense effect on Hopton, he added, 'for the Royalist commander sustained the loss of [Boles'] regiment with extraordinary trouble of mind, and as a wound that would bleed inwardly; and therefore was the more inflamed with desire of a battle with Waller, to make even all accounts.'[9]

CHAPTER NINETEEN

The Siege of Arundel

On Friday 15 December 1643, Waller gave orders for the London brigade to assemble at Farnham. Some propositions for a march upon Arundel were put to the regiments, 'which most of our men utterly misliked and refused, as conceiving the recovery of that castle to be a thing not to be effected, time enough for us to be upon our march homewards before Christmas.'[1] Waller granted the desire to be discharged according to his promise, but asked them to act as an escort to the prisoners who had refused the Covenant. The citizens accepted this condition and set out on the following day towards London.

With perhaps 5,000 Horse and Foot Waller left Farnham on Sunday 17 December, and quartered that night at Haslemere. Next morning, upon a report that Hopton had garrisoned Cowdray House with four troops and 100 Foot, Waller sent ahead two cavalry regiments to surprise them, but the Royalists were not to be found. The army camped near Cowdray House for the night, and marched to Arundel on Tuesday 19 December. Late in the evening the weary soldiers halted in Arundel Park, and prepared to sleep under the 'best spread trees in the park'.

Arundel Castle stands upon a spur of the Sussex Downs. Swanbourne pond, at the foot of the precipitous east flank of the spur, and the River Arun, around the base of its northern tip, together form a section of natural moat. On the hillside to the west sprawls the town of Arundel, separated at that time from the castle by a narrow belt of trees. A double line of earthworks, the flanks of the outer one resting on Swanbourne lake near the mill and the town wall close by St Mary's Gate, guarded the only open avenue – along the back of the spur from the north. The Royalist's garrison, under the governorship of Colonel Sir Edward Ford and his deputy, an Irish officer named Colonel Joseph Bamfield, numbered at least 800 Foot and four troops of horse.

The Parliamentarian plan envisaged a main assault on the northern field fortifications with several minor attacks elsewhere to divert the enemy's attention. Soon after daybreak on Wednesday Waller's guns began 'to scour a weedy hill', as he called it, some 300 yards away from

147

the first line of entrenchments where a Royalist 'forlorn hope' had taken up a stance.[2] When these skirmishes had been driven back, three columns of Parliamentarian Foot advanced cautiously along the grassy down towards Arundel.

Secretary Roe reminded Lieutenant-Colonel Birch: 'And to my best remembrance the falling on was thus: Sir William Waller's Lieutenant-Colonel [Ramsey] was marching up the narrow lane, with about three hundred musketeers. Which your self perceiving, and being near ready your self to fall on, not liking his rash attempt, you unhorsed the London scout master who at that instant stood by where you were drawing the men into divisions, and speedily rode that horse to the van of that party of foot, and turned again the Lieutenant-Colonel and his party, and drew them into the hollow of the lane out of the enemy's shot, which took place on 7 or 8 of that party as you were speaking before they could be secured, which retreat caused a great shout from the enemy, not fearing your coming on again.

'About a quarter of an hour after this, you were ready with your men in 3 divisions. On the left hand marched the aforesaid lieutenant-colonel with about 200 musketeers; on the right hand your own Major Cotsforth and two hundred musketeers; in the body yourself, 40 paces back with the rest, pikes and muskets.

'Thus marching on, the enemy letting fly very thick, you not liking your major's pace who was marching before you on the right hand, but indeed more softly then you used to do in such a shower, you commanded the captains where you were to come on speedily, and you ran up to the major's party then about 40 paces short of the enemy's line. Where, they being almost at a stand, your example drew them on instantly to enter that line, unto which yourself first entered, though it was intricate to get over that steep line.

'But, one assisting another, instantly there was near 200 entered. In which instant of time, before the rest could enter, (and the great fishpond being between our army and the place where you entered, so that the enemy saw you could not quickly be relieved) out came they with about 100 gentlemen reformadoes on horseback besides foot and other troops of horse, and gave your disordered foot at that very instance of entry such a charge, that they laid many flat to the ground, as well as yourself.'[3]

Colonel Bamfield himself led this Royalist counter-charge. 'Perceiving not far from me that a considerable body of the enemy's foot had passed the line, with eight or ten blue colours which were of Sir Arthur Heselrige's regiment, commanded by Colonel Birch (who I think still lives), and began to range themselves in order, I desired Major Bovel [commander of the three troops of Lord Bellasis' regiment] to charge them with me, for if we brake them not the castle might be lost as well as the town. We charg'd, routed and drove them back over the line.'[4]

In this moment of crisis Waller spurred forward among the retreating musketeers. 'In the middle of the danger and difficulty of the assault,' wrote one, 'our noble vigilant and heroic commander Sir William Waller did so cheer up our resolutions and put such new fire into our blood, as it raised in us all the spirits of fortitude to fall upon our enemies, everyone of us striving to exceed each other in valour, or absolutely resolve to endure the loss of our lives to the last man.'[5] Inspired by their leader, the Parliamentarians stormed back over the first fortification and formed up in Castle Park to assault the second entrenchment near the town wall.

The Royalist defenders behind this work fired with little effect upon the 1,400 enemy Foot and 400 Horse they could see being arrayed before them. After a brief time Birch's musketeers replied with several heavy volleys, firing three ranks at a time, and then advanced towards them. The Royalists fled into the town, hotly pursued by the Parliamentarians. 'At which instance,' Roe recounted, 'Sir William Waller's Lieutenant-Colonel, who but then you encouraged by clapping your hand on his shoulder, your hand no sooner of but he was shot dead. And yourself not gone above 20 paces further received that wonder of God's mercy, the shot in your belly.'

In spite of this hail of shot from the castle walls Waller led his men after the Royalists, attempting to follow them into the inner court of the stronghold. 'We beat them into the Castle,' wrote Waller, 'and entered the first gate with them. The second they made good and barricaded; and there they are welcome. I am resolved to block them up, for I know they are in a necessitous condition.'

On Thursday Waller concluded his despatch with an appeal for more soldiers. 'Truly, my Lords, I am very weak in foot, and my horse so hackneyed out that they are ready to lie down under us. I expect Colonel Behre here on this day, and Colonel Morley. Likewise the Kentish foot are not come up, and I expect them not these two days. The last night I received an advertisement from Winchester that Prince Rupert was expected that night there, and there were 120 carts sent out for his train and baggage. All the country there is summoned to come in with their arms.

'My neighbours of Petersfield, when they quitted that quarter, upon the alarm at Alton, left many of their arms behind them, which on Tuesday were fetched to Portsmouth. If I had some fresh horse, I might easily have cut off ten or twelve troops of the enemy's horse that are quartered betwixt this and Braintree, but being so weary and in so weak a condition I am forced to keep home for a while, and to watch the nine that are in the Castle. I summoned them, but they refused either to give or take quarter, so confident they are of succours. My trust is in God. I humbly desire my commission may be sent down, for without it I shall not be able to settle these counties.'[6]

That evening Colonel Behre, a German officer, entered the town of Arundel with 600 Horse from the Lord General's army. Perhaps to excuse so meagre a reinforcement, Essex reported to Parliament that this regiment was 'so well commanded' that it could face a thousand Cavaliers. Behre's men soon complained of their quarters at Arundel and left shortly after the fall of the castle.[7]

Colonel Herbert Morley's more useful Sussex regiment of horse arrived not long afterwards. From Kent came a trained band regiment of foot and some companies of dragoons. With Livesey's Horse and Springate's Foot these now formed the Kentish brigade, in total 893 soldiers, commanded by Major-General Sir Henry Heyman.[8] The Committee of Surrey sent a few companies from the garrison regiment of Chichester. Clearly Kent and Sussex laid great store upon recapturing Arundel Castle.

The blockade of the fortress lasted from Thursday 21 December until Saturday 6 January. Waller counted upon starvation and thirst doing his work for him. The garrison possessed plenty of beef, both powdered and on the hoof, but much of their bread and malt had fallen into Parliamentarian hands when the town surrendered. For want of fodder the troopers tore ivy off the castle walls, but after a few days many chose to turn loose their horses through a breach made in the unassailable eastern ramparts. Towards the end of the siege Bamfield had cut down the wheat ration of each soldier to 'two sodden spoonfuls' a day. Some experienced soldiers used gunpowder as a substitute for salt. To make matters worse for the garrison, an ox tumbled down one of the two walls and polluted the water. In an attempt to lower the level of the second well, Waller's men drained Swanbourne pond and feasted that night on fine fat carp picked up from the pond mud.[9]

Not that they lacked food, for the Commissary-General commandeered a shop in Arundel whence he issued quantities of provisions of all kinds. Cowling even ordered tobacco from London for the soldiers. For his Christmas dinner Waller sat down with his chief officers to 'a roasting pig, pigeons and chicken', washed down with wine and beer.[10]

For the relief of Arundel the King despatched Lord Wilmot's brigade of 1,000 Horse to Winchester: 'a gallant body,' Hopton commented, 'yet was it not proper for that service.' Nevertheless, by 31 December Hopton brought his army within three miles of Arundel, but an officer who had escaped from the castle assured him that the garrison could hold out without want for fourteen days. Hopton asked him if he had seen their stores, especially their wheat, to which the Captain answered that he had the day before seen a heap of wheat in a room, which as he described was computed not to be less than 40 quarters. Satisfied with this reply, Hopton drew back his army west of Chichester to await infantry reinforcements.[11]

1. Sir William Waller.
(National Portrait
Gallery)

2. Lady Anne Waller,
his second wife.
(Courtauld Institute
of Art)

In the engraving, within the banner:

S.ʳ WILLIAM WALLER Knight Sargeant
Maio.ʳ Generall of yᵉ Parliaments army and
a member. of yᵉ Hono.ᵇˡᵉ House of Commons

C.J. pinxit   1643   Rodimondi incidit
Pieter Stent Excudit

3. A contemporary engraving of Sir William Waller when he was at the height of his fame in 1643.

ROBERT DEVEREUX EARLE OF ESSEX HIS EXCELLENCY, LORD GENERALL OF
the Forces raifed by the Authority of the Parliament, For the defence of the King and Kingdom &.

4. Robert, Earl of Essex, Captain-General of the Parliamentary forces. (British Museum)

5. *Sir Arthur Heselrige, Waller's Lieutenant-General of Horse, 1643/4. (Lord Hazelrigge's Collection)*

THE HON.ᵇᵉˢ COLONEL
NATHANIEL FINES.
MIREVELT. PINX.

6. Colonel Nathaniel Fiennes, Governor of Bristol. (Lord Saye & Sele)

7. *Patrick Ruthven, Earl of Forth. Waller's opponent at Cheriton. (The Bodleian Library, Oxford)*

8. *Lord Ralph Hopton, King's General in the West and Waller's chief opponent. (Petworth House, The Egremont Collection (The National Trust): photograph, Courtauld Institute of Art)*

I shall readily apprehend any occasion that may enable me to serve
you in this particular concerning the restitution of your children. itt
is my unhappiness that I am not capable of performing your
comand they beeing by an order from the Parlament re=
moved to London. I was a meere stranger both to their takin
and removall, and therefore accountable for neither I presume
your nobleness will impute nothing to me in either.
if there be any thing with... power, wherein I may be ser=
viceable ... ready to give demonstration
that I am

My Lord
I have had the honour to receive a letter from your Excellency
upon the ... of your Ex.cy parolle, I have released Lieu=
tenant Colonell Lunsford, not doubting your noble performance
in setting att liberty Lieutenant Colonell Carr. I should not have
putt your Excellency to the trouble of this signification under
your hand, but that I humbly conceive I could not otherwise have
justified my self to my superiors, but by shewing such ... security

Noble Sir
I must ever honour your proceeding
you have ... in this treaty for the exchange of Lieutenant Colo=
nell Lunsford with Lieutenant Colonell Carr, proceeded with so
much candor and nobleness, that I must ever honour you for itt.
I have released Lieutenant Co=
lonell Lunsford, but I cannot part with him, without giving him the
character of a noble gallant gentleman; His Ex.cy parolle 4. I shall
never thinke your

Sr I have had the honour to receive a letter from your highness
touching the exchange of Prisoners wherein, as in all other things
within the possibility of my obedience, I shall be ready to serve
you. with these lines I have sent inclosed the list of such as are
now with me; and if I may knowe who of mine prisoners ... with
your highness, I shall willingly traffick for them.

My Lord
upon the notice from your Excellency that Captain Keightly is
living, I have taken the boldness to send his servant to attend
him in his weake condition. itt is no more, then I have permitted
to those gentlemen that are prisoners with me, into whome
I shall not be wanting to express all the civility I can.

9. Sir William Waller's letters written to Royalists in June 1643, mainly concerning
exchanges of prisoners. The page includes the only draft in his own hand of his famous
letter to Lord Ralph Hopton. (The Bodleian Library, Oxford. MS. Clarendon 22, fol. 113r)

In the first week of the siege the Royalist officers in Arundel Castle put on a bold front, even asking Waller under a flag of truce for wine, tobacco, cards and dice 'to merry away this idle time'.[12] In order to keep as many hungry mouths as possible within the walls, Waller issued a proclamation threatening death to all deserters who fell into his hands,[13] and gradually shortage of meal, coupled with a visitation of 'the bloody flux and spotted fever',[14] and the absence of Hopton's army, produced a mutinous humour in the garrison. Moreover, by constant pinprick attacks at all hours of night and day, Waller deprived the inmates of much sleep. Nor were his guns silent for long. For example, a 'saker drake' and a leather gun sited on the top of St Nicholas Church tower played hard on the inner gatehouse and the round Norman keep, at a range of under 250 yards.[15] Rather than await a battering from six heavy siege pieces on their way from Portsmouth,[16] Sir Edward Ford resolved to yield the castle on terms.

Waller wrote: 'The parley began on Thursday [4 January], when they sent me a letter signifying their willingness to surrender the place, if they might have honourable conditions. I returned answer, that when I first possessed myself of the town, I summoned them to yield upon fair quarter, but they were pleased to refuse either to give or take quarter. I now took them at their word, and bid them yield to mercy. That night I heard no more of them.

'The next morning [Friday 5 January] the drummer came to me again with another letter from Colonel Bamfield, and all the principal officers wherein they disclaimed that incivility to my trumpeter laying the fault upon two who had no soldier in them who unadvisedly, without their consent or knowledge, returned that answer. They looked upon my offer of mercy, and great undervaluation of them with a protestation, [declaring] they would all rather choose to die gallantly, than yield sheepishly to fetters. All the mercy they desired was on behalf of the Lady Bishop and some gentlemen with her, that they might have liberty to repair to their several homes. I sent them answer that I was very satisfied, that in the disavowing of that harshness, they had made some courtesy and that I was content to give them fair quarter. If they should refuse the proffer I assured them it should be the last, and [their] blood should be upon their own heads. The ladies have free leave to come out, with a safe conduct to their homes. If they had a mind to treat upon particulars, they should send out to me 3 officers of quality and I would employ 3 of equal quality to them.

'Within a short time after there came out Colonel Bamfield, Major Bovile and Captain Hodges, who pressed me very much that they might have liberty to march out like soldiers, otherwise they vowed to choose death rather than life, and so broke off. About 2 hours after, they sent out to me Lieutenant-Colonel Rawlins and Major Moulins, who after some debate came to an agreement with me, that this morning, the castle should be surrendered to me by 10 of the clock with all colours, arms, ammunition entire. And that the commanders and gentlemen should have fair quarter and civil usage, the soldiers, quarter. For performance of covenants Sir Edward Ford and Sir Edward Bishop were immediately to be yielded, which was accordingly done.'[17]

That Friday, in the forenoon, Waller entertained the Royalist commissioners and some gentlewomen from the castle to dinner. The ladies remained with Sir William 'who feasted and entertained them that night'. On the following morning, Saturday 6 January, the Parliamentarians entered Arundel Castle.

Waller informed the Speaker: 'We have taken 17 colours of foot and 2 of horse. We have one thousand prisoners, one with another, besides about 160 which we took at the first entering of the Town, and such as ran from the enemy during the siege . . . I humbly desire the London regiments may be speedily sent hither to secure this place (of as great importance as any I know). [I shall] advance with what strength I have towards the enemy. If this be done speedily I doubt not by God's assistance, but to give you a full account of this service. The life of all consists in expedition. God direct your counsels . . .'

'I shall presume to appear as a humble suitor to you on behalf of these God has delivered into my hands. They have carried themselves nobly and bravely, and, I humbly beg they may receive fair and civil usage – in a special manner I am a petitioner for Colonel Bamfield. Some men of ours were taken prisoner by them, and were very fairly used. I ask a like favour for them.'[18] Bamfield was in particular jeopardy. As he wrote in his memoirs, 'I never signed the Capitulation and might have been denied the benefit of the Articles, and quarter, had General Waller been cruel'.

Five hundred common soldiers emulated the example of the Alton prisoners and took the Covenant; four troops of horse escorted the remainder to London. But Waller could not descend upon Hopton's quarter as he had planned for shortly after the fall of the castle the weather broke and snow blizzards rendered the roads impassable.

On 12 January Waller informed the Speaker of the necessity of raising a body of foot with all speed if there was any intention for him to march westwards. This letter was probably written before the change in the weather.[19] Meanwhile, the two regiments of London Foot, which had set out on 5 January to replace Harrington's brigade, made a slow progress through Surrey. By 8 January the regiments lay at Kingston, but the refusal of Captain Edmund Scott [Kent volunteer troop of horse] to accompany them further delayed their advance to Guildford.[20] Not until the 29th did they reach Petworth. By this time most of Waller's regiments had gone into winter quarters in the towns and villages of West Sussex, and the Londoners gratefully followed suit.

Before returning to London Waller rode down to the seashore to inspect a lucrative windfall. Three Dutch privateers had driven aground a large Dunkirk ship mounting twenty-two brass guns and laden with Hollands, Lockrams, lace, silver and 'thread plush' in one part of its hold and 200 arms and 100 barrels of powder in the other. Rather than yield his ship to the Dutchmen the captain surrendered it to Waller's soldiers who had gathered at the creek where the ship had struck land.[21]

On Monday 8 January Waller went aboard, and stayed for a time supervising the removal of the cargo by wagons to Arundel. The military cargo designed for Ireland or Bristol, some Royalist officers aboard, the ship itself, and the brass guns (the whole valued at £20,000), passed into the possession of Parliament, but the merchandise became the subject of a lengthy legal wrangle in the Admiralty courts. Eventually Waller received £700 as his share of the salvage money and 'a little painted cabinet and some toys, worth twelve or fourteen pounds, presented to my wife by the merchants of that forementioned ship as a token of their thankfulness for the care I had shewed to preserve their goods'.[22]

Having settled his men into their winter quarters and cleared the Royalists out of one important Sussex ironworks, Waller journeyed to London, which he had reached by 25 January. Once more his stock had risen high in the capital. In verses presented to Lady Waller and printed at the end of a published account of the fall of Arundel,[23] one London poet wrote prophetically:

> Methinks, I already read that large page
> Of Chronicle, in the ensuing Age,
> Which shall contain his Name, unless that he
> Go on so far, it must a Volume be:
> Then, as I turn the leaves, perhaps, I finde
> Some lofty strain to speak his gallant minde,
> And tell our after-nephews part of all
> That made him up a perfect Generall.

CHAPTER TWENTY

A Great Victory at Cheriton

'The war is like a football-play, where one side does give the other a kind of overthrow, and strikes up anothers heels, but presently [immediately] they rise up and give the other as great a blow again.'[1] Thus a writer in *The British Mercury* described the changing military fortunes in the late winter of 1643.

In the West, Prince Maurice, who had taken Exeter and Dartmouth in the previous autumn, now besieged Plymouth. Byron, honoured in October 1643 with a peerage for the victory over Waller at Roundway Down and his service on Newbury field, commanded a new Royalist army in Cheshire composed mainly from regiments brought over from Ireland. He had gained some early successes, but he was defeated at Nantwich by the Fairfaxes and Sir William Brereton's local forces (25 January 1644). Professional soldiers, versed in the endemic warfare of the Continent, may have accepted this state of affairs with equanimity, especially as they were enjoying the prospects of promotion, pay and booty. But the 'vehements' in Parliament and City clamoured for a decision in the field.

John Pym had died of cancer on 8 December, and his death – following on that of John Hampden at Chalgrove Field in the summer – threatened to leave a gaping hole in the political and strategic leadership of the war, for this pair had worked together like two consuls of Rome. Pym had lived to see Scotland's entry into the war on Parliament's side. Fortunately, two articles in the treaty, signed with the Scots on 29 November 1643, made provision for a Committee of Both Kingdoms to be established, which could in principle assume the necessary military direction.[2] An ordinance which was read twice in the House of Commons on 30 January 1644, defined the functions of the proposed committee as 'to advise, consult, order and direct, concerning the carrying on and managing of the war'.[3]

The Earl of Essex, who survived one rumoured attempt of securing his resignation,[4] reacted in a predictably negative way. His party in the House of Lords lodged an objection against the words 'order and direct', claiming that these executive powers belonged to the office of the Captain-General alone. But a scrutiny of the Earl's commission by a joint committee of both Houses confirmed that Parliament had not delegated to him such a complete authority for the direction of the war. According to one contemporary political diarist, the refusal of Alexander Leslie, Earl of

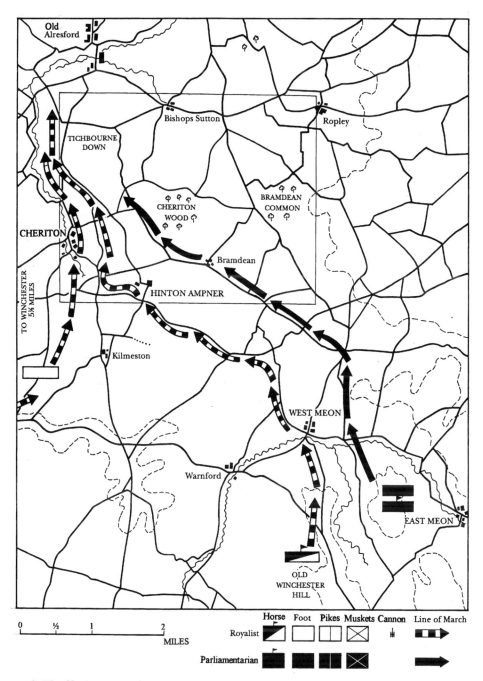

Old
Alresford

TICHBOURNE
DOWN

Bishops Sutton

Ropley

CHERITON
WOOD

BRAMDEAN
COMMON

CHERITON

Bramdean

TO WINCHESTER
5¼ MILES

HINTON AMPNER

Kilmeston

WEST MEON

Warnford

OLD
WINCHESTER
HILL

EAST MEON

	Horse	Foot	Pikes	Muskets	Cannon	Line of March
Royalist						
Parliamentarian						

MILES

0   ½   1   2

8. The Cheriton campaign

Leven and the general of the Scots army, to serve under Essex, 'especially his officers being so bad', proved to be the deciding factor.[5] In January, Leven had led the Scots south through the snow into northern England.

Then Essex himself intervened to point out the practical difficulties of entrusting the day-to-day strategic control of field armies to a central committee in London. After some debate the Commons insisted on having their own way, leaving the disgruntled Lords with little choice but to pass the ordinance complete with the disputed phrase (16 February). Essex did, however, receive an important reassurance, almost a concession, that in the field he could act according to the military situation without reference to London. Thus, haste to set up the first Committee of Both Kingdoms, together with a desire on the part of the moderates to mollify the Lord General, led to a compromise, a fudging of the issue which would have serious consequences during the coming year.

The composition of the committee revealed the growing ascendancy of militants in the Lower House. Prominent members of that faction, including both Vanes, Oliver St John, Heselrige and Cromwell, occupied at least eight of the fourteen commoner seats. Although Essex sat in the committee as one of the six peers, Denzil Holles, his most vocal political advocate in the Commons, was not elected. Sir William Waller, voted fourth onto the committee, possessed, at least potentially, a strong influence over its debates, for he not only remained with the 'vehements' but also enjoyed the friendship of Sir Philip Stapleton and Sir Gilbert Gerrard, both colonels in the Lord General's army and members of the committee.

'Sir William Waller intends to become Lord of the West,' declared *Mercurius Aulicus* in the second week of January. The recruit of Waller's army for the impending reconquest of the West came high on the agenda of the committee during its early meetings at Derby House. On 12 February the Committee of the Southern Association had introduced an ordinance for raising 3,000 Foot, 1,200 Horse and 500 dragoons.[6]

Concern for local security induced the political leaders of the four counties to struggle hard to retain a measure of control over the regiments they were compelled to assign to Waller's army. This opposition, coupled with disagreement over certain financial clauses and Sir William's objection to an amendment emphasising his subordination to the Lord General, delayed the passing of the ordinance in Parliament until 30 March. Yet the Committee of Both Kingdoms took strong action to establish Waller's authority over the military forces in the association and to anticipate the ordinance by drawing regiments out of the member counties for service under him.

So successful were these measures that on 4 March the Committee of Both Kingdoms could resolve that Waller would advance forthwith against Hopton with 3,000 Horse, 5,000 Foot and 600 dragoons of his own, supported by a cavalry brigade under Sir William Balfour from the Lord General's army.

As Lieutenant-General of the Horse under Essex, Balfour was senior enough to be placed in command of Waller's cavalry over Heselrige's head, the latter still suffering from his rumoured part in the rout of Roundway Down. Balfour, a Scot, had seen military service with the Dutch. At the time of the Earl of Strafford's trial he had been Lieutenant of the Tower of London. He had distinguished himself at Edgehill, and he seems to have been an excellent officer.

In order to prevent the King from reinforcing Hopton with part of the Oxford Horse the committee directed the Earl of Manchester to make a diversion against that city.[7] With this bold plan to coordinate the actions of three armies, the new Parliamentarian high command at Derby House made its first attempts at directing strategy.

In the second week of March Waller rejoined his men at Arundel. On Wednesday 13 March Waller issued 'A proclamation for the better performance of Duty and observations of the Laws of War'. The following crimes would be punished: failure to hand over prisoners to the (Provost) Marshal General, or to appear at the appointed rendezvous, straggling from the colours, the private sale of captured horses, private fights in quarters, molesting civilians and foraging without warrants. The subsequent minutes of Waller's courts martial throughout 1644 contain many illustrations of these and other common misdemeanours in the armies of the Civil War.[8]

On Tuesday the 19th he set out towards Petersfield, his rendezvous with Balfour. Meanwhile, Major-General Richard Browne led the winter-weary Londoners from Petworth to Midhurst. On 21 March Waller, who had quartered his regiments in the villages around Petersfield, sent word for the Londoners to march to Treyford, 5 miles south-west of Midhurst, where they remained until Sunday 24 March.

After the arrival of Livesey's Horse and Weldon's Foot from Kent,[9] Waller decided to concentrate his forces for a move on Winchester and on Monday Browne's regiments marched to their appointed quarters at Warnford and West Meon, 'where we found a party of the enemies horse when our quartermasters entered the town, which occasioned some action, though not much considerable'.[10]

Waller's headquarters lay at East Meon, 3 miles by road to the south-east. On Tuesday he despatched six troops of horse to scout towards Winchester, and they returned that night with three prisoners captured in a skirmish with superior numbers of Royalist cavalry. Now fully aware, having learnt that Hopton had sallied out of Winchester, Waller ordered a rendezvous for his army on the heath by East Meon next morning.

At the appointed hour sixty-three troops of horse mustered for Waller's inspection, twenty-two from the Lord General's army and the remainder from his own two brigades. Two regiments of dragoons and five of infantry completed the array.[11] Probably while Waller was still riding about this field, news came in that 3,000 Royalist Horse had drawn near to the quarters of the London brigade at West Meon.

Some weeks before this date General Patrick Ruthven, Earl of Forth, joined Hopton at Winchester with considerable reinforcements from Oxford, increasing the Royalist army there to a strength of 3,800 Horse, 3,200 Foot and perhaps ten guns. The Earl assumed command of the combined army. He was an officer of long experience in the Swedish army under the great Gustavus. Over seventy years of age and decidedly fond of the bottle, he suffered much from gout. Yet he was still a brave and competent officer. Forth seems to have delegated the executive work of command to Hopton. Consequently, it was the latter who led the Royalist army away from its quarters in and around Winchester on the evening of Tuesday 26 March. After a 3 mile march the soldiers camped for the night, and then before dawn Forth, 'though with pain and difficulty enough', wrote Hopton, came up and supervised the advance of the Royalist Horse to Warnford hoping to surprise the Londoners in Warnford church observing the Wednesday fast.

Major-General Browne, however, had received warning of the Royalists' approach, probably from the prisoners taken the day before, and consequently they found Warnford completely deserted. At first the London brigade stood in battle order near West Meon, but then a despatch from Waller directed Browne to march his men back to a high wooded down, known today as Westbury Forest, midway between the two Meon villages, 'which accordingly we did, in the forlorn hope expecting the enemy every hour to fall upon us, so that we were forced to make a stand a mile or more from the town in extreme danger till Sir William Waller's forces came up from East Meon to join with us'.[12]

It was the sight of the Cavalier host massing on Old Winchester Hill which compelled the Londoners' rearguard to face about near the crest of the Westbury feature, where the Royalist Colonel Slingsby sighted them: 'We spied a full regiment with white colours stand in order facing us upon our left hand about a mile and a half from us but could by no means discover where the enemy's body lay.'[13]

Waller marshalled his main forces on the reverse slope of the Westbury down, no doubt hoping that the Royalist generals would commit their army to a march up the broken hillside. But Hopton, possibly recollecting his experience at Lansdown, could not be so easily enticed, and instead he sent Major-General Sir John Smith with some cavalry towards the enemy 'to seek to draw him from his advantage to engage from the woods, and nearer the plain'. Waller countered by sending some of his own troops down into the valley to drive off the Cavaliers, and this service they performed without much loss to either side.

Behind the broad back of Westbury Forest the Parliamentarian Horse found the hours of waiting tedious, and enjoyed some light relief at the expense of the apprentices in the London regiments, town lads who rarely strayed from the crowded streets of the city. The White and Yellow Regiments had not been out of London before. 'Here you should have seen the Londoners, run to see what manner of things cows were,' wrote Captain Robert Harley to his brother. 'Some of them would say they had all of them horns, and would do great mischief with them, then comes one of the wisest of them crying "Speak softly". To end the confusion of their opinions they piled up a council of war, and agreed it was nothing but a kind of looking glass.' Harley may not have been alone among Waller's officers from the West in regarding lightly 'the wooden city brigade under their true colonel, Colonel Browne'.

In the early afternoon (Wednesday 27 March) Waller gave orders for his army to march to Alresford, 10 miles to the north-west, a move which would outflank the Royalist Horse and almost cut them off from their base at Winchester. Balfour led a vanguard of thirty-five troops of horse, the Foot marched in the centre and Waller brought up the rear with his three Western cavalry regiments. To shorten his line and therefore reduce the effects of an attack upon his own flank, Waller commanded the Horse to ride four troops abreast. The army set out beside the leafy lane which ran through the wooded hills to the village of Bramdean and thence to Alresford.

Meanwhile, Hopton, who knew the local countryside very well, became suspicious. Remembering that the Westbury Down stood somewhat nearer to Alresford than his own position on Old Winchester Hill, he sent out scouts to see if Waller had ordered any of his cavalry to secure that 'reasonable strong quarter'. As soon as these scouts returned with tidings that the whole Parliamentarian army was marching towards Alresford, the Royalist generals resolved at once to set out with their army towards the same objective.

In order to be sure of getting there before Balfour's vanguard, Hopton raced ahead with Stowell's brigade of horse and his own two regiments of horse and dragoons. 'And the business was so hard pressed on both sides, as the Lord Hopton, a mile and a half before he came to Alresford, marching himself with Sir Edward Stowell in the head of his brigade, did plainly discover Sir William Balfour's troops marching in the lane level with them, and they were not a mile asunder.' Hopton galloped on half a mile to join his own regiments and told them to hasten into the town and hold it until the rest of the army came up.

As soon as Balfour saw that the Royalist horse would reach Alresford before him he halted his troops, probably on East Down, a long hill east of the large village of Cheriton. Both generals then spent the evening consolidating their new positions. As dusk descended, Forth brought the Royalist infantry and the rest of the Horse on to Tichborne Down, just south of Alresford, where they stood in arms that night facing towards the enemy quarters.

The London brigade had marched up to Balfour's horse in time to catch their first glimpse of the Royalist Foot hurrying towards Alresford and among the citizen companies 'you could hear no other word of command than "Stand straight in your files"'. Like all inexperienced young soldiers, the apprentices may well have been nervous about their own behaviour in the impending battle. That night, they slept uneasily in Lambourn meadow, on the floor of the valley behind East Down.[14]

From his own headquarters in Lady Stewkley's manor house of Hinton Ampner, higher on the southern slopes of the same valley, Waller could look down upon the camp-fires of the Londoners. So also could those Royalist scouts in search of Waller's army, who rode out 'to discover where this yet invisible body lay, and at last found his whole strength, horse, foot and artillery, in a low mead within half a mile of us, where he [had] shadowed himself in his march by a lane, and in that ground by a thick high hedge'. Not until midnight did Waller's rearguard draw into the valley, a delay 'which was caused by our often facing about to face the enemy', wrote one of their number, Captain Harley.

Next morning (Thursday 28 March) Hopton despatched more scouts towards Waller's camp, but they hastily withdrew after meeting with some troops of Parliamentarian Horse. 'There was but a little hill and a little vale between us,' Hopton recollected. 'The hill they endeavoured to keep, because it cover'd them from us, and gave them the advantage of looking into us. We disputed that ground that day with little parties, and loose skirmishes, but towards the evening we got the top of the hill and the view of the enemy's quarters, where they encamped as it is said before in a low field enclosed with a very thick hedge and ditch and their ordnance planted upon the rising of the hill behind them.'

Most of the skirmishing revolved around a house and two barns full of corn which the Parliamentarian troopers had partly ransacked for fodder. Captain Harley described as 'a great oversight in us' the fact that the Parliamentarian infantry were not employed to guard this farm 'until we had fetched away the corn, which was much wanted in our army', but Waller's failure to embattle his foot on East Down may be judged as a more serious error, for it allowed Colonel George Lisle with 1,000 Royalist musketeers to occupy this hill 'at an easy rate' before nightfall.

Forth and Hopton rode onto the captured down and after a brief reconnaissance placed Lisle with his musketeers in a fenced wood almost immediately above Waller's camp. To prevent a surprise attack up Alresford lane the generals stationed 500 Horse in the area where the track skirted Lisle's wood. Returning to Tichborne Down they appointed quarters for the rest of their army and gave orders for the soldiers to spend a second night in arms. Then Hopton retired to his coach at the head of the army and Forth to his lodgings in Alresford.

Waller's apparent neglect in not occupying East Down with his Foot may have arisen from a deep division of opinion in the Parliamentarian council of war. On Tuesday 26 March letters from the Committee of Both Kingdoms brought Waller the dire tidings that Prince Rupert had relieved Newark on 21 March, and that Manchester's army had marched into the Midlands to join with a brigade of the Lord General's Horse and retrieve the situation. Not only had the expected diversion against Oxford fallen through, but also the Lord General's much reduced army could no longer be relied upon to protect the capital in the event of Waller's defeat. Therefore, the committee begged Sir William to be cautious and not to fight unless he could do so with clear advantage.[15]

Consequently, at the Parliamentarian council of war in Hinton Ampner manor house on the afternoon of Thursday 28 March, some urged a withdrawal, leaving camp-fires burning to deceive the enemy. (According to Birch's secretary, for example, the council of war resolved 'to make fires and retreat', and only his master's activities as captain of the watch that night made such a move impossible – an unlikely tale.) Others countered by pointing out that such a move with the Royalists occupying East Down would be virtually impossible. No doubt in accordance with Waller's own mind, the meeting advised that the army should stand its ground and give battle if necessary next morning.

The events of the night illustrated the wisdom of not attempting a retreat. In the small hours of the morning Lisle heard sounds of wagons being spanned and driven off, and deducing that Waller had started to march away he sent word at once to Hopton, who relayed the message to Forth. As a result Sir John Smith received orders on Tichborne Down to make ready 1,000 Horse to fall on the Parliamentarian rearguard, but hours passed and the expected withdrawal did not take place.

As the shape of the ground became once more visible in the light of dawn, Hopton rode up to Lisle's position to see for himself what was happening in the valley below, but a thick mist lay like a shroud over Waller's camp. About two hours after sunrise the Royalist general perceived that far from retreating, Waller had secured just before dawn 'a

9. *The battle of Cheriton, 29 March 1644*

high woody ground' on the right hand of his quarters, and was making ready his regiments for battle.

'In the morning when I went to view the army,' wrote Captain Harley, 'I saw such cheerfulness in every one's countenance, that it promised either victory or a willingness rather to die than lose the field. Only the citizens' silver lace began to look like copper. There was on the right hand of us – as we now faced – a wood which we did conceive might be of great advantage to us if it were maintained; for which purpose their was a party of a thousand musketeers, Colonel Potley's regiment and the Londoners white regiment, sent thither, and three hundred horse to second them.'

Colonel Leighton led these Parliamentarian musketeers to the high eastern end of East Down, a place 'very well set with hedges and trees (such as Waller loves) where his men were bestowed at thick as the hedges', noted *Mercurius Aulicus*. Here, Leighton's musketeers stood some 100 feet higher than those of Lisle in their enclosed wood less than a mile along the ridge.

Waller arrayed the bulk of his infantry 'in battalia' at the foot of the down which curved between Bramdean and Hinton Ampner; the remaining regiments he placed on the somewhat higher ground which lay east of Lamborough field.[16] Heselrige and Balfour commanded the left and right wings of the horse respectively, and may have placed their regiments behind the Foot in a position where they could guard Waller's main line of retreat – the road through Bramdean. In order to anchor his left flank, Waller despatched another very strong party of musketeers, drawn partly from the London brigade, to line the hedges before Hinton Ampner. Clearly, Waller believed that the Londoners would fight best if stiffened with more experienced soldiers.

Meanwhile, Forth, still suffering the agonies of gout, had joined Hopton on East Down, where he gave orders for the whole Royalist army to be drawn up to them, a move accomplished by perhaps 11.00 a.m. Hopton's Horse and Foot occupied the Royalist left wing east of Alresford lane, and those which Forth had brought with him from Oxford marched into line on the right wing extending towards Cheriton.

Having carefully surveyed the approaches to the wooded ground held by his Roundhead neighbours on East Down, Hopton commanded Colonel Matthew Appleyard to select 1,000 musketeers, including no doubt his own Yellowcoats, and assemble them in four divisions on the reverse slope of East Down. Having done this, Appleyard advanced according to his orders towards the Parliamentarian position, but as soon as his men came into sight Leighton's musketeers and two small drakes 'gave fire very thick and sharp' and pinned them down in the open.

Hopton rode forward and shouted at one of the divisions, as he himself wrote, 'to run with all possible speed into the wood upon the enemy's flank, where there was likewise a cross-hedge to cover them, which they had no sooner done and given one volley from thence but the enemy fell in disorder and began to run, and Colonel Appleyard with his party pursued them, and had the execution of a part of them through the wood, and possessed himself of all their ground of advantage, and took a horse colours and some prisoners, but none of their cannon, for they being light guns were drawn off.' Thus by noon the Royalists had secured the whole length of East Down.

The sight of 1,000 musketeers flushed out of the wood like hares and running in panic down the hillside momentarily dashed the morale of Waller's watching army. Each accounted for the disaster according to his own prejudice. Birch believed that Leighton swore too much to have God with him, while Captain Harley blamed it all upon the cowardice of the Londoners, who 'no sooner did they see that the bullets would come otherwise then they would have them but they made a foul retreat – I am confident I smelt them – with a fair pair of heels, which did so discourage the rest that they all left their charge with a shameful retreat. Our three hundred horse which were to second our foot as soon as the enemy offered to charge came away in the same confusion on the left hand.' If Secretary Roe may be believed, Heselrige turned to Birch and asked him, 'Now, Colonel, have you fighting enough?' Without hesitation Birch replied with a metaphor from the game of bowls: 'Sir, this is but a rub; we shall yet win the cast.'[17]

According to one officer in the left wing of the Royalist army, 'this defeat put the rebels into such a fright that we could discern several companys of thirty, or forty, and more in some, running over the fields in the rear of their army half a mile and as well discern their horses spann'd in their carriages and to their artillery'. Waller despatched Heselrige's Foot from the centre of his battle line to stabilise his right flank and check the pursuit of the fleeing musketeers, tasks which Birch's men performed promptly. Meanwhile, on the left, some of Forth's soldiers had driven back the Londoners from their hedgerows near Hinton Ampner. 'Now the day began to look black on our side,' wrote Captain Harley, 'and if God had not wonderfully showed Himself we had lost the field, yet I did see something that promised victory. All were still willing to go on, and the soldiers put the fault on their officers, and the officers on the soldiers.' Necessity may have fathered this spirit of resolution, for the Royalists from their newly-won high ground could easily charge down on any attempted retreat through Bramdean.

'Now was his Majesty's army in a most happy posture, for though they offered a great price for this last hill yet they paid it not, the attempt costing a very few men.' The cheapness of the purchase did not, however, blind Hopton to the tactical advantages the hill gave him, and after he had settled strong guards upon all the approaches to it he sent word to Forth offering to fall upon the right flank of Waller's army with 1,000 Horse and 1,000 musketeers. The aged army commander decided against such a move, for 'having now possessed all the ground of advantage on our side, his opinion was that we should not hazard any further attempt, for that he conceived the enemy would now be forced either to charge upon their disadvantage, or to retire.' Hopton professed himself 'extremely satisfied with that solid advice', and after issuing the necessary orders to his colonels he rode along the down at about 1.00 p.m. to confer with Forth on the right wing.

Meanwhile, like a chess player moving his most important piece to a dominating position in the centre of the board, Waller had ordered his cavalry into the valley. Forth's Cavalier regiments had already spurred forward onto the upper slopes of East Down as if they intended a charge. 'That we might not be outdared by their horse,' wrote Harley, 'we drew down all our horse into a heath, which stood betwixt the two hills where they did fight, but under favour of the enemy's ordnance, the hills being one from another not whole culverin shot – which was well known to some of the enemy's horse which were dispersed by our shot. Here my lieutenant lost his horse and part of his foot, but I hope we will recover speedily. Their cannon did very small execution amongst us, the enemy thinking all were his own if he could but possess himself of the village and those hedges we had lined.'

At about half an hour after noon Forth had apparently disregarded his own advice and sent down 1,500 commanded musketeers with some troops of horse to take Hinton Ampner. Waller countered by reinforcing his own men in the village with 1,200 musketeers,[18] but before they could arrive, the courage and resolution of the Royalists had carried them into the small cluster of houses. Hoping no doubt to improvise a smoke screen, they set the thatch roofs on fire, only to discover that the wind had turned, blowing the smoke back into their own faces. This accident allowed the Parliamentarian musketeers to return by degrees into the hedgerows which they had been compelled to abandon. Meanwhile, Livesey's Kentish Horse scattered a few Royalist troops supporting their musketeers in front of Hinton Ampner. Livesey's major, Anthony Weldon, would later accuse his colonel of running away on this occasion.[19]

Perhaps in order to establish a line of retreat from this village to East Down, Forth despatched the 28-year-old Colonel Henry Bard with his regiment of foot to take up a position somewhere between the two, but just before noon 'with more youthful courage than soldier-like discretion', wrote Hopton, he led his Greycoats into the thick of the fray near the burning houses.

Seeing a great gag opening up between the Royalists on the down and those in the heath, Sir Arthur Heselrige commanded out ten horsemen from each of the thirty troops in his brigade and formed them into three parties under Captain John Butler, Colonel Richard Norton and Captain John Fleming. Captain Butler's 100 troopers, mostly Lobsters, then rode into the gap and wheeled onto the rear of Bard's regiment. To the vast discouragement of the spectators on East Down the Parliamentarian horse 'performed their charges so well that through God's blessing they routed them all, slew about a hundred and fifty and took a hundred and twenty prisoners with divers commanders of quality. We received not much loss, only Captain Fleming hurt in the arm with a captain's leading staff.' Colonel Norton's party then 'scoured the lanes' and drove the remnants of Bard's regiment into the woods. Some 150 men in Bard's regiment were killed and another 120 captured, leaving only 176 Greycoats at a muster three days after the battle. Bard himself was taken, with a bad wound that cost him the use of an arm. According to *The Scottish Dove*, Norton was the 'first instrument' to turn the day at Cheriton.[20]

At approximately this time Hopton, as previously related, had set out from the left flank to confer with Forth, 'and being near the midway upon the brow of the hill he saw troops of the right wing too far advanced and hotly engaged with the enemy in the foot of the hill'. The army commander, much troubled with the situation in the west end of the valley, which he ascribed to Bard's disobedience to his orders, told Hopton 'to draw out 1,000 horse, and to command them to advance to the enemy's horse that were in the common at the foot of the hill, and to charge them'. Hopton selected Sir Edward Stowell and his brigade for this service and began to array it for a descent into the valley.

Meanwhile, a sharp fight had developed on Waller's right wing, where part of the Parliamentarian Foot stood with Balfour's thirty troops of horse and a regiment of dragoons near them. Colonel Slingsby, an infantry 'tertia' commander in the left centre of the Royalist line, who claimed in direct contradiction to Hopton's account that 'we were order'd to fall on from both wings', apparently sent down some Foot 'in battalia' towards the Parliamentarian position north of the Bramdean road, where they were charged by a strong party of Balfour's Horse at about the same time that Captain Butler's Lobsters were cutting Bard's regiment to pieces.

These Royalist Foot repulsed Balfour's first onslaught, but 'they immediately tried the second charge in which Captain Herbert of my Lord Hopton's regiment was slain, with a fresh body and were again repulsed, and so again the third time, the foot keeping their ground in a close body, not firing till within two pikes length, and then three ranks at a time, after turning up the butt end of their muskets, charging their pikes, and standing close, preserv'd themselves, and slew many of the enemy'.

The 22-year-old Lord John Stewart, a third cousin of the King and Lieutenant-General of Royalist Horse, despatched the Queen's regiment to protect the Foot from further attack, but these troopers, many of them Frenchmen, retreated after only one 'unhandsome charge'. By this time Waller had sent 1,000 musketeers beyond his right flank and, under the leadership of Lieutenant-Colonel John Birch, they began a slow climb towards the woods on East Down, driving back the Royalist Foot before them.

The focal point of the battle now shifted to the open heath and enclosed fields and meadows which lay along the bottom of the valley. Forth knew that he must attack Waller's horse on that common in order to check the incessant flank charges upon his infantry, now gradually giving ground upon either wing, but to do so his cavalry would have to abandon the heights of East Down. By this time, about 2.00 p.m., his right wing had become so inextricably engaged with the Parliamentarian musketeers at Hinton Ampner, who had been reinforced by Waller's own dragoons, that he had no alternative but to give the orders for Stowell's 1,000 Cavaliers to make their way down into the heath for what he hoped would be the decisive charge of the day.

'Then we drew down most of the horse,' wrote Colonel Slingsby, 'and endeavour'd to draw up upon that plain ground before our foot, in which our enemy's horse stood rang'd in nine fair bodies, but having one lanes end only to pass into it, they came upon great disadvantages, for by that time one body was in the ground and drawn up (before another could second it), it was over charged with number.' Despite this initial hazard, Stowell's troopers hurled themselves against the Parliamentarian cavalry with a boldness verging on desperation. Balfour's Horse took the brunt and were temporarily broken before the Parliamentarian reserve recovered the situation. After 'a sharp and close charge that continued near half an hour, Stowell's body of horse was broken and routed, and himself charging home to their cannon was taken prisoner with five wounds upon him.'

Observing the distress of Stowell's brigade, Forth committed all but Sir Humphrey Bennet's nine troops of Hampshire Horse to the fierce cavalry struggle raging below him. Like bundles of dry twigs cast onto a dying fire these two brigades of perhaps 2,000 Cavaliers blazed up the fight. A confused struggle of charge and counter-charge raged over the heath. From the thick-hedged lanes running along the forward slope of East Down a line of musketeers poured fire at the Parliamentarian Horse whenever they saw an opportunity. Through the whirling smoke it became increasingly difficult to distinguish friend from foe, especially as the soldiers on both sides wore white tokens in their hats and initially had adopted the same password, 'God with us'. To stem this source of confusion, Waller at some stage in the battle changed his password to 'Jesus bless us' or 'Jesus help us'.

In this inferno Sir William Waller narrowly escaped capture, 'the enemy having by a charge given upon some troops of mine shut me off from my own men, I having then but three in company with me, but it pleased God they were repulsed again, and thereby a way opened for my retreat.' He rode everywhere, encouraging his troops to keep their order and leading them frequently against the Cavalier troops. 'I reckon it a mercy,' he wrote, 'that upon a sudden occasion that day, charging without my headpiece, and being known to the enemy (as I afterwards understood from some of them), I came off safe and unhurt.'[21]

By 4.00 p.m. a number of Royalist cavalry commanders had fallen dead or mortally wounded, among them Lord John Stewart and Major-General Sir John Smith. Slingsby noted that 'our horse (discouraged and enfeebled with the loss of so many or almost all their principal officers) were not so fit to fight again, especially in regard their number began to lessen apace.' Hopton, who had ridden into the valley with Stowell's brigade, gathered together 300 Horse and stood guard on the entrance to Alresford lane (under a galling fire from Waller's demi-culverins) while the remaining Cavaliers made a fair retreat to the top of the down where their Foot still stood. When he had regained the hill, Hopton discovered Forth already supervising the departure of the wagons and making preparations for the infantry to follow after them towards Alresford.

Meanwhile, Waller's two wings of musketeers had inexorably driven in the flanks of the Royalist army. 'Colonel James Carr and Major Strachan had so plied their business on the left of our army that they forced the enemy to draw off their ordnance, and quickly engaged all the enemy's foot on them,' wrote Harley. At first, Forth's regiments in bristling battle order fought hard with pike and musket against Colonel Carr's musketeers on the more gentle western slopes of East Down, but the sight of the Cavalier Horse pounding up to the brow of the hill after their defeat in the valley so unnerved the Royalist Foot that they began to give ground. With Waller's soldiers on either end of the down and a large body of his Horse and Foot moving towards the centre 'it was with great difficulty', wrote Hopton, 'that we got off all our cannon'.

Secretary Roe, marching with Lieutenant-Colonel Birch and his musketeers, emerged from the wood recently quitted by Lisle's men in time to witness the retreat of the Royalist Foot. 'The first thing that I could perceive, they pulled off their colours, thrust them in their breeches, threw down their arms, and fled confused. Yourself [Birch] and others hot in pursuit had not followed them above 100 paces into their own ground, before one, whom I shall not name, overtook you, commanded you to stand. But for what end I never yet could tell, except it was to give the enemy leave to run away, and carry away their cannon. Sure I am you stood there three quarters of an hour, until the enemy was far enough.'

The fear that the Parliamentarian army would not press hard on the enemy's heels seems to have been widespread, for Captain Harley declared: 'I believe we should not have pursued if Colonel Weims had not showed himself very violent for it. To him next under God doth belong much of our victory. Through his persuasions it was ordered we should again fall on them and given them a general charge.' Secretary Roe hinted at a deep political motive for the delay, but almost certainly Waller had paused only to regroup his army on East Down, a cautious act of generalship wholly wasted upon his more excited junior officers.

Once some semblance of order had been restored Waller lost no time in unleashing a 'forlorn hope' of 300 Horse after the hurrying columns of Royalist soldiers on the shallow plain leading to Tichborne Down. Then he followed at a more sober pace with the main body. Waller's Horse caught up the enemy rearguard. Colonel Richard Neville's regiment turned and faced them, buying some precious time for the Foot. But most of the Cavaliers rode for their lives. The flying troopers streamed past the Royalist Foot, 'who cryed out (as the country people say) "Face them, face them, once more face them" which they did, but to small purpose'.[22]

The Royalist army stood for an hour or more on Tichborne Down in order to allow the artillery to get a head start towards Winchester, but as soon as Waller opened fire with six or eight cannon the two generals decided to split their army and withdraw under cover of night. While Forth rode westwards with the cavalry to Winchester and beyond, Hopton conducted the Foot and artillery with truly professional skill through the thickly wooded hills to Basing House. The Parliamentarians galloped into Alresford and cut down about a hundred Irish soldiers who had been left as a rearguard with instructions to set the town ablaze. By midnight Waller and Balfour arrived with their Horse before Winchester, but apart from capturing some stragglers and abandoned wagons they made no contact with the enemy.

The Royalists had lost an impressive list of officers killed or taken prisoner and at least 300 soldiers, whereas only 60 Parliamentarians had fallen.[23] No field officer in Waller's army suffered serious wounds except Lieutenant-Colonel Thompson, whose leg had been swept off by a cannon ball, and he bore his pain stoically, declaring that 'he had yet another leg to lose for Jesus Christ'.[24]

In the context of the national military situation Cheriton was indeed a great victory for Parliament. 'Truly, I tremble to think how near we were to the very Precipice of Destruction', wrote the Earl of Essex,[25] but although Waller had walked that dangerous ground with considerable strength of mind his achievement added little to his reputation as a general. Perhaps too many officers magnified their part in the battle at the expense of his own. Sir Arthur Heselrige,[26] Colonel Wemyss and Lieutenant-Colonel Birch claimed or were given credit for some of the field decisions while Essex pointedly placed Balfour before Waller in his references to the generals.[27]

These claims can be set aside. Heselrige probably did no more than his duty. Denzil Holles, however, has left a venomous account of Heselrige's cowardice at Cheriton. He was found 'weeping under a hedge,' Holles alleged, 'moaning "Ah, woe is me! All is lost, we are undone!" and that "a great Scotch officer" reproved him severely for it, and bade him leave the field, and not stand there gudding [crying] to dishearten the soldiers.'[28] Such a story from the biased pen of Holles must be taken with a pinch of salt. Certainly Heselrige had acquired a reputation with the Royalists and his political enemies as an outwardly bombastic yet inwardly timid man. He may not have lacked courage, but he did rather overplay the part of the martial man.

As for Sir William Balfour, he wrote to Essex on 30 March as if he had been in sole command. 'I caused all our Horse to draw out in a little heath before our quarters, and the Foot to be drawn up in battle [order] in a large spacious field within our quarters in a heath.' The Lord General lost no time in publishing this despatch.[29]

It is hardly conceivable, however, that Waller did not control the battle, at least until the main tactical moves had been irrevocably set in motion and he could do no more than lend his own sword to the defeat of the much-vaunted Royalist Horse. That shrewd appreciation of ground which marked the Parliamentarian tactics throughout the battle and the key decision to advance the Horse into the valley thereby transforming the Parliamentarian concave line into a convex one, came undoubtedly from Waller. Thereafter it was a matter of exploiting the Royalist mistakes. The presence of Colonel Carr and his own regiment of dragoons at the most threatened point, Hinton Ampner, may be taken as some evidence that Waller responded promptly and effectively to the changing complexion of the battle.

Critics may be allowed their disappointment at the escape of the Royalist army, but Waller wisely restrained the pursuit until his own forces had gathered in strength on East Down. The Royalist army withdrew in a disciplined formation, and like a stag it could turn and inflict death wounds unless the pack hunted together. In conclusion, it is perhaps worth noting that, for the first time, Cavalier Horse in strength had been defeated in the field by an equal body of Parliamentarians, and this significant victory fell not to Cromwell's Ironsides in the Eastern Association's army but to Waller's cavalry at Cheriton.

'We acknowledge the great goodness of God for so seasonable a mercy after the unhappy business at Newark,' wrote the Committee of Both Kingdoms to their victorious generals on 30 March. 'We are very sensible of the great advantage that will come to the kingdom by a careful and diligent im-service.'[30]

At first it seemed that Waller would indeed lead his regiments into the western counties. On Sunday evening he halted 8 miles beyond Winchester, having briefly occupied that town but failed to take the castle, and the day after, his regiment of horse took some stragglers in Andover.[31] Hearing that Forth's Cavaliers had ridden hard for Newbury, Waller sent Captain Richard Fincher, his Quartermaster-General, with three regiments to beat up that quarter; the party returned to Stockbridge on Thursday 4 April with a hundred prisoners.

Meanwhile, Waller himself led the remaining cavalry to Christchurch, where he captured 400 Royalist Foot and 100 Horse.[32] On Saturday 6 April, as Waller's forces moved south to Romsey, the London brigade procured the surrender of Bishops Waltham, a Royalist stronghold east of Winchester. Yet apart from a minor success at Winchester itself next day – when a party of Heselrige's Foot stormed into the town, taking 100 prisoners and as many horses – and beating up an enemy quarter at Sonning, near Reading – where he took five officers but missed two regiments that had been there the day before – Waller could achieve nothing else in Hampshire or Berkshire. He turned back to Bishops Waltham and then marched north towards Farnham Castle, where he arrived on 17 April.

Two main reasons induced Waller to turn aside from the course suggested by the Derby House Committee. In the first place he lacked both soldiers and money. Secondly, Waller learned by 4 April that the King was gathering a formidable army at Marlborough with the express purpose of preventing him from advancing into the West, and avenging if possible the defeat at Cheriton. In response, the Committee of Both Kingdoms decided to concentrate all their forces south of the Trent at Aylesbury, but these could not reach the rendezvous before 19 April. Browne's brigade left Bishops Waltham for home on 8 April. Waller had no choice but to move nearer to the relief brigade at Kingston.

By 22 April the City brigade, which had been sent to replace Browne's homeward, drew near to Farnham, and although Waller lacked sufficient Horse since Balfour's departure, the prospect of recovering the West once more beckoned him. On 4 May Waller wrote to inform the Speaker that Hopton was at Blewbury (some 14 miles north-west of Reading), and if he had but a month's pay his army would advance.[33] On 6 May he rode into London and shortly afterwards informed the House of Commons that as the enemy had now withdrawn from their quarters in Newbury, the way lay open to the West where thousands would join him.[34] He found, however, a growing desire that the Parliamentary armies should now combine against and bring the King's main army to battle.

Seen in retrospect, the battle of Cheriton may be said to have marked the real turning-point in the struggle between King and Parliament. For the King's secretary, Sir Edward Walker, observed that this victory of Sir William Waller and his forces 'necessitated His Majesty to alter the scheme of his affairs, and in the place of an offensive to make a defensive war'.[36]

PART FIVE
A Fading Star

CHAPTER TWENTY-ONE

To Oxford

After victory at Cheriton nothing less than 'a grand Battle' would satisfy Parliament.[1] To this end it was resolved to adhere to the old plan of concentrating the armies of Essex, Waller and Manchester, which would total 28,000 men, and then 'to wait upon his Majesty at Oxford'.[2]

No doubt the Committee of Both Kingdoms endorsed this strategy before Sir William's arrival in London, and he appears to have embraced it wholeheartedly on the understanding that once the King's army had been beaten or driven north he could turn into the West in order to recover that region for Parliament.

Meanwhile, Waller retained a more than nominal responsibility for the conduct of Parliament's military affairs in the West. The Derby House Committee had already sent one of Waller's regiments, Colonel Edward Harley's Foot, to augment the garrison of Plymouth, and early in May two of his better officers, 'an able and trusty man' Colonel James Carr and Major Archibald Strachan, became respectively governor and commander of the horse in that town.[3] In response to urgent appeals from Lyme Regis, now besieged by Prince Maurice, Waller despatched by sea three companies of Heselrige's Foot under Major Cotsforth, which weakened his army by perhaps 120 men.[4]

The committee of 'Western gentlemen', the Members of Parliament responsible for Western affairs and in particular for financing the war in those parts, had apparently desired Lord Robartes as Governor of Plymouth and commander in Devon and Cornwall. Robartes had raised a regiment of Redcoats which fought at Edgehill (the double turncoat Scottish officer Alexander Urry became its major until he was captured at Second Newbury). Whether or not it was the Earl of Essex who nominated Robartes for the Western command in May is not known.

On Monday 13 May 1644 the Lord General joined his army at Beaconsfield, and Sir William resumed his command at Farnham two days later, having tarried in London to plead successfully in the House of Commons for the life of his poet cousin, Edmund Waller, who had entered into a conspiracy with the Royalists at Oxford.[5]

When a letter from Essex (15 May, Buckingham) reached the Lower House desiring that Waller might come to him speedily as he thought a battle likely sooner than he had expected, Heselrige moved that same day that Waller might be 'let off going', as the differences between the two Houses had not been settled.[6] Presumably these unresolved matters related, at least in part, to the respective commissions and authorities of the two generals, one drawing his main support from the Upper House and the other from the Lower. Clearly neither the factions of Essex or Waller were happy when it came to the issue of who was really in command.

At Farnham, Waller found a muster of his army already in progress. He had good reason to be satisfied with what he saw. Sixteen regiments of horse and foot, some 10,000 men, were drawn from their quarters in or about the town. Of the Western brigade only Heselrige's regiment was missing: it remained with its colonel in London until 25 May. Sir Thomas Peirs and the four troops of Kentish Horse which had accompanied the City brigade passed into Livesey's regiment, but the failure of Colonel Richard Norton's Hampshire horse to appear at the rendezvous offset this accession of strength.

Lieutenant-Colonel Thorpe, as he had become by 26 April, had taken command of Colonel Turner's old regiment, known more commonly as 'the City horse'. The other London regiment under Colonel Harvey was still at this time under orders to join Waller at Farnham.[7] Perhaps touched by the flattery implicit in Harvey's desire to serve under him rather than Waller, Essex enabled the London colonel to flout the wishes of the Derby House Committee. Among his reasons he declared that Waller was an 'unfortunate' general. A compromise solution, however, was worked out whereby Waller received some troops from the main Parliamentarian army in place of Harvey's regiment. They were mainly the troops of Scottish commanders who no longer felt at home in the Lord General's army.

As a consequence, at about this time Waller gained the services of Colonel John Middleton, 'a brave man and as well understood in the command of horse as any of our side', as *The Parliamentary Scout* called him. Major-General Skippon described him as 'a very worthy sober man'.[8] Still only twenty-four years old, Middleton had begun his career as a pikeman in a Scots regiment in the service of France. Later he would change sides and serve the King with distinction, winning an earldom for himself. In company with Colonel James Holborne and other Scots commanders in the Lord General's army, Middleton had been scandalised by some observations made on his nation by the German professional officer Commissary-General Hans Behre, and with them he had readily accepted a transfer to Waller's army, bringing his regiment with him.

Incidentally, Hans Behre also had to defend himself against the revealing charge that he said that if Parliament and the Lord General be at variance he would fight for the latter. In addition, he had quarrelled with another of Essex's officers, the Earl of Denbigh, Parliament's commander in the northern counties of the Midlands. But the bad feeling between English and Scots officers in the Lord General's army was of long standing. A serious quarrel had broken out as early as 16 March 1643, which had resulted in sword fighting and some bloodshed.[9] In the changed context of the political situation in early 1644, when Parliament had entered into the Solemn League and Covenant with Scotland, the Earl of Essex should clearly have stamped out this national discord in the army, rather than tolerating, if not encouraging, such men as Behre.

Waller's brave array of horse was matched by an equally impressive body of infantry. Waller had disbanded the partially formed foot regiments of James Carr and Edward Cooke. The common soldiers of the latter, the more considerable of the two, recruited Lieutenant-Colonel Birch's regiment. All the foot regiments under Waller's command at Cheriton remained with the army, while the two London regiments had been replaced by three − the Southwark White Auxiliaries, the Tower Hamlets and the Westminster Auxiliaries, brigaded under Major-General Sir James Harrington.[10] In addition, Waller could expect a regiment of foot from Sussex as soon as Colonel Edward Apsley had raised it.[11] Two companies of Bluecoats, guards of an enlarged train of twenty-four field guns, leather pieces and 'wagons of war', completed the muster.[12]

On Friday 17 May the Royalist garrison in Reading, having slighted the fortifications around the town, withdrew towards Abingdon and on that same day Waller gave orders for his remodelled army to march next morning. Probably he intended to join forces with Essex in order to besiege Reading, for he quartered on Saturday and Sunday nights at Bagshot.

From this town Sir William wrote to the Speaker saying that he had learnt from prisoners of war that the King's army intended to march northwards and would not offer battle. If it did so Waller 'conceived' that the Lord General might follow, supported by Manchester's Eastern Association forces and the garrisons of Northampton and other adjacent places, while his own army returned to the West. But if the Royalists drew westwards he suggested that then the Lord General and himself might pursue them, and give a good account of themselves.[13] It was an eminently sensible piece of strategic thinking.

After riding to Henley to confer with the Lord General, who was making ready to occupy Reading, Waller marched to Basing House no doubt expecting that ripe pear to fall with a mere shake of the branch and allow him to draw out more soldiers from the Southern Association. On his way he paused at Hartley Row to write another letter to the Speaker.

Besides announcing his intentions Waller desired recruits, arms and equipment for his own and Vandruske's Horse. He added that it would be 'a great weakening of the King's army if he could show mercy to men of quality who came in'.[14] Here, Waller shows that his policy of fighting as in a 'war without an enemy', and of conducting himself 'in a way of honour and without personal animosities', was actually grounded in political and military commonsense. For, ultimately, civil wars cannot be ended by the sword, only by reconciliation. In the meantime, as Waller wrote, such a policy of kindness and mercy to those who surrendered or changed sides would have the practical consequence of encouraging more deserters from the Royalist ranks. As so often, virtue and practical advantage marched hand in hand.

Waller arrived in the afternoon of Tuesday 21 May. 'They welcomed us with 2 or 3 pieces of ordnance, and hung out 3 or 4 several colours,' wrote young Lieutenant Richard Coe. 'The ordnance did not hurt, only scared our under-marshal, the blast blowing off his hat. Our horse went round, faced the house, the enemy charged upon them, slew 2 horses and one man of ours. We saw 2 of their men fall on the breastworks but no more to our view. There we lay until evening and it not being thought convenient to lay siege to the house, we marched round the park to Basingstoke. The enemy, thinking we had an intent to beleaguer the house, burnt all the houses and 2 mills near adjacent because we should have no shelter there.'

Perhaps apprehensive of another reverse at the beginning of a campaign, Waller allowed his men to quarter in the town of Basingstoke without making any further attempt upon Basing House. On Friday the 24th the army set out towards Abingdon. It is not difficult to catch the spirit of excitement in the ranks of Waller's army: it was in the very morning of the campaign, and hopes mounted higher with each step on the road to Oxford.

After a night spent in the fields at Aldermaston the soldiers took to the road again and 'we descried this day some of my Lord General's colours to march wide of us towards Abingdon. That night we lay at Compton, a dirty town but we had good respect of our moneys. On Saturday the 25th, as the army drew near to Abingdon, Sir John Merrick came to us, who saluted our commanders nobly and was welcomed of us with much joy and shoutings. He told us my Lord General's forces were that night to quarter in Abingdon.' Merrick commanded a regiment of Greycoats, raised in London, in the Lord General's army.

The two armies were now close neighbours. Essex wrote from Abingdon that night to Parliament to ask that if Waller went into the West, the Eastern Association army might be sent to him. He reported that some of his regiments were at Sandford and some of Waller's forces quartered in Cumnor to the west of that village.[15]

As the Lord General's soldiers already occupied Abingdon, Waller made his headquarters for the next two nights at Marcham, 3 miles west of the town.[16] The two generals now addressed themselves to the problems of besieging Oxford, a city girt about on every side but the north by rivers which formed natural moats for the extensive ring of fortifications erected by the King's military engineers.

At first the Earl of Essex seems to have decided to concentrate both his and Waller's armies against the eastern defences. Accordingly, on Monday 27 May he moved his regiments beside the River Cherwell towards the villages of Cowley, Headington and Islip, the latter being some 5 miles north of Oxford. Apart from a garrison left in Abingdon, Waller's army followed hard on their heels, pausing to sleep through the rain of Monday night under cover of Nuneham woods. 'Next morning,' wrote the London subaltern, 'we marched forward in sight of Oxford, and my Lord's army marched within a mile of our army or thereabouts – we heard how kindly the City and my Lord's guns entertained each other.'[17]

But after only one night at Sandford, 3 miles south-west of Oxford, Waller received new orders to remove his army to the west side of the city so that the attention of the garrison would be divided and its line of retreat towards Worcester sealed off. This counter-march, the first hint of confusion, could have been avoided by a more thorough reconnaissance on the part of the Lord General.

Waller's regiments retraced their steps to Abingdon and, as Essex required several days to complete his preparations for an assault, the soldiers spent two nights in that comfortable quarter, a sojourn marred by the destruction of the ancient Eleanor Cross which stood in the market-place.[18]

On Friday 31 May Waller advanced from Abingdon towards Witney and his soldiers slept that night in Appleton woods. As 100 Royalist dragoons held New Bridge, where the road from Abingdon to Witney crossed over the Isis,[19] Waller drew out the Foot, 2 miles from each company, to storm their position. Finding that the Royalists had broken down a section of the bridge, the commanders of this party threw planks across the river, using punts as pontoons, and then led their men over and compelled the enemy to withdraw, leaving in their hands a captain, sixty-four common soldiers and forty camp followers, mostly Irish, including a woman 'who was whipped and turned away'.[20] The army spent the sabbath day in the fields around New Bridge while pioneers laboured to make it strong enough to take the weight of wagons and guns.

Meanwhile, Waller received orders from Essex not to advance further towards Woodstock until the Lord General had recovered the pass over the river at Islip, which was not effected until the following morning (Monday 3 June). 'About 12 o'clock we heard it was taken and that the King's army was drawn back into Oxford,' wrote Waller and Heselrige to the Speaker the next day from New Bridge. 'Thereupon we sent out a party of 300 horse to see if they could get to his Excellency and also for gaining intelligence.' They concluded their letter to the Speaker with a request for reinforcements either from the City or Parliamentarian garrisons in the southern Midlands, otherwise the Royalists in Oxford – defended by the rivers – would hold them at play for the greater part of the summer.[21]

However, receiving intelligence that Essex intended to storm the city next morning, the King resolved to leave Oxford that Monday night (3 June). According to Royalist sources the Oxford garrison made a 'grimace' towards Abingdon to draw Waller back from the New Bridge, and then under cover of darkness at 11.00 p.m. the King, with 3,000 troopers and 2,500 musketeers riding pillion behind them, together with thirty carriages and eight guns, rode out westwards across Port Meadow towards the Witney and Burford road.[22] Early on Tuesday afternoon Waller's scouts brought him word of the King's flight and at once he ordered his army to march in pursuit, hoping to intercept the Royalist party at Witney.[23]

'We marched after [them] all day and night,' wrote Richard Coe, 'and came a little before day near Witney where we were quartered under a hedge 3 or 4 hours, it rained extremely as it had done for the most part since our advance from Farnham till then.' That same night Waller entered Burford with his cavalry, but he was too late: the King had supped there some hours earlier and then ridden north-west towards Worcester.

Yet as soon as the Foot drew near Burford, 'we stayed not at all, not so much as to get beer, bread or water, but were commanded by Major-General Potley, under Sir William's command to march around the town with all speed, affirming the King's forces and our horse to be in sight, which was nothing so,' added Coe. Learning from his scouts and the fifty stragglers 'gleaned' in Burford that the King had marched six or eight miles north-west through the rain-soaked Cotswolds, some of his party quartering in Bourton-on-the-Water and some in Stow-on-the-Wold, Waller made haste after him and halted for the night in the latter town.

'We are now in pursuit of the King's army,' Waller and Heselrige informed the Committee of Both Kingdoms in haste from Stow that evening (Tuesday 4 June). 'This day the King was at Eversham by 2 o'clock. His army could not march so fast. . . . This night, we send out a strong party of horse, and if we miss in that we shall not be able to overtake them at this run. . . . The weather proves very bad, which has been a great hinderance to us, yet the soldiers march cheerfully.' Waller's cavalry came within a mile of Evesham, capturing a lieutenant, three cornets and about sixty prisoners, but returned to Stow on Thursday 6 June with the news that the King and his cavalcade had safely reached Worcester.[24]

A Dance in the Midlands

On the morning of Thursday 6 June 1643 the Lord General met Waller and Heselrige at his headquarters in Chipping Norton, and announced that he now intended to march himself with his army into the West to raise the siege of Lyme, leaving to Waller the task of following the King.

This astounding decision was taken without summoning Waller to a council of war, to hear his views and commit him in a joint decision. It ran counter to the natural expectations of Waller, and also, as it happens, to the wishes of the Committee of Both Kingdoms. Yet by a breakdown in communication, the committee's letters to this effect, dated 30 May, reached neither general in time. Both letters had requested them to send a relief force to Lyme. To Waller's letter, however, they had added the significant sentence: 'We shall not need to recommend this further to you, having always had experience of your forwardness, and considering the safety of the western parts is committed to your care and many of your forces designed to that end.'[1]

To avoid any misunderstanding, the committee on Monday 3 June had resolved to send one of their number, John Crewe, to the generals with a specific direction that Waller should undertake the service in the West,[2] but events moved too fast for this emissary who obviously took his time. On Wednesday 5 June the Lord General had informed Waller by letter that he would undertake the Western service himself, and on the next day, after the conference at Chipping Norton, he began his march south towards Lyme.

Waller and Heselrige wrote to the committee that same day: 'Being thus put out of our way and his Excellency commanding that an eye should be had which way the King takes, we resolve to follow the King wherever an army can march. Our reasons are, we believe the war can never end if the King be in any part of the land and not at the Parliament, for break his army never so often his person will raise another; all the stories of England, and our experience at Shrewsbury, will manifest that sufficiently. And the King has no other hope but that delay in time may bring changes, and we know there is a season which, when God offers, wisdom embraces. . . . We fear lest this army consisting of several forces,

City, Association and Waller's, they should not be paid, and so for want dissolve. We hope the several powers will consent and open their purses as well to this as the Western design. We beseech you to move the House and to give us satisfaction in this point. . . .

'Our horse are much beaten out with their march, and so are our foot, the weather proving extremely bad. We intended this night to have gone to Sudeley Castle, but we doubt the rain will hinder it. Our soldiers plunder malignants, do what we can, and embezzle their goods. There is no way to prevent it unless a committee be appointed in the army that may seize their goods for the public and be liable to account. We have sent up some names, and if the Houses please to grant an ordinance much may be saved that otherwise would be lost. We know this is a ticklish point, only these counties are out of the Parliament's power, and we take it the like was granted to his Excellency the Lord General. The truth is nothing troubles us more than to see the Kingdom's wealth thus misspent. If it be thought fit to grant any such power we desire it may be despatched, for we find the City gentlemen tender in acting without an ordinance.'[3] There was doubtless more to be said at Derby House, however, than Waller cared to entrust to a despatch and therefore Heselrige set out towards London bearing this letter.

Believing that the King intended to retreat northwards to join Prince Rupert in Lancashire, Waller laid plans for 'a universal conjunction of forces against the enemy which with God's blessing, will make the work short'.[4] At that time the Earl of Denbigh, Parliament's Major-General in the northern Midlands, was besieging Dudley Castle, near Stourbridge, and Waller asked him to inform Sir William Brereton and Sir John Gell of the design so that they could augment Denbigh's brigade with their Cheshire and Derbyshire forces, thereby interposing a large army between the King and his nephew.

Meanwhile, Waller resolved to attempt Sudeley Castle, 9 miles to the west of Stow. Tewkesbury had fallen to the local Parliamentarians some days earlier, and Waller believed that the capture of Sudeley would enable him to raise money and recruits in the eastern parts of Gloucestershire. Moreover, he hoped that his friend, Colonel Massey, would meet him with as many men as possible from the Gloucester garrison, so that after the siege, which Waller resolved to lose no time over, they could march together to the rendezvous with Denbigh's forces.

Saturday 8 June turned out to be so wet that the Foot and artillery could not march, 'whereupon leaving them with two regiments of horse and my dragoons', narrated Waller. 'I marched to Sudeley Castle in some hope it might yield upon summons, but the enemy seeing no foot looked upon it as a bravado and let fly great and small shot roundly amongst us, whereupon I sent order to the army to advance to me next day. . . . That night the enemy burnt some houses and the stables belonging to the castle, but had not time to slight the hedges about it, so that we lodged our dragoons within little more than pistol short of their works, and laid all the passages with our horse.

'The next morning early the enemy fell out with some horse, but were quickly beaten in by our dragoons. About noon the body of our army appeared upon the top of the hills, whereupon they craved a parley by a drum, and sent out Lieutenant-Colonel Sayer and Major Aldam to treat, who stood upon points of honour, that they should be allowed to march out with their full arms and be conveyed to Worcester, or have my parole for their safety thither. But that being refused and assurance given they should have no other conditions but fair quarter, they parted with a resolution to hold it out to the last man, and upon their return in a bravery gave us a volley of shot.

'They were immediately answered with interest, and in a short time we possessed the barn which was within a stone's cast of their works. Our men were drawn up in preparation to give a general assault, and diverse of our horsemen, without orders, rode up to their very works and discharged their pistols at them. Night coming on we deferred the assault till the next morning, but about an hour within night their drum beat a parley again and brought a letter from the Governor, Sir William Morton, and officers, signifying that they yielded upon my own terms, but desired they might be used like gentlemen. I assured them they should receive no other entertainment, and sent for the Governor to come out to me, which he did, and the next morning I took possession of the place.'[5]

Having secured Sudeley Castle and its garrison, Waller now marched north, reaching Abbots Morton, 9 miles east of Worcester, by the night of Wednesday 12 June.[6] In response to an appeal from the Earl of Denbigh, now threatened by 4,000 Royalists under Lord Wilmot from Prince Rupert's army, Waller sent his Horse ahead to support him, but the Earl had beaten off the enemy, abandoned the siege of Dudley Castle and retired to Stourbridge before they could come up.

On Thursday evening Waller left the Foot in quarters at Bromsgrove and rode to Stourbridge where his cavalry awaited him. 'That night, upon information that the enemy was in Kidderminster, I took nine troops of horse and fell upon that quarter, being two miles from Bewdley, where the King and his army lay and yet remain. We found the town little better than an empty farm, only we lighted upon Lieutenant-Colonel [Edward] Stamford [of Lord Digby's regiment of horse] and a captain of foot and some poor soldiers whom we took. We gave the alarm to Bewdley Bridge. The enemy, instead of falling out, fell to breaking the bridge, which they sufficiently performed. . . . The King's army is in a most discouraged, broken condition, and if it be well plied will be utterly broken. I humbly suppose, if my Lord General would speedily advance into these parts, the work would be easy.' Shielded by the broad Severn from the Parliamentarian forces at Stourbridge, the King had little cause for anxiety. Unless, of course the Committee of Both Kingdoms adopted Waller's sensible strategy and brought into play both their two main field armies against him. But Essex had no intention of falling in with that plan.

In London the Committee of Both Kingdoms, stirred up by an angry Heselrige, determined to exert their authority over the Lord General.[7] On Tuesday 11 June the House of Commons had voted that it was 'most convenient' for Waller to march at once into the West.[8] The committee sent word immediately of this resolution to Essex, desiring him to send a party of horse to Lyme and to remain where he was with the rest of his army until further instructions arrived.

To their letter dated 13 June, directing him to retrace his steps to the environs of Oxford, the Lord General replied from Blandford with a rambling and ill-tempered letter. He justified his decision to undertake the relief of Lyme and the subjugation of the West on the grounds that his army was the more suitable of the two for that service, asserting that 'the army which has the greatest strength of foot will be the most able to reduce the West, and I believe that I have the most resolute foot in Christendom'. Although Essex was undoubtedly justified in boasting about his Foot, at least in comparison with those in Waller's army, his premise was incorrect. He was going to relieve the siege of Lyme, not to besiege it, and a 'flying army' of Horse and dragoons, with some regiments of foot and local support could best achieve that end. In fact his army was the less suitable of the two for that particular objective.

Beneath the other reasons Essex put forward for regarding Waller as unsuitable or disqualified for the Western design, may be glimpsed an underlying resentment of the high standing which Sir William enjoyed at this time. 'I shall not stand to dispute how well Sir William Waller is beloved in the West, you know something of Bristol and Plymouth,' he continued in characteristically sarcastic vein. Among the attributes of his nominee for command in that region, Lord Robartes, Essex included the fact that 'he is entrusted with a higher place in the army than a Major [General] of a brigade'. In fact Robartes held the office of field marshal, probably with the rank of a lieutenant-general.

Essex implied later (see p. 201) that in coming to his apparently inexplicable decision he had succumbed to persuasions of those in his army with interests in the West. Lord Robartes must be the prime suspect. His Cornish father had made a great fortune from wool and tin – the Duke of Buckingham had extorted the enormous sum of £10,000 from him as the price of the Baronry of Truro. Clarendon described the son as a 'sullen, morose man, intolerably proud'. Having successfully commanded a brigade at the battle of Newbury, Robartes now aspired to become Parliament's Major-General in Devon and Cornwall, with his headquarters in the Parliamentarian base of Plymouth. The petition to Parliament in May having failed to secure him that command, Robartes, it may be surmised, saw another way of establishing himself in his own county, by using Essex's army to clear out the Royalists.

But did the Earl of Essex any longer possess the necessary authority? He certainly claimed that such appointments belonged to his executive prerogative. But the issue of who should command in the West was as much a political as an executive decision, and by deliberately ignoring that fact, Essex was once more stirring up the hornet's nest. No doubt Essex chose his words carefully when he proceeded to browbeat the committee on paper: 'pardon me, if I make bold to order and direct my own Major [General], for in truth I do not see how Sir William Waller can take care of all the counties along the seaside from Dover to St Michael's Mount. He refused to protect a county or two, and said that was only to lie at receipt, and yet he thinks that service honourable enough for his General. If you think fit to set him at liberty and confine me, be pleased to make him General and me the Major [General] of some brigade, that my soldiers may have free quarter, free plunder, and fair contributions besides, as his have without control.'

In fact the Lord General's next shot – that if the armies were now interchanged Parliament would lose the benefit of both of them that summer – should have made some impression upon the committee. But the sensible decision was to keep the two armies together in the centre of England, not to interchange them. Waller clearly sensed that this was the right thing to do. Having now received the committee's direction to march into the West on 15 June, he tried to limit the damage by suggesting that he should remain at Stourbridge until Essex's army came up, a request which the Earl of Denbigh and the other general officers at a council of war strongly supported.[9]

Next day Waller played for time by reporting that he had received a coded message from the Parliamentarian and Scottish commanders near York. As it could not be deciphered (Heselrige having taken the key to London) and as it might contain news which could influence their decision, Waller told the committee that he would wait at Stourbridge for further orders. 'His Majesty yesterday retired again to Worcester,' he added, 'I have given orders for the present reparation of Bewdley Bridge, which will make me master of both sides of the river and give me a readier opportunity to follow His Majesty whensoever he dislodges. His army is mouldered away to a very small proportion, and I think it lessens every day. . . . If the Lord General march speedily up towards Bristol side, his [the King's] retreat into the West is cut off, which is the only hope left for him.'

Although the Royalist Foot had indeed withdrawn from Bewdley, some strong bodies of horse were left in quarters near the bridge. Supposing the retreat to be a feint in order to make him lose ground, Waller faced Bewdley until noon on Sunday 16 June, before learning that the King, together with the main Royalist forces, had shot away from Worcester towards Oxford by way of Evesham under cover of darkness in the early hours that morning.

'Leaving my foot with two regiments of horse to attend them, I advanced with the rest of my horse and dragoons after him to Evesham, 22 miles distant,' Waller informed the northern commanders, the Earl of Leven, Manchester and Sir Thomas Fairfax, whose armies were besieging York. 'But when I came hither I found that His Majesty had gained 20 miles before me, so that I conceived I should not ruin my horse to pursue him further, and therefore gave over the chase. I resolve now, since in these parts I can do nothing in correspondence with our northern armies, to apply myself to the service of the West.'[10]

On 17 June Lord Digby, the King's Secretary of State and chief adviser, informed Prince Rupert by letter of the dramatic change in the military situation. Whatever his own merits as a soldier, Digby could see clearly the strategic blunder of the Earl of Essex and its consequences. 'The truth of it is, had Essex and Waller jointly either pursued us or attacked Oxford, we had been lost. In the one course, Oxford had been yielded up to them, having not a fortnight's provision and no hopes of relief. In the other Worcester had been lost, and the King forced to retreat to your Highness, and our remove from Worcester to Bewdley was with that design in case Waller should have advanced on the one side and Essex on the other, as we certainly imagined they would have done.

'But either Essex's unskilfullness, or his desire to ruin Waller,[11] has made him draw his army westward as far as Salisbury, and send Waller after the King who, conjecturing by our remove to Bewdley that our intention was to Shrewsbury, made such haste that way as far as Stourbridge that he gave us the opportunity of slipping back to Worcester upon Saturday, and of gaining yesterday the pass of Evesham, and this morning Broadway Hills, from whence I now write, before his being able to get further towards us than Bromsgrove, as we can learn. So that now we suppose we cannot be hindered from rejoining our Oxford forces and train of artillery, nor from the election which of the two armies we will deal with single, both which are very much weakened, or whether we will think fit to make a diversion by marching into the heart of their quarters, since Oxford is now thoroughly provided and secured. This is the best face of our condition, which, though very hazardous still, yet comparatively with the former may be thought comfortable.'[12]

With hope that he would double the strength of his army once he entered the Western counties Waller arrived in Gloucester on Thursday 20 June.[13] But next day his scouts informed him that in the absence of the Lord General, who – according to instructions from the committee – should have reached the neighbourhood of Oxford by this time, the King's army had marched westwards to Witney and Burford. Waller therefore intended to alter his course to Cirencester where he would be better placed to intercept the Royalist army if the King chose to march down into Devon to support the Royalists who had invested Plymouth.

By this time, however, the House of Commons had unwisely accepted the Lord General's Western adventure as a *fait accompli* and, somewhat mollified by the relief of Lyme, agreed to overlook his disobedience and let him continue to advance further into the West.[14] Hearing that the King had left Oxford, the committee now countermanded their last order to Waller and directed him to follow the King wheresoever he chose to go, promising him reinforcements of 520 Horse and 1,500 Foot drawn from Parliament's garrisons in the Midlands.

Feeling 'very much confirmed' in his own decision to remain in the centre and to oppose the King's march, Waller appointed a rendezvous for the promised reinforcements. Moving eastwards from Gloucester he re-entered Stow-on-the-Wold on Monday 24 June. Here he learnt that the King had marched towards the Eastern Association in a double bid to draw the Earl of Manchester's army outside York away from Prince Rupert's northern army and to relieve Oxfordshire from the burden of provisioning the Cavalier regiments. The Committee of Both Kingdoms ordered Waller to pursue the King eastwards. Meanwhile, they planned to form a second-line army at Hertford, consisting of the local trained bands stiffened by a fresh London brigade under Major-General Sir Richard Browne.[15]

On Tuesday the 25th Waller learnt that the Royalist army had marched into Buckingham on the previous Saturday, well on its way towards the threatened counties. That night Waller's Horse quartered in and around the village of Oxhill after an 18 mile ride northwards, and the Foot lay down to sleep in Shipston-on-Stour, only 5 miles behind them. In order to refresh the army Waller commanded his soldiers to have a day's rest by observing a fast day on Wednesday. Here 7 troops of horse, 600 Foot and 11 pieces of ordnance from the garrisons of Coventry and Warwick joined the army, a welcome recruit.[16]

Professing his willingness to obey their directions, Waller wrote to the committee that evening: 'I only desire to be excused from taking long marches without rest sometimes in this extremely hot weather, especially with the foot, who are very much diminished and would quickly be ruined if I should not spare them as much as possible. The King had advanced his horse near Wellingborough, but upon intelligence that we were upon the march drew all back to Buckingham again. By the best intelligence we can get they are 10,000 horse and foot, 8 field pieces, four pieces of battery, and a great mortar piece.'[17]

During the rest on Wednesday (26 June) an officer in Waller's own regiment took the opportunity of writing to a friend in London, and his letter illustrates the high tide of morale in the army at this time: 'Sir, we have again taken divers prisoners, and do chase the King's forces every day, they run from us, and indeed be too light of foot for us. I should not have believed they could have run so well had I not seen it so. Some few days since they drew up their forces into battalia, and made the countryfolk believe they would fight, saying: "Now let the Roundheads come, that dare not march out of the lanes and hedges." But we appeared, since they ran from us, but we took some of them.'[18]

Waller resumed his march on Thursday the 27th, heading directly east to intercept the King if he persisted towards the counties of the Eastern Association. He halted that night at Hanwell Castle, which stood on high ground west of the River Cherwell. There, Waller's scouts told him that the King's army had also halted not 5 miles beyond the river at the village of Edgecote. 'Upon more certain notice that Waller was not far from Banbury,' wrote Sir Edward Walker, 'it was thought best to march thither, and to lay hold of a fit opportunity to give the rebels battle.' The readiness of the Royalists to have a battle is significant. Doubtless it would have been a very different story if they had been faced by the combined armies of Waller and Essex. As it was, the King's generals could take on each army in turn.

Walker continued: 'Wherefore early next morning, being Friday the 28th of June, the army advanced in good order towards Banbury, and about ten of the clock had a rendezvous on Leigh-Grounds about a mile on the east side of that town. It was so rainy and misty a morning that we could not discover the rebels. But it presently immediately growing fair, we discovered their army drawn up in Hanwell Warren, about a mile before us on the west side of the Cherwell. Presently upon the discovery of each other it did appear that both armies had the same desires to get some place of advantage to fight on; and to that end our army advanced, intending to have marched through Banbury, and to have possessed Crouch Hill, half a mile west of the town. But our march being longer than their's, and more difficult in respect of passing through the town, they first got the possession of that hill; upon which our's retired, and lay in the fields under Grimsbury Hill, half a mile east of Banbury, the Cherwell being between us and them.'

My Dishonourable Blow at Cropredy Bridge

Like a climber who had at last glimpsed the summit after a weary ascent and many disappointments, Waller experienced some elation at the prospect before him. 'This day in all probability will prove a deciding day,' he informed Derby House, 'the Lord prosper his own cause, for his great name's sake. I praise God I find a great deal of cheerfulness in the army, and I doubt not we shall render you a good account of our service. We are drawing into the field, and therefore I can only give you this short assurance.'[1]

Both armies stood in battle order throughout Friday in their own ground and sent out skirmishing parties, for neither commander would hazard a river crossing beneath the guns of the other. It was a time for sizing up each other.

Equally matched in Horse and dragoons (with perhaps 5,000 apiece) and in artillery, the only important difference between the armies lay in the proportions of infantry. Waller possessed about 4,500 Foot and the King not more than 3,500. But Waller's regiments of foot included the London brigade who lacked any battle experience. Waller's army was roughly the same in size and proportion as the one he had commanded at Cheriton. The King's army, by contrast, was no stronger in Foot than Hopton's army on that day, but probably possessed an extra 1,500 Horse and dragoons. They were all battle-seasoned regiments. In addition, of course, they enjoyed the presence of King Charles himself – a powerful factor in their morale. Even so, Waller had good grounds for confidence. Despite that long march of some 500 miles around the Midlands his soldiers, inspired by their officer and chaplains, were eager for another victory – this time the decisive one.

One of the King's Lifeguardsmen, Richard Symonds, tersely recorded the day's skirmishing: 'The enemy's horse endeavoured to pass the river on the right hand of Banbury, but were repulsed; one Captain Martin of horse killed after he had charged twice; his men did not follow. Some scouting beyond Banbury that evening. Little or no hurt on either side.'

On the next morning, Saturday 29 June, Waller again drew out his men from their bivouacs in the cornfields and resumed his position on the high ground of Grimsbury Hill. As if he wrote from the saddle with his telescope in one hand, he scribbled this note to the committee at Derby House: 'the King's army is drawing up [to] the hill, most of his horse are fallen down towards Cropredy, whether it be to secure their retreat or to make their passage that way to fight upon more equal ground is yet not certain, but we shall quickly know. If they have a mind to it they will as gladly be welcomed as ever men were.'

Perceiving, however, that, rather than storm his position on Grimsbury Hill, the King intended to march north-west towards Daventry (with an open road from there into the Eastern Association's counties), Waller took swift action: 'With all possible haste I rose and marched to [Great] Bourton, which brought me full in upon the flank of the enemy and gave me a very great advantage. Whereupon I and Lieutenant-General Middleton, with some regiments of horse advancing, seized upon the bridge at Cropredy and the other passes near it, and gave order to have them secured with foot and artillery.'[2]

Meanwhile, the King's army, marching in three long columns and beginning to diverge away on the road to Daventry, had become somewhat strung out. On a report that a body of 300 Parliamentarian Horse had been sighted beyond Hay's Bridge (where the Daventry road crossed the Cherwell), the King had sent orders to the vanguard division to make haste in order to secure it. He himself followed on their heels with the middle division as fast as he could. Consequently, an interval of about a mile and a half had opened up between the rear of the King's main division and the leading regiments of the one bringing up the rear. This rearguard, moreover, was now extended into 'a tail of five miles long'. Sir Edward Walker gives the strength of this straggling column as 1,500 Horse, 1,000 Foot and 11 cannon. The fact that it included the train of artillery must have slowed it down considerably.

Only a general of Waller's imagination and verve would have seen the opportunity and taken it, hazarding all on a throw of the dice. He ordered Lieutenant-General John Middleton and Captain John Butler, now Adjutant-General, to lead Heselrige's and Vandruske's regiments of horse into the attack across the river, using the bridge in order to do so. Meanwhile, Waller led a second and larger thrust of 1,000 Horse over the river by an unnamed ford below the bridge. In order to provide some support, Lieutenant-Colonel Jeremy Baines, Quartermaster-General of Foot, also marched over the river at Cropredy Bridge, together with four companies of his own Surrey Greencoats and five companies of Waller's regiment of foot, their colours flying at their heads, together with a few light guns.

Under a cloudless blue sky early on that hot Saturday afternoon

Middleton's brigade splashed over the river and encountered a body of Cavaliers whom they took to be their target – the King's rearguard division. In fact they were some regiments under the command of Lieutenant-General Lord Wilmot, who had turned back from their march in the rear of the main division. Middleton's charge broke the Royalist Horse, and Wilmot was temporarily taken prisoner.

A lieutenant in Heselrige's regiment of horse wrote: 'We pursued them above a mile till we came to a bridge [Hay's Bridge], where their foot made a stand, drew up and fac'd us; we being with musket shot of them only our four eldest troops, (viz) Sir Arthur's, Captaine Okey's, Captaine Foley's, and Captain Gardiner's. They overthrew a carriage to barricade the bridge and planted it with musketeers. This occasioned our retreat back again, being unwilling too far to engage ourselves, having no foot within above half a mile of us, and discovering their army behind us. Upon our retreat we discovered the party of foot (drawn over with us) by an unresistable body of the enemy's horse, of some thirty troops, and two regiments of foot, put to disorderly retreat, which hastened our march back again.

'And coming back we found the way to the [Cropredy] bridge within a quarter of a mile stopped with the enemy's horse and foot, who were got between our foot and the bridge. For whose relief (although our way back lay on the right hand) we advanced up to their body on the left hand up the hill [west of Wardington village], and with our four troops charged the King's own regiment, and put them to a retreat. But the other troops coming down upon us, (there being of them in all some three regiments) with whom we were in no case able to deal, we were necessitated to retreat very disorderly . . .'[3] Middleton's regiments were routed by the Earl of Cleveland's brigade, five regiments in all. Although the King had sent his Lifeguards under Lord Bernard Stuart back over Hay's Bridge to threaten the enemy's rear, according to a Royalist source they were not charged by the Lobsters.

Meanwhile, Sir William Waller at the head of his brigade of cavalry had crossed the river and begun the assent of the hill on which Wardington stands. 'I had a steep hill to mount, not far from the top whereof the enemy was drawn up in a strong body,' he wrote in his despatch the next day. Facing him from the rear division stood the Earl of Northampton's brigade of four regiments of horse, supported by Sir Bernard Astley's tertia of foot.

Waller continued: 'Some of the regiments came up slowly, whereupon I turned back leaving my regiment to march on, but coming to the foot of the hill I was advertised that the Lieutenant-General [Middleton] had charged the enemy and broken him, and chased them above a mile in a most fair way to have ruined their whole army, but a great body of the enemy, having rallied and charging him, broke him and forced him to a quick retreat, not without loss. . . . Whereupon the whole army of the

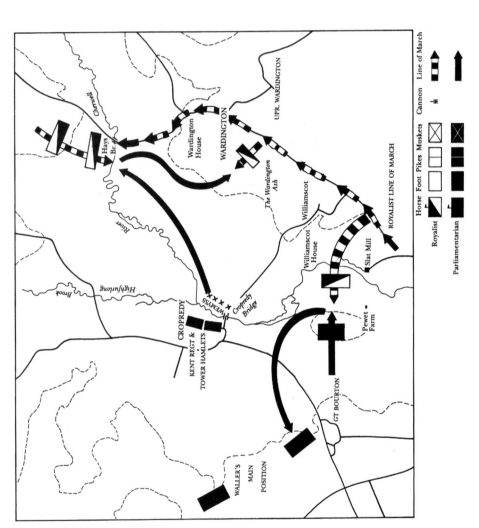

10. *The battle of Cropredy Bridge, 29 June 1644*

enemy being rallied, I thought it best to make an orderly retreat to our foot, which we did without loss, and drew up upon the hill on the right hand of [Great] Bourton, where we faced the enemy's army which was drawn up on the other side of the passage.'[4]

While the brigades of Middleton and Waller were thus engaged, there was 'hot service at Cropredy Bridge'. Major-General Andrew Potley's regiment of foot, together with eight brass cannon and the Bluecoats of the artillery train to guard them, had advanced to the bridge. The Parliamentarian Foot under Lieutenant-Colonel Baines, who had advanced too far forwards and came under attack, now fell back in disorder towards them.

According to Lieutenant-Colonel John Birch, these Parliamentarian foot across the bridge still amounted to no more than 1,200 men. To make matters worse, many of their musketeers had been drawn out into a commanded party on the previous Thursday, and still remained in the main body of Waller's army. Equipped only with pikes and supported by no more than a few light leather guns, this Parliamentarian body of infantry soon broke before the fire of the Royalist muskets and some Cavalier charges. Some ran in panic back over the narrow bridge, crying 'The field's lost! The field's lost!'. Others threw down their pikes and endeavoured to swim to safety across the river.[5]

In the panic of the moment the Bluecoats abandoned the eight brass cannon that Colonel James Wemyss had taken over the bridge to exploit Middleton's early success and to support Potley's over-confident advance. These guns were lost, Waller wrote, 'through the indiscreet courage of those that engaged them in pursuit of the enemy further than they had orders'.[6] Wemyss would not leave his guns and he was taken with them.

But the Tower Hamlets regiment marched to the rescue, supported by Colonel Ralph Weldon's Kentish foot, and they stemmed the rout by securing the bridge. With two drakes they claimed credit for keeping the Royalists at bay through the rest of that hot afternoon.

Waller's position on Bourton Hill was virtually unassailable, 'having the advantage of springs and bogs before his front, and both on his flanks and back strong hedges (you know his conditions of old, hills, bogs, hedges, ditches, these you must grant him, he'll not fight else)'.[7] From this ground the Parliamentarians' heavy artillery banged away at the Royalist army which had massed behind the captured ford at Slat Mill as if it intended to make a crossing, and compelled it to move further back up the hill towards Williamscot village.

Just before sunset that evening a trumpeter arrived with a message from the King to the effect that if Waller consented, his Majesty's herald-at-arms would proclaim 'a gracious message' at the head of the Parliamentarian army. Waller replied that he had no commission to entertain any message from the King without the permission of Parliament and therefore the message must be addressed there.

Waller did not include in his official report an intriguing incident which followed hard upon this exchange. In his *Experiences* he confided: 'When I had given my answer, I turned shortly round. When the trumpet said he had a private message for me, and prayed me to hear him, I replied there need be no privacy, not caring to give a handle to mine enemies, but some that were near me did persuade me to hear the man, and went out. He then presently [immediately] pulled forth a letter, which to my great shame and surprise came from the Lady *****. In it she besought me to betray my cause; and this she did so wittily and kind that I had much ado to be angry. Before this lady's marriage I had been her suitor, and did dearly love her, and she remembered me of this, and some soft passages. Whether or not she was put on this by some greater than herself I never knew, but I returned for answer that as I had never been traitor to my love, so I would not to my cause, which I should be, if I did as she would advise, and after this I heard no more.'[8] The identity of this mysterious lady remains a secret.

After a night of fitful sleep the two armies faced each other again on Sunday 30 June without incident, except that an unholy Royalist gun scattered a congregation of Parliamentarians gathered for prayer in Cropredy meadow. That morning Waller wrote his despatch on the battle to the Committee of Both Kingdoms, apologising for not doing so the previous evening: 'I was utterly tired out with the labour of the day.' By this time he could give some account of his chief losses. 'Colonel Wemyss, Lieutenant-Colonel Baker [Waller's regiment of foot] and a Dutch captain were taken prisoners, and Lieutenant-Colonel Baines taken or slain, and what was extreme wounding to me, 8 pieces of ordnance lost, being unhappily, in that heat of the pursuit of the enemy, drawn out beyond the passage of Cropredy bridge.'[9]

According to the Royalist sources Waller in fact lost eleven brass cannon. Their haul also included an ingenious invention by Wemyss – the first armoured vehicle to appear on an English battlefield! *Mercurius Aulicus* describes them as 'two blinders for muskets and leather guns'. Sir Edward Walker gave more detail: 'two barricades of wood drawn with wheels, in each seven small brass and leathern guns, charged with case shot.' Certainly it was the loss of those 'unlucky pieces' which galled Waller most. In a later year the memory of those brass guns came back to him when he reflected upon the spiritual causes of his military failures: 'my presumption upon mine own strength and former successes, justly humbled at the Devizes by an utter defeat, and at Cropredy with a dishonourable loss of a part of my train of artillery.'[10]

Of those killed or captured, Colonel Wemyss was the most important on Waller's side. According to the Royalist newspaper *Mercurius Aulicus*, when Colonel Wemyss came before the King he declared that 'Gud faith, his heart was always with his Majesty'. 'So is mine with the State-Committee' was the humorous editorial comment. For their part the Parliamentarians had captured or killed two Royalist colonels, a major, two captains of horse, and a cornet. About a hundred common soldiers had been killed or made prisoner on either side. Many more had suffered severe wounds. James Sleamaker, for example, a trooper in Captain Thomas Marshall's troop in Waller's own regiment of horse, had 'received a cut from the enemy throughout the face and had his bowels trod out with a horse, and was then run through with a tuck [rapier] to the unparalleled hazard of his life'. Years later, still 'in a very sad and miserable condition', he would be petitioning Parliament for a pension.[11]

On Sunday morning (30 June) an unpleasant accident almost killed Sir William. 'Being with my officers at a council of war, the floors of the room (where we were) sunk, and we all fell into a cellar that was underneath it. I lay overwhelmed with a great deal of lumber that fell upon me, and yet I bless God I had no hurt at all.'[12] Waller did not mention the fact that old Major-General Andrew Potley had landed first on the cellar floor and broke his own fall. As the stout figure of Colonel Holborne collapsed on top of Waller, followed by the rafters of the faulty floor, Potley at the bottom of the pile sustained the worst injuries, and he appears to have retired from active service shortly afterwards.[13]

Towards midnight the King marched away with his Foot and train, leaving his Horse to face Waller until morning, when they also departed. 'I moved not till I had full assurance from my parties, prisoners, and spies that the enemy was clearly gone, lest it might have been but a feint to draw me from my vantage ground,' Waller wrote from Towcester on Tuesday 2 July.

'Being assured the King was gone towards Buckingham I was in great anxiety lest he might fall upon Major-General Browne, and therefore marched with all speed after him. But his Majesty, making a sudden halt at Farthinghoe, turned off to Aynho on the hill and crossed the river, taking up his quarters at Aynho and towards Doddington. I had in the morning sent divers advertisements to Major-General Browne to draw his forces towards Towcester as the safest rendezvous for us both to meet at in regard of the river. That Monday night I marched to Preston-on-Hill [Preston Capes], and this morning I came hither.

'During these two days march I was extremely plagued by the mutinies of the City brigade, who are grown to that height of disorder, that I have no hope to retain them, being come to their old song of "Home! Home!". The Major-General met me here and has quartered his forces within three miles of me. I found his men [in] no very good temper, some of his Essex soldiers threatening already to quit him, and the Hertfordshire men expressing their impatient suffering during a night or two's ill quartering. My Lords, I write these particularities to let you know that an army compounded of these men will never go through with their service, and till you have an army merely your own that you may command, it is in a manner impossible to do anything of importance.'[14] There could be no clearer statement of the case for reforming the armies of Parliament than this the first suggestion from Waller's pen.

To illustrate Waller's thesis, incidentally, there were a number of trials of the more serious infringements. Several cases of mutiny were brought before his council of war during the next few weeks. At the 12 July meeting (Daventry), for instance, two mutineers were sentenced to be hanged, another to be shot, and a quartermaster (who failed to suppress a mutiny) to be cashiered by the hangman. Major Edward Wood was ordered (on 23 July) to be arrested for having killed a man. Wood was subsequently released when it was found that he had shot a mutineer in the Southwark White Auxiliaries with a pistol, in performance of his duties as Adjutant-General of the Foot.[15]

Waller expected the King to return to Oxford, but on Wednesday 3 July he informed the committee at Derby House: 'I have just now received information that the enemy has given me another turn upon the toe and marched last night to Stow and Morton-in-the-Marsh, on his old road to Worcester. Tomorrow I intend to march after them with all possible speed with my horse and musketeers, leaving some behind to line the pikes and help guard the colours, which will follow easily. I cannot follow to overtake them in a direct line, but in coasting them by the way of Leicester I hope to gain ground of them . . . I am of the opinion, before this business be done, we shall be the longest winded army in England. I hope we shall never be weary of well doing, let the way be never so long and rugged.'[16]

The King's decision to march once more into the Midlands reflected his desire to spare Oxfordshire from being utterly denuded of provisions, but his advisers shrewdly calculated that the move would serve 'to discourage the Londoners to follow the same dance again',[17] a judgement which proved correct.

News that the Earl of Leven's Scots army, the Yorkshire army under the Fairfaxes, and the Eastern Association forces led by the Earl of Manchester and Oliver Cromwell had defeated Prince Rupert at Marston Moor (Tuesday 2 July), halted the King in his tracks at Evesham. That victory demonstrated what could be done when three armies combined and worked together, a commentary on the lack of such cohesion in the South. Even so, the rival armies had been almost equal in strength, the Royalists numbering about 17,500 and the Parliamentarians about 24,000. The Royalists were said to have lost 4,150 men in the battle, together with their artillery and baggage, 100 colours, and 10,000 pikes and muskets. Yet, after Marston Moor the three victorious armies separated and went about their separate tasks, instead of staying together and marching south to defeat the King and take Oxford. The Fairfaxes contented themselves with the reduction of the surviving Royalist fortresses in Yorkshire. The Scots had to send forces home to deal with the Marquess of Montrose. Manchester now showed his extreme 'backwardness' – he did virtually nothing with his army for the next four months!

Waller reached Northampton on the evening of Wednesday 3 July, intending to march up Watling Street and to intercept the King's expected march northwards.[18] 'My instructions are to follow [the King], which I will observe as long as I have breath,' he informed the Bedfordshire Committee. 'But the complexion of this army is not suitable to this design, the forces thereof consisting mostly of foot. I have therefore moved the Committee of Northampton[19] to make a levy of all the horse they own to mount musketeers upon, with this rule that to every nine horses so raised for the service there shall be added a county man and a horse who shall take charge of the nine to hold them upon service and return home again. If any be embezzled the captain of that company must be responsible and for such as are lost upon the service the State must answer.'[20] The Committee at Bedford acted promptly to send some horses to Waller, thereby earning both his thanks and those of the Derby House Committee.[21]

Browne's new regiments joined him at Northampton next day with surprising results: 'the City forces under Sir James Harrington,' wrote Waller, 'when they saw the new forces cried out that their relief was come, and notwithstanding they were paid, away went the White Regiment for London, and many men of the other regiments did the like. Besides, those remaining have Sir James' promise to depart at the end of three weeks.'

To make matters even worse, on Saturday 6 July Browne's mutinous soldiers physically assaulted their general, hurting him in the face. 'Such men are only fit for a gallows here and a hell hereafter,' Waller remarked with unusual bitterness.[22] Next day Browne led away his disorderly regiments to besiege the Royalist garrison at Greenland House near Henley-on-Thames, Waller stayed in Northamptonshire, mounting nearly 1,000 musketeers on horses provided by that county and building up his cavalry with every available local troop of horse. With the defeat of Prince Rupert at Marston Moor, the need to prevent the King from marching northwards from Worcester had faded.

At Evesham, the Royalist Council of war had certainly considered that option, weighing its merits against marching into the West to join Prince Maurice, 'so to attempt Essex with our forces joined, or to get him between our Armies, and to distress him before Waller could possibly come to his assistance'. 'This debate lasted at least three days without any certain resolution,' wrote Sir Edward Walker, many arguments being made of almost equal force for either design. 'And truly had Waller in the interim either attempted or drawn towards the West, it is possible we had taken the first; but his marching up and down from Buckingham towards Daventry, Northampton and to Warwick (being severed from Browne) gave us assurance of his weakness and irresolution.'

With the departure of the London brigade, and Browne's inability or unwillingness to stay with him, Waller was undoubtedly much weakened, especially in Foot. Moreover, he must have given the impression of indecision as he marched and countermarched. Perhaps he did not know what to do, the intentions of the King being difficult now to read. In the end, misled by a Royalist feint towards Woodstock, Waller marched south-east towards Aylesbury on Saturday the 13th to attempt an interception, but at nightfall he wrote from Towcester to inform the committee that the King had certainly moved into the West.

Waller's orders were to follow the King wherever he marched, and yet he now hesitated before obeying them literally and marching after him into the West. He sent Sir Arthur Heselrige to the Committee of Both Kingdoms to explain the present situation and to seek a clarification of his next task. Meanwhile, he skirted north of Oxford with his depleted army on his way to Abingdon. 'I long extremely to receive some instructions from you that may give me direction what course to steer,' he wrote to the committee from Bicester on 17 July. 'I have no particular interest, and if I may advance the public service, I have the end of my ambition.'

That same day the committee sent him a letter with their answer. He was to quarter his Foot and train of artillery at Abingdon in order to block up Oxford, and to despatch a strong party of Horse and dragoons to secure Dorsetshire. Waller, in the meantime, had besieged the strong Royalist fortress of Boarstall House in north Buckinghamshire, while another force from his army had taken prisoner a handful of Royalists in their quarters at Woodstock. Waller entered Abingdon on Saturday 20 July.

Next morning, having by now received the committee's written instructions, he replied that he would comply even though he did not favour dividing his army in this way unless reinforcements came to replace the missing Londoners and Midland garrison contingents. He had written to Major-General Browne, now at Reading, to join his forces with his own, so that 'I could leave my train with him and with the train horse mount the remainder of my foot and clear Dorsetshire and all those parts, and possibly do some further service according to emergent occasions'.

While awaiting the committee's reply Waller found himself faced with another mutiny. 'I am necessitated to inform you of the mutinous carriage of Sir Michael Livesey and Sir Thomas Pierce,' he wrote to Derby House, 'who, without acquainting me with their discontents, have falsely suggested to the Committee of Kent that I abused and slighted their regiment consisting of 800 horse, which I am confident is the bravest regiment in England, and that I should put them upon the hardest duty and worst quarter. Yesterday, without any notice given to me, four troops of that regiment marched away by their command. The rest I am informed, for they have private counsels of their own, will follow speedily.' Realising that 'if this disorder pass unpunished I may bid farewell to all power of commanding in this army', Waller requested as a right that the troops should be returned to him and the two chief offenders, whom he had put under restraint, called to account.

On 24 July the committee replied, agreeing with Waller's suggestion that Browne should move to Abingdon. But more trouble now stemmed from the fact that as Major-General of Oxford, Buckinghamshire and Berkshire, Browne now seems to have regarded himself as Waller's equal. He had not complied with Waller's earlier request that he should march his forces to Abingdon. Nor would he deign to see Sir William when the latter came to Reading for a conference. Letters from Derby House induced the 'Woodmonger' to change his mind about marching to the rendezvous, but he would not surrender his new independence. In order to lay charges against Livesey, and to resolve the muddles over strategy and command in the region, Waller left his army at Abingdon and went to London on 26 July.

From Farnham on 18 May to Abingdon on 20 July – a space of sixty-three days – Waller's regiments had covered some 500 miles. Latterly they had chased the King's army more like sheepdogs patrolling a moving flock than staghounds after a royal beast. Yet Sir William had certainly prevented the King from either joining Prince Rupert in the North or invading the Eastern Association to draw Manchester and Cromwell homewards; solid strategic achievements. But the King had wisely avoided battle on Waller's terms.

For his part, Waller acted with his customary prudence and caution; the one possible exception, that unique encounter battle at Cropredy, arguably deserved a better result. As it was, Waller preserved his army but at a cost to his honour and prestige as a general. For he had lost there those symbols of his military power, his field cannon, 'the taking of which in all is accounted the greatest sign of victory', wrote Sir Edward Walker, not without some satisfaction. Still more serious had been the effects of the protracted campaign in the Midlands on Waller's composite army, especially as it ended without a great victory over the King to cement them together again.

The real trouble, as Waller had discerned, lay in the fact that regiments raised originally for the defence of their city or counties could not be kept in the field for long, far from home, on an offensive campaign. The Earl of Essex had chosen to ignore this factor when (in May) he had left Waller with orders to march northwards and to follow the King wherever he went. Shortly afterwards Waller had reported to the Committee of Both Kingdoms: 'the Western men are much dejected to see me diverted this way, and truly I believe it will cause the breaking up of Colonel [William] Sydenham's [Dorset] regiment [of horse], many of the soldiers having already run away, and more likely to follow.'

Nor would counties associated for mutual defence show much alacrity in supporting Waller's efforts to raise reinforcements in their territory or at their expense. Upon representation from the leading Parliamentarians in Sussex, for example, the Committee of Both Kingdoms directed Sir William to withdraw the commissions he had granted to Colonel Edward Apsley and his officers, then raising a foot regiment for him in that county. Waller agreed, adding with some bitterness 'because I would not have anything to do with the gentlemen of Sussex, from whom I have received nothing but constant uncivilities'. Hampshire proved equally recalcitrant about sending him Colonel Richard Norton's regiment of horse.

By the end of July, Waller's forces had fallen to no more than 5,000 Horse, Foot and dragoons, together with his depleted train of artillery. It was but a shadow of that army which had marched so bravely towards Abingdon not two months earlier. Those weary and largely fruitless marches after the King in the summer of 1644 had gradually worn down and exhausted the precious reserve of spirits, giving that 'dishonourable blow' at Cropredy Bridge an effect upon Waller's forces out of all proportion to its weight. Indeed, as Clarendon perceived, 'it even broke the heart of his army'.

CHAPTER TWENTY-FOUR

Facing Westwards

'London is now in a sad posture,' Lady Brilliana Harley informed her brother from Westminster on Sunday 8 September 1644. 'They cry out extremely against Sir William W[aller] that he made no more haste.'[1] Thus the capital reacted to the extraordinary news that the Lord General's army had surrendered to King Charles at Lostwithiel in Cornwall. Shortly before this disaster, the Earl of Essex wrote to the Committee of Both Kingdoms to prepare them for the bad news and to identify Waller as the scapegoat for the blame. 'But had I known that Waller, who was to attend the King's army, had wanted power or will to have a care of it, no persuasions of those who are interested in these counties should have engaged me so far in a country so ill affected to the Parliament.'[2] It is doubtful if Essex saw the irony of the situation. The previous year it had been *his* failure to 'attend' to the King's army which had led to Waller's utter defeat at Roundway Down. Now he had suffered as bad a ruin in the West, and he employed the same reasoning as Waller's officers to explain things. Later the redoubtable Hugh Peter, then a chaplain in Essex's army, speaking at the bar of the Lower House, laid the blame on Waller's General of Horse, John Middleton.[3] Nor were there wanting those in London who took up the cry that Waller had maliciously abandoned the Earl to his fate. Charges of such a serious nature require investigation.

Waller's main defence was given in a conversation by him with Sir Simonds D'Ewes. As a Presbyterian moderate, D'Ewes could not be regarded as hostile by Waller, and so the latter had no cause for dissimulation. At the time of their conversation, too, both Essex and Waller had withdrawn from active command, and so no political or personal interest would be served by Waller distorting the truth. 'When it was too late, and that both had been laid aside,' wrote Sir Simonds D'Ewes in his diary, 'they then saw their error and became very firm friends. Yet Sir William Waller did in private discourse between him and me seriously protest that he did not know that ever he had done anything wittingly or unwittingly to disservice the Earl of Essex. And when I asked him why he did not then move in time to him from Farnham in Surrey when the said Earl was distressed in the West, he answered me that he had express order from the Committee of Both Kingdoms not to stir.'[4]

Waller could perhaps have better replied than when he had received a clear order to march westwards, he lacked the necessary strength to constitute a real threat to the King's army. And, further in his own defence, he could well have argued that by sending as far forwards as possible his Horse and dragoons under Middleton, he had done all that anyone could reasonably expect to save Essex from the fate he had brought upon his own head. Only a brief narrative of the events in those five weeks from Waller's visit to London on 26 July and the collapse of Essex's army in early September can substantiate this conjectured defence.

After Sir William had attended the House of Commons and meetings of the Committee of Both Kingdoms at the end of July, the latter disposed of his army along the lines it had indicated, respecting Waller's personal desire to stay near his remaining Foot and train of artillery at Abingdon.[5] Here, presumably his objective was to put a bridle on the Royalist garrison in Oxford.

On Sunday 18 August news reached London that Essex was 'environed by four armies' and in great want of provisions. Apparently contrary to what Waller told D'Ewes, the Committee of Both Kingdoms did then resolve that Sir William Waller himself should march into the West with a body of horse and dragoons. As part of the disposition already made, the committee had directed Lieutenant-General Middleton's brigade of 1,500 Horse and 500 dragoons to abandon the siege of Donnington Castle and to move into Dorset in order to hinder the raising of Royalist levies and to disrupt the collection of provisions.[6]

At the committee's behest during the following week Waller sent Lieutenant-Colonel Baker (exchanged after Cropredy for a Royalist officer) with his own foot regiment, now converted into 400 dragoons, to strengthen Middleton's force.[7]

Incidentally, Sir William Waller's efforts to convert his Foot into dragoons was constantly hindered by lack of horses. Yet he came under some criticism on this score. Although Waller took steps to ensure that his troopers delivered up captured mounts, he did not order any economies in the number of horses which his officers could possess. In a comment upon their rolls the muster masters assigned to Waller's forces reported to the Committee of Accounts: 'it was generally taken in the army for a burden to the country that the officers kept too many horses, which was observed by so great a company of loose horses that usually followed the troops.' One gathers the impression that just as Waller proved to be an indulgent father to his sons, he overlooked some of the extravagances of his officers.[8]

For his own 'flying army' Waller would have to rely upon the remaining regiments at Abingdon, those of the Southern Association and such men as the Western counties would provide along the road to Lostwithiel. But local commanders had staked their claim to these forces, and they would not loosen their grasp without a time-consuming struggle. Having convinced the committee at Derby House that Abingdon should be fortified as a check on Oxford, he had volunteered to undertake this work in person. As the situation in the West deteriorated, however, Waller decided to remain in London. Therefore 'out of his own free will' Waller had placed his foot regiments and train of artillery at Abingdon under the temporary command of the 'Woodmonger', Major-General Sir Richard Browne, who lost no time in moving his headquarters to the town.

Browne neglected his new charges to the point of starvation, so that disease ran through their overcrowded quarters. But he proved most reluctant to part with them when Waller requested them back, alleging that until the forces being raised for service around Oxford came in he could not let them go.[9] According to *Mercurius Aulicus*, as much as one third of Waller's soldiers were sick. When Waller reached his old base at Farnham, the appointed rendezvous for his forces in the third week of August, he forwarded to Derby House a report on the 'Woodmonger's' intransigence, written for him by Colonel James Holborne (now Major-General of Foot), 'whereby you may perceive how I am blocked up with faggots at Abingdon', showing that he had not lost his sense of humour.[10]

Predictably, the Southern Association proved to be as tardy in sending any regiments to Farnham. By diplomatically desiring the Committee of Both Kingdoms to pass over the charges he had laid against Sir Michael Livesey, Waller once more secured the services of the disgruntled Kentish Horse. Yet neither they nor a regiment of 1,000 Kentish Foot raised by an ordinance of 12 July had set out towards Farnham by 24 August. On that day the Derby House Committee wrote to the Kent Committee at Knole House, informing them that Waller's 'speedy marching into the west for the assistance of the Lord General . . . is retarded by the non-marching of your forces.'[11] Not until Monday 2 September, three days after Colonel John Birch arrived to take command of the new Kentish regiment, did its first companies set out from Knole to join Waller's forces.[12]

As for the other counties in the Southern Association, it was not until late in August that the Derby House Committee directed that 400 Greencoats from Farnham Castle in the regiment of Colonel Samuel Jones, together with 400 mounted Foot from the several Sussex garrisons, should be sent to Waller with sufficient money for their wages. Hampshire escaped a similar request, probably because Colonel Norton had now drawn all its forces in another siege of Basing House.

'I have this evening received informations, some from the King's army, others from Basing [signifying] so much of the weak condition of both, as it much inflames me to go on, if I may be speedily supplied with force,' Waller informed the Committee on Tuesday 27 August.[13]

Despite many preoccupations he found time to remonstrate with the committee over the arrest of a Worcestershire gentleman who had come to London with his safe conduct: 'My Lords, this is so contrary to my pledged faith that I cannot but think myself infinitely concerned in it, and must beg his instant release. I am the more importunate in this as it concerns your service, for I must never expect to be trusted in any treaty if I suffer a safe conduct under my hand to be violated. I have no more to add.'

Next day, Wednesday 28 August, there was still no sign of the Kentish regiments. Waller asked the committee, 'I pray take a present course that my train may be sent to me . . . and that the 20 barrels of gunpowder appropriated by Browne may be made good out of the store at London, likewise that Colonel Holborne may not be interrupted in what he shall do there [at Abingdon] according to your order, towards mounting my men, most part of them being so weak that I am persuaded they will not be able to march on foot. I want 50 dragoon colours, there being 10 colours to a regiment, 100 dragoon drums, 5,000 belts for their muskets, and 2,000 swords. Be pleased to send your order to the [Committee of] Militia for those four drakes of 3 lbs. bullet, and direct that such of these things as are ready may be immediately sent down hither. The rest may be sent by sea to Weymouth.'

Instead of this necessary dragoon equipment, on Sunday 1 September – the date of the surrender of Lostwithiel – Waller received a letter from Derby House enclosing a complaint from the Surrey Committee against his Commissary-General's attempt to establish a weekly tax for provisions in certain hundreds of the county. Waller examined the warrant and wrote back next day with wry humour: 'I can justify in all but the two dozen chicken, of which I never expected so much as one leg.' In the same letter, however, he could report the good news of the belated arrival from Abingdon of his Foot and train.

Even with 300 new recruits out of Kent, Waller's infantry at Farnham still only amounted to 1,400 soldiers. 'I have not one foot soldier mounted, Major-General Browne having sent notice to the constables of the hundreds that we intended to take their horses and all they had, so you may imagine that they provided for us accordingly.

'This day a company of dragoons under Captain [Nathan] Butler arrived out of Kent, and I expect 3 companies of the new Kentish regiment tonight or tomorrow. All these poor men have brought their mouths with them, and my Abingdon blades, they are the pictures of famine and poverty. And I fear the money still at London will not amount to three weeks' pay, for I must reserve for the payment of my good men in the West. I desire it may be considered that these poor creatures are to be repaired from head to foot, and I must out of this pay make provision for a march of near 300 miles, so I cannot imagine what will be remaining to them to defray their quarters. The parts about Farnham are very poorly provided, having been exhausted when we lay here last winter, so I thought I done well to send for provisions further off, but I shall not so abound in my own sense . . .'

Waller's letters to the Speaker and the Committee of Both Kingdoms (both dated 1 September) contain similar statements of his need for men, money and horses. Waller also asked permission to storm Basing House, believing that if he could take it many more local forces could be drawn to the West. He had made a brief appearance at the siege a few days earlier.[14]

Four days later (on Thursday 5 September) Waller still lacked the remaining 500 soldiers of the Kentish regiment of foot. As for the Sussex forces and 400 infantry assigned him from the Isle of Wight, they were to take ship along the coast and join him at Salisbury, the next rendezvous. 'In pursuance of your commands I shall not fail to make all possible speed into the West. I only desire there may be no more expected than is possible. . . . The only invincible obstruction that lies before me is the difficulty, not to say impossibility, of mounting my men, without which accommodation I leave it to any man's reason to judge in what time I shall be able to march to my Lord General's assistance, being clogged with a train without which I cannot march on foot, and not having one team of horses towards it.' Waller's infantry, however, had already covered 16 miles, quartering at Wootton St Lawrence to await the train of artillery.[15]

From Farnham on Saturday 7 September, Waller reported to the committee that his plans for augmenting his force with Wiltshire and Dorset cavalry had just received a severe blow. 'This day Colonel Ludlow came to me with orders from the Committee of Wiltshire to surrender to me his commission which he had from me. There are likewise orders sent from that committee to those troops of his which were at Salisbury, to draw away immediately to Malmesbury, and not obey their Colonel if he came with my commission to them.'

Waller took prompt action to resolve the situation. 'Last night, hearing that those troops were at Salisbury, I sent directions to them not to stir from thence till they received orders from me, and in the meantime to send out continual parties into the West to gain intelligence. How far this will now be obeyed I cannot tell. I have refused to accept Colonel Ludlow's commission, and have given him order to repair immediately to his troops and to see my former orders performed, which I make no question but he will do as far as he can.'

According to Ludlow, because he would not surrender his commission from Waller and obtain a new one from the Lord General, 'those of my country-men who were of the faction of the Earl of Essex, obstructed me in the raising of my regiment.'[16] Obviously, the long-standing feud between the supporters of Essex and Waller even reached down to the county level of military organisation.[17]

'My Lords, so long as I have a life I will lay it out freely in your service, but it is a very great discouragement to me to meet with nothing but opposition and in such a time wherein we cannot admit those clashings without betraying God's cause. I have reason to expect the like opposition in Dorsetshire, where the committee has vacated my commissions to Colonel Sydenham and Colonel FitzJames, and are going about to cashier 13 or 14 troops which are now actually raised, and most of them in a very serviceable posture. I have sent them order to draw either to Ilchester or Salisbury as they may with most conveniency.

'I moved the House concerning this point of command, that they would declare how far my commission stood good, in regard my Lord General had made Colonel Massey Commander-in-Chief of the Gloucestershire forces, and the Committee of Wilts had likewise voted the command of theirs to Massey. The House determined that my commission stood entire, and that nothing should be done to diminish it.

'I humbly desire if it seem good to your Lordships that this may be so settled that I may not be subject to these contestations, which I conceive are extremely prejudicial to your service. For mine own part, I would willingly surrender this command to whomsoever you shall appoint and march with my regiment under whose command you will.'[18]

Meanwhile, in Cornwall, the Earl of Essex had succeeded in getting himself cut off not only from London and Waller's army, but also from the friendly fortress of Plymouth nearer at hand. Charles had drawn the Western Cavaliers to his standard and with a good-sized army he surrounded Essex at Lostwithiel. The Parliamentarians suffered defeat at Beacon Hill and Restormel Castle (21 August) and at Castle Dore (31 August). Balfour and the cavalry broke out (27 August), and though Essex himself escaped from Fowey by sea, Skippon, with the Foot and the artillery, was compelled to surrender. 'I thought it fit to look to myself,' wrote Essex in order to excuse his flight, 'it being a greater terror to me to be a slave [object] to their contempts.'

Later, on Saturday 7 September, Waller took up his pen once more at Wootton to report to the committee, 'the sad confirmation of our loss of the western army [Essex's army at Lostwithiel], which is doubled to me in the desperate condition of my poor troops under Lieutenant-General

Middleton'.[19] In his third despatch that evening, written at Overton, 21 miles from Farnham, Waller suggested that he should leave his 2,000 Foot at the siege of Basing House and press on with his 800 horse and 150 dragoons to join Middleton but the committee's reply on the 7th drew him back to Wootton to supervise the march of the whole army westwards. Meanwhile, Middleton's plight was eased by the arrival at Weymouth of a London regiment of dragoons commanded by Major John Warren.

On 9 September Waller could relay to Derby House the more cheerful news of a junction near Taunton between Middleton's brigade and the Lord General's Horse. Moreover, Essex's disarmed Foot marching east of Honiton, had been abandoned by their Royalist guards, and 'if it be true the enemy have broken their articles, our men are free to take up arms immediately, if you can tell how to supply them, which I humbly conceive is the work that now lies before you. . . . My men are upon their march, and I will lose no time in my advance.'[20] On 23 August the Commons had already dismissed the charges of 'unnecessary procrastination' made against Waller.[21] In the light of these despatches it is indeed difficult to give much weight to those 'base calumnies', as Waller called them, which held him accountable for the disaster at Lostwithiel.

Sir Arthur Heselrige joined Waller at Salisbury and on Thursday 12 September they sent the committee at Derby House news of the Parliamentarian cavalry in Dorset, now threatened by the advance of the King towards its western borders. Middleton's Horse lay at Sherborne and the Lord General's at Dorchester, some 17 miles away, but none other than Hans Behre – the troubler of the Scots – held command over the latter and unless he was made subordinate to Balfour or removed for a time, the cooperation of the two bodies would be impaired. 'Something must be done in this without delay. If we fight divided both are lost,' wrote Waller and Heselrige with urgency. By this time they had decided to stiffen the south coast garrisons with their infantry and to try once more to assemble the Dorset and Wiltshire Horse. To pursue these ends Waller departed to Blandford and Heselrige to Poole.[22]

Two days later, on Saturday 14 September, Waller and Heselrige met again at Blandford. As for the local Horse, 'there is not one come in yet,' reported Waller, 'neither am I likely to have any when the country shall observe how little authority I have to command them and how easily I am overpowered everywhere.'[23]

The state of the south coast ports caused the two commanders even more concern. 'Lyme being likely to endure the first shock we hope to ship this day Colonel [Ralph] Weldon's [Kent] regiment, which is under

300, to secure that place, and this day the rest of our foot will be at Wareham, where we intend to be this night, and to leave so many foot as may defend it. We look upon it as a place of great consequence, neither can the works be slighted.

'Tomorrow we purpose to be at Weymouth, where we shall labour to ship Colonel Birch with the last regiment which came out of Kent, making about 700 for Plymouth. . . . The train and about 80 firelocks we shall leave at Poole, because of their want of ordnance. We desire the foot from Sussex and the Isle of Wight, and those two companies of Farnham that are before Basing may be speeded. When the Earl of Manchester comes up we can, if need require, draw our foot quickly out of garrison.'[24]

For a multitude of unconvincing reasons, however, the Earl of Manchester made no great haste to obey the Committee of Both Kingdom's directive and march south from Reading, which he had reached some days earlier. Upon receiving this direction from the Committee of Both Kingdoms, for example, he is alleged to have exclaimed in a jocular vein, 'Still they would have me march westward. Westward ho! But they specify no place, for ought I know it may be to the West Indies or to St Michael's Mount.'[25]

The Committee of the Eastern Association had predictably opposed the march of their army into the South, and even more so into the West. Yet the Commons did not rest satisfied either with Manchester's excuses or his action in sending some Foot to Newbury and Horse to Marlborough. On 9 October copies of a dozen letters which the committee had sent Manchester to get him to join Waller were produced and 'the House seemed to marvel much at his advancing no further'.[26]

For his part, the King showed every sign of abandoning the siege of Plymouth, whither he had marched after Lostwithiel, and advancing on London. From Weymouth Waller journeyed north-west to Shaftesbury, where he wrote to the committee on Saturday 21 September giving them an account of his dispositions and a list of the forces still obstructed from joining him. 'I hear the King has advanced to Cullompton, ten miles on this side of Exeter. If it be so I expect to hear from His Majesty shortly.'[27]

Three days later (24 September) he reported that the King would quarter that night at Chard. Meanwhile, no word had come from the Lord General, who had abandoned his first refuge in Plymouth – leaving Lord Robartes as Governor – and had taken ship to Portsmouth where he had begun the work of rebuilding his shattered regiments.

Even if he was reinforced by Middleton's cavalry, who had fallen back to Shaftesbury, Waller knew that he could not engage the King's army without Foot except upon an extreme disadvantage. That day Waller wrote a letter to Essex at Portsmouth, informing him that 'we are a gallant forlorn hope. Our horse are very considerable, as good and as many as when we went first to Oxford, with the exception of our saddles and arms.' The £5,000 promised by the House of Commons came not: 'our wants are so extreme that a major of horse has been fain to borrow sixpence for the shoeing of his horse,' wrote Waller on 25 September.[28] 'As for the point of command between the Earl of Manchester and myself I doubt not but we shall agree well enough. I am so heartily weary of this war that I shall submit to anything that may conduce to the despatch of it.'[29]

Five days later (Monday 30 September) Waller wrote again from Shaftesbury to urge a conjunction of the three Parliamentarian armies in the South. 'If this be timely done,' he informed the committee, 'we may most easily restrict the miseries of our war within a narrow space.' Meanwhile, the Parliamentarian horse skirmished daily with parties of Cavaliers. 'We have taken divers prisoners, and upon Friday last the enemy killed Major [Jasper] Clutterbuck. He was religious and valiant; we have cause to lament his loss. We shall not yield any ground but what we must needs.'[30]

With the King at Sherborne, not 15 miles to the west, Waller drew out his horse on Thursday 3 October. They stood and slept on the barren hills, wind-blown by day and chilled by night, until Tuesday 8 October. But by quitting his quarters some 12 miles to the south at Blandford because there were not enough provisions left in the neighbourhood to feed his men or horses, Quartermaster-General Dalbier (now commanding Essex's Horse) had exposed Waller's left flank, compelling him to withdraw to Winterbourne Stoke, 17 miles to the north-east of that town, before the Royalist army could envelop him.[31]

'Horse alone will not do your work against a strong body of horse and foot with artillery,' Waller and Heselrige reminded the committee at Derby House on Thursday the 10th. 'If your foot come not with all speed you will suffer in some place or other. We hope God intends mercy to us in that the King's army has done no more since our great loss in Cornwall. . . . The King we believe resolves to fight and to put all upon this. According to our understanding it is his only course, all his contributions failing. Hopton went last week to Bristol to draw out the garrison. We may yet do well, there is a little time left.'

Having at long last received orders to join up with the armies of Essex and Manchester in Hampshire, Waller commanded his 3,000 Horse and 1,500 dragoons to fall back to Andover. On his way there, on Friday 18 October, he wrote a letter from Wallop (7 miles south-west of Andover) to the House of Commons, reporting that 500 Royalist Horse had come the night before to Salisbury and killed some Parliamentarian soldiers there.[32]

At Andover, Waller's forces faced about once more, fearing that the King would reach Basing House, some 20 miles to his rear, before the two other Parliamentarian armies, one converging from Reading and the other from Portsmouth, could meet near Winchester and march to join him. Late on the Friday night a strong party from the Royalist camp suddenly descended upon Andover, and Waller was (unusually) taken by surprise. After a sharp cavalry skirmish in which Colonel William Carr was captured, Waller skilfully withdrew his forces to Basingstoke.[33] Meanwhile, the Horse from the armies of Essex and Manchester stood by to give support if need arose. 'It was a great mercy of God,' he wrote later, 'that when the King came suddenly upon me with his whole army at Andover, and I had then nothing but a mere body of horse and dragoons with me, I made a fair retreat to Basingstoke.'[34]

From that familiar town on Sunday 20 October Waller and Manchester wrote to inform the Committee of Both Kingdoms that with Essex's army at Alton, and with a fresh London brigade of no less than five regiments under Major-General Sir James Harrington not far off 'you may now look upon the forces as joined. We hope there will be a battle shortly; to our understandings it cannot be avoided. We desire the prayers of all our friends.'[35]

The Second Battle of Newbury

On the rainy night of Monday 21 October the Royalist army halted at Kingsclere. Suspecting a design on Reading, the Parliamentarian commanders moved their armies north-east next day to intercept the enemy, but the King turned instead towards Newbury. That evening the Parliamentarian cavalry off-saddled at Aldermaston, but the infantry still trudged the roads, now deep in mud, to their next quarters in the fields around the village of Swallowfield. By Friday 25 October, the combined Parliamentarian armies had drawn westwards to Thatcham, within 3 miles of Newbury on the north bank of the River Kennet. That evening, while rival parties of dragoons skirmished with each other on the outskirts of the town, the chief generals resolved to view the ground that separated them from the Royalist main body early next morning. The Lord General, however, had an excuse – perhaps political in nature – for not joining them. He had trudged through the rain-soaked Berkshire lanes at the head of his beloved Foot, caught a chill and taken to a feather-bed in his coach. He was now unwell in bed in Reading.

The reconnaissance of the Parliamentarian generals on Saturday 26 October and the news brought by Sir John Urry, who had changed sides a second time, gave them both a good idea of the terrain over which the battle would be fought and also an accurate picture of the Royalist forces and their dispositions. The King's army of 9,000 Horse and Foot occupied Speenhamland, a great open field crossed by a few hedgerows between Royalist-held Donnington Castle and Newbury. The bulk of the Royalist cavalry were grouped in the centre near the train of artillery, but strong parties of Foot and Horse guarded the perimeter of what was in effect a strong defensive position between the Thames and Lambourn rivers. In particular the King's generals had secured the bridges over the Lambourn at Shaw village and near Donnington Castle.

On the open west side stood the village of Speen, midway between the two rivers, which flowed not a mile apart at this point. Here, the King had placed Prince Maurice's Western Horse and a contingent of seasoned Cornish Foot. They stood to arms in and around the hamlet of Speen at the foot of a high heath which rose quite steeply to the west. 'At the entrance to the heath between two hedges,' wrote Sir Edward Walker, 'we cast up an [earth], which cleared [commanded] the heath and all the fields to the north, even to the river to the south. Within the hedge there was one narrow field, and from thence a perpendicular descent into a marish [marsh] between that and the River Kennet. This was our position, wherein, had the traverse [defensive earthwork across an approach] been finished and made down to the marish (although we were inferior in number) yet we should have been sufficiently provided to have withstood their force.' In reserve, somewhere between Speen and Newbury, the King stationed Sir Humphrey Bennet with a body of some 600 Horse. To guard against surprise, the King's generals also sent detachments of Horse to the villages of Bagnor and Boxford, in order to secure the next crossing points over the Lambourn above Donnington.

The combined Parliamentarian armies were almost double in size to the King's army. They mustered some 8,000 Horse, 11,000 Foot, together with a train of 24 guns. While a battery of these cannon on Clay Hill thundered down on the Royalists ensconced at Shaw bridge and its bastion, the medieval manor of Shaw House surrounded by earthworks, a Parliamentarian council of war resolved upon an unusually bold plan which more than suggests the influence of Waller. 'We then (considering the King expected present [immediate] supply from Prince Rupert and that two brigades of his horse were gone to Banbury) thought it fit not to delay,' wrote Waller and Heselrige to the Speaker, 'and upon advice resolved to divide our army and to fall on two ways.'[1]

The army divided into two parts. Sir William would lead one on a long night march, hooking right around Donnington Castle on the north, and come down to surprise the Royalists on the west in Speen. Meanwhile, Manchester would launch a simultaneous assault on the Shaw House as soon as he heard gunfire on the west of the King's position, signifying that Waller's forces had arrived and engaged.

Later that evening (Saturday 26 October) Waller set out to implement this imaginative plant, marching to Hermitage with a strong contingent: the Lord General's Foot, the City brigade and all the Horse (except for 2,000 left with Manchester), in three brigades under Lieutenant-Generals Oliver Cromwell, Sir William Balfour and Major-General Philip Skippon.[2]

Early on the sabbath morning, the 27th, the long-awaited battle began in earnest with a dawn attack on the east flank by Manchester's Foot across the River Lambourn at Shaw, but Sir Bernard Astley's musketeers drove them back in confusion. The louder roar of cannon now replaced the crackle of musketry as Manchester's soldiers laid low awaiting the sounds which would herald an onslaught upon Speen.

Not until after noon did Waller's forces reach the end of their long 10-mile march around the King's position. The soldiers paused to sleep for several hours in the fields south of Chieveley, about halfway on their journey. The soldiers took the road again before dawn, drove 500

Royalists out of Boxford, crossed the River Lambourn there and turned south-eastwards along the back of the heath towards Speen. Waller wrote: 'By two in the afternoon we were within a mile an a half of the town upon a large heath. Then we fell into the lanes and hedges and marched not above one quarter of a mile before we came in sight of the enemy who had blocked up our way with a strong breastwork and in it five pieces of cannon, and for their better advantage they were under the favour of Donnington Castle, their best pieces being there. Upon our approach their cannon played hard upon us, the place being a narrow heath gave no leave to bring up our body. The hedges hindered our horse very much. Their cannon made our ground very hot. There was no way left but to fall on with horse and foot, and that without delay.'

The Royalist soldiers in the earthwork observed the determined advance of Waller's army. 'At that time the rebels having passed the river, first possessed themselves of a wood on the west end of the heath beyond Speen, and thence discharged their ordnance and marched in good order, with very great bodies of foot winged with horse. Our horse made good the heath awhile, but being overpowered were forced to retreat,' wrote Sir Edward Walker.

Eager for revenge upon the hated Cornish, some 800 musketeers drawn from Essex's regiments of foot stormed the half-completed Royalist earthwork, manned by 400 soldiers with four or five guns.[3] Although case-shot took its toll from their ranks, the Parliamentarians carried the work. On their right the City brigade of three regiments swept down upon Speen village, only to be hurled back by the Western veterans under Prince Maurice and Hopton. After an hour's bitter fighting Speen fell to the Parliamentarians, and jubilant veterans of Lostwithiel recognised six of the nine brass guns captured, clapping their felt hats to the touch holes to prevent them from being spiked.[4] The Royalists, firing from every bush and hedgerow, made a fighting withdrawal to the western edge of the Speenhamland where the King's army stood.

At 4.00 p.m. cracking of volleys of musketry and the loud bangs of field guns reached a crescendo away to the east, signalling the start of the much delayed main attack of Manchester's forces on Shaw House. With Speen now in his hands, Waller ordered his cavalry to continue their advance eastwards, passing above and below the village. In the thrust forwards on the south side, Balfour's Horse drove back Sir Humphrey Bennet's troops, while to the north on the Lambourn side, Cromwell's regiments of horse encountered the redoubtable Earl of Cleveland's brigade.

As the storm of this cavalry battle moved eastwards towards the edge of Speenhamland, the King, riding about with drawn sword in hand to encourage his men, found himself in danger of being surrounded by Parliamentarian troopers, and only a valiant charge by his Lifeguards rescued him.

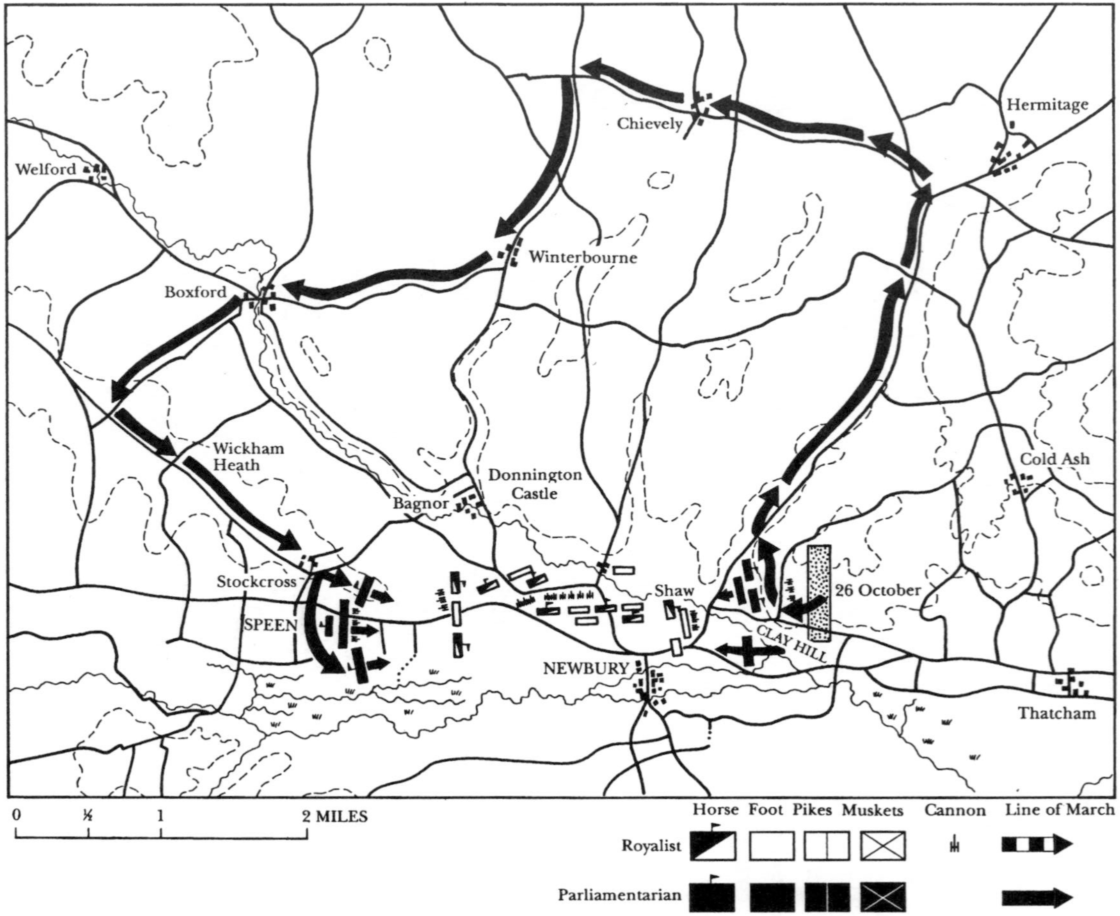

11. *The second battle of Newbury, 27 October 1644*

Hermitage

Cold Ash

Thatcham

26 October

CLAY HILL

Chievely

Shaw

Winterbourne

NEWBURY

Donnington Castle

Bagnor

Welford

Boxford

Wickham Heath

Stockcross

SPEEN

0   ¼   ½   1   2 MILES

Horse Foot Pikes Muskets Cannon Line of March

Royalist

Parliamentarian

Waller had a similar experience.[5] His regiment took part in the first charge. 'When I fell on with my troopers by way of Speenfield and we were there mingled with the enemy, I had a great deliverance, for one of the adverse party coming behind me, and being ready to fire his pistol in my reins, in that instant one of my Lifeguard killed him, or otherwise in all likelihood he would have killed me.'[6]

Eventually, Bennet's brigade, having rallied near the Royalist Western Foot who were now lining the long hedge and ditch bordering the Speenhamland field, stemmed the storm tide of Balfour's advance south of the village. Richard Symonds related the counter-charge of the regiment of the Lifeguards in which he took part: 'the King's regiment being near, drove at them, which made them wheel off in confusion, and followed them in the chase, made all their bodies of horse run in confusion, killed many, besides musketeers that had lined the hedges and played upon us in the chase till we cut their throats. Before these horse came up to us, while our regiment stood on the brink of the hill, their musketeers killed Mr Jones of the King's troop.'[7]

Sir Edward Walker wrote: 'At the same time the Rebel's horse of their left wing [under Cromwell's command] were advancing towards the north side of the great field, but before they got thither, General Goring put himself into the head of the Earl of Cleveland's Brigade . . . and being accompanied by the Earl himself, he fell upon them, and forced them back in great confusion, and then got over the hedge, where he was again charged by another body, but he quickly defeated them also, and slew divers of the rebels on the place.

'In this charge the courageous Earl of Cleveland engaged himself so far, and by the illness of his horse which fell with him, was taken prisoner. This charge was the more gallant because this brigade of horse, not only went over the ditch to meet the Rebels, but passed by three bodies of the Rebel's foot, who shot at them both when they pursued the Rebels and as they came back.'[8]

According to one critical Parliamentarian officer, 'by the report of the best there, if Cromwell had played the part that became him, the enemy had been totally routed. All the horse under his command stood still when Colonel Barclay's brigade was charged three times.[9] Not-withstanding all that, they stood still, Cromwell himself not being upon the head of them. Lieutenant-General Middleton came, seeing no great absurdities and oversights, and desired the said Cromwell's horse to charge, who refused firm till he went with one of the squadrons and charged the enemy, who was routed and left unseconded to fly for his life, being in the middle of his enemies, so that day there was no service performed at all by Cromwell.'[10] How far this accusation against Cromwell may be sustained remains doubtful.

The fighting continued sporadically for an hour into that 'fair and moonshine night', but already Waller's commanders had drawn back their brigades and regiments 'to avoid confusion in the dark by that scattered way of fighting'.[11] Unknown to Waller, the Royalist defenders had hurled back Manchester's sturdy assaults on Shaw House, but even so the King's army could scarcely spend the night confined between two hostile armies or endure another day of battle, and so a withdrawal was decided upon.

While his generals marshalled their forces northwards along the dark muddy lanes to Wallingford, the King paused for half an hour at Donnington Castle, watching from the battlements the stabbing flashes of musket fire in the moonlit fields behind him; then, accompanied by only 500 Horse, he rode off towards Bath where Prince Rupert awaited him with fresh forces.[12]

Waller, Heselrige and Cromwell followed the main body of the Royalists as far as Blewbury, 10 miles from Donnington. Some Foot accompanied the Horse to Blewbury, the troopers carrying their weapons for them. There they learnt that the enemy had safely crossed the Thames at Wallingford early on Monday morning and they decided to abandon the pursuit. Having quartered their men in the surrounding villages, they returned to Newbury, hoping to persuade Manchester to advance with his Foot to support their forces as soon as possible.

CHAPTER TWENTY-SIX

Missed Opportunities

Although the losses in killed and wounded at Second Newbury were probably equal (perhaps 500 men on either side) the Parliamentarian generals had at least gained the field. 'The King's army is exceedingly dispersed, and if ever a victory might be followed up with advantage this is one,' wrote Waller and Heselrige to the Committee of Both Kingdoms on Wednesday 30 October. Characteristically, Waller urged an immediate advance into the West. The clarity of his strategic thinking is impressive. 'We all know the activeness of the enemy to rally, especially Prince Rupert having so good a foundation for an army at Bath, and the King in person with him. We conceive that if you suffer your forces to disperse before they either scatter Prince Rupert's or drive them to their winter quarters, the enemy will continue masters of the West. If you command your forces to go up towards Bath, either the King will give us battle or retire to Bristol. If a battle we have cause to desire it; if to Bristol we have as fruitful parts as are in England to quarter in, and then our victory will be prosecuted to the Parliament's honour and profit. The King's contributions and levies, both for men and money in the West will be absolutely frustrated, and Taunton, now besieged, relieved; and so your enemies will have no armies in the spring.

'Some think of the [enemy's] falling into the [Western] Association's [country]. We apprehend that will not be, for, if the King should see forces draw towards him, he must call up altogether, and it is not for men with horses here in winter to go far from their garrisons, for there are so many rivers in every county, and so much enclosure, and the lanes so deep [in mud], that cut up but one bridge and in places of advantage 500 foot might beat 5,000 horse.

'And upon this stroke, if we move suddenly, we may do that work. Then our forces may safely divide, but for the present it is visible division is most dangerous. We feel the season of the year, we see the soldiers wants and sufferings, yet our sensibleness of the desolation and utter ruin which falls upon all sorts of people where armies come, makes us more earnestly desire to end the war than to enjoy our own ease. We presume not to direct, only being upon the place we conceive it our duties to declare our thoughts, submitting all to your resolutions, and are ready to obey what you may please to command.'[1]

Although the committee of Western gentlemen in London supported this proposal, the Committee of Both Kingdoms decided against a march westwards until the King's intentions were known. Meanwhile, the Royalist regiments had marched from Wallingford to Woodstock, their appointed rendezvous with the King and Prince Rupert, who were expected from Cirencester with a reported strength of 2,000 Horse and Foot.

Heselrige subsequently gave evidence that he and Waller 'moved the Earl, Major-General Skippon and other foot commanders, for the present advance of the foot, and he is of the opinion that if this course had been followed they might have seized on Woodstock or other places of consequence, to hinder the King's army from rallying, but the foot did not march until Friday [1 November], when a command was received from the Committee of Both Kingdoms to that effect.'[2]

Having sent a party to watch the garrison of Donnington Castle and the Royalist artillery train which had been left standing within its walls, the Parliamentarian generals occupied themselves in preparations for a march to the environs of Oxford to prevent the King's return to his base. On Saturday 2 November the army advanced as far as Hanwell, 4 miles from Oxford and at council of war it was proposed that they should turn westwards to Highworth, in order to interpose between Prince Rupert's forces, General Charles Gerard's Welsh levies, and the Royalist army already at Witney and Woodstock. But the Earl of Manchester, who had been averse to leaving Newbury in the first place on the grounds that neither the task nor the weather suited his infantry, led the opposition to this design in the council, alleging that 'even then the foot began to run from their colours'.[3] Consequently, the Parliamentarian army rather lamely turned back to besiege Donnington Castle.

On Friday 8 November the King and Prince Rupert brought their combined army from Wallingford towards Donnington, intending to relieve the castle and to recover the artillery. The Parliamentarian council of war considered the possibility of moving the army between the King and Donnington Castle, but chiefly out of fear that the Royalists might outflank them and gain Newbury, they resolved to remain on the defensive at Newbury. Besides, as Skippon informed the Lord General in a letter, 'the certain intelligence of the enemy's army being on this side of Wallingford came to us so late the night before they relieved the castle, which was the next day in the morning, that it was impossible (our horse lying so far quartered up and down from us) to prepossess the foreviewed ground for interposing between the enemy and the castle, without too manifest hazard of those who that had been first upon the place without the other.'[4]

Next day the Royalist army stood in array once more on Speenhamland, having reoccupied its original ground, facing the Parliamentarians in Newbury. Lord Byron estimated the rival strengths as

14,900 Parliamentarians and 8,000 Royalist, but the latter were probably over 9,000.[5] Having secured his train of artillery and skirmished boldly with the enemy, the King drew off that Saturday night (9 November) to Winterbourne Heath, where a body of Parliamentarian Horse found his regiments standing in battle order on Sunday morning. By 11.00 a.m. that morning the Parliamentarian army had begun to march out of Newbury to the open fields north of Shaw, expecting another battle. But the Parliamentarian council of war, meeting in a cottage near Shaw, could not agree on whether or not to fight again. Some officers urged that the King must be defeated before foreign contingents, especially one expected from France, could come to his aid. But the Earl of Manchester assured them that no such forces would come out of France, and then gave his opinion against a battle, adding: 'Gentlemen, I beseech you let's consider what we do. The King need not care how oft he fights, but it concerns us to be wary, for in fighting we venture all to nothing. If we fight 100 times and beat him 99 he will be King still, but if he beats us but once, or the last time, we shall be hanged, we shall lose our estates, and our posterities be undone.' Whereupon Cromwell replied, 'My Lord, if this be so, why did we take up arms at first? This is against fighting ever hereafter. If so, let us make peace, be it never so base.'[6]

Sir William Waller almost certainly voted with the 'loved party, Skippon, Cromwell etc.' for a battle, but Manchester, Lawrence Crawford and Sir William Balfour were all against it and they carried the day.[7] Crawford, a 33-year-old professional officer with experience under Gustavus Adolphus, was the Major-General of Foot in the army of the Eastern Association. He was on bad terms with Cromwell, the root of the trouble being their religious differences, but he was a brave officer 'sufficiently forward to engage', as Manchester's chaplain, Simeon Ashe, put it. While the King marched off to Lambourn and Marlborough, the Parliamentarian regiments retired once again into their quarters in and around Newbury. Yet the Committee of Both Kingdoms still hoped to keep the army in the field until the King's forces had gone into winter quarters, in the belief that both Basing House and Donnington Castle would fall to compensate them for the 'dishonour' incurred at Newbury.

On Wednesday 6 November the committee had written to Waller asking him to send 1,000 Horse to the relief of Taunton, and if the King drew that way, to march himself with the rest of his cavalry to second them. In reply five days later, Waller expressed his 'particular inclination to do service in those parts', but pointed out that his cavalry were now so weak that 'if you deduct 1,000 horse from them, the remainder will be so small as I cannot with any countenance stay with them'. Instead he suggested that regiments of Colonels Ludlow and FitzJames, with 200 commanded horse under Commissary-General Vandruske, should be sent at once, while Major General Holborne drew out his Foot from the south coast garrisons and then joined the party as its commander-in-chief. The Derby House Committee accepted these proposals, interviewed Holborne and then despatched him into the West.

Yet in the second week of November the Parliamentarian forces quitted their half-hearted siege of Basing House and went into winter quarters at Reading, Henley, Abingdon and Farnham. Waller's army were assigned quarters between Staines and Farnham.[9] On 19 November, Waller wrote to Prince Rupert negotiating over a proposed exchange of prisoners.[10] Part of the King's army then occupied Newbury, 'so that our great army,' wrote one Parliamentarian, 'is now shamefully beaten and cudgelled out of the field into their winter quarters, nay, into our own quarters, whereas we should have lived upon them to our great dishonour and discouragement, not having fought any considerable action.'[11] The committee at Derby House envisaged Waller's remaining regiments as holding a line from the sea near Portsmouth to Farnham, and thereby protecting the Southern Association from Royalist incursions.[12]

The Parliamentarian generals had already judged it expedient to send Sir Arthur Heselrige up to London to explain their actions to Parliament. On Thursday 14 November, Denzil Holles saw him as he strode into the House of Commons 'all in beaten buff, cross-girt with sword and pistols as if he had been killing his thousands . . . and there, like a great soldier in that habit, he gave a relation of what had passed, highly extolling the gallantry and conduct of all the commanders and the valour of the soldiers.'[13] The House was not entirely satisfied with the explanations offered to it by Heselrige. Nine days later Waller and Cromwell, both newly arrived in London, received orders to speak in the Commons. Therefore on the 25th, Waller gave to the House his own version of the campaign. Yet Whitaker reported that both Waller and Cromwell laid the blame on Manchester for the failure to defeat the Royalists decisively at Second Newbury, and so it is possible that Waller opened the attack upon Manchester.[14]

The long-smouldering quarrel between Cromwell and Manchester now exploded. Cromwell accused his commanding officer before the House of 'continued backwardness to all action'. To a committee subsequently appointed to receive evidence concerning this charge, Waller made a deposition cataloguing the delays and evasions of the Earl, notably his failure to advance to Shaftesbury or Salisbury in October, and his attempts to halt the pursuit of the enemy after Second Newbury. As Waller made no mention of the decision not to interpose the army between the King and Donnington Castle on 8 November, it may be assumed that he assented to it, but he repeated Manchester's imprudent words uttered on the 10th at the council of war in the cottage near Shaw. Waller's statements added little to the case against Manchester and, compared with the other depositions, it was decidedly mild in tone.[15]

This inquest into missed opportunities at Newbury and Donnington gradually developed into a searching assessment of Parliament's generals. 'God seems not to favour the great officers: certainly we are ill served by them,' noted one political diarist.[16] Nor did Waller escape criticism, for the chief officers of Essex's army came up to London and circulated rumours against him. Though he was 'for fighting and Balfour not, yet they endeavour to render him the cause of it and ascribe it to his unfortunateness, and to say the truth, the wiser sort of men do not believe him so fit for the conduct of an army, though in this particular it passed by the major part of votes in the council.'[17]

The failure of the Parliamentarian forces at Newbury and Donnington played into the hands of those radical members of Parliament who wanted to refashion them into a single army after their hearts' desire. On 23 November the Commons directed the Committee of Both Kingdoms 'to consider of a frame or model of the whole militia' and to present their report to the House.[18] Waller attended the meetings of the Committee of Both Kingdoms regularly after his return to London, and on Tuesday 31 December he was voted onto a subcommittee to consider in detail the composition of the proposed New Model Army.[19]

By this time it had become clear that Sir William Waller would not be offered the command of the New Model Army, though had it come his way he may well have led it with as much distinction as Sir Thomas Fairfax. In a great Parliamentary speech on Monday 9 December, Cromwell had persuaded the Commons to bring in the proposed Self-Denying Ordinance, whereby members of both Houses would surrender their commissions, a measure which had the obvious merit that 'it stills any difference between the Lord General and Waller, and Lord Manchester and Cromwell.'[20] 'Moreover,' wrote the same diarist, 'the present commanders had parties and factions who retarded the work, and made them not care (as their places were general) how long it lasted.'

According to Edmund Ludlow, Parliament laid Waller aside under the terms of the ordinance 'rather to show their impartiality, than for any distrust of him, he having never discovered to that time any inclination to favour the King's cause'.[21] Yet by this time Sir William had grown 'so perfectly tired with the drudgery of it' that he supported both measures despite their somewhat unjust consequences in his case. 'Truly I was so little fond of the trade of a soldier (notwithstanding those temptations of honour and profit that accompanied it), that I gladly gave my vote to the Self-Denying Ordinance, and the New Model.'[22]

Thus the winter of 1644 saw the end of Waller's military prospects, despite his continued employment as a military caretaker before the New Model Army could take the field in the following spring. Perhaps only the exchange of the elderly Countess of Forth for his eleven-year-old daughter Margaret, who had been taken prisoner by the Royalists contrary to the King's commands and held at Exeter, relieved this December gloom.[23] Their reunion may well have served as an earnest of those private joys of family and estate to which his heart increasingly turned, although for the time being he consented reluctantly to remain Parliament's 'General of the West'.[24]

Hopeless Employment into the West

On Wednesday 15 January 1645 the House of Commons voted Waller as commander-in-chief of a force of 6,000 Horse and dragoons for service in the West.[1] Plans to form such a body from the rump of Waller's army, augmented by contingents from those of Essex and Manchester, had been afoot since mid-December, but a sense of urgency only developed when the Royalist General Lord George Goring – Waller's old opponent at the siege of Portsmouth in 1642 – swept through Dorset and Wiltshire at the head of a field army and even rode into Farnham on 9 January. Fortunately for Parliament, after menacing Portsmouth and Christchurch he had returned into Wiltshire.

Waller remained in London working hard upon the composition of his army until the 29th, when the House resolved that he should go down from the capital and lead the expedition into the West. Within three days Waller arrived at Farnham and set about taking an inventory of his forces.[2]

'The Lord General's horse are about 600, his and Manchester's foot 2,000, and Manchester's horse near 700,' he reported to the committee on 2 February. 'I cannot yet give a particular account of my own forces, both in regard they are quartered more remote from me, and I know not what proportion they are recruited. Tomorrow morning I propose to take a view of the foot, and in the afternoon of the Lord General's and Manchester's horse. On Tuesday [4 February] I intend to be at Petersfield and to muster my own horse and dragoons, and on Wednesday or Thursday, if money be sent down, to advance to Alresford and Bishops Waltham, from whence I can move as you may direct me. . . . It is in vain to talk to the soldiers of marching till the money comes. The officers this day represented some particulars wherein their regiments were defective, viz. 600 pikes, 1,000 swords, 1,000 bandoliers, 2,000 knapsacks and 2,000 pairs of stockings.'[3] Waller had already requested the House of Commons to send him 3,000 pairs of shoes for the army.[4] 'The charge of these things will not be great, and it will give the soldiers a great encouragement to have them supplied.'[5]

ROUNDHEAD GENERAL: *The Campaigns of Sir William Waller*

Five days later Waller sent Derby House the results of his musters, 'by which you will see how far short they fall of your reckoning, and you will perceive by the commissioners that the Lord General's troops hold out no better. It was your resolution that these troops in all should make up 1,500 horse, besides 7 troops which were appointed of the remainder of Lieutenant-General Cromwell's regiment to join with me by way of addition to my forces.'[6] Two expected regiments of foot – Morley's from Sussex and Alexander Berkeley's out of the Reading garrison – had not yet arrived, the latter awaiting a replacement from Aylesbury before it could move. According to *Mercurius Aulicus*, Waller's forces numbered no more than 500 Horse and 700 Foot in the first week of February, but these may only have been the soldiers billeted about Farnham.[7]

While awaiting further directions from Derby House, Waller acted promptly upon scout reports. On Tuesday 11 February he informed the committee: 'Upon information that the enemy had three regiments of horse with some dragoons quartered at Andover, I gave order to a party of my Lord General's horse and some regiments of mine own to advance to Ropley [7 miles north-west of Petersfield] intending to attempt the beating up of that quarter. But when I came thither I received advertisement that the enemy by some intelligence from Old Alresford – had taken the alarm, and was retired to Newton Tony [6 miles east of Amesbury].

'The enemy from Salisbury have sent out their warrants for the bringing in of carriages upon pain of death, which is a clear implication that they intend to march, and I guess it will be westward, in regard I hear Major-General Holborne has engaged Sir Lewis Dyves' forces [Dyves was the Royalist Major-General in Dorset, with his headquarters at Sherborne Castle]. It will be of very great consequence to despatch away forces to their present relief, with a strength answerable to so great a work. I am now labouring to get the foot here to march, but I know not how far I shall prevail with them.

'I hear nothing yet of [the] Aylesbury regiment, neither is Colonel Morley's foot yet come to me. The commissioners can give you an account how far I fall short of the number of my horse.' On 12 February Waller's cavalry strength was given to the Commons as '3,400 horse on muster and 700 dragoons'.[8]

'If all his Excellency's foot might be drawn out of Reading,' Waller continued, 'and a course taken to secure that place in their absence, I shall – by God's assistance – be enabled to be master of the field, and go through with that work in the West, which I look upon as the greatest service that now lies before you. Whereas if through the weakness of this party I should receive any blow, it would be very dangerous to the East and West. I humbly desire that the particulars mentioned in my former letters may be immediately despatched to me.'[9]

Tidings that the Royalist besiegers at Weymouth had stormed and carried the outworks of the town brought Waller orders from London to march westwards at once, or at least to send ahead a strong party of Horse and dragoons.[10] In obedience to this command, Waller replied on Thursday 13 February: 'I am this morning taking horse to Alresford, whither I give order to all the horse and dragoons to draw up, excepting some troops left for the guard of the foot and train in their following march. Immediately upon receipt of that unhappy news from Weymouth, I wrote to the Governors of Weymouth and Poole not to be dismayed, but to make good their trust like soldiers, and I would not fail to march to their relief with all speed. I hope they will not fail in their duties. However, I will not be wanting in mine as far as I am possibly able. I have written divers times both to you and the Commons' House concerning the condition of this army and of my position in it, but I have been so unhappy that I have never received one word of answer to any particular. I have discharged my conscience, and now if I perish, I perish. I shall from the rendezvous give you an account what troops will march with me.'[11]

Within a day Waller heard that Horse of the Lord General and the Earl of Manchester had mutinied in their quarters. Lack of pay and necessities lay at the root of this trouble, exacerbated in the former case by old rivalries. 'Colonel Grenvile commanded the first,' wrote an anonymous political diarist in London, 'but basely refused and said he would not go with such a rogue, and so came away plundering the country. Having reduced himself from 1,500 to 600 they went from Croydon to Wickham, and then about Stile plundering as they went . . . and daringly sent propositions to the House to have their pay and then my Lord General may command them, to his great dishonour who takes no care to quiet them.'[12]

The House of Commons had directed the Southern Association to raise a composite regiment of 500 Horse for Sir Richard Grenvile, a prominent West Country landowner newly returned from military service in Ireland. Waller had given Grenvile a commission as Lieutenant-General of Horse, and the Western Committee promised him the governorship of Plymouth (in place of Lord Robartes) when it could be relieved. The southern counties dragged their heels over raising his regiment. When Grenvile, weary of the more extreme religious views among his fellow commanders, deserted to the King in March that year, no more than four troops had been raised. In fact discontent was rife among the Parliamentarian cavalry in these early weeks of 1645. Short of pay, they took to plundering the countryside. The Lord General's Lifeguards and the regiments of Behre and

Dalbier (many of them Dutch and Walloons) were 'the most exorbitant of all'.[13]

The Committee of Both Kingdoms sent down Sir William Balfour and Phillip Skippon to quell the mutiny in the Lord General's Horse and Foot respectively. Then the committee made the mistake of ordering Essex's three disorderly cavalry regiments into Gloucestershire to serve under Massey, promising them a fortnight's arrears of pay in their pockets.[14] Despite their high protestation that 'they would rather go under any [commander] whom the Lord General should appoint without money, than with Sir William Waller with all the money in England',[15] they mutinied again in Berkshire, and only with difficulty could Balfour disperse them into quarters. By contrast, Essex's Foot remained at Farnham, though still grumbling for want of their wages, and Manchester's Horse also appear to have swallowed their discontent by the end of the month.

Fortunately for Waller, the Parliamentarian defenders of Weymouth recovered the outlying fortifications by their own efforts, and the Committee of Both Kingdoms cancelled their order to him to march immediately into the West.[16] Meanwhile, on Monday 17 February Sir William had viewed his own cavalry at Petersfield, whence he wrote that evening to secure the return of Lieutenant-General Middleton from London to his command.[17]

Hearing that Goring intended to besiege Melcombe Regis, the committee directed Sir William to send Colonel Morley's Foot by sea from Portsmouth. They had already sailed once for Weymouth, but contrary winds had blown them back to the Isle of Wight.[18] Waller went himself to Portsmouth about this business and from there on 22 February he reported yet again the state of his forces to the House of Commons.

By this time Middleton and Sir Hardress Waller had informed Sir William Waller of yet another mutiny among Manchester's Horse. Hardress Waller, William's first cousin, had newly-arrived from service in Ireland. Waller made him colonel of Potley's depleted regiment and, while he was endeavouring to recruit it, Hardress acted as captain of the Lifeguards troop. Told to collect provisions for four days, 'by reason the countries which they were to go were so wasted that they were like a wilderness', Manchester's troopers came to the rendezvous with none. Moreover, the Eastern Association regiments wanted both recruits and the weapons needed to arm them.[19] As a result the House resolved five days later that Lieutenant-General Oliver Cromwell should be asked to go down in person and march with Waller to relieve Melcombe and the garrisons adjacent, and then to disperse the Royalist levies being mustered in that area.

Accompanied by three more troops of his own regiment of Ironsides from Henley, together with his Quartermaster-General, Henry Ireton, Cromwell joined the Eastern Association's Horse in Sussex by the end of February, bringing their number up to about 2,000.[20] Meanwhile, Waller had returned to Farnham by way of Wickham and Owlsbury, sending up to London from the last named an intercepted letter from Sir Lewis Dyve concerning the state of Weymouth and the Royalist designs upon that town.[21]

On Tuesday 4 March, Waller and Cromwell received explicit instructions to march into the West, with their cavalry, 'all excuses set aside'.[22] Together with Cromwell's command, Waller's 3,000 Horse and dragoons rode from Owlsbury to Andover on Saturday the 8th, and thence on the following day towards Amesbury, 'which I thought the furthest way to our journey's end, Taunton, yet for quarters sake we were compelled to march', commented Colonel Edward Cooke.[23]

Not far from Amesbury, Waller received intelligence that Colonel Sir James Long and his regiment of 400 Cavaliers planned to halt at Devizes upon their return journey to Oxford from Bristol, whither they had escorted the Prince of Wales with his court and council. Deciding to interpose his forces between the Royalist regiment and Devizes, Waller changed the direction of his march north-westwards towards Amesbury, where he halted his army on Monday 10 March.

Here, Waller learnt that his prey, Colonel Long, had reached Devizes, and that a number of levies summoned by virtue of his authority as High Sheriff of Wiltshire, awaited him. Colonel Cooke and Captain Butler wrote: 'This intelligence caused Sir William to advance towards the Devizes that night, having also advertisement that the enemy's works about the town were very slight. And when his army were on their march about a mile from Amesbury, he drew them up into a body, and four out of every troop to go on the forlorn hope.

'On Tuesday morning very early, our forlorn hope gave the enemy an alarm (the whole army marching all night) upon which all Colonel Long's regiment, which were quartered in and near Devizes, drew into a body. And news being brought thereof to Sir William, he made some stay, and at first seemed rather to prepare for defence than to give an assault, and divided his horse into three brigades: the first commanded by himself, quartered near Potterne [2 miles south of Devizes], Woodington [Wedhampton], and the Devizes; the next brigade was commanded by Lieutenant-General Cromwell; and the third by Sir Hardress Waller, a kinsman of Sir William's, which brigade joined together and wheeled about and fetched a large compass, that they might not be discovered by the enemy, and fell in between them and the Bath.

'On Wednesday morning Sir William Waller drew up his forces to fall upon the enemy, and they having discovered that Sir William had a purpose to give them a visit, Colonel Long with the horse left the Devizes and retreated towards Bath, not having notice of General Cromwell's readiness on that side to receive them. And Sir Charles Lloyd, the Governor of the Devizes, with most of the foot slighted their works, and retreated into the castle thinking that they were not able to defend the town.

'Sir William hearing that Colonel Long was marching away, he pursued him very close in the rear, and when the enemy were a little past Milchin [Melksham], thinking by the swiftness of their march to make their escape away, Colonel Cromwell appeared in the van, betwixt him and Bradford, which, having notice of, Colonel Long would have returned back again, but could make no way of escape, the passages being narrow and the country so fortified with quickset hedges that he was, as it were, in a pound.'[24]

Sir William recounted his own part in the capture of Long's regiment more fully in a despatch to the Speaker: 'It was my fortune to find an empty form, the enemy being drawn off to Westbury and Steeple Ashton, but the rest had better fortune, and in the end I had my share too. Cromwell lighted upon two troops at Potterne, Sir Hardress Waller upon the rest of the regiment at Westbury and Steeple Ashton, who beat the enemy in upon my quarter, where my regiment lighted upon them.'[25]

Perceiving that they had been cornered the Cavalier regiment offered only a token resistance. In a short letter appended to the printed account of the action Waller added: 'Colonel Cooke and Captaine Butler have written at large unto you, and therefore I shall only confirm it, that with God's gracious assistance we have routed the best regiment of the King had in the West. Of four hundred horse there escaped not thirty, the Colonel, Sir James Long, eight captains and seven cornets were taken, and most of the other officers with about three hundred prisoners. This fell out in Wiltshire between Trowbridge and Shepston. We are now marching towards honest Holborne [at Taunton], with whom (on the grace of God) we will join, or stick halfway.'[26] First, however, Waller halted for the night to refresh his Horse in West Lavington, 'after this toilsome march and service in the worst ways and basest weather that I ever saw'.[27]

The capture of Colonel Sir James Long's regiment had been exceptionally well executed in the best style of the 'Night Owl'. Yet Waller had discerned a new bird of prey in the military sky. Acknowledging the good service of Cromwell's Horse at this occasion in his *Experiences,* he later recorded his impression of the future dictator. 'And here I cannot but mention the wonder which I have oft times had to see this eagle in his eyrie. He at this time had never shown extraordinary parts, nor do I think that he did himself believe that he had them. For although he was blunt, he did not bear himself with pride or disdain. As an officer he was obedient, and did never dispute my orders nor argue upon them. He did, indeed, seem to have great cunning, and whilst he was cautious of his own words – not putting forth too many lest they should betray his thoughts – he made others talk, until he had, as it were, sifted them, and known their inmost designs.

'A notable instance was his discovering in one short conversation with one Captain Giles (a great favourite with the Lord General, and whom he most confided in) that although his words were full of zeal, and his actions seemingly brave, that his heart was not with the cause. And in fine, this man did shortly after join the enemy at Oxford, with three and twenty stout fellows.

'One other instance I will here set down, being of the same sort, as to his cunning. When I took the Lord Percy at Andover, having at that time an inconvenient distemper, I desired Colonel Cromwell to entertain him with some civility; who did afterwards tell me, that amongst those whom we took with him (being about thirty), there was a youth of so fair a countenance, that he doubted of his condition. And to confirm himself, willed him to sing. Which he did with such a daintiness that Cromwell scrupled not to say to Lord Percy that being a warrior, he did wisely to be accompanied by Amazons. On which that Lord, in some confusion, did acknowledge that she was a damsel. This afterwards gave cause for scoff at the King's party, as that they were loose and wanton, and minded their pleasure, more than either their country's service, or their master's good.'[28]

Intending to pursue Goring, whom he believed was retreating to join forces with Sir John Berkeley, Governor of Exeter, Waller appointed a rendezvous for his own army and Holborne's garrison from Taunton at the Dorset town of Cerne Abbas on Wednesday 19 March. But the prospect of a glittering bargain diverted Waller from this design. Leaving Cromwell to continue southwards towards Cerne, he turned about and marched in the opposite direction to face Bristol. On 4 January the Derby House Committee had ordered £50 to be given to Waller and Oliver St John, the Solicitor General, no doubt to serve as a golden key to the gates of Bristol.[29] Yet the plot fell through and the city remained securely in Royalist hands. From Marshfield on Sunday 23 March Waller reported as much in a despatch to the committee. 'I am come into these parts about a business that Mr Solicitor was acquainted with when I was in London. Though the business failed through the faintheartedness of those that undertook it. Yet I cannot but lament my want of foot, and dare speak it with confidence, that if I had but those 3,000 that were assigned unto me, you might be masters of the West, and of the places of the greatest importance in it, the people being universally disposed to receive us, but unwilling to engage till they see me with such a body as may give them assurance. I mean to stay with them, and not to be gone tomorrow.[30]

'I hope in the Lord, Lieutenant-General Cromwell and Major-General Holborne are joined before this. I am like to have the hardest task to get to them, the enemy interposing between me and them at Shaftesbury. If your Lordships think fit to send down foot, or to command those that were at Farnham, with some other regiments in addition to march to me, I shall be in the way to receive and secure them about Wimborne. I desire to hear speedily what I shall do.

'I received a letter yesterday from Colonel Massey signifying that there is a party in Herefordshire and Gloucestershire that have besieged Hereford near 16,000 strong, and that they have 6,000 muskets among them. They will not yet declare of either side, but only for the defense of their own country. The people in all these countries are likewise prepared to rise, and if I had a body of foot in the field I am confident they would speedily be with me.'[31]

Only three days later (Wednesday 26 March), when Waller took up his pen again, he wrote from Downton, 6 miles south of Salisbury and 40 miles from Marshfield. 'In regard to my Lord Goring's labouring to impede my march I went to Lavington, and from thence upon the advance of a long march over the plains. I came safe (I praise God) hither. Upon my way between Calne and Lavington I passed by the Devizes, where it pleased God to give me a good success. The enemy's horse sallying out, we charged them and beat them into the town pell mell with them, and if I had had foot I might have bid fair for the castle. We took a Lieutenant-Colonel and divers officers and 200 very good horse.[32] Cromwell (I hear) is advanced from Ringwood towards Dorchester. I am now going after him, to know what condition he is in, as fast as weary legs can carry me. Our want of money is extreme.'[33]

Waller reached Ringwood next day (Thursday 27 March) and called a halt. While the men found quarters in and around the village Waller wrote to the Derby House Committee describing the situation: 'Our duty and marches have been extreme, so that we are here a tired company, and necessitated to make some stay for our refreshing. Lieutenant-General Cromwell, I presume, is this day joined with Major-General Holborne, for he was last night at Bridport. I hope General Goring's drawing down after me towards Mere and leaving Grenvile with his and Barclay's forces at and about Chard, may afford our forces some good opportunity. I have sent an express with all speed after Lieutenant-General Cromwell to know where and how I may join him, and I shall apprehend the first opportunity to do it. I cannot but advise you that since my coming thither I have observed a great smoke of discontent rising among the officers. I pray God no flame breake out, – [three lines carefully blotted out]. The ground of all is the extremity of want that is among them, indeed in an insupportable measure.'[34]

Meanwhile, Holborne had marched out of Taunton with about 2,000 Horse and Foot towards the Cerne Abbas rendezvous. Harassed by Sir Richard Grenvile (now fighting on the King's side) and some Royalist regiments drawn from the siege of Plymouth, Holborne reached Axminster by Thursday 27 March.[35] Goring sent parties of Cavaliers to surprise Cromwell's Horse at Dorchester, but the attempt failed and he could not prevent a union of the two Parliamentarian forces on the last day of the month. Waller joined them shortly afterwards and together they marched north against Goring, who therefore abandoned Shaftesbury and retired to Bruton, 13 miles to the north-west, where he could effectively oppose any advance upon Bath or Bristol.[36]

By beating up Waller's outquarters at Cucklington, near Wincanton, the Royalists stung their enemy into action. On Friday 4 April, a Parliamentarian body of 2,000 Horse and dragoons advanced towards Bruton. The patchwork of small fields would not permit large formations, but 400 Parliamentarians charged a party of Cavaliers and chased them back to Bruton.[37] At once Goring withdrew to Wells and Glastonbury, 'whither we felt it unsafe to follow him,' wrote Cromwell, 'lest we should engage our body of horse too far into that enclosed country, not having foot enough to stand by them, and partly because we doubted [suspected] the advance of Prince Rupert with his force to join with Goring, having some notice from Colonel Massey of the Prince's coming this way.'[38] As Waller's 'very poor infantry of about 1,600 men' might tempt the enemy into a 'too unequal engagement', the Parliamentarian commanders agreed to fall back to Salisbury, little knowing that only Goring's weakness in foot regiments had prevented him from forcing a battle.

Like a player in a chess game, Goring followed up Waller's withdrawal by returning to Bruton and the villages about it. There his regiments could quarter much closer together than those of Waller in the more scattered hamlets around Salisbury. 'General Goring taking this advantage,' wrote one of his officers, 'sent out parties almost every night to beat up the enemy's quarters in Wiltshire, which was done with such good success that in a short time we took many prisoners and colours,' which occasioned Waller to write this ensuing letter to General Goring:

Noble Lord,

God's blessing be on your heart, you are the jolliest neighbour I have ever met with. I wish for nothing more but an opportunity to let you know I would not be behind in this kind of courtesy. In the mean time, if your Lordship pleases to release such prisoners as you have of mine for the like number and quality that I have of yours, I shall esteem it as a great civility, being

Your Lordship's most humble and obedient servant,
William Waller.[39]

As a result of this letter Colonel Innes and Major Butler from Waller's army met two Royalist commissioners to discuss the details of the exchange. One of the latter, Sir Richard Bulstrode, noted: 'The country folk, believing we were appointed to make a peace, flocked in great numbers to Shaftesbury, where we stayed fifteen days to release all prisoners of quality on both sides from Lands End in the West to Portsmouth. Sir William Waller sent us a great present of wines, which came from London, believing we could have none such elsewhere.'[40]

Both Bulstrode and his general exaggerated these Royalist successes. Sometimes the Cavaliers found their enemy waiting for them. On Wednesday 9 April, for example, Cromwell wrote to warn his kinsman Lieutenant-Colonel Edward Whalley, a commander in the regiment of Ironsides that the enemy would attack their quarters at dawn on the morrow.[41] Nevertheless, Goring's despatches made good reading in Bristol where the Prince's Council believed that these aggressive tactics would foster desertion from Waller's army. Doubtless with a smile on his face, Lord Culpeper, a member of the Prince's Council, rated Goring in a friendly letter for being 'a very cruel man' in his pursuit of Waller; 'Certainly you will break the poor man's heart, and then you will have no more fine epistles from him.'[42]

Lack of money and the failure of Parliament to send him his promised recruits caused Sir William more distress than these skirmishes.[43] By Wednesday 16 April, when it had become apparent that the Royalists contemplated no major offensive from the West, Waller made ready to surrender his commission under the terms of the Self-Denying Ordinance. On that day a member of the Commons noted down in his journal the receipt of a letter from Waller at Salisbury, probably his last despatch as a commander. In it he related 'in how comfortless a condition he was left there, not having money to pay his soldiers which made them every to fall from him and to undervalue him, and not to obey him as their commander, which made him desirous rather to give his "yea" and "no" in the House of Commons than to remain amongst his troopers so slighted and dis-esteem'd by them.' Two of Waller's officers, Colonel FitzJames and Fincher accompanied the letter from him in order to make known to the Commons in what condition he was.[44]

The House referred to the Committee of Both Kingdoms and the Committee of the West about whether to send Waller reinforcements or to order his withdrawal to Kingsclere in Hampshire, where some regiments from the New Model Army could come to him. Apparently, the committees decided upon neither course, for in the third week of April, Waller's troops and companies at Salisbury began to disperse according to their several instructions, while Sir William himself rode to his parliamentary seat of Andover to settle some private affairs before going up to London.[45]

Five years later, when Sir William could view this last Western campaign in perspective, he saw it as a crowning example of the difficulties he had laboured under throughout the war. These he ascribed, not entirely with justice, to the machinations of those who had became known by the time he wrote as the Independents. Besides keeping him short of money, 'they would be sure I should never have an entire body of mine, but so compounded of city and country regiments that when they pleased they might take me in pieces like a clock.

'And this was the true reason why I could never improve any successes. Because these adventitious borrowed forces, having no dependence upon me but upon those that sent them, would not follow me further than pleased themselves, but would be ready to march home when they should have pursued their point, as if they had done enough when they had done any thing. Yet such were the charities which I met with in the world, that it was made my fault, that like Joash [in the Second Book of Kings] I gave over shooting sooner than I should have done; when, in truth, I had no more arrows left to shoot.

'From time to time I was put upon all disadvantages that might lessen me in my reputation and expose me to ruin. Witness, among other particulars, the hopeless employment into the West, as it was rightly styled by John Lilburne in one of his pamphlets, when I was commanded to march without delay to the relief of Taunton with a body of horse and a few dragoons and a vote for 3,000 foot (of which I never received the benefit of one man), and this against a complete formed army, far exceeding my strength, in a deep enclosed country, where it was known that every field was as good as a fortification and every lane as undisputable as a pass.'[46]

Laid Aside Like a Broken Vessel

The New Model Army consisted of eleven regiments of Horse, each of 600, a regiment of 1,000 dragoons and twelve foot regiments of 1,200 apiece. The foot regiments of Essex and Manchester provided 3,048 and, 3,578 soldiers respectively for the New Model, whereas only 600 men were selected from Waller's army.[1] These joined the New Model's Commander-in-Chief Sir Thomas Fairfax at Windsor as two regiments, Colonel Ralph Weldon's and Colonel James Holborne's, the former being an amalgamation of the Kentish Foot and the latter probably a mixture from all Waller's other remaining regiments of foot.[2] In the event, however, Holborne declined his designated commission; probably as a Scotsman, he disliked its promised religious temper. As his replacement Sir William selected his cousin, Sir Hardress Waller. Some of Waller's other infantry companies found employment in the south coast garrisons, while others followed the lead of Colonel Edward Harley's regiment and attached themselves to Major-General Edward Massey, now commander in the Western Association.[3]

By contrast, probably more troops of horse sought vacancies under Sir Thomas Fairfax than the new establishment could accommodate. The commissioners selected the regiments of Sir Michael Livesey[4] and Lieutenant-General John Middleton, but the Self-Denying Ordinance and a record of disobedience, if not cowardice, debarred the former colonel. As for Middleton, his Scottish Presbyterian faith seems to have dissuaded him from accepting the offered commission. No doubt at Waller's recommendation, his Adjutant-General of Horse, John Butler, was chosen to command the second regiment in place of Middleton, which again probably represented an amalgamation of the better troops in the army, including some troops of Lobsters.[5] The Kentish Horse were given to Cromwell's associate Henry Ireton, though he had no connection with that county.

Some of Waller's remaining cavalry stayed together and found employment in the Western campaign of summer 1645. The regiments of Colonels George Thompson[6] and Edward Cooke[7] with 600 Horse, inclined first towards Massey and then accompanied Fairfax to the relief of Taunton. Some of the county-sponsored regiments, however, had disintegrated before the year's end.[8] The train of artillery and Waller's Lifeguard lingered in Surrey for several months before being paid off.[9]

Many of the junior officers in Waller's army entered other regiments in the

New Model, but others were reduced in April.[10] On the 16th of that month, Colonel FitzJames and Quartermaster-General Fincher had also brought with them to the House of Commons a petition of some sixty officers in Waller's army who expected to be soon unemployed and sought the same terms as those under the commands of Essex and Manchester upon their reduction.[11] This figure, therefore, probably represents the number of officers actually ending any kind of military employment. The House duly voted that they should receive a fortnight's pay, but many months elapsed before either Waller's former officers or his soldiers saw even a part of the pay arrears owing to them for having, as Waller wrote, 'willingly exposed themselves to tedious marches and hard duties by day and night, both summer and winter'. As late as June 1647, for example, former soldiers in Waller's army joined with those of Essex and Massey and 'did bother the House and kept in the members till £10,000 was ordered to be distributed among them for arrears'.[12]

The reduction of Sir William Waller's army also closed a chapter in Lady Anne Waller's life. In September 1644 the Venetian ambassador reported some gossip which ascribed Sir William's failure to advance into the West to Lady Anne's presence at Farnham, 'the soldiers being indignant at marching under the command of his wife, who being zealous in religion, grown ambitious of the popular favour and predominant over her husband, has usurped the General's baton. To please them Parliament has recalled her . . .'[13] These words of the ambassador, a Royalist sympathiser, merely repeated the substance of many satirical attacks upon Lady Anne made by the Oxford newspaper *Mercurius Aulicus* throughout 1644, when 'no week can pass hardly without an unmannerly flirt and fling at her'.[14]

First, *Aulicus* accused Waller's 'Wonderful Lady' of preaching in public, a sectarian innovation which the Royalists detested. Yet in the August edition for the 33rd week the editor reported: 'Lady Waller sent a message to us (in earnest 'tis true) that we have hitherto spoken unrighteously of her, for as yet (she protests) she never preached, but says she knows not what we may drive her to.' Lady Anne assured her critic that she only interpreted some difficulties in the Word, 'which her Ladyship called "Undoing hard chapters" according to which phrase her husband's Army is quite expounded'.[15]

The week before *Aulicus* had reported that since Cropredy Bridge, Waller's army had shrunk from 10,000 to about 1,500, 'which makes Colonel Waller so little throng'd at Westminster that he needs not say (as his Lady did at Abingdon Church) – "Stand off, good people, that the soldiers may see me"'.[16] A fortnight later the newspaper described her as 'wondrous earnest for Master Henry Marten to be Governor of Reading'.[17] Therefore, it seems that Lady Anne wished to share in her husband's work as a general, and to employ such political influence which she might possess as his wife to forward the interests of her political friends.

Thirdly, *Aulicus* painted Lady Anne as a woman who dominated her husband throughout the war as 'she used to do at Winchester Church, where if he offered to speak about Doctrines or Uses, her Ladyship would rebuke him, saying, "Peace, Master Waller, you know your weakness in these things". Since which time Sir William has ever gone for the weaker vessel.'[18] Upon one occasion she thrice greeted her husband with: 'O thou man of God, come kiss me!'[19] On another occasion, the Royalist editor alleged, she pushed Sir William into going up to London to protest against Major-General Browne's usurpation of his authority in the Oxford area.[20]

To some extent *Mercurius Aulicus* simply maligned Lady Anne as a model or pattern of Puritan womanhood. The Parliamentarian broadsheets replied with the same ammunition: 'She is not like your court-madam, Aulicus; uses no oil of talk, no false teeth, no wanton frisking gait, no catter-wauling [loud plaintive noises like a cat – singing?] in Spring Garden. She bestows not all her time upon her body and leaves none for the soul. She cannot measure out a whole morning with curling irons, and spend the afternoon in courting and vanity, and toying in Hyde Park; but every morning her soul is made ready before her body. She looks not so much what clothes, as what virtues are convenient to wear.'[21]

More important, the Royalist ridicule of Lady Anne served to explain to a wide circle of readers why such a noble gentleman as Sir William Waller should be found among the ranks of the King's enemies.[22] Also by caricaturing him as a henpecked husband, *Mercurius Aulicus* no doubt hoped to lessen the respect in which the Royalists clearly held him as a general, especially in the first year of the war. Although not too much weight must be placed upon propaganda of this nature it must be admitted that these anecdotes do not bear the marks of complete fabrication, only of the truth writ somewhat large.

Perhaps above all Sir William valued his wife's strength in adversity, and it is likely that he turned to her once more in the spring of 1645. As a sensitive and honourable man he could not but feel some slight at the fact of his dismissal. With the passage of years, when the wound had healed into a scar, a badge of his devotion to Parliament, he could interpret (and therefore accept) the event as yet another example of a divine admonition: 'It was just with God to lay me by [from] all employment, as a broken vessel, in regard of the corruption of my heart in my first engagement, and neglect of reformation in the officers and soldiery under me.'[23]

By his 'corruption of heart' Waller probably meant personal ambition, and by that 'neglect of reformation' of his soldiers no more than what any Puritan gentleman of the day would have said about his sons or household servants. Such explanations in terms of God's rods and afflictions, however, did not prevent Waller from sifting out the critical factors in his military career. He defined the real problem in his *Vindication*: 'I could never improve upon any successes.'

The reasons for this impotence, as he had several times pointed out to Parliament, boiled down to the nature of the army at his command, together with Parliament's neglect of its recurring needs for money, recruits and weapons. 'Possibly I might have made more bricks,' he concluded, 'if I had more straw.'

Moreover, at this level of analysis, Waller accepted the role that chance or luck plays in war. His reputation for 'unfortunateness' after Roundway Down had some grounds. 'If at any time I miscarried in my attempt (as who may not? the dice being nowhere so uncertain as in the field),' he wrote, 'it was *operosa infaelicitas* unto me.' Sometimes, he admitted, in his eagerness for victory, he had overreached himself. 'I strained myself in missing my aim, and my failing was my punishment'.[24]

'After I had quitted the service of the Parliament in the field, and was returned to London and there settled with my family, my estate began to fall short, part thereof lying in the King's quarters; and the rest (through the distraction of the times) affording me very little sustenance. To supply my necessities, I was fain to sell several things; and in the end I was at such a pinch, as that without selling my plate (which I had kept as my last reserve of value) I knew not how to send to market.

'Whereupon my wife and I have recommended our condition to God, resolved the next morning to send our plate to the goldsmiths and to make money of it. But the next morning I was wakened by my servants, who let me know there was one come from Barnstaple with some money for me. The sum was not above fifteen pounds, but that served my present occasions, and before that was spent I received a further relief, so as I was put to no more such exigencies.'[25]

As a general in command of an army, Waller should have received £10 a day, the same pay as the Earl of Essex (a Major-General under Essex was paid £2 a day).[26] On one occasion his 'vanity in furniture' got the better of him and he exchanged part of his arrears for £300 worth of 'goods and household stuffs' sequestered from the royal palaces.[27] 'A considerable part of mine arrears amounting to above £1,000, I freely remitted (upon the passing of my account) when the House of Commons would have allowed it; and a remaining part of it (to the sum of £800), I was glad to compound for, at 12 shillings in the pound, when I was a prisoner at St James.'[28]

Heselrige's attempt in 1644 to secure for Sir William the office of Master of the King's Bench suggests that he endured some financial hardship before the close of the war.[29] He estimated his losses during it at over £30,000 – over a million pounds in modern money – and denied that 'what I lost in the hundred, I got in the shire'.[30] In donatives, salvage money, gifts and plate he received no more than about £1,000.

Moreover, 'I was necessitated to live above mine own condition, that I might not live below that quality which the favour of the Parliament had put upon me, so that what I received I spent, and much I spent before I received it.'[31] As a commander-in-chief, for example, Waller had to dispense considerable hospitality to his officers. Heselrige, who received £5 a day as commander of Waller's Horse, subsequently claimed a large sum of arrears, but (according to his enemy, Holles) 'had been at no charge, having lived still upon Sir William Waller'.[32] Although Waller attended the Committee of Both Kingdoms assiduously for the remainder of 1645,[33] and served on the Hampshire Committee – he witnessed the capture of his home Winchester Castle in October 1645[34] – these labours carried no remuneration, and in the autumn he sought to pursue his late vocation as a soldier in order to restore his fortunes.

On 24 October 1645 the Venetian ambassador in Paris reported to the Doge that he had received from the secretary of the Committee of Both Kingdoms a proposal by which an unnamed officer offered to enter the service of the Republic of Venice with 4,000 men and 20 or 25 ships. 'He feels sure that Parliament will give him leave at the least hint,' added the ambassador. Eventually the secretary named the officer as Sir William Waller, requesting 'that if the affair comes to nothing it may be forgotten and buried'.

Professing that his purpose was not pecuniary but founded upon piety and honour, and that he intended to live and die with Venice in this cause, Waller proposed 'a powerful diversion possibly at several points' on the coast of Turkish-occupied Candia, to be mounted by a mercenary fleet operating out of a strong base harbour – Cephalonia, Cursola or Liesina. For himself, Waller asked a commission as general of this fleet and forces, and also as commander over all other English and Scots in the Republic's service, by land or sea.[35] It was a remarkably self-confident and bold proposal for one who publicly eschewed any desire for self-advancement or any further military ambition.

Nothing, however, came of this scheme, partly because the Venetians realised that Waller's permit to travel abroad would be subject to countless delays, if not revocation, and partly perhaps because his financial prospects at home had improved. For in December 1645, as part of some proposals offered to the King, the Commons recommended that Sir William Waller should be made a baron with an annuity of £2,500.[36] 'I was puffed up with a presumption that I should never be moved,' he wrote, 'whereupon God most justly, within a few months after, sent those several chastisements upon me: banishment, imprisonment, sickness, the death of my wife, poverty.'[37]

PART SIX

Triumph of a Moderate

The Road to Exile

Although the great Parliamentarian victory at Naseby (14 June 1645) shattered the King's main field army, not until August of the following year did the New Model snuff out the last embers of Royalist resistance. Then Sir William and his family, in company with many others, could enjoy a brief season,

> When gardens only had their towers,
> And all the garrisons were flowers;
> When roses only arms might bear,
> And men did rosy garlands wear.

The author of these lines, Andrew Marvell, was tutor at the time to Sir Thomas Fairfax's children at Nunappleton House in Yorkshire, and may well have inspected there the regiments of blue, white, red and yellow-coat flowers with the general, as they walked and conversed up and down the broad paths of the garden.

The Earl of Essex, however, did not long outlive the return of the flowers. While hunting stag in September 1647 he felt unwell, and then a few days later he suffered a fatal stroke. In the next month Parliament gave him an impressive state funeral. In the long military procession that followed the draped coffin on a gun-carriage, Waller did not ride with those officers who had served under the Earl's immediate command; instead, he marched alone behind the first three regiments of foot drawn from the New Model Army, trailing a pike.[1]

Thus Waller escorted to the grave the former Lord General who had eventually incurred the displeasure of the majority in the House of Commons and accepted the consequences. But the victorious New Model Army, who marched that day with muffled drum and furled colours would not go so easily to the graveyards designated by its paymasters in Parliament.

In the spring of 1647 Parliament voted to reduce the New Model Army from some 14,000 soldiers to one less than half that size, mainly Horse and dragoons. Out of the supernumeraries, seven regiments of foot, four of horse and one of dragoons would be chosen for service in Ireland – still in the throes of rebellion – while the remainder were to receive two months' pay on disbandment.[2] The House referred to the Committee for Affairs of Ireland, which met at Derby House, the task of selecting the forces assigned to that country and not unnaturally the committee relied heavily in this matter upon one of its leading members, Sir William Waller.

On 1 April a member of the Commons would even propose Waller as Commander-in-Chief for Ireland, but it was not put to the vote, doubtless because Waller declined the nomination. Next day Waller nominated Skippon for the post, and the House of Commons duly voted in favour of him.[3] According to Clarendon, Cromwell was among those who opposed Waller's appointment. Apparently, Waller had been sounded out for the Irish command as early as December 1645. In a letter to Sir Hardress Waller (22 December 1645), Sir Philip Percival reported a conversation with Sir William, who said that he 'had so much discouragement when he was near at hand that he cannot think of being engaged again . . . though he wishes the cause as well as any'.[4]

By this time it was clear that raising a new army, phoenix-like from the ashes of the New Model Army, was not going to be an easy matter. In March the Irish Committee had selected Sir William to lead a small deputation to the Army's headquarters in order to present their proposals for enlisting the new regiments for Ireland.

Accompanied by Sir John Clotworthy, Waller arrived at Saffron Walden on 20 March. 'That evening we made application to the General [Sir Thomas Fairfax],' wrote Waller, 'and communicated our business unto him, whereupon immediately he gave order for a convention of the officers the next day. In the mean time, according to the latitude given to us by the committee, we took occasion to sound the affections of those officers and gentlemen that did us the honour to visit us, how they stood inclined to the service of Ireland, declaring unto them what terms the Parliament offer'd that employment.' Some of their visitors showed themselves willing to engage, but very many either would not commit themselves or proposed 'difficulties and unreasonable demands'.[5]

Next day Waller and Clotworthy delivered their message to a general assembly of officers and withdrew while they discussed it. Eventually the officers answered 'that they were not, for the present, in a capacity to give their positive resolution whether they would engage for Ireland or no, until it were declared. First, what particular regiments, troops, or companies of the army were to be continued in the service of this country. Secondly, under whose conduct, or command-in-chief, they should go, that did engage for Ireland. Thirdly, what assurance they should have of pay and subsistence during their employment there. And, fourthly, that they might have satisfaction in point of arrears and indemnity for their past service in England.'[6]

Dissatisfied with 'this way of answering propositions with propositions' Waller, Clotworthy and another Member of Parliament, Richard Salway, who had joined them that day, asked Fairfax to summon a second convention on the next day, which he agreed to do. But at this meeting the officers adhered to their former resolutions.[7] As the Derby House commissioners would not accept the convention's four conditions, the matter had reached a stalemate.

'That evening,' wrote Waller, 'we had information given us from very good hands that there was a petition of dangerous consequence pretended to come from the soldiers, but framed and minted by some of the principal officers, which that afternoon had been tendered to the convention (in the General's own house, where he quartered) . . . and that it was there pressed with so much passion, that an officer of quality and eminent merit (by name Quartermaster-General [Richard] Fincher) offering his sense against it, was reproach'd by Colonel [Nathaniel] Rich, as a person not deserving to live in the army.' But Fairfax flatly denied to them the existence of such a petition or that he would ever allow such a document to pass through his hands. With this assurance the delegation returned to London.

Waller's visit to Saffron Walden put in motion a long train of events. The Army's petition, embodying the four points made on 21 March, duly arrived in London. Parliament's reaction was to pass a declaration recording its 'high dislike' of the men's actions, and warning them that unless they desisted they would be 'looked upon and proceeded against as enemies of the state'. Bold words, but in the circumstances it was a somewhat empty threat. Parliament now became aware of the divisions in the Army between those who supported the petition, headed by a coterie of officers which included Lieutenant-General Thomas Hammond, Commissary-General Henry Ireton, Colonel John Lilburne and Lieutenant-Colonel Thomas Pride, and those who dissented from it and expressed immediate readiness for service in Ireland. Many of those who signed the declaration in favour of Ireland without further delay or debate, had held commissions in Waller's army. His old Adjutant-General of Horse, for example, who had signed an affectionate letter to him after the capture of Bristol in 1645 'your corpulent servant for ever, John Butler', now sided with Fincher in opposition to the more militant and intransigent party.[8]

In his report to the House of Commons, Waller gave a full account of the proceedings at Saffron Walden, 'sticking the guilt of the whole design upon the person of Commissary-General Ireton and the rest of the above named officers'.

About an hour later, Henry Ireton strode into the chamber, took his seat in the House and, by general request, Waller repeated his speech. Ireton then stood up and coolly described the charge as 'a pure fiction'. 'Not knowing whom to believe the House continued in a great suspense until . . . there came a letter to Colonel [Sir Edward] Rossiter from his major out of Lincolnshire,' wrote Waller, 'signifying that a petition had been sent to him from the headquarters, to be subscribed by the regiment with directions that he should send the returns to Commissary-General Ireton and the rest of the officers formerly named by me.'

Ireton then brazenly admitted the existence of the petition, but claimed that he had only given countenance to it in order to prevent a worse issue from 'the great inflammation in the army'. Thoroughly aroused, the House voted for the suppression of the petition and late that night, when the potential dissenters had retired to bed, passed a strongly worded declaration against all those who had supported it.[9]

The majority in House of Commons now attempted to force through its programme for the New Model Army, making certain concessions to humour the soldiers. Yet these conciliatory measures did not include the crux of the matter: the settlement of the Army's arrears of pay, not less than eighteen weeks for the horse and forty-six weeks for the foot. Waller did not condone this gross oversight, which he regarded as an injustice. 'The ordinance of indemnity, the votes in favour of the apprentices, for provision of maimed soldiers, widows and orphans, for exemption from press, had everyone of them my concurrence. And for the payment of arrears, I may say I was for it to the uttermost farthing. . . . And, truly, herein I did but discharge my conscience. For I was ever of the opinion that a soldier's pay is the justest debt in the world.'

This failure of the House of Commons to vote sufficient money for arrears, however, did not justify in Waller's mind the subsequent disobedience of the Army, nor make him falter in his own allegiance. Perhaps he was being rather unrealistic in this respect. Be that as it may, he set out once more to Saffron Walden with the Earl of Warwick, Lord Dacres, Clotworthy and Massey to proceed with the enlistment of officers and men for Ireland. Here, on 14 April, they discovered a new and intractable spirit in the Army. There was a vehement opposition to the Irish service on Parliament's terms in the Army, together with a growing discontent in the rank-and-file of the regiments directed against Parliament itself. In spite of pressure from Waller and his colleagues, Fairfax refused to issue a proclamation against those who opposed enlistment for Ireland. In reply to the Earl of Warwick's speech at yet another convention of officers, Colonel John Lambert merely reiterated the four conditions of 21 March amid shouts of 'All! All!' from most of those in the room. As, given their terms of reference, nothing more could be achieved by the Parliamentary deputation at Saffron Walden, they returned to London and made their report to the Committee for Ireland at Derby House. As a snub to the Army, the committee continued its efforts to secure volunteers, helped by the fact that on 27 April the Lords voted the Army six weeks' arrears of pay. 'By the end of April,' wrote Waller, 'divers of the officers relating to 10 troops of horse and 50 companies of foot were drawn to declare their resolution to engage in the Irish service.'

Throughout May the Army maintained its posture of defiance to the wishes of Parliament, and a majority of the soldiers, stirred up by the 'Agitators' or 'agents' they elected, successfully intimidated those who had already signed for Ireland. Feelings ran high, and Fairfax now found himself squeezed between the incompatible demands of his soldiers and Parliament. On 25 May Parliament announced that the disbandment would begin on 7 June, although it now offered the men eight weeks of arrears. Only with difficulty could Fairfax maintain his authority over the Army.

On 4 June Cornet George Joyce seized the King at Holmby House and brought him under the wing of the Army at Newmarket. An officer and a man from each regiment were now elected to form a General Council of the Army, together with its general officers. Thereafter the Army brushed aside some late conciliatory measures from Westminster and directly challenged the authority and the very existence of this present Parliament, framing a Declaration (14 June) at St Albans on its march towards London which called for the expulsion of delinquent, corrupt or unfairly elected members from the Commons, immediate progress towards a final settlement, and a date for its dissolution. Parliament sent a month's pay in cash to St Albans, but to no avail. Hard on the heels of this document came the Army's demand for the expulsion of eleven Members of Parliament, the leaders of the Presbyterian party who had been foremost in making plans for resistance, among them Sir William Waller.[10]

Parliament asked the eleven accused members to withdraw, and then it entered into new negotiations with the Army at High Wycombe on 1 July, which brought a temporary respite. But the crisis was not over. Under the sway of Cromwell and Ireton, the General Council of the Army now sent up to London its own programme for a settlement in the Kingdom. Meanwhile, the City broke ranks with Parliament and voted to bring the King back to London and negotiate with him for a compromise settlement based on a three-year introduction of the Presbyterian system – a somewhat unrealistic idea in the circumstances. Tumultuous rioting broke out for five days. On 26 July a mob of City apprentices entered both Houses vociferously protesting at Parliament's apparent weakness in stooping to appease the Army. Using this as an excuse, those more radical members, the Independents, who supported the Army – the Speaker, eight peers and fifty-seven members of the Commons – took refuge with Fairfax for their own security, not unlike those of both Houses who had fled to join King Charles at the start of the Civil War. The remnant of Parliament summoned back the eleven excluded members. They also prepared to defend themselves against the Army, with Edward Massey in command of London's ring of fortifications.

For in late May, foreseeing the probability of conflict with the New Model Army, Parliament had resurrected the Committee of Safety and charged it with raising an army for self-defence. Much of this work had devolved upon its experienced former generals, Waller, Browne and Massey. The support of the City of London was a critical factor, however, because the City could provide no less than eighteen regiments of foot, ranging in strength from 800 to 2,000 men. In addition, Waller estimated that Parliament might have up to 5,000 Horse, composed of 'reformado officers and gentlemen of quality'.[11] Thus Parliament might well field an army which compared favourably with the New Model Army, at least in numbers. With considerable energy Waller set about listing those reformadoes into regiments of horse and dragoons, doubtless planning to lead them out to harry the flanks of the New Model if it assaulted the City militia as they manned the fortifications around the capital.[12] Outside London the main rendezvous for Parliament's 'new army' was at Worcester.

In his *Vindication* Waller denied the charge that he had promoted that week of riots by the London apprentices. He explained what had really happened. 'It pleased the House of Commons to command my service, in taking care for the drawing up for the Ordinance in favour of the apprentices touching their times to be allowed for recreation. Upon which account some apprentices (who negotiated that business for the rest) made their application to me. Shortly after, when that petition from the City was to be presented, which was followed with so much disorder that it gave occasion or pretence to the Speaker and divers others of the House to withdraw to the army . . . there came two persons to my house in Drury Lane to speak with me, who, when I came out unto them, told me they were apprentices of the City, and came to be advised by me how they should manage their petition. To whom I replied that I knew no advice to be given but that they should be careful to attend the House as early as they could before they were pre-engaged in other business.

'But this did not serve their turn, who came only to ensnare me. Whereupon they moved further, and said that myself and the other impeached gentlemen were concerned in their petition, and that they must and would have us into the House again. To which I returned no more, but that I should have no more to do in that business, and so I left them. This was all that passed, and yet those false impudent creatures made their report at the Army, that I abetted that disorder and assault upon the House, and co-operated with the apprentices in it, which served to exasperate the Army so much the more against me.'[13]

Only cold feet in the City and in Southwark prevented Parliament from meeting force with force. Fairfax advanced down to Hounslow Heath in Middlesex, where on 3 August he impressed a City delegation with a muster of 20,000 Horse, Foot and dragoons, all well-equipped and maintaining perfect discipline. 'When the Army first marched up to the City of London and made that breach upon the Parliament, I was voted to command a body of horse and dragoons in the nature of a flying army, for the defence of the King, Kingdom, Parliament and City,' wrote Waller. 'And whilst I was acting (with others) according to my duty at the Committee of the Militia sitting at Guildhall to advance that levy we were all unexpectedly deserted and betrayed by the City and left out of all capitulation. So that, upon the entering of the Army [on 6 August], we were enforced to lie hid, and within a few days after to make use of the passes which the House of Commons had formerly given us and quit the Kingdom. The Lord all that time preserved me from falling into the hands of the Army, though I was pursued by land and sea.'[14]

Accompanied by an informal lifeguard of some fifteen or sixteen mounted men, Denzil Holles, Sir William Lewis, Sir Philip Stapleton, Sir John Clotworthy, Walter Long and Waller left London on 12 August and rode hard towards the Essex coast, narrowly escaping capture on the road.[15] Embarking on a ship moored in a private creek, they set sail beneath lowering grey skies. Soon the storm broke with a sudden gust of wind which would have overturned the vessel, as Waller related, if 'the rope that fastened the main sail had not slipped, whereby the sail flying loose, the wind had no more power upon it'.[16] Just outside the haven of Calais harbour, an English warship caught up with them and escorted the ship back to the Downs. But, mercifully for the accused Members of Parliament, a council of war held aboard Vice-Admiral William Batten's flagship discharged them, and they made a safe journey back to Calais.[17] Batten was subsequently placed under the command of the rigorous and humourless Colonel Thomas Rainsborough, an imposition much resented by the sailors who had already lost (through the Self-Denying Ordinance) their popular admiral, the Earl of Warwick.

Here, Sir Philip Stapleton succumbed to the plague. At a considerable personal risk Sir William visited the sick man and, as he said, 'was with him and had him by the hand not above five or six hours before he departed'.[18] Waller then sailed on to Flushing, again not without incident. 'I was very like to have been a cast away, upon the quick sands, called the Pert Maerts near Sluys, where the ship struck fifteen or sixteen times, but never stuck.'[19]

Waller reached Holland with no more than £46 at his disposal. Shortly afterwards, Lady Anne, who had been staying at Herstmonceux Castle during August with the children, together with their household of one gentlewoman, a nurse, four maids and six men servants,[20] now joined him in exile. She brought with her a sum of £500, and Waller also soon began to receive rents from his estates. About two months earlier, doubtless as a contingency measure, he had taken the wise precaution of sending some of his furniture and household effects across to Rotterdam, and, surrounded by these possessions, Sir William and his wife settled down to a quiet life in Holland, initially in Leyden.

Later Sir William and his family moved to The Hague, where he paid his respects to that 'queen of women, the Queen of Bohemia'. He also exchanged civilities with some of the Royalist exiles; they are not named, but it would have been surprising if they did not include his old friend Lord Ralph Hopton. It is pleasing to think that they may perhaps have refought their battles after a good dinner, before turning to the events of the day. These meetings, however, did give rise to the kind of rumours that Waller had foreseen in his famous letter to Hopton in June 1643: 'I know the conference could never be so close between us, but that it would take wind and receive a construction to my dishonour.' In this instance, it was widely noised in England that Waller had now accepted a commission from the Prince of Wales.

Meanwhile, in England the King made his escape from the Army (November 1647), only to become a prisoner at Carisbrooke Castle, Isle of Wight, but at least out of the immediate grasp of both Parliament and Army. His devious dealings with Parliament, including double-crossing them by entering into a secret arrangement with the Scots, brought about the series of scattered uprisings known as the Second Civil War in the following year. Waller found it necessary later to deny that he knew anything about one of the trouble spots, a mutiny that swept through the ships in Parliament's navy (May 1648) as they lay at anchor in the Downs, 'till it was common news and matter of discourse in every barber's shop in the Hague', or that he visited the rebellious ships of fleet when they dropped anchor at Sluys, only a few hours distance from The Hague. There they had taken on board the Prince of Wales as their admiral, and sailed for England in mid-July, accompanied by four Dutch warships, to support the Royalist uprisings in England. But soon afterwards Vice-Admiral Batten defected back to Parliament, with the *Constant Warwick*, though he had been knighted by the Prince. Eventually, all except five ships, followed Batten's example.

While acknowledging his love for the Scots as a nation, Waller felt they had deserved the defeat inflicted upon their army by Cromwell at the battle of Preston (17 August 1648). Moreover, he declared, as a patriot he could never have supported the Scots against his own country. 'For myself I would have it known that I am an Englishman and the son of an Englishman, and no consideration shall ever make me forfeit that interest.'[21]

While Cromwell lingered in the North, the Presbyterian majority in the House of Commons decided to reopen negotiations with the King. In

September they sent commissioners to meet him at Newport on the Isle of Wight. Although Charles prevaricated for over two months, at last he agreed to the establishment of the Presbyterian system of church government for three years, but he would not countenance the abolition of the Church of England's bishops.

The changed political situation was such that Sir William judged it safe to abandon his exile. In June, the House of Commons had revoked the order disabling him from membership, and by the middle of August – a year after his flight abroad – he was back in London.[22] But impatience had overruled caution. Waller had returned home too soon.

CHAPTER THIRTY

Three Years in Captivity

Once back in London in the summer of 1648, Sir William Waller resumed his seat in the House of Commons, and he now took his part in the autumn's debates on how to best resolve the outstanding issues between Parliament and King. The unwillingness of either party to surrender ground had led to a breakdown in their negotiations (27 October). Meanwhile Fairfax and the Council of Officers sent their own terms direct to the King, which the latter rejected (18 November). The Army now fell back on the radical *Remonstrance* emanating from Henry Ireton and the Levellers, which called for the King to be brought to justice and the monarchy abolished. On 30 November Fairfax reoccupied London, having given orders for the King to be brought onto the mainland under strict guard. Some of the leading Presbyterian Members of Parliament now fled, but Fairfax's idea of establishing a caucus of Independent members as a provisional government was rejected by the House. On 5 December, after an unprecedented all-night sitting, Waller voted with the majority that the King's removal to Hurst Castle in Hampshire was illegal. He also voted to reopen negotiations, giving his yea to the motion 'that the answers of the King to the propositions of both Houses are a ground for the House to proceed upon for the settlement of the peace of the Kingdom'. It was carried by 129 to 83 votes.[1]

Retribution from the Army came swiftly: next day musketeers from the regiments of Colonel Pride and Colonel Sir Hardress Waller turned away 186 members from the doors of the House and arrested 41 others, including Sir William. A further 86 subsequently stayed away in protest, leaving a 'Rump' of 154 members. 'Seized upon by the Army as I was going to discharge my duty in the House of Commons and, contrary to privilege of Parliament, made a prisoner in the Queen's court,' Waller wrote of his experience. 'From thence led ignominiously to a place under the Exchequer called Hell, and the next day to the King's Head Inn in the Strand. After[wards] singled out (as a sheep to the slaughter) and removed to St James.'[2] This fate he shared with Clotworthy, Massey and other moderate or Presbyterian leaders. Before accompanying the soldiers to his new prison, Waller presented them with a paper protesting against this 'high violation of the rights and privileges of Parliament and of the fundamental laws of the land'.[3]

Waller remained a captive in St James's Palace from 12 December 1648 until 27 July 1650. Then the Council of State ordered his removal to Windsor Castle.[4] While he was still in London, he may have witnessed the daily departures of his fellow prisoner in St James's Palace, King Charles, to stand trial in Westminster Hall during the third week in January 1649. On the 26th Charles was sentenced to death, and on the morning of the 30th he walked with his guard across the park to the Banqueting House in Whitehall and from thence to the scaffold outside, where he faced execution with dignity and composure.

During his eighteen months of imprisonment in London, Waller received good treatment from his guards. Yet one former subordinate tried to trick him. 'I had a message sent me from one Colonel FitzJames [a colonel of horse in Waller's army in 1644] with the signification of his respect to me and compassion of me, representing the extreme danger in which I was and the inevitable destruction that attended me if I did not endeavour to prevent it by some escape. In order to that, he made me a tender of his assistance, engaging himself that he would set me safe aboard a ship that lay ready in the river for me to transport me beyond the reach of all mine enemies. But it pleased God to prevent the effect of his treachery, both by giving me confidence to stand upon mine own innocency and by discovering . . . that that perfidious man (in the midst of all his protestations of friendship to me) had privately offered himself to give evidence against me at the bar of the House of Commons. So that it was a mere train, laid to bring a guiltiness upon me, and to take away my life.'[5] During her husband's confinement in Windsor Castle, Lady Anne had the good sense to turn down a similar offer from one Captain Kempe of Colonel Pride's regiment.

Waller needed to be constantly vigilant, for such former subordinates as FitzJames could not be trusted. As he narrates, Waller had a similar experience in his new prison. 'Shortly after my coming to Windsor Castle, having opportunity to send to my dear wife the Lady Anne (whom I had left in a disconsolate condition at London great with child and within a few weeks of her delivery) as I had sealed my letter and was ready to despatch it away, I had notice given me by the soldier that attended me, that the Governor [Colonel Christopher Whichcott] must see whatever letters I wrote or received.

'Whereupon I bade him carry it unto him that he might open it if he thought fit. But the Governor returned it back unto me again untouched with this compliment: that I was very much mistaken in him if I thought he would be so unworthy as to open letters between a man and his wife, and with some other further expressions of respect to me in regard he had formerly served as a Lieutenant-Colonel under me [probably in the Green Auxiliaries during the autumn of 1643].

'This I took as a civility from him, but I found it after to be no other than a mere insidious practice. For after an uninterrupted passage of letters between my wife and me for about a fortnight or three weeks, by which time he supposed we might be grown to a confidence to write freely, he suddenly seized upon all my letters. But by the Providence of God there was nothing to be found in them that could prejudice me, and so that train took no effect.'

One of Waller's letters from Windsor Castle has survived. It was in reply to a brief note, dated 11 May 1649, accompanying a gift. Old Sir Robert Harley, whose eldest son, Edward, also languished in prison, had written to Sir William: 'It is a duty which these sad days call for, that we should help to less one another's burden, especially when we can say we suffer not as evil doers.'

Waller replied on 21 June with a characteristically humorous and yet noble letter: 'I am ashamed to think how backward I have been to acknowledge your kind remembrance of me and must beg your pardon for it. I really intended to have written to you again, by the next opportunity, but to tell the truth and shame the devil, I forgot it, and in that forgot myself. All the charity I beg from you is, that you will be assured, however my memory may be false, my heart is and shall be true to you. I see by your enclosed, you are in very good company when you are alone. I wish I may edify by the good example. It is the chemistry of a true Christian to extract good spirits out of the evils of this world. The Lord sanctify his hand to us all, and teach us to learn righteousness out of his judgements. I desire these lines may present the tender of my most affectionate service to your self and your noble sons.'[6]

After a second spell in St James's Waller wrote of himself as 'tossed like a ball into a strange country, to Denbigh Castle in North Wales, remote from all my relations and interests'.[7] Apparently some 'designs on Windsor' led to this change of prison. Between St Albans and Towcester his coach swayed dangerously over a narrow bridge above a deep river but Sir William safely reached his Welsh prison upon an April day in 1651.[8]

'And here let me call to mind how much reason I had to be thankful to him who chastens those whom he loves for the great consolation experienced in the dear partner of my captivity,' wrote Waller in appreciation of his wife Lady Anne. 'She came to me disguised in mean apparel when I had groaned in my bonds seven months, thinking it the duty of a wife to risk all things for the satisfaction of her husband. Much difficulty had she in coming and was frequent on the brink of being discovered, but at length over mountains and unknown roads, sometimes with a guide and sometimes with none, she arrived at my prison. And she seemed when she discovered herself to me to be like the angel who appeared unto Peter in like circumstances. She did not indeed bid my prison gates fly open, but by her sweet converse and behaviour she made those things seem light which were before heavy and scarce to be borne.'[9]

Lady Anne certainly restored her husband's spirits. On 1 September 1651, after thirty-two months of imprisonment, he wrote cheerfully to Colonel Edward Harley in London: 'I know not into whose hands these presents may come, but if any be so impertinent to open them, I would have them know from the highest to the lowest, from cat to bobtail, that I am, Sir, your most affectionate ever faithful friend, William Waller.'[10]

In at least one respect, however, Sir William found his Welsh prison irksome. For some reason the Governor, Colonel George Twistleton, would not allow him to attend the public divine service on Sunday. 'My not attending unto, nor improving by sermons, when it pleased the Lord to come under my roof and to visit me by his ministers at St James's, was justly punished at Denbigh by a restraint from all ordinances.'[11]

During his imprisonment Sir William wrote his *Vindication*, defending himself against the charges 'that from the time I quitted my employment in the field I took leave of my first principles and deserted the godly party, siding with those who had the pestilent tokens of malignancy upon them. That I carried myself as an enemy to the Army, Parliament and Kingdom, by endeavouring to break the Army, to force the Parliament and to kindle a new flame of war in the Kingdom. That upon the failing of these designs I withdrew beyond sea, transporting great sums of money; and that during my abode in Holland I took a commission from the Prince of Wales, and was interested in the revolt of the ships and in the drawing of the Scottish army into England.'[12]

Waller appended to the historical sections examining and refuting these slanders a short exposition of his thoughts upon both the institutions of Church and Monarchy. As for the Church, he abominated its disunity due to the 'promiscuous toleration of all sects'. These divisions formed 'the principal cause of atheism in this our age, wherein men of corrupt minds, taking offence at the discordant and cross opinions that are among us, do grow to a contempt of all religion'. But Sir William admitted that variety could exist in one Church and therefore (echoing his mother-in-law Lady Lucy Reynell's sentiments) thought it 'necessary to have a fit distinction held between those whose tenets are destructive to the fundamentals, the essentials of religion . . . and those who differ from us only in circumstances and deduced points'. To the former Sir William would allow no place; to the latter 'much tenderness and condescensions'.

The observance of this distinction between fundamentals and circumstantials, perhaps the most hopeful development in the Puritan theological thinking of the day, would indeed bestow 'the Christian liberty of the primitive times', but Sir William disliked those who used their freedom to become lax in the outward forms of worship. 'I could wish that in declining those ceremonies and rites which carry an appearance of superstition and vanity men would not run into a contrary extreme irreverence, neglect and profaneness. . . . God delights to be served in a sober but yet orderly and comely way; and as he is not taken with pomp and ostentation, so he abhors sordidness and sluttery in his church as well as in his camp. No Christian church in the world is, or can be, without the use of some ceremonies. . . . For my own part I am not, nor never was, against a modest dress of religion, but I like not affected decorations.'

In his conclusion on Church order, Waller suggested that the Westminster Assembly, still then sitting to determine the shape of the national Church, 'might be enlarged to [become] a general synod of all the reformed churches, with admission of a fit number of divines of all parties . . . for if none but those of the predominant parties govern it they will make it but the second part of the Council of Trent'. He entertained little hope, however, that his suggestion would ever be heeded, and nor was it.

He now turned to the institution of Monarchy. Here the position was plain. 'I hold myself obliged to the laws of the land, the oath of allegiance and the Covenant (as by a threefold cord), to the preservation of monarchy, with all the just rights and prerogatives thereunto belonging.' Sir William appealed to biblical and classical examples to prove the venerability of the institution and to give authority to his views. Yet he knew the limits of such arguments. 'These are ancient things; and the remaining memory of them appears unto us no otherwise then like a crack'd mouldred picture, whereof we may discern here and there some decayed lineaments and touches, but cannot possibly make out the full and entire proportion.' Nevertheless, Sir William probably enjoyed the mental exercise of marshalling these 'philogies and fancies' drawn from his favourite authors to support his case. It is not difficult to picture him in his room at Denbigh Castle, his brown hair thinner now and his figure rather more solid than the soldier of Lansdown and Cheriton, poring over the dark leather volumes and discussing their contents with a gentle-tempered Lady Anne in their 'sweet converse'.

Cromwell's various experiments in the period following the execution of the King in January 1649, when he sought to clothe the power of the sword in some constitutional dress, provided ample evidence for Waller's assertion that 'the Commons and the Lords have their respective operations, but without the influence of a king upon both there would be nothing but confusions and exorbitancies'. He advocated a re-establishment of what would later be called a constitutional monarchy, circumscribed by good laws. 'In plain terms, my heart's desire is to have that government restored again, by King, Lords and Commons, under which we and our forefathers for many ages have happily flourished.' He was deeply shocked by the King's execution, and prayed for the safety of his son during the campaign which ended so disastrously for the Royalists at the battle of Worcester on 3 September 1651.

As for the rule of the Rump in 'a confusion called a Commonwealth', Waller looked upon it 'as a mere usurpation and tyranny; upon their votes and orders as null and void; and upon all they have acted, as treason in the highest degree' – brave words for a political prisoner. He summed up his thoughts by declaring: 'I was born under a monarchy, and I desire to die under it.' His wish would be granted, for he lived to see the triumph of the moderation in politics and religion that he exemplified.

In a moving passage, Sir William professed again his love for Parliament. 'My affection to the Parliament (that is the Public) was no morning dew. Though the sun has look'd upon me and scorched me to a degree of blackness, though I have suffered many ways in my estate, in my liberty, in my reputation, yet nothing has been of force to exhale that. They write of Creon, in the tragedy, that he hugg'd his beloved daughter in his arms in the midst of the fire and would not quit his hold, but when he could not help her, willingly perished with her. I have embraced the Parliament cause in the hottest flames of the war, and by the grace of God, so long as I can retain my soul within my teeth, I will never desert it. And if I can do it no further, I shall contentedly mingle my ashes with it.'

Not for the first or the last time, physical captivity gave a man insight into the nature of true liberty and bondage, and Sir William closed the *Vindication* with some sentences which reveal an unfolding of his spiritual and reflective powers: 'I am both a prison and a prisoner to myself. The world is but a common gaol. A prison wherein those that have greatest power and authority have greatest bonds upon them, and are greater prisoners than those whom they imprison. . . . In the straitest confinement that can be put upon me, it is the refreshing of my soul that I can walk with God and have my conversation in heaven. I may be shut up, but God cannot be shut out.'

On 2 January 1652 the Council of State ordered the Governor of Denbigh to send Sir William to London, as he had petitioned for liberty. The Committee of Examinations also received direction to interrogate Waller and make a report. Consequently, Cromwell's soldiers brought Waller back to his old lodging in St James's Palace, now employed as a prison.

Lady Anne had died during that cold winter in North Wales, leaving Sir William once more a widower. 'When after the death of my late dear wife I had sent out my sons to school, and removed my daughters with some part of my goods to the Lady Blanye's house in Long Acre (myself remaining in that desolate condition, a prisoner at St James's) there was a base information give to the Council of State by a servant of mine (whom for a falseness I had put away) that I had deposited plate and jewels to a great value in that good Lady's custody. Whereupon (without any cause alleged or anything at all in charge against me) they sent a warrant signed by Bradshaw, by a sergeant-at-arms, to seize upon all that I had there, as belonging to an enemy of the State.

'But it pleased the wisdom of God to befool their malice that they made me search in mine own house where all that I had of value was, but only in that place where there was nothing but so inconsiderable a parcel of plate that they were ashamed to keep it when they had it, and so they sent it back again. In the mean time I had leisure to dispose of what I had by me to a place of safety.'[13]

Before the end of March, the Council of State at last granted Waller's petition and set him free. 'After above three years imprisonment . . . it pleased the Lord to turn my captivity and to restore me to the comforts of my poor family again.' He fully appreciated the extent of his good fortune. 'I must ever acknowledge it also a very great and special mercy that having been so long subject to so great a malice, armed with so great a power, I was not given up as a prey; and that after all endeavours used to find or make me criminal I came off with an entire innocency not only uncondemned but unaccused.'[14]

So Ensnaring a Time

'After my return from Denbigh when I took up a resolution to marry again, I besought God for his direction in my choice, who heard my petition and sent me the Lady Harcourt to repair the breach in my poor family, which was so rich a blessing both to me and my children that I can never sufficiently acknowledge it.'[1] On 13 April 1652, probably while still under house arrest near St James's, Sir William married his third wife, Lady Anna Harcourt.

After a strict Puritan upbringing in the household of her father William, Lord Paget, Anna had married Sir Simon Harcourt, whom she described as 'a useful and much desired man'. Harcourt rose to be the Royalist Governor of Dublin in the Civil War, but he was killed before its close. Upon her marriage to Sir William she wrote, 'I was in such a condition as I needed him most: my children grown up, my estate still filled with doubt and other troubles so that in likelihood it could not without much scarcity have supplied me and him too, my mind so worn with public and private troubles that I began apparently to sink in my bodily health and strength. Then did God give me a religious, wise, and faithful loving husband.'[2]

Lady Anna cared for Sir William's younger children by his second wife as if they were her own. William, Thomas and Anne flourished under her maternal eye, obediently eating up their food and drinking 'the medson' she gave them.[3] Soon Lady Anna could be thankful that the children 'prove so hopeful and do improve daily under my care, and that they are all alive and do enjoy their healths better than they did when they came to me, and do grow'. Waller's older daughters, Margaret and Dorothy, had already married: the former to Sir William Courtenay of Powderham Castle in Devon, and the latter to John de Warrenne in 1649, a gentleman who obligingly adopted his wife's surname. Yet Lady Anna faithfully repaired even these breaches: in 1653 she presented her husband with 'a hopeful and likely son', Walter, and a year or two later with a girl, Moll Waller.[4]

In the fullness of his gratitude for his deliverance from prison and for the blessing of his marriage to Lady Anna, Sir William resolved to dedicate himself more completely to God's service:

My Vow 1652

'In acknowledgement of God's infinite mercy and goodness of which I have had all these experiences I vow, by his grace assisting and enabling me, to restrain them in a thankful memory, and to transmit the recordation of them to my children, that they may never be forgotten, neither by me nor my posterity.

'I humbly renew my vows both against the practice or purpose of every gross sin or the allowance of any, though never so small; and resolve (so far as I am able) to shun the occasions of them, and in particular I protest (by the help of the divine grace) against giving any entertainment or lodging in my heart to O. I. S. © ☺ £ [these are shorthand symbols – possibly depicting the 'seven deadly sins'].

'As a poor thank-offering for so many undeserved mercies I humbly renew the consecration of the tenth of whatsoever I receive in my estate to pious uses, and (besides the £100 formerly devoted to those ends in acknowledgement of my deliverance out of prison) I vow one hundred pounds more as an oblation to God for the blessing and happiness I enjoy in my present married condition, to be employed in such ways as I shall be directed by my godly friends.

'And if I be repaid the debt owing me from L.K.[5] I engage myself to dispose forty pounds of it (with the addition of ten pounds more unto it) to the town of Newton Abbot in Devon, for the making up of their stock, which was employed for the setting of the poor at work, in the workhouse there erected by me.

'I humbly devote my life to God, who has so often preserved it and so many ways blessed it, resolving by his grace to do all I can for the setting of him up in my heart: to love, fear and trust him more; to pray, read and hear more, and more zealously than I have done hitherto; to walk in my particular calling more uprightly, constantly, cheerfully, fruitfully; and to endeavour to become better in all relations, both to the public in church and state whensoever I shall be in a capacity to service them; and in private, as a father, husband, master.

'As a father, endeavouring to bring up my children in the nurture and admonition of the Lord, teaching them his fear, both by precept and example, with a spirit of meekness that they may not be discouraged.

'As a husband, dwelling with my dear yokefellow according to knowledge, loving her as mine own body, as mine own self, as Christ loved his Church, so taking care with her for the things of this world, that as we study to please one another, we may likewise remember the homage we both owe to God, and labour above all things to please him.

'As a master, so carrying myself towards my servants, forbearing threatening, giving them what is just and equal, as knowing that I also have a master in Heaven, and making provision for my family, according to my duty.'[6]

By 1654 Sir William had accumulated some capital from the rents of his lands and the proceeds of prisage and butlerage. With this money in that year he purchased Osterley House in Middlesex, described in a contemporary survey as 'a fair and stately building of brick erected by Sir Thomas Gresham, knight, citizen and merchant-adventurer of London, and finished about 1577. It stands in a park by him also impaled, well-wooded and garnished with many fair ponds, which afford not only fish and fowl, as swans and other water fowl.'[7] Besides becoming lord of the manor of Heston, Sir William now became the owner of some 758 acres in the neighbouring parishes. By 1655 he had raised £5,000 by mortgages on this estate and he maintained this sum by new indentures until 1663, when he sold the western half of the estate, 367 acres in all, for £5,250 and paid off most of the remaining debt.[8]

In the *Vindication* Waller had clearly stated his desire that the monarchy should be restored, but at first he would not promise his support to the Royalist agents plotting for the overthrow of the Protectorate. Sir William's natural wariness reinforced by his experience of those traps that had been deliberately set to incriminate him, and perhaps also by a resolve not to be parted again from his new wife and young family, led him to talk with great circumspection to those who came to him seeking his engagement in schemes for armed risings.

Some of Sir William's words penned in 'A Daily Directory' between 1652 and 1655 reflected his own need for caution in these matters: 'I would so govern my carriage (if I could) as neither to trust too far, nor to seem to mistrust at all. . . . The best way in conversation is the middle way, between ungirt and straight-laced; between a confidence, and a diffidence; an open facility, and a close reservation. But in case of suspicion, I should think the fairest way to clear it were the openest, that is, to communicate it freely to the party suspected.'[9]

Early in 1655 some Cavaliers approached Sir William at his house in Aldersgate Street, no doubt hoping to persuade him to join the risings planned for that year. Whatever Sir William's reply, Lord Willoughby of Parham, a Presbyterian leader already committed to cooperating with the Cavaliers, felt sure enough of him to promise his new friends that both Waller and Browne would support them on the day.[10] Probably at this time John Thurloe, Cromwell's astute Secretary of State, received information from an anonymous Cavalier that the latter two gentlemen were enmeshed in a widespread plot, and that Browne would command the City forces in the coming rebellion, while Waller would lead those of Westminster and Middlesex.[11] Yet Waller almost certainly gave no firm undertaking to the Royalists beyond perhaps a general expression of sympathy for their designs. As Penruddock's Rising collapsed that spring, Sir William had cause for some thankfulness: 'I have reason to acknowledge it a great mercy of God,' he recorded in March 1655, 'that he preserved me in so ensnaring a time, wherein the Lord heard my prayer.'[12]

Two years later Sir William came face to face with the military dictator of England whose power and politics he had so strenuously opposed nearly a decade before. Upon 22 March 1657, so Lady Anna wrote, 'my husband being in my brother [Sir Thomas] Irby's house, we having lived peaceably in town most part of the winter, there came two messengers from my Lord Protector to search the house, to seize his papers and to bring him in safe custody to Whitehall. Whither he was carried about 9 of the clock in the morning, and there attended all day, was examined by my Lord [Protector] himself of many particulars, and sent home again at night, which was a mercy quite above my hopes and contrary to the expectation of all people and a thing very unusual with those in power. The Lord receive the praise and glory of this his wonderful goodness, which he shewed so personally to me when my heart was very much afraid, both in regard of what my husband had suffered so long together, without any declared cause, and in regard of the infirmities that his former imprisonment made him liable too; also in regard of the great charge that imprisonment was like to be him, and the hindrance that would have followed in his estate . . .'[13]

Cromwell, as a supreme realist, betrayed no awareness of his former relationship with the prisoner. 'He did examine me as a stranger,' wrote Sir William, 'not as one whom he had aforetime known and obeyed, yet he was not discourteous. And it pleased the Lord to preserve me that not one thing objected could be proved against me.'[14] Part of the subject matter of their conversation may be deduced from the interrogation of Major Robert Harley in the Tower on the following day. He told Secretary Thurloe that he had indeed discussed with Sir William the presence of the Marquess of Ormonde, a prominent Royalist, in the capital, a fact which they had learned, so he claimed, only from the weekly journals. Thurloe also enquired about two suits of armour in Waller's Westminster house. Cromwell, who looked upon Ormonde's coming and going as the first sign of a Royalist invasion, probably wanted to assess for himself how far Sir William and the other Presbyterian leaders were implicated in this dangerous plot. Without more convincing evidence than widespread rumour, Thurloe could write to Henry Cromwell towards the end of the following month: 'It's certain Sir William Waller was fully engaged.'[15]

An uneasy year passed. In February 1659 'the Lord was pleased to visit my husband with many sad distempers, as with an ague which being joined with the scurvy and the remainder of an ill fit of the gout, did threaten much danger to his life'. Barely had Sir William recovered from the ague and 'whilst he was very faint with fasting and sweating, he was threatened with a sore fit of the stone, of which I was greatly afraid. But the Lord has hitherto stayed his hand, so that his extremity has neither been long nor great.'[16]

By this time Sir William had secured a favourable judgement in a case which had long lingered in the courts and before the Council of State. Apparently in 1654 his old enemy, Colonel Edmund Harvey, now a commissioner for customs, had attempted to levy his taxes on the barrels of wine selected by the Waller family's lessee of prisage and butlerage, despite the crown rent of £500 already paid each year.[17] The ups and downs of litigation added to the anxieties of Sir William and his wife, and no doubt they experienced considerable relief when it was all over. One other financial matter, Waller's bid for a barony in Ireland, produced no result, but it perhaps illustrates his continued interest in a country which he never seems to have visited.[18]

CHAPTER THIRTY-TWO

The Restoration

On 3 September 1658 Oliver Cromwell died, and his son Richard became Protector in his place. His nominal rule ended some eight months later with the restoration of the Rump (7 May 1659). While a divided and hydra-headed Army quarrelled with an unrepresentative Parliament, the Royalist conspirators and their Presbyterian allies resolved upon one more appeal to arms, planning a series of simultaneous risings through England in the summer of 1659.[1]

By this time Sir William Waller had become much more committed to such measures, a change of attitude partly explained by the political situation and partly by the emergence of a more effective Royalist organisation in England. Alongside the 'Sealed Knot', which was composed of Royalist conspirators, the 'Great Trust' had been set up by order of the King in Holland. The aim of this second group was to bring about a joint rising of Royalists and Presbyterian moderates among the Parliamentarians.

The moving spirit behind the 'Great Trust', John Mordaunt, second son of the Earl of Peterborough, had clearly won a promise of Waller's support. They may perhaps have met for the first time in 1648 during Waller's exile in Holland. If so, it is possible that Queen Elizabeth of Bohemia introduced them to each other, for both had waited upon her in that year at her home in The Hague. Mordaunt's wife was a close friend of the Queen's, and this fact in itself would be a sufficient recommendation for her husband when he first spoke with Sir William.[2]

Not all of those loosely called Presbyterians, however, would accept the unconditional restoration of the King as the stated objective of these clandestine endeavours. Many preferred to work for a free and full Parliament to replace the Rump, while still others insisted upon the terms of the Treaty of Newport as the basis for a return of the monarchy. At one of his meetings with Mordaunt, Sir William apparently prophesied that such proposed limitations would not be burdensome for long after the Restoration, an encouraging thought for the Royalists.

On 24 March 1659, the day after this conversation, Mordaunt wrote as much to the King: 'He [Waller] is of the opinion that all the restrictions the fears of the most guilty of the Presbyterians will at first tie your Majesty to, will suddenly and visibly be taken off by your Majesty's sweetness of disposition and temper, and though the violence of some few should

262

endeavour to keep your Majesty to them, yet he is absolutely of the opinion that the next free Parliament will restore you fully to your rights and prerogative. . . . He assured me that the persons that are of quality among them detest to have a hand in any imposition, but the other party are more numerous, and unless he and others keep faith with them, it would be impossible for them to draw them off when time serves.'

It seems that, in the summer of 1659, Waller had sounded out Richard Cromwell on behalf of the restoration movement. But he could not return a good report. 'As to Cromwell he believes him very mean and highly false, having given his word to follow his advice, or at least to conceal it, yet discovered it to Thurloe.'

The Royalist scheme for overthrowing the government by force of arms in the summer of 1659 was a complex one. When regional risings had drawn away the Army from London, Sir Richard Browne would lead a *coup d'état* in the City. Meanwhile, south coast ports would be seized and the King would then land at the head of foreign troops.

In the event, Booth's Rising (so named after Sir George Booth, one of its northern leaders) collapsed without achieving its aim, and for this failure many reasons may be adduced. One of the main causes, the inadequate briefing of those who were to take part in it, may be illustrated by the case of Waller. It is virtually certain that Waller's part in the rising lay in Kent, and he probably received a commission from the King, by way of Mordaunt, to command in that county. It could be no accident that he travelled into Kent with his family in July. Yet on 27 July, when he had received warning that the rising was imminent, Waller wrote the following letter to Mordaunt:

Sir,

I reckon it a great unhappiness, that your first letter of the two I received from you came not so seasonably to my hands that I could have taken the opportunity to have met with that noble gentleman. I have a great desire to kiss your hands, and to have the honour of his acquaintance; and wish that sometime this day (if it be possible) I might meet either with one or both of you; for I cannot resolve what way to take till I have spoken with you.

And I would gladly know in what capacity I shall be desired to act. If either you or that worthy person will appoint a place of meeting, I desire it may be as near the waterside as may be, for I have neither coach nor horse here, but came by water to this place. I beseech you let me have the favour to hear speedily from you, for I shall not willingly make any long stay here. The good Lord prosper you. I am,

Your very humble servant
[unsigned][3]

Before any further instructions could arrive from Mordaunt the government had taken steps to nip the rising in the bud by arresting as many of the suspected leaders as possible, including Sir William Waller.

'Upon the 5th of August in the year 1659,' wrote Waller's wife, Lady Anna, 'being in Kent to drink the waters for the health of myself, children and divers of our family, Sir William was taken prisoner by Captain Barrington at two of the clock in the night, and caused to rise out of bed and to ride 4 miles at that time in the night which might have been a great prejudice to his life, or health at least.'[4]

Although no charges could be found, the government cast about for an excuse to detain him. 'After he had been prisoner a fortnight, then they made him an offender by tendering some promise to him, which, he refusing, was sent to the Tower. I account it a very great mercy that neither Sir George Booth, who they report is very fearful, nor any of the Cavaliers, have accused my husband, to please those now in power.'

In the event, Waller's sojourn in that grim fortress did not prove burdensome. Lady Anna wrote: 'Whilst we were prisoners in Kent, the trouble in that condition was sweetened by the great kindness of many there, and when we were in the Tower we found great kindness from the warder, which was a great lessening of our trouble; and the more to be taken notice on, because it is a rare thing, as I perceive by the relation of what other gentlemen suffered from their keepers, to find any amongst them that were not severe, cross and covetous, to the great prejudice of their prisoners. We found it quite contrary, although we were utter strangers, and therefore are bound wholly to attribute it to the over-ruling hand of God, that we should be directed at 10 of the clock at night (when we had no time to look about us or to choose or inquire what might have been best for us), to the only man's house in the Tower which was best for us.'[4]

Waller remained in this comfortable house with the kind warder for ten weeks. Indeed his enemies 'made themselves sport with his trouble, saying he chose to be at the Tower that he might retire, whereas our charge was much greater in there than it would have been at another place'. On 31 October, however, his lawyers procured his release with a writ of habeas corpus, and the couple returned to their town house in Westminster.[5]

The collapse of Booth's Rising and his imprisonment in the Tower recalled Waller to his policy of wariness. Obviously in reply to a letter from him, Mordaunt wrote back on 26 November promising not to expose either him or his fortunes lightly. Mordaunt added that the King had left it to him to decide when to call Waller to arms, and said that he would be very cautious in doing so.[6]

In December Waller discouraged Browne from attempting an armed coup in London.[7] That same month one of Mordaunt's correspondents informed him that the 'old Presbyterians have grown up again', with their insistence on the Treaty of Newport as the condition for restoring the monarchy, and that they have 'a little poison'd' Sir William Waller.[8] Consequently, it appears that Waller had somewhat shifted his ground, as far as the conditions issue was concerned, since his earlier conversation with Mordaunt in March 1659.

While Sir William enjoyed his 'retirement' in the Tower of London, the Army had finally ejected the Rump, a body that had long outstayed its welcome on the political stage, but divisions of opinion among the generals had led to the restoration of this last vestige of the Long Parliament in December. With considerable courage, Waller, in company with Sir Gilbert Gerrard, Sir Richard Onslow, William Prynne and seventeen or eighteen other excluded members, sought admission at the door of the House, only to be turned away at the doors by the guards. But their action served to underline the totally unrepresentative nature of the Rump. Subsequently, they issued a sharp declaration against this breach of privilege, one more nail in the Rump's coffin.[9]

Once more the high-handed actions of that most insensitive body, the Rump Parliament, aroused the wrath of the Army in and near London, and only the southwards march of General George Monck with his regiments from the North, preserved it in being. But, after experiencing for himself the perversity of the Rump, Monck determined to secure a free Parliament. As a step in this direction, he prudently summoned those surviving members who had been excluded by Pride's Purge (December 1648) to a meeting, and there he secured their written consent to his political agenda. By this agreement, these Members of Parliament promised to settle the question of command in the Army, produce money for arrears of pay, send out writs for a new Parliament and dissolve their sitting by a fixed date.

On 21 February Samuel Pepys witnessed the procession of the excluded members into Westminster Hall. As a boy at St Paul's School and an ardent supporter of the cause of Parliament, Pepys had stood among that silent shivering crowd who watched the execution of King Charles I, a fact that he much hoped would be forgotten in the coming reign as it was potentially so damaging to his career prospects. On this day his sharply observant eye noted an amusing incident: 'Mr Prynne came in with an old basket-hilt sword on, and had a great many shouts at his going into the hall.'[10] These popular plaudits doubtless required some acknowledgement, and in the excitement of the moment Prynne lost control of 'his long rusty sword, longer than ordinary'. Upon perhaps the crowning day of his Parliamentary career it was Waller's misfortune to walk behind this crop-eared political veteran. 'As he went into the House, William

Prynne's long sword ran between Sir William's short legs, and threw him down, which caused laughter.'[11]

The renewed House of Commons faithfully carried out Monck's programme. This included the setting up of a new Council of State, and among those appointed to it stands the name of Sir William Waller. As a member of the council, he used his influence to obtain the release from prison of his first cousin, Sir Hardress, whose actions as a major-general in Ireland rendered him obnoxious to the government.[12]

Sir William's main contribution at this time was to foster the all-important concern for the good relations between the House of Commons and General Monck, the midwives of the Restoration. For example, he visited General Monck at his headquarters to allay some doubts aroused among some of his officers by the passing of Parliament's Militia Act. On 16 March Sir William sat as a Member of Parliament for the last time, when he gave his vote for the long-awaited dissolution. The citizens of Westminster did indeed elect him to the Convention, the Parliament summoned without royal writ, but he did not take his seat. Therefore Waller played no part in the final scene in this act of the drama: those negotiations which made possible the peaceful and joyful entry of King Charles II into his capital on his thirtieth birthday, 29 May 1660.

'We are both upon the stage and must act out those parts assigned us in this tragedy,' Waller had told Hopton seventeen years earlier. He had played his part well, and his only reward was to see the final curtain fall on that tragedy of a 'war without an enemy'.

A Clear Evening

After the Restoration Waller retired completely from public affairs. Unlike the Earl of Manchester, Massey and Browne, for example, he received no reward from King Charles. But Massey and Browne had actively supported King Charles II in the Worcester campaign when Waller, languishing in his Welsh prison, could only pray for his success. In the event, Waller counted it a blessing that he was allowed to retain his estates. At least he could now enjoy a private life in freedom and some comfort.

At sixty-one years of age, Waller still suffered from occasional attacks of gout and the stone. A portrait of him by Sir Peter Lely at Goodwood House in Sussex depicts the face of an unwell man. On 13 October the anxious Lady Anna, herself ailing, could record in her journal 'a very great mercy concerning my husband, who being ill of his eyes, had a mind to take pills for to purge his head, and made me write for them when it was late, and accordingly took them at night, which made him so ill that I greatly feared his life. But, for ever blessed be the Lord, who restrained the working of the pills, and brought out the iresyplus [?inflammation of the eye], and has supported him all this while in bed, and has prevented any ill accident hitherto, so that he is pretty well.'

A week after this deliverance, Sir William took up his pen to write to Colonel Robert Harley, now Governor of Dunkirk. His eldest son, William, had first gone abroad with a tutor in 1656, and thereafter swiftly acquired a reputation as a quarrelsome spendthrift. Indeed, the young man's headstrong behaviour and subsequent hatred of popery are traits which suggest some inheritance of character from his mother. Sixteen years before, Robert Harley had received his baptism of fire as a cornet at Lansdown under Waller's command; now Sir William entrusted his second son, Thomas, to this dependable friend to whom he penned this touching expression of the hopes and fears of parenthood:

1660, October 21. Osterley Park.

Dear Sir,

I cannot but esteem it a great happiness to me that having now but one son left whom I can own with the affection of a father, I have the liberty – by your favour – to deposit him in your noble hands, where he may enjoy the benefit of your advice and example. I have freely given you his character already, and I presume his overt nature will quickly verify it. You will find him to be of flexible, ductile disposition and ready, I hope, to embrace your good counsel, if his easiness do not betray him to ill company.

The only thing I fear in him is his love to play [gambling], which has put him upon borrowing and shifting to his great disadvantage, and will still endanger him, if there be not a severe hand carried over him. I make it my humble suit that you will be pleased to keep him as busy as you can, that he may not be at a leisure to misspend his time.

His allowance is fifty pounds a year, and if he may receive it there from you, by such proportions as you shall think fit, I shall punctually from time to time upon sight of your bill pay it here to whomsoever you shall appoint. Or, if that may be any way inconvenient, I shall take some other course to return it unto him, as this bearer, my servant, shall acquaint me with your mind.

Sir, I intimated in the beginning of these lines, that this poor youth is now in effect my whole stock; my eldest son being gone away from me in a rebellious way, which I have reason to take so much the worse, as it is without any provocation at all offered to him, and flatly contrary to his own protestations of duty and obedience made more than once upon his knees, with tears, unto me. He is now – as I am informed – at Calais, from whence the passage is so short that I have just reason to fear he may quickly form some design from thence to debauch his brother. This I the rather apprehend because he has already attempted it here, and – as the case now stands with him – he has no other way to secure himself against his brother's interest but by involving him in the same guilt.

I make it my humble suit therefore, that you will exercise your noble friendship in holding an eye upon him so far as that if he should make any visit to his brother – upon what pretence soever – you would discharge him out of the town, and not suffer them to be together.'[1]

In the following spring Sir William attended the marriage of his third daughter, Anne, to Sir Philip Harcourt – Anna's son – in the chapel at Osterley Park. Travel on the Continent had developed Waller's stepson from a 'very weak lean child' into a healthy young man. His mother, Lady Anna, could feel grateful that he 'did not resolutely fix upon some unworthy person, vain, or poor, or of ill condition'. Yet at first Lady Anna had not looked with favour on the match, as she confessed in her journal. 'My mind, being in some respects very averse, was over-ruled and quieted by the goodness of God.' Clearly some facet of young Anne's character had caused her anxiety, for later she could acknowledge it as a mercy 'that I have had so much encouragement concerning her since, more than I had before'. Apparently, Sir William spoke up for the young couple, for his wife added thanksgivings to God:

'that there is so little unkindness between Sir William and I in the disputes about such a business'.[2]

In October 1661 Lady Anna fell mortally sick. Freed on her deathbed from 'a slavish fear of death' which had much troubled her in recent years, she spoke to friends about that 'unhappy difference between her husband and one of his sons'. The day before her death she even asked Sir William to deny rumours that she had added fuel to that fire. This he did, adding that once she had effected a reconciliation between the two Williams, son and father, by her tears. Edmund Calamy, the eminent pastor of Aldermanbury, painted this touching portrait of Lady Anna in the funeral sermon he delivered for her in the New Chapel, Westminster; it was later published at Waller's request. In it Calamy eulogised Lady Anna for such Puritan practices as her support of ministers, her attendance at Sunday morning and evening sermons, her catechism of maid servants and serving boys, and her monthly worship at Holy Communion. She was 'a very prudent lady', he concluded.[3]

Lady Anna's daughter, little Moll Waller, had survived 'a terrible fever' and then a bout of pleurisy in November 1658, but she probably died before her mother. Neither did her young brother Walter, nor a baby sister, Katharine, born on 30 August 1657, evade fatal maladies in their childhood.[4] In truth, none of Lady Anna's progeny enjoyed good health, for Frederick Harcourt had also died in 1657.[5] But Waller's bereavements were not confined to his children. Anne, young Philip Harcourt's wife, died in August 1664, possibly in childbirth.[6]

On a happier note, Margaret had grown into young womanhood in Devon. She had survived her seizure by the Cavaliers in 1644, and doubtless met Sir Thomas Fairfax and Oliver Cromwell when her grandmother gave them hospitality at Forde House during the siege of Exeter (1646). When she married Sir William Courtenay, who had entitlement to the Earldom of Devon, probably in 1648, she would have been fifteen and her bridegroom about twenty. They made their home at Forde House. At least nine of their nineteen children were baptised or buried at Wolborough, the remainder mostly at Powderham Castle, for death much depleted her family. Some of Margaret's personal possessions still exist at Powderham Castle, notably a copy of Waller's *Vindication* inscribed in his own hand, and a portrait of him painted in 1648, when he was one of the seven Presbyterian leaders imprisoned in Windsor Castle.

With that brace of prodigal sons abroad, and his two surviving daughters safely married, Sir William turned to prayer and meditation, reading and writing. Four months before his daughter Anne's death he attended a fast, held in three crowded rooms at the Countess of Exeter's house: the last glimpse of him in public.[7]

During the last seven years of his life Sir William composed his spiritual legacy, twenty-two meditations published together posthumously in 1680 as *Divine Meditations Upon Several Occasions: With a Dayly Directory*. This book represents the peak of his development as a formal writer and it also contains many gleams of his mature Christian wisdom, gold refined by a master alchemist from much experience. 'Let us then content ourselves that we have here a window into his breast through which we may observe the inward workings of his soul,' declared the writer of the preface to the first edition.

His purpose in writing the *Divine Meditations* was not self-revelation. To understand it, we must turn back to his 'Vow of 1652', the year of his release from prison, when he wrote: 'I humbly devote my life to God, who has so often preserved it . . . resolving by his grace to do all I can for the setting of him up in my heart.'

The *Dayly Directory*, written shortly after the 1652 Vow, represented Sir William's plan of campaign. In Denbigh Castle he had found a world in a prison, a kingdom in a mind. Now he took the paradox of the great within the small one step further: 'Every day is a life in little; in the account whereof we may reckon our growth from the womb of the morning; our growth from thence to noon (when we are as the sun in his strength) after which (like a shadow that declines) we hasten to the evening of our age, and so to our sunset, when we come to close our eyes in sleep, the image and representative of death. Our whole life is but this tale of a day told over and over. I would therefore so spend every day as if it were all the days I had to live; and in pursuance of this resolution I would by the assistance of divine grace endeavour to observe this following daily practice.'[8]

No man could follow even such moderate precepts as those which Sir William set for himself without discovering the intractability of his own human nature. Beneath a calm and modest demeanour Sir William had always owned a natural self-confidence without which he could have neither commanded men nor made military decisions. Therefore, the endeavour to open himself to God, and to allow this strong personality to be transformed, now the central purpose of his life, could not be easy, for self-confidence and humility can make quarrelsome bedfellows. 'O let the power of your gracious vocation have a perfect work upon me', he prayed, 'to change me and I shall be changed, to convert me, and I shall be converted; so though by nature, I am enmity against you, by grace I shall be reconciled to you.'

The earliest version of his *Experiences* was written to honour his pledge: 'In acknowledgement of God's infinite mercy and goodness. . . . I vow by His grace . . . to retain them in thankful memory and to transmit . . . them to my children that they may never be forgotten by me, nor by my posterity.'

Waller clearly felt that he did not always hit his mark, which was to 'set up' God for the praise of his family. In a second manuscript of the *Experiences*, prepared for his eldest daughter, Margaret, some years later, he felt it necessary to omit many of the biographical anecdotes and reminiscences of purely human interest and to rephrase many others, eliminating any possible grounds for self-satisfaction.[9] For example, 'At the Devizes when I beat the Lord Marquess Harford . . .' became 'At the Devizes when it pleased God to grant me that success.' In fact the last traces of a pride, especially in the section of 'several prosperous successes', were carefully erased, literary corrections which illustrate the workings of Sir William's mind and will at this period of his life.

The *Divine Meditations* both complemented and improved upon the *Experiences*. In the former Sir William sought God in his own history; in the latter he looked for him in the present, in nature and art. Whereas in the *Experiences* Waller wrote down biblical quotations and anecdotes separately, in the *Divine Meditations* he skilfully blended the two together. In a similar way, his lighter and more discriminating use of classical authors compares favourably with the treatment of them in the *Vindication*.

Owing to its purpose, Waller's *Divine Meditations* is general rather than autobiographical. But, like most writers, he drew on personal experience. Therefore there are, as it were, some flies caught in the amber, relics of his personality held firm in this translucent material. His love of books, for example, shows in the fifth meditation, 'Upon the contentment I have in my books and study', accompanied by some gentle criticism of what might be called literary hypocrites: 'in vain do they boast of full libraries that are contented to live with empty head', and of those who run 'from one book to another, as birds skip from one bough to another'. Yet quantity of reading mattered little to him. 'It is in reading, as it is in making many books; there may be pleasing distraction in it, but little or no profit. I would therefore do in this, as merchants use to do in their trading; who in a coasting way, put in at several ports, and take in what commodities they afford, but settle their factories in those places only, which are of special note. I would by-the-by allow myself a traffic with sundry authors, so I happened to light upon them, for my recreation; and I would make the best advantage that I could of them; but I would fix my study upon those only, that are of most importance to fit me for action, which is the true end of all learning, and for the service of God which is the true end of all action.'

In the sixth meditation, 'Upon an entertainment of godly friends', Sir William extolled mirth as 'a divine thing'. He continues: 'It is an anticipation of the joys of Heaven in the delightful society of a good conscience when we are alone; and together with that of conscientious friends, when we are in company. They are the merry hearts that keep the continual feast. It is one of the Devil's lies, and that of which he has made as great advantage as of any, that religion is a dull, flat, melancholy thing; whereas in truth, there is no such clear, delicate mirth as that which comes from the springs above.'

There are indeed some humorous passages in the *Divine Meditations*. 'Upon the sight of bowlers in a green' calls forth these reflections: 'It is a measuring cast, whether it be a better sport to see the bowling, or the bowlers; of the two, the last would make one laugh most; and therefore I think the best part of the sport lies on their side. Certainly there cannot be a better jest seen, than the antic figures into which they screw themselves; nor a greater absurdity heard, than the sensible advice that they cast after their senseless bowls; now and then, to have them rub; now and then to have them fly; and to observe their impatience (many times to a degree of desperation) if they chance not to run correspondently to their flexures and cringes.'

Only two meditations deal with subjects outside the orbit of Waller's retired life at Osterley Park and the surrounding Middlesex countryside: 'Upon my imprisonment' and 'Upon my release'. Their presence in the book perhaps indicates the importance of those three captive years for the development of Waller's reflective mind. These chapters follow the two meditations 'Upon a fit of the Gout' and 'Upon my recovery out of the Gout', and with them they form a compact section on Christian fortitude in all suffering short of death, taught not by precept but by Waller's own example. This 'dear blessed gout', for example, could serve God's end: 'So shall your rod . . . be productive.'

Sunrise and sunset, hunting and fishing, a fair house and a pleasant garden, good music and pictures in a gallery, a prancing horse and even a parrot in a cage, all these subjects are the starting-points for short chapters of meditation. The image of the garden, for example, prompts him to reflect that it is better to be pruned by the divine gardener than weeded out: 'Lord, do anything to me, rather than nothing. Let your pruning knife be never so sharp and cutting, it can do me no hurt, so long as it tends to make me good.'

Not least of the attractiveness of the meditations is the way in which they abound in images called from Sir William's long life. Upon the regaining of his liberty he could write, 'now that I am abroad I may say I have more sea room, but withal I am more exposed to foul weather'. Sometimes he conjures up vivid memories from his younger days. While coursing, 'I have often seen a hunted hare, when she is hard run, get into a flock of sheep, and put the hounds to a loss by keeping among them in their walk'.

Elsewhere, Sir William criticises the new fashions in banqueting: 'What is this but to play with God's blessings, as little children play with their meat when they have weak and squeamish or no stomachs.' Years of observing children at table may have prompted the thought that he can now take what God gives 'without being so unmannerly as to reach over my neighbours plate, for a better'.

It is perhaps remarkable that there are so few military images in the book, although one or two sentences betray Sir William's experience in war. 'Fear and courage may many times act alike, and are not incompatible in the same subject. One may generate the other. Desperation, which is the depth of fear, does many times (being sharpened by necessity) excite courage and beget hope. Temerity, which is the height of courage, does often (from experience of danger) breed caution, which is a discreet fear.'

One may suspect Sir William of a play upon his old Royalist sobriquet as the 'Night Owl' in these words: 'How strangely do those people live, that begin their morning at noon, and their noon at night; that turn day into night, and live backward? But it is no wonder to see owls fly abroad at late hours! O my soul, God never created you to live in a feather-bed! Life consists in action; idleness is but a living death.'

Waller evidently completed the *Divine Meditations* in 1665, when he was 67 years old. 'When I look back to the morning of my life, and consider my time past, methinks it is but a very little while since I came out of the chamber of my mother's womb. How soon is the tale of three score and seven years told!' In his closing chapter, 'Upon my lying down to rest', he wrote: 'Methinks, I have had a long day's journey in the world, and a wearisome; accompanied with blustering weather, and rugged ill ways; and now, a bed would do well. . . . Nay, I am not only dead, but in a great part buried: how much of myself is already laid in the dust? Death has taken three of my ribs from me, and so many limbs as I have lost children by his stroke. My dearest relations are gone to bed before me; to what purpose serves this fragment, this remainder of me here? Lord, take all to you; let me not lie half in the bed and half out. Your bed is not too little, nor your coverlet too narrow, but you have room enough for me.'

On 27 April 1668 Waller made his last will and testament,[10] appointing as his executors Lord Fitzwilliam, Sir Robert Barnham [whose father, Sir Francis, had acted as Chief Butler of England during the minority of William] and his son Francis, Solicitor-General Heneage Finch and Dr Thomas Cox. Turning first to his servants, he left Mistress Martha Veale the handsome sum of £150, and Martha Allen, widow, £10 for herself and a like sum to each of her sons 'for binding of them to be apprentices or otherways for the good of the said children'. Two late rectors of St Martin-in-the-Fields, evidently the church where Waller attended divine service, received £200 for charitable purposes and £10 a piece.

Sir William directed his executors to sell the rest of the Osterley Park estate, buy more land in the name of William, and allocate both sons a suitable annuity from the rents. From this arrangement it may be deduced that Waller did not trust the young men to manage their inheritance. He also arranged that, in the event of their decease, his estate would pass to his grandchild, Simon Harcourt, and failing him to the daughters of William and Thomas. (Thomas' grandson, who died in 1802, was Waller's last male descendant.[11]) By two codicils dated 11 and 20 July, he left £250 'to my faithful and dearly respected friend, Master Thomas Cox', and made some provision for his eldest son's debts.

Sir William died on 19 September 1668. In the New Chapel, Westminster, according to Thomas Jekyll in a letter to Anthony Wood, 'he was buried in great pomp and state, with several flags and other ensigns of honour, suitable to his quality, born by persons in rich heralds coats and by them hung up in the church over his grave.

'But those persons not being true heralds but only servants of Sir William's son dressed up to save charges, the true heralds that were thus fobb'd of their efforts, resented it so highly as to come about a week [after] into the church (whilst the sweeper was making of it clean) and pull down all the flags, leaving no marks of remembrance . . . beyond which the poorest beggar that is, will always have.'[12]

According to another anonymous contemporary, however, on 17 October 1668 the heralds removed the arms and trophies of Sir William Waller as 'being false and beyond his quality'.[13] Perhaps his prodigal sons had been over-generous in remembering their kind and wise father. Not that it matters much. For, as Sir William wrote himself, 'It is not flags and pedigree but a noble heart that makes a noble person. True goodness is true greatness, and God's blessing the true riches.'

New Chapel is no more now, reduced to rubble when German bombers in the Second World War destroyed much of Broadway (where it stood) in Westminster. Such bones as could be recovered were reinterred in a common grave in the City of London's public cemetery. This book is now Sir William Waller's monument. As for an inscription, what better than the moving words with which he concluded the *Vindication* of his life and career in the English Civil War and its aftermath:

If I shall find favour in the eyes of the Lord, he will reintegrate me. . . . But if he thus say, I have no delight in you; behold, here am I, let him do to me as seems good unto him.

Notes and References

In these references I have followed the practice of citing the author and title of a book, article or pamphlet in full in the first place, and subsequently in an abbreviated form. In the case of documents and pamphlets I have given the repository on the first citation in each chapter. Also for the sake of brevity the following abbreviations have been used:

Add. MSS	Additional Manuscripts, British Museum
B.M.	British Museum
Bodl.	Bodleian Library, Oxford
C.B.K.	Committee of Both Kingdoms
C.J.	*Journals of the House of Commons*
Clarendon	E. Hyde, Earl of Clarendon, *History of the Rebellion and Civil Wars in England*, ed. W.D. Macray, 6 Vols (1888)
C.S.	Camden Society
C.S.P.D.	*Calendar of the State Papers, Domestic Series*
C.S.P. Ireland	*Calendar of the State Papers, Ireland*
C.S.P. Venetian	*Calendar of the State Papers, Venetian*
D'Ewes	Sir Simonds D'Ewes, 'A Journall of the Parliament begunne Nov. 3. Tuesday, Anno Domini 1640.' British Museum, Harleian MSS 162–6
Divine Meditations	Sir William Waller, *Divine Meditations Upon Several Occasions: With a Dayly Directory (1680)*
D.N.B.	*Dictionary of National Biography*
E.H.R.	*English Historical Review*
Experiences	Waller's 'Experiences' printed in *The Poetry of Anna Matilda* (1788)
Experiences	MS of Waller's 'Experiences' in Wadham College Library, Oxford
Harl. MS	Harleian Manuscript
H.M.C.	Historical Manuscript Commission
Hopton	*Bellum Civile. Hopton's Narrative of his Campaign in the West (1642–1644)*, ed. C.E.H. Chadwyck Healy, Somerset Record Society, Vol. 18 (1902)
Journal	'The Journal of Lady Anna Waller', *Harcourt Papers* (privately printed), Vol. I
L.J.	*Journals of the House of Lords*
Luke	*Journal of Sir Samuel Luke*, ed. I.G. Philip, 3 Vols, Oxfordshire Record Society (1947–53)

P.	Parliamentarian
R.	Royalist
R.O.	Record Office
Slingsby	'Relation of Colonel Walter Slingsby', printed in *Bellum Civile* (see above)
S.P.	State Papers in Public Records Office, London
T.T.	Thomason Tracts, King's Library, British Museum
Vindication	*Vindication of the Character and conduct of Sir William Waller, Knight, written by himself* (1793)
Whitaker	L. Whitaker, 'Diary of proceedings in the House of Commons, 8 Oct. 1642–8 July 1647', British Museum, Additional MS 31116

CHAPTER ONE: EARLY LIFE

1. Experiences, p. 106
2. A. Wood. *Athenal Oxoniensis*, Vol. 3, p. 814, (1817); Sevenoaks Parish Register
3. Experiences, ff. 6–7, 27
4. W. A. Waller, *Our Family Record* (1898)
5. P.C.C. Capell, Will of Sir Thomas Waller; Kent R.O. Sir Edward Dering's MS 'List of Lieutenants of Dover Castle'
6. *C.S.P.D., 1603–10*, p. 46
7. *Register of the University of Oxford*, ed. A. Clark, Vol. 2, p. 328, (1887–9)
8. Experiences, f. 9; A. Wood, *op. cit.*, p. 814
9. *Experiences*, pp. 113–14; Experiences, f. 27. See also M. Ashley, *Life in Stuart England*, Chap. 9, (1964)
10. *Experiences*, pp. 108–9; G.R. Markham, *The Fighting Veres*, p. 423, (1888); Venetian State Archives: Despatches of Super-intendent-General in Istria to the Senate, 20 May 1617, Collection 339
11. J. Latimer, *The Annals of Bristol in the Seventeenth Century*, pp. 87, 376–7, (1900)
12. *Palgrave's Golden Treasury*, Bk. I, LXXXIV
13. *Vindication*, pp. 213–14. Capt. J. Butler to Waller, 15 Sept. 1645, *The Nicholas Papers*, ed. G.F. Warner, C.S., Vol. I, p. 65, (1886)
14. Experiences, f. 13
15. D. Lloyd, *Memoirs of . . . Excellent Personages . . .*, p. 342, (1668) (annotated copy cited in C. Oman, *Elizabeth of Bohemia* (1938), pp. 230–1)
16. Experiences, ff. 36–7

CHAPTER TWO: MY LITTLE WORLD

1. W.A. Shaw, *The Knights of England*, Vol. 2, p. 171, (1906); Clarendon, Bk. VII, § 100; S.G. Harris, 'Notes on the History of Newton Abbot', *Transactions of the Devonshire Association*, Vol. 31, p. 285, (1899); P.C.C. Seager 27, Will of Sir Richard Reynell; *Visitations of Devon*, ed. J.L. Vivian, p. 643, (1895). See also M. O'Hagan, *A History of Forde House* (1990) and Edward Reynell, *The Life and Death of the Religious and Virtuous Lady, the Lady Lucie Reynell, of Forde in Devon: Who died the 18th April, 1652. Whereunto is annexed a Consolatory Epilogue for dejected Soules* (1654). The sole surviving copy of this small printed book is in the Bibliothèque Nationale, Paris
2. Devon R.O. Quarter Sessions Order Books. Waller served once more as a JP in Hampshire (Epiphany, 1647, Hampshire R.O. Quarter Session Order Books)
3. *Diary of Walter Yonge*, ed. G. Roberts, C.S. (1847), pp. 86–7; Yarde deed (1623) in Devon R.O.; P.R.O. Star Chamber Proceedings (James I), Bundle 311; Experiences, f. 62
4. R. Granville, *History of the Granville Family* (1895); *C.S.P.D. April–Sept. 1639*, p. 215
5. M. Coate, *Cornwall in the Great Civil War*, pp. 84–9 (2nd ed 1963)
6. R. Granville, *op. cit.* p. 176. Letter undated
7. *Diary of Walter Yonge*, ed. G. Roberts, C.S., pp. 86–7, (1847)

8. Experiences, ff. 19–21
9. S.P. 14/182, f. 17; B.M. Sloane MS 3816, Harl. MS 1583, ff. 76–7; J. Rushworth, *Historical Collections*, Vol. I, p. 153, (1659–1701); Hampshire R.O. 5 MS 153, f. 81; *C.S.P. Ireland, 1647–60*, p. 47; *The Visitation of Kent 1619–21*, ed. R. Hovenden, p. 130, (1898)
10. Experiences, ff. 53–4; *Visitation of Devon*, p. 643
11. R.W. Cotton, 'Forde and its Associations', *Transactions of the Devonshire Association*, Vol. 33, p. 702 (1901)
12. Experiences, f. 55
13. Bath Guildhall R.O. Chamberlain's Accounts, 16 Oct. 1635
14. *Experiences*, pp. 127–8
15. *C.S.P.D., 1637–1638*, p. 447
16. *Experiences*, pp. 127–8

13. *Acts and Ordinances of the Interregnum, 1642–1660*, ed. C.M. Firth and R.C. Rait, Vol. I, p. 9, (1911); *C.S.P. Ireland, Adventurers for Land 1642–1659*, p. 48; *C.J.*, Vol. 2, p. 601
14. S.P. 28/131, f. 4
15. *Vindication*, pp. 108–9; *The Army Lists of the Roundheads and Cavaliers 1642*, ed. E. Peacock, pp. 47–8, (1874)
16. W.B. Devereux, *Lives and Letters of the Devereux, Earls of Essex, 1540–1646*, Vol. 2, (1853); J.L. Sanford, *Studies and Illustrations of the Great Rebellion* (1858); *D.N.B.*
17. *C.J.*, Vol. 2, p. 651
18. Cf. D. Lloyd, *State Worthies*, p. 1008 (1679): 'The one (Hopton) was the best soldier the King had; the other (Waller) the most experienced that the pretended Parliament boasted of.'
19. I. Roy, *The Royalist Army in the First Civil War* (Oxford D. Phil. thesis, 1963), Chap. I
20. *Vindication*, p. 7
21. *Ibid*, p. 8

CHAPTER THREE: THIS WAR WITHOUT AN ENEMY

1. Experiences, ff. 6–7; *Experiences*, p. 131; P.R.O. S.P. 28/129
2. B.M. Stowe MS 618; Experiences, f. 24; *Correspondence of the Scots Commissioners in London*, ed. M. W. Meikle, p. 142, (1917)
3. M.E. Keeler, *The Long Parliament, 1640–1641*, p. 49, (1954)
4. R. Granville, *History of Granville Family*, pp. 235–6
5. Clarendon, Bk. VII, § 100
6. *Vindication*, pp. 303–4
7. C.V. Wedgwood, *The King's War 1641–1647*, p. 132, (1958)
8. *C.S.P.D., Apr.–Aug. 1640*, p. 569
9. C. Hill, *Intellectual Origins of the English Revolution*, p. 100, (1965)
10. *Vindication*, pp. 27–8. The reference is to *Eikon Basilike: The Portraiture of His Sacred Majesty in His Solitudes and Sufferings*, (1648), p. 14. 'What flames of discontent this spark (though I sought by all speedy and possible means to quench it) soon kindled, all the world is witness.'
11. Clarendon, Bk. IV, § 343–4
12. *C.J.*, Vol. 2, pp. 130, 554, 568; *Vindication*, p. 108

CHAPTER FOUR: FIRST SUCCESS: THE SIEGE OF PORTSMOUTH

1. *C.S.P. Venetian, 1642–1643*, p. 128
2. Clarendon, Bk. VI, § 32; Plan of Portsmouth, B.M. Add. MS 16370; W.G. Ross, 'Military Engineering during the Great Civil War, 1642–9', *Papers of the Royal Engineers*, Vol. 13, p. 101, (1887)
3. *C.S.P. Venetian, 1642–1643*, p. 128
4. 'The Account of Sir William Lewis', P.R.O. S.P. 28/129, f. 1
5. Main P. sources: *A True Report of the Occurrences at the Taking of Portsmouth*, T.T. E. 112 (8); *A Relation from Portsmouth, wherein is declared how the Castle was taken*, E. 116 (15); *The Taking of the Castle at Portsmouth*, E. 116 (21); J. Vicars, *Jehovah-Jireh. God in the Mount*, pp. 158–61, (1643). Main R. source: *A Declaration of all the Passages at the Taking of Portsmouth*, E. 117 (10). Chief secondary account: G. N. Godwin, *The Civil War in Hampshire 1642–56*, Chap. 2, (1904)

6. Clarendon, Bk. VI, § 84; S.P. 28/140, f. 40

CHAPTER FIVE: WILLIAM THE CONQUEROR

1. *England's Memorable Accidents*, 7–14 Nov,. T.T.E. 242 (10). Ramsey was not held responsible, but later retired to Scotland
2. *Experiences*, p. 109
3. P. Young, *Edgehill 1642*, (1967)
4. Experiences, f. 13; Rushworth, *Historical Collections*, Vol. 2, p. 92
5. 'A Relation of my Lord Ogle's Engagements before the battle of Edgehill and after', Add. MS 27402, ff. 85–91. Main P. pamphlets for campaign: *Truth in two Letters, 9 and 17 December, from the Regiment of Col. Browne, upon the designes of Marlborow and Winchester*, E. 83 (11); *The latest printed Newes from Chichester, Windsor, Winchester, Chester, Manchester and York*, E. 83 (8); *Brave Newes of the taking of the City of Chichester . . .*, E. 83 (36)
6. *Truth in two Letters . . .*
7. Experiences, f. 63
8. Waller's own account in a letter to the Speaker was printed in *Jehovah-Jireh*, pp. 235–8. Main secondary account: see C. Thomas-Stanford, *Sussex in the Great Civil War 1642–1660*, (1910)
9. Waller, Heselrige and Cawley to Speaker (6 Jan. 1643), *Military Memoir of Colonel John Birch*, ed. T. W. Webb, C.S., pp. 202–3, (1873); *C.S.P.D., 1645–1647*, p. 447; Receipts, S.P. 28/298
10. Thomas-Stanford, *Sussex in Great Civil War*, p. 589
11. Whitaker, f. 20

CHAPTER SIX: THE NIGHT OWL

1. *C.J.*, Vol. 2, p. 937
2. G. Wither, *Justitiarius Justificatus*, T.T. E. 506 (30); *Mercurius Aulicus*, 26 Feb.–4 March, E. 86 (41)
3. *Acts and Ordinances of the Interregnum, 1642–1660*, ed. C.H. Firth & R.S. Rait, Vol. I, pp. 79, 85, 100, (1911). For Parliament's proclamation (10 Feb. 1643) giving Waller authority to raise assessments in Gloucestershire and its neighbouring counties, see Bodl. Tanner MS 64, f. 167
4. Claim for arrears of pay, P.R.O. S.P. 28/46, Pt. IV, f. 351
5. *Mercurius Aulicus*, E. 86 (41); *A Famous Victoree obtained against the Cavaliers by Sir William Waller at Padsworth*, T.T. E. 90 (24). For the reasons for believing that the latter refers to Alton, see Godwin, *The Civil War in Hampshire*, pp. 71–2
6. Vicars, *Jehovah-Jireh*, p. 276; *Mercurius Aulicus*, E. 86 (41)
7. *Jehovah-Jireh*, p. 276
8. Keeler, *The Long Parliament*, pp. 101–2, 225; *D.N.B.*; *The Memoirs of Edmund Ludlow 1625–1672*, ed. C.H. Firth, Vol. I, pp. 440–3, (1894)
9. *Ibid*, Vol. 2, p. 133
10. Clarendon, Bk. III, § 128
11. *Mr. William Lilly's True History of King James the First and King Charles the First*, pp. 48–9, (1715)
12. *D.N.B.*; Keeler, *The Long Parliament*, p. 213; G.H. Brown, *The Place of Sir Arthur Heselrige in English Politics 1659–1660*, pp. 4–8 (Oxford B. Litt thesis, 1949)
13. *Jehovah-Jireh*, p. 276; Bayley, *Civil War in Dorset*, Chap. 3
14. E. Warburton, *Memoirs of Prince Rupert and the Cavaliers*, (1849), Vol. 2, p. 141
15. *Mercurius Aulicus*, 19–25 March, T.T. E. 247 (26)
16. Ludlow, *Memoirs*, Vol. I, p. 52; *Mercurius Aulicus*, 19–25 March, E. 247 (26). For Thomas Essex, see J. Latimer, *The Annals of Bristol in the Seventeenth Century*, p. 167. For the Yeoman's Plot, see J. Vicars, *op. cit.*, pp. 277–8; *A Full Declaration of all particulars concerning the march of the forces under Col. Fiennes to Bristol. Also a relation of the late conspiracy against the city of Bristol*, T.T. E. 97 (6). For Fiennes, see *D.N.B.* and Keeler, *The Long Parliament*, p. 310; Luke, p. 15
17. *A Full Declaration of all particulars . . .*, E. 97 (6)
18. *Mercurius Aulicus*, E. 247 (26)
19. Letters of Colonel N. Fiennes to his father and Essex, both dated 20 March, in *A Relation made in the House of Commons by*

Col. Nathaniel Fiennes, concerning the
Surrender of Bristol, T.T. E. 64 (12)

CHAPTER SEVEN: WESTERN
SUCCESSES

1. *A Letter from Sir William Waller to the
Earl of Essex of a great victory he obtained at
Malmesbury*, T.T. E. 94 (12). Other P.
accounts: Luke, pp. 42–3; *Jehovah-Jireh*,
pp. 292–3. R. account: *Mercurius Aulicus*,
19–25 March, E. 247 (26)
2. Clarendon, Bk. VI, § 292–3
3. Luke, pp. 50–1
4. A letter from Waller and Heselrige to
the Speaker (12 April 1643), printed as *The
Victorious and Fortunate Proceedings of Sir
William Waller and his forces in Wales and other
places since they left Malmesbury*, E. 97 (2).
Other P. sources: Luke, pp. 53–4; J. Corbet,
'The Military Government of Gloucester',
Bibliotheca Gloucestrensis, ed. J. Washbourne,
pp. 28–9, (1825). Corbet was Massey's
chaplain
5. *Sir Edward Hungerford's Vindication for
the Surrendering of Malmesbury to Sir William
Waller*, E. 100 (3). Cf. P.R.O. S.P. 28/15, Pt.
2, f. 210. Capt. Richard Gifford's
deposition concerning Hungerford's
money-grasping ways; Bodl. Tanner MS 62,
f. 75, Capt. Henry Archbold to Col. J.
Fiennes (6 June, Malmesbury) expressing a
desire to leave Hungerford's service. Cf.
Ibid, f. 111, Capt. Samson 'is quite weary of
his service'
6. Kent R.O. Waller's letter to Devon
Commissioners (29 March 1643), Earl de la
Warr MSS U. 269C. 290/(56). Cf. Waller's
later proclamation against neutrality in
Sussex, *Mercurius Britanicus*, 15–22 Apr.
1644, E. 43 (19)
7. *Historical Collections*, J. Rushworth,
Vol. 5, p. 263. Bodl. Clarendon MS 22, f. 97
8. *Victorious and Fortunate Proceedings*...
9. *Experiences*, p. 109
10. *The Vindication of Richard Atkyns*, ed. P.
Young, entitled '"The Praying Captain" A
Cavalier's Memoirs', *J.S.A.H.R.*, Vol. 35,
p. 7, (1957)
11. *Victorious and Fortunate Proceedings*...

12. Corbet, *op. cit.*, pp. 34–5. *Mercurius
Aulicus*, T.T. E. 99 (22) contains
contemporary material, including the
possibly truthful tale that Waller's horse
had thrown him in the conflict. Parliament
ordered the printing of Waller's despatches
'with alterations by Sir Thomas Barrington'
(*Mercurius Aulicus*, 16–22 April, T.T. E. 100
(18)), but may have declined to print his
account of Ripple Field. Barrington, an
Essex gentleman, was a friend of Pym's and
a respected member of his party. A.H.
Burne and P. Young, *The Great Civil War,
1642–1646* (1959), pp. 70–4, gives useful
topographical information on the
battlefield

CHAPTER EIGHT: HEREFORD
TAKEN

1. The Accounts of Capt. Thomas
Blayney, military treasurer in Gloucester,
P.R.O. S.P. 28/129, 299
2. *Mercurius Aulicus*, 5–11 March, T.T. E.
247 (20). A report that of a loan of £60,000
desired by Parliament only £25,000 had
been brought in, of which £16,000 went to
Essex and £8,000 to Waller; *C.J.*, Vol. 2, pp.
964, 971. Waller contributed himself to a
£4,000 loan on 14 February, which was to
be repaid by sequestrations, *C.S.P.D.*,
1641–1643, p. 443. Other methods were
also employed. Cf. P.R.O. S.P. 28/298:
Warrant to Giles Hickes 'to march with
troop to Sir Richard Ducy's house and raise
£1,000 from him or bring him back to
Gloucester as a prisoner'.
3. Corbet, *op. cit.*, p. 35; *Mercurius
Bellicus*... *Wherein is the relation of the taking
of Hereford by Sir William Waller*, E. 100 (7)
4. Willis-Bund, *Civil War in Worcestershire*,
p. 91
5. Corbet, *op. cit.*, pp. 16, 36

CHAPTER NINE: WORCESTER
ATTEMPTED

1. Erle to Speaker (3 June 1643),
H.M.C., *Portland* MS, Vol. I, p. 710

2. *Colonel Fiennes his reply to a Pamphlet entitled: An Answer to Colonell Nathaniel Fiennes Relation concerning his surrender of Bristol,* T.T. E. 70 (1), (6 Oct. 1643); Popham to Fiennes (24 May 1643), Bodl. Clarendon MS 22, f. 43

3. J. Fiennes to N. Fiennes, (26 May), Clarendon MS, 22, fo. 45

4. Sir Robert Cooke to Speaker (2 June), H.M.C., *12th Report,* I, p. 709

5. Quoted in E. Warburton, *op. cit.,* p. 95

6. Sir Robert Cooke, Colonel Burghill *et al.* to Speaker (3 June), H.M.C., *Portland MSS,* Vol. 1, p. 712

7. Blayney's Accounts, P.R.O. S.P. 28/129, 299

8. Clarendon, Bk. VII, § 401; F. I.R. Edgar, *Sir Ralph Hopton,* 'Conclusion', (1968)

9. *Experiences,* f. 50; *Vindication of Atkyns,* p. 11; Alnwick Castle: Duke of Northumberland MSS, Letters and Papers, Vol. 16, ff. 50–1; Hopton, pp. 48–50; Slingsby, pp. 90–1

Chapter Ten: Preparations for Battle

1. Waller and Heselrige to Speaker (22 June), Bodl. Tanner MS 62, f. 128

2. Clarendon, Vol. 3, p. 89. Cf. *Bellum Civile,* p. 51; *Weekly Intelligencer,* 13–20 June, T.T. E. 55 (8) 'Six gallant troops of horse went to him from London last week under the command of Sir Arthur Heselrige'. The troop commanders were Capts. Samuel Gardiner, Richard Fincher, John Butler, Edward Foley and John Okey, P.R.O. S.P. 28/7, f. 540. Heselrige spent considerable sums of money procuring suitable horses for his heavily armoured troops. In 1644, when Edmund Ludlow joined the regiment as major, Heselrige bought 100 horses for him in Smithfield, *Memoirs,* Vol. I, p. 90. For Heselrige's colours, see 'Banners of the Parliamentarian Army', B.M. Add. MS 5247

3. G. Markham, *The Souldier's Exercise* (1643), pp. 35–6. Cuirassiers or 'pistoliers' ought to be 'men of the best degree' and

'the meanest is a gentleman'

4. Bodl. Clarendon MS 22, f. 87

5. *A Relation made in the House of Commons by Col. Nathaniel Fiennes, concerning the surrender of Bristol,* T.T. E. 64 (12). The letter may well have been edited by Col. Fiennes for he produced it as evidence that he had sent 1,200 men to Waller at this time. Both his own and his brother's half-completed foot regiments in Bristol certainly remained there, as well as the remaining half of Popham's Foot.

6. Clarendon MS 22, f. 113

7. S.P. 28/7, f. 535; 28/8, Pt. 1, f. 63; 28/14, Pt. 1, f. 70

8. MS in Prideaux-Brune MSS, printed in M. Coate, *Cornwall in the Great Civil War,* 2nd edn, p. 77, (1963). This is not the original of Waller's letter, as Miss Coate believed, but a copy. It differs only in unimportant details from Waller's draft in Clarendon MS 22, f. 113. The gist of the letter appeared in *A Weekly Account* 3–10 July, E. 249 (25). Another copy exists in the Duke of Somerset MSS, H.M.C., *15th Report,* App. VII

Chapter Eleven: Victory at Lansdown

1. Hopton, p. 51; *A True Relation of the Victory obtained by Sir William Waller . . . against the Marquesse Hartford, Prince Maurice and others,* E. 60 (12), the main P. source for the Lansdown campaign. See also Vicars, *Jehovah-Jireh,* pp. 376–80

2. H.M.C., *Portland MSS,* Vol. 3, pp. 112–13. Capt. Edward Harley to Sir Robert Harley (15 July, Bristol). Sir Robert Harley of Brampton Castle, Herefordshire, a prominent Puritan gentleman and M.P. for his county (see M.F. Keeler, *The Long Parliament 1640–1641* (1954), p. 203; *D.N.B.*), was one of the leading Parliamentarians concerned with the West. Edward Harley, a troop commander in Waller's regt., had marched into the West with Heselrige's Lobsters in June, *Letters of*

Lady Brilliana Harley, ed. T.T. Lewis, C. S., (1853), p. 203. He ascribed the loss of the passage to the failure of the 'seconds' to arrive in time, but *A True Relation* implied that the reinforcements (3 troops of horse and 3 companies) were sent in good time, and placed Dowett and not Burghill in command of the original party. But as Harley's troop was in the same regiment as Dowett he would have noted such a fact

3. Slingsby, p. 91
4. *Vindication of Atkyns*, p. 52
5. Edward Harley's Letter, *op. cit.*, p. 112; *A True Relation . . .*, p. 4
6. Waller to Speaker (12 July), Tanner MS 62, f. 164
7. *Experiences*, p. 123
8. *A Weekly Account*, 3–10 July, T.T. E. 249 (18). The officers' names are given in 'Royalist Casualties at Lansdown', a list compiled by P. Young as Appendix 'B' to the account of Atkyns, *op. cit.*, p. 68

CHAPTER TWELVE: MY DISMAL DEFEAT AT ROUNDWAY DOWN

1. *Vindication of Atkyns*, p. 55
2. *Ibid*, p. 62
3. Luke, p. 116
4. *C.J.*, Vol. 2, p. 163
5. *Mercurius Aulicus*, 9–15 July, T.T. E. 70 (8)
6. *A True Relation . . .*, p. 5
7. Hopton, p. 55
8. Waller to Speaker (12 July), Bodl. Tanner MS 62, f. 164. Letter of Waller to his wife, reported in House of Commons by Anthony Nicholls on 12 July, B.M. Whitaker, Add. MS 31, 116, f. 12
9. Experiences, ff. 15–18
10. Wilts. Quarter Sessions Records, H.M.C., *Various Collections*, Vol. 1, p. 111
11. Tanner MS 62, f. 164
12. *Vindication of Atkyns*, p. 57
13. Edward Harley's Letter, *op. cit.*, p. 113; Whitaker, f. 12
14. *The Kingdome's Weekly Intelligencer*, 11–18 July, E. 61 (1); *C.S.P. Venetian, 1642–1643*, pp. 304–5; *Experiences*, pp.

123–4; W.B. Devereux, *op. cit.*, p. 374. For an unconvincing reply on behalf of the Lord General for his failure to make a diversion, see *A Remonstrance to vindicate Robert Earle of Essex from some false aspersions cast upon his proceedings*, E. 71 (7)

15. Bodl. Tanner MS 62, f. 164. The House received the letter on 15 July, D'Ewes, Harl. MS 165, f. 127
16. Hopton, p. 57
17. Edward Harley's Letter, *op. cit.*, p. 113
18. The fullest account of the battle on either side: *Sir John Byron's Relation to the Secretary of the last Western Action*, B.M. 1103 d. 77/5. A useful secondary account: J. M. Prest, 'The Campaign of Roundway Down', *The Wiltshire Archaeological and Natural History Magazine*, Vol. 53, (1949–50)
19. Clarendon, Bk. VII, § 118
20. *Vindication of Atkyns*, pp. 58–60
21. 'Sir John Byron's Relation' . . .
22. Edward Harley's Letter, *op. cit.*, p. 113
23. *Experiences*, p. 123
24. *Ibid*. For the Lord General's letter (9 July, Great Brickhill), which triggered off this reaction, see H.M.C., *Cowper* MSS, Vol. 2, p. 335. For evidence that the 'zealous' had been planning their army before this letter reached London, see *Instructions and Propositions containing incouragements to all good men to subscribe for the raising of an Army of ten thousand men of godly conversation, as additional forces to the Army under the command of Robert, Earle of Essex* (8 July), T.T. E. 59 (15)
25. 'The Journal of the Siege of Bristol', E.G.B. Warburton, *Memoirs of Prince Rupert . . .* (1849), p. 238
26. *Colonell Fiennes his reply . . .*, E. 70 (1); 'The Testimony of Colonell Edward Cooke', *A Catalogue of the Witnesses and Testimonies produced by the Prosecutors of Colonell Nathaniel Fiennes at his Tryall*, E. 255 (17)
27. Experiences, ff. 27–8
28. *C.S.P. Venetian, 1643–1647*, p. 1
29. Sir John Denham, *Poems*, p. 107, (1671)
30. *The Letters and Speeches of Oliver Cromwell*, ed. S.C. Lomas, Vol. 1, p. 150, (1904)

CHAPTER THIRTEEN: A WARM WELCOME

1. *The Knyvett Letters*, p. 121

2. Wm. Constantine, MP to unknown correspondent, 5 Aug. 1643, Bodl. Tanner MS 62, f. 263. 'The Earls (Essex) party goes under ye stile of moderate, ye other vehement' Clarendon called them 'violent', Bks VII–VIII, *passim*

3. *Vindication*, p. 11

4. J.M. Hexter, *The Reign of King Pym* (1941), pp. 70, 97; G. Yule, *The Independents in the English Civil War* (1958), Chap. 3

5. 'The Diary of John Greene (1635–57)', ed. E.M. Symonds, *E. H. R.*, Vol. 43 (1928), p. 392

6. Clarendon, Bk. VIII, para. 100

7. Whitaker, B.M. Add. MS 31, 116, f. 63; P. Young, *Marston Moor 1644*, p. 80

8. *The Kingdome's Weekly Intelligencer*, 18–15 July, T.T. E. 61 (22)

9. *D.N.B.* See also, C.M. Williams, 'The Political Career of Henry Marten, with particular reference to the origins of republicanism in the Long Parliament' (Oxford D. Phil. thesis, 1954)

10. *C.J.*, Vol. 3, p. 176. All were Independents, see J.H. Hexter, *op. cit.*, p. 123. Although the petitioners requested permission to 'all rise and joyne together as one man' they also sought power for their committee to compel those unwilling to contribute money or service, D'Ewes, Harl. MS 165, f. 128

11. *A Perfect Diurnall*, 24–31 July, T.T. E. 249 (30)

12. D'Ewes, B.M. Harl. MS. 164, f. 368. Cf. B. Whitelocke, *Memorials of the English affaires* . . . (1853 edn) Vol. 1, p. 70. For other evidence of Waller's popularity, Anthony Nicholl to Judith Barrington, 'Correspondence and Papers of the Barrington family', B.M. Egerton MS 2646, f. 297; Countess of Sussex to Sir Ralph Verney (19 July), Verney MSS at Claydon House, Bucks, cit. in J. Hexter, *op. cit.*, p. 120

13. *Vindication*, pp. 15–16. Cf. an earlier attempt in the previous winter by the 'violent party' to set up a volunteer army independent of Essex, J. H. Hexter, *op. cit.*, pp. 109–10

14. *C.J.*, Vol. 3, p. 183. Marten's first draft measure for the new army's establishment brought from the Merchant Taylors' Hall committee had been rejected as it contained no list of officers to be commissioned. On 26 July Marten proposed Waller (who was then in the House) for the chief command 'which choice the house very well approved', reported Whitaker, Add. MS 31, 116, f. 66. The House of Lords concurred on 29 July (*L.J.*, Vol. 6, p. 187) and the Common Council of the City on the same day, *Ibid*; *Letter of Mercurius Civicus to M. Rusticus*, T.T. E. 65 (32)

15. *A Perfect Diurnall*, T.T. E. 249 (30). *A Declaration of the Proceedings of the Honourable Committee of the House of Commons at Merchant Taylor's Hall for Raising the People of the Land as one Man Under the command of Sir William Waller*, T.T. E. 63 (10). For Henry Marten's speech concerning Waller on this occasion, see *Three Speeches delivered at a Common-Hall*, T.T. E. 63 (8). J.H. Hexter (*op. cit.*, Chap. 6 and 7, *passim*) mistakenly supposed that two new armies were to be raised, one by the Independents and the other by the Committee of Militia each with Waller as their general. In fact the Committee of Militia was busy raising the 6,500 Horse for the Earl of Manchester

16. *A True Relation of the Taking of Bristol*, T.T. 669, f. 8 (19). The letter referred to was probably that read in the Lower House on 22 July alleging Parliament's neglect of the army, D'Ewes, Harl. MS 165, f. 129

17. *L.J.*, Vol. 6, p. 160. Cf. Essex to Speaker (6 Aug.), Bodl. Tanner MS 62, f. 233, where the Lord General stated that his army had been three weeks without pay, and if money was not sent he could no longer hold it together

18. *C.J.*, Vol. 3, p. 183

19. *Ibid*, pp. 190–1; Whitaker, Add. MS 31, 116, f. 67

20. *C.J.*, Vol. 3, pp. 191–2. For a discussion of the council's membership see J. H. Hexter, *op. cit.*, p. 144

21. *C.S.P. Venetian, 1643–1646*, p. 6

CHAPTER FOURTEEN: HOW THE WEST WAS LOST

1. *A True Relation of Colonell Fiennes his Trial,* T.T. E. 255 (16), p. 106

2. *Experiences,* pp. 123–4; W.B. Devereux, *op. cit.,* p. 374

3. *The Journal of Sir Samuel Luke,* p. 120. Cf. *The Kingdome's Weekly Intelligencer,* 11–18 July, T.T. E. 61 (1), 'I say no more, but that it is a great pity two such valiant Commanders, [Waller and Heselrige] should suffer through neglect of others.'

4. *C.S.P. Venetian, 1642–1643,* pp. 304–5

5. *Mercurius Aulicus,* 6–12 Aug., T.T. E. 65 (26). Cf. Guildhall R.O., 'Journals of the Court of Common Council', Vol. 40, f. 69 (1 Aug. 1643): 'some ill affected persons have indeavoured to raise some mis-understandings and jealousies between his Excellency . . . and the Citty, by spreading abroad some false rumors and untrue assertions against his Excellency and his Army tending to their dishonour . . .' A committee was sent to Essex to represent the good opinion of the City and offer their best assistance for recruiting the army.

6. *A Remonstrance to vindicate Robert Earle of Essex from some false aspersions cast upon his proceedings,* T.T. E. 71 (7). This was written by one or more of Essex's officers out of loyalty to their general. Cf. the action of Col. Sir Philip Stapleton and Col. Arthur Goodwyn, who compelled Sir Henry Vane the younger to apologise in the Commons twice for slighting the Lord General, D'Ewes, B.M. Harl. MS 165, ff. 123–4

7. *The Parliament Scout,* 15–20 July, T.T. E. 61 (13)

8. *The Life, Diary and Correspondence of Sir William Dugdale,* ed. W. Hamper (1827), p. 53

9. I.G. Phillip, *op. cit.,* pp. ix–x. Cf. Essex's faulty intelligence before Edgehill, Clarendon, Bk. VI, para. 81; E. Ludlow, *op. cit.,* p. 41

10. Essex to Speaker (12 July, Gt. Brickhill), Tanner MS 62, f. 166

11. Whitaker, Add. MS 31, 116, f. 12

12. D'Ewes, Harl. MS 165, ff. 123–6; according to D'Ewes the House thought the Lord General's letter 'to bee spoken in a pipulizing or scoffing way'.

13. 'Memorial of Denzil, Lord Holles', *Tracts on the Civil Wars in England,* ed. F. Maseres, Vol. 1 (1815), p. 197. As early as 20 April, *Mercurius Aulicus* (16–22 April, T.T. E. 100 (18)) had marked down Heselrige as 'no very ventrous fighter', and Holles may have imbibed this rumour

14. J. Heath, *A Brief Chronicle of the late Intestine Warr . . .* (1663), p. 78

15. E. Ludlow, *op. cit.,* Vol. 1, p. 53. Heselrige later recommended Ludlow for a place in the New Model Army, which may explain why Ludlow does not name Heselrige specifically

16. *Colonell Fiennes Letter to my Lord Generall concerning Bristol,* T.T. E. 65 (26); *A Relation made in the House of Commons by Col. Nathaniel Fiennes, concerning the surrender of Bristol,* T.T. E. 64 (12)

17. Clement Walker, *An Answer to Col. Nathaniel Fiennes, relation concerning his surrender of the City and Castle of Bristol,* T.T. E. 67 (36). Clement Walker and William Prynne prosecuted Fiennes at his trial

18. Letter of Wm. Constantine, MP. (5 Aug. 1643), Bodl. Tanner MS. 62, f. 263

19. *Mercurius Civicus,* 8 Aug., T.T. E. 65 (4)

20. D'Ewes, Harl. MS 165, ff. 134–5. Whitaker listed them as Pym, Strode, Crewe and St John, Add. MS 31, 116, f. 67. D'Ewes, Harl. MS 165, f. 145

21. D'Ewes, Harl. MS 165, ff. 145–8. Sir Christopher Yelverton, John Glyn and William Jephson also changed their minds

22. B.M. Harl. MS 165, f. 149

23. Essex to Lord Mayor etc. (16 Nov. 1642, Hammersmith), Guildhall R.O., 'Journals of the Court of Common Council', Vol. 40, f. 41

24. D'Ewes, Harl. MS 165, f. 146; Yonge's diary, Add. MS 18, 778, f. 13; J. Rushworth, *Historical Collections,* Vol. 5, p. 357

25. Harl. MS 165, f. 149

26. Whitaker, Add. MS 31, 116, f. 70

27. D'Ewes, Harl. MS 165, f. 157; Whitaker, Add. MS 31, 116, f. 73

28. Essex to Speaker (25 Aug., Colnbrook), Bodl. Tanner MS 62, f. 293

29. Whitaker, Add. MS 31, 116, f. 74
30. D'Ewes, Harl. MS 165, f. 158
31. *C.J.*, Vol. 3, pp. 197–8, 219
32. Essex to Anthony Nicholl (29 Aug. 1643), Bodl. Tanner MS 62, f. 309
33. Bodl. Tanner MS 62, f. 293

CHAPTER FIFTEEN: RAISING A NEW ARMY

1. Cols. William Carr, James Carr, Potley, Wemyss, Lt.-Col. Ramsey and Maj. Archibald Strachan (Waller's Dragoons)
2. *Correspondence of the Scots Commissioners in London, 1644–1646*, ed. H.W. Meikle (1917)
3. *Letters of State written by Mr. John Milton . . . 1649 till the year 1659*, ed. E. Phillips (1694), p. xxviii
4. *Vindication*, pp. 16–17. Cf. *A Remonstrance to vindicate Robert Earl of Essex . . .*, T.T. E. 71 (7), which included a claim that by August 1643 Essex had not received £600,000 since the beginning of the war
5. *C.J.*, Vol. 3, p. 238. The proportions were as follows: London and Middx. 1,500; Surrey 300; Sussex 400; Kent 600; Hants 600
6. *C.S.P. Venetian, 1643–1646*, p. 18
7. H.M.C., *Portland* MSS, Vol. 3, p. 116
8. P.R.O. S.P. 28/132. According to this regimental account, Turner's regiment of horse was raised on 23 August as part of the 6,500 cavalry voted on 18 July
9. *The True Informer*, 23–30 Sept., T.T. E. 67 (38). 'On a MS List of Officers of the London Trained Bands in 1643', ed. H.A. Dillon, *The Archaeologia*, Vol. 52 (1890). The MS list is to be found in B.M. Harl. 986 with annotations by Richard Symonds
10. *A Perfect Diurnall*, 4–11 Sept., T.T. E. 250 (8). P.R.O. W.O. 55/460. Ordnance entry book (not paginated)
11. *L.J.*, Vol. 6, p. 242
12. *C.J.*, Vol. 3, p. 266; *L.J.*, Vol. 6, p. 247
13. Whitaker, Add. MS 31, 116, f. 82
14. *C.J.*, Vol. 3, p. 269
15. *A Perfect Diurnall*, 9–16 Oct., T.T. E. 252 (2)
16. *Ibid*: Clarendon, Bk. VII, para. 236;

C.S.P. Venetian, 1645–1646, p. 34
17. *Vindication*, p. 16. Cf. Harl. MS 165, f. 179, where D'Ewes expressed the same opinion
18. H.M.C., *13th Report*, 1, p. 133
19. *C.S.P. Venetian, 1643–1646*, p. 27
20. *C.J.*, Vol. 3, pp. 455–6
21. *Mercurius Aulicus*, 22–8 Oct., T.T. E. 75 (13)
22. Popham served with Waller's army at the siege of Arundel, see Bodl. Tanner MS 62, f. 508. On 23 May 1644 the Commons voted that he should be recommended to Waller for some employment worthy of him, and that he should have leave to go down upon that service, *C.J.*, Vol. 3, p. 505. He was then sent to raise recruits in the West, see E. Ludlow, *Memoirs*, Vol. 1, pp. 90–1
23. H.M.C., *Portland* MSS, Vol. 3, pp. 116, 119–20
24. Major Ralph Cotsforth of Heselrige's foot had been third captain in Lord Brooke's regiment (Peacock, p. 34). Captain Edward Foley of Heselrige's horse, served under Brooke as a troop commander (P.R.O. S.P. 28/34, Pt. 2, ff. 377, 383), while Captain John Okey acted as quartermaster to Brooke's own troop in August 1642 (Peacock, p. 48)

CHAPTER SIXTEEN: A FLING AT BASING HOUSE

1. Hopton, p. 61
2. B.M. Harl. MS 6804, f. 224
3. 'On a MS List of Officers of the London Trained Bands in 1643', *The Archaeologia*, Vol. 52 (1890), ed. H. A. Dillon, pp. 12, 16
4. E. Archer, *A True Relation of the trained-bands of Westminster, the Green Auxiliaries of London, and the Yellow Auxiliaries of the Tower Hamlets; under the command of Sir William Waller; from Monday the 16 of Octob. to Wednesday the 20 of Decemb. 1643*, B.M. 101, b. 64
5. Archer, p. 2
6. P.R.O. S.P. 28/8, Pt. 1, ff. 75, 77
7. P.R.O. S.P. 28/135, ff. 1–12. The accounts of Col. Samuel Jones of all money

received and paid out for his regiment and the garrison of Farnham Castle. A dragoon company also formed part of the Farnham garrison

8. P.R.O. W.O. 55/460, Ordnance entry book; B.M. Add. MS 34, 315, Ordnance issue book, 1643–4, ff. 19, 22, 25

9. B.M., Add. MS. 32, 477, f. 83

10. P.R.O. S.P. 28/135, ff. 1–12, 122–55, account books of Commissary-General Nicholas Cowling. In Nov. 1643 the officers were Lt.-Col. Ramsey, Maj. John Hillersdon, Capts. Edward Willett, Lewis Pemberton, Andrew Mainwaring, Philip Stevens, Gravenor, Roe

11. Waller (16 Nov., H.M.C., *Portland* MSS, Vol. 1, p. 154) and E. Archer (*A True Relation . . .*, B.M., 101, b. 64, p. 2) both gave the cavalry strength as 16 troops and 8 companies of dragoons. The dragoon captains included John Clarke, Matthew Draper, John Bennet, Nicholas Moore and William Turpin, P.R.O. S.P. 28/10, ff. 105–12

12. C.H. Firth, *Cromwell's Army* (1902), p. 88

13. *C.J.*, Vol. 3, pp. 299, 302

14. *L.J.*, Vol. 6, pp. 294–6

15. *The True Informer*, 28 Oct.–4 Nov., T.T. E. 75 (21)

16. See *Certain Informations*, 22–7 Nov., T.T. E. 77 (6) for further use of term 'Southern Associated counties'

17. Hopton, p. 65

18. Waller to Speaker (16 Nov.), H.M.C., *Portland* MSS, Vol. 1, pp. 154–5

19. A copy of a letter from a lieutenant in the army in *Remarkable Passages*, 19–25 Nov., T.T. E. 77 (3). For an old drawing of Basing House in the Bodleian Library see frontispiece of G.N. Godwin, *The Civil War in Hampshire 1642–1645* (1904). *The Souldiers Report concerning Sir William Waller's fight against Basing House*, 12 Nov. 1643, T.T. E. 76 (5), contains a brief contemporary description of the house

20. C.R. Peers, 'Excavations on the site of Basing House, Hampshire', *Archaeologia*, Vol. 61, pp. 553–64. A copy of the contemporary engraving of Wencelaus Hollar is printed in this work. Yet the pattern of the earthworks has only become

evident from aerial photographs. P.R.O. W.O. 55/458 and Bodl. Rawlinson MS D. 395 contain numerous Royalist ordnance warrants for issues to Basing House

21. Waller to Speaker (16 Nov.), H.M.C., *Portland* MSS, Vol. 1, pp. 154–5

22. *Mercurius Aulicus*, 12–19 November, T.T. E. 77

23. E. Archer, *A True Relation . . .*, B.M. 101, b. 64, p. 4

24. H.M.C., *Portland* MSS, Vol. 1, pp. 154–5; *Mercurius Britanincus*, 20–7 Nov., T.T. E. 77

25. *Mercurius Aulicus*, 12–19 Nov., T.T. E. 77

26. *Mercurius Britanicus*, 20–7 Nov., T.T. E. 77 (7); E. Archer, *A True Relation . . .*, B.M. 101, b. 64

27. Waller to Speaker (16 Nov.), H.M.C. Portland MSS, Vol. 1, pp. 154–5

CHAPTER SEVENTEEN: DELIVERANCE AT FARNHAM

1. Waller to Speaker (23 Nov.), H.M.C., *Portland* MSS, Vol. 1, p. 159; Wm. Cawley to Speaker, *Ibid*, p. 161; *C.J.*, Vol. 3, pp. 314, 319, 320; *Mercurius Civicus*, 23–30 Nov., T.T. E. 77 (15)

2. P.R.O. S.P. 28/135, ff. 1–12, 122–55, account books of Commissary-General Nicholas Cowling. Cowling had been commissary of victuals in Bristol under Col. N. Fiennes. *A Catalogue of Witnesses and Testimonies . . .*, T.T. E. 255 (17), p. 20

3. E. Archer, *A True Relation . . .*, B.M. 101, b. 64, p. 7

4. Hopton, p. 67

5. Experiences, f. 18. Cf. Waller to Speaker (28 Nov.), H.M.C., *Portland* MSS, Vol. 1, pp. 163–4; *A Great Overthrow Given to Sir Ralph Hopton's whole Army by Sir William Waller near Farnham . . .*, T.T. E. 77 (14); *Mercurius Civicus*, 23–30 Nov., T.T. E. 77 (15); *The Weekly Account*, 23–30 Nov., T.T. E. 77 (16)

6. E. Archer, *A True Relation . . .*, B.M. 101, b. 64, p. 9. Hopton, however, in *Bellum Civile* (p. 67) placed this raid before his attempt on Farnham

7. Clarendon, Bk. VIII, para. 6; Hopton, p. 68; *Colonel Joseph Bamfield's Apologie, written by himselfe and printed at his desire* (1685). Apart from stating that the Royalist army was divided into four, not three brigades, Bamfield differs from Hopton only in detail. Bamfield was an Irish officer in Hopton's army

CHAPTER EIGHTEEN: THE STORMING OF ALTON

1. *Mercurius Aulicus*, 3–9 Dec., T.T. E. 79 (1)
2. Bodl. Tanner MS 62, f. 410; *The Kingdome's Weekly Intelligencer*, 28 Nov.–5 Dec., T.T. E. 77 (29), reported the King at Basing House with 2,000 Horse, and as intending to advance into Kent
3. Clarendon, Bk. VIII, para. 9
4. R. Baillie, *Letters and Journals* (1775), Vol. 1, p. 403
5. *Military Memoir of Colonel John Birch . . . written by Roe, his Secretary*, ed. J. Webb, C. S., (1873), p. 4; E. Archer, *A True Relation . . .*, B.M. 101, b. 64, p. 8
6. *A Narration . . .*, T.T. E. 78 (22), p. 7
7. *Experiences*, p. 124
8. Both letters from Hopton and Crawford are printed in G.N. Godwin, *op. cit.*, p. 148
9. Clarendon, Bk. VIII, para. 9

CHAPTER NINETEEN: THE SIEGE OF ARUNDEL

1. E. Archer, *A True Relation . . .*, B.M. 101, b. 64, p. 13
2. Waller to House of Lords (21 Dec.), *L.J.*, Vol. 6, p. 350 (first half), H.M.C., *10th Report*, Pt. 6, p. 150 (second half)
3. *Military Memoir of Colonel John Birch*, pp. 6–7. The entrenchment known locally as Rhodes Ditch, can still be seen beneath the trees of Castle Park. Even today it justifies Waller's description as 'very strong' (Waller to House of Lords (21 Dec.), *L.J.*, Vol. 6, p. 350 and H.M.C., *10th Report*, Pt. 6, p. 150)
4 J. Bamfield, *op. cit.*

5. Jacob Travers, *An Exact and True Relation of the taking of Arundel Castle by Sir William Waller*, T.T. E. 81 (12), pp. 2–3
6. *L.J.*, Vol. 6, p. 350 and H.M.C., *10th Report*, Pt. 6, p. 150
7. *Journal of Sir Samuel Luke*, p. 233
8. The account book of Commissary Bowles, P.R.O. S.P. 28/130, ff. 111–26, lists the Kentish brigade at the siege of Arundel, giving officers' regiment names and strengths
9. Hopton, p. 73; *The Journal of Sir Samuel Luke*, p. 229; Revd John Coulton to Samuel Jeake, 'Extracts from the MSS. of Samuel Jeake', *Sussex Archaeological Collections*, Vol. 18 (1878), Coulton was present at the siege as chaplain to a Sussex troop of horse
10. Cowling's account book, P.R.O. S.P. 28/135, f. 16
11. *Bellum Civile*, pp. 73–4. Cf. a report in D'Ewes, Harl. MS 165, f. 268, that Waller drew out his forces to give battle, but Hopton refused to fight, and returned to Winchester leaving Wilmot to face Waller with a part of his army
12. *A Full Relation . . .*, T.T. E. 81 (10)
13. *Ibid*
14. J. Bamfield, *op. cit.*
15. J. H. Hillier, *The Sieges of Arundel Castle* (1854), p. 35
16. *A Perfect Diurnall*, 27 Nov.–4 Dec., T.T. E. 252 (10)
17. See *Certaine Propositions made by Sir William Waller at the Surrender of Arundell Castle* (6 Jan.), T.T. E. 81 (21)
18. Bodl. Tanner MS 62, f. 497
19. Bodl. Tanner MS 62, f. 508
20. *Mercurius Civicus*, 4–11 Jan., T.T. E. 81 (22)
21. *Mercurius Bellicus*, 4–11 Jan., T.T. E. 81 (22); *The Journal of Sir Samuel Luke*, p. 233. 'Extracts from the MSS. of Samuel Jeake', p. 53; Whitaker, B.M. Add. MS 31, 116, f. 108
22. *Vindication*, pp. 208–9
23. *Certaine Propositions . . .*, T.T. E. 81 (21). The full text of these 'Gratulatory' verses is given in J. H. Hillier, *op. cit.*, pp. 56–8

CHAPTER TWENTY: A GREAT VICTORY AT CHERITON

1. *Mercurius Britanicus*, 27 Nov.–5 Dec., T.T. E. 77 (28)

2. W. Notestein, 'The Establishment of the Committee of Both Kingdoms', *American Historical Review*, Vol. 17 (1912)

3. *L.J.*, Vol. 6, p. 430

4. *C.S.P. Venetian, 1643–1647*, p. 78

5. 'Journal of Occurrences 1643–1646', B.M. Add. MS 24, 465. This is a later transcript of a contemporary journal written by an Independent

6. *C.J.*, Vol. 3, p. 39

7. *C.S.P.D., 1644*, pp. 33–4, 49

8. Reprinted in full in J. Adair, *Cheriton, 1644*

9. *The Journal of Sir Samuel Luke*, p. 270

10. *A Fuller Relation of the Victory obtained at Alsford, 28 March, by the Parliaments forces* (presented to the Lord Mayor and Committee of Militia by an eyewitness employed to attend the London Brigade), T.T. E. 40 (1), p. 4; *The True Informer*, 23–30 March, T.T. E. 43 (24)

11. Capt. Harley to Col. Edward Harley (12 April, Bishopstoke), H.M.C., *Portland* MSS, Vol. 3, pp. 106–10. Capt. Harley described his account of the Cheriton campaign as 'these scribbled lines which are nothing else than a confused thing patched up by a short memory'.

12. *A Fuller Relation* . . ., T.T. E. 40 (1), pp. 4–5

13. Colonel Walter Slingsby's Relation of the Battle of Alresford, printed from Clarendon MS 23 in *Bellum Civile*, pp. 100–3

14. *A Letter from Captain Jones* . . ., T.T. E. 40 (12). This officer served in one of the city regiments

15. *C.S.P.D., 1644*, pp. 70–1

16. Previously historians (probably following the map on p. 322 of S.R. Gardiner, *History of the Great Civil War 1642–1649* (1893), Vol. 1) have placed the Royalist army on Tichborne Down at this point, and have believed the battle to have been fought in the valley between that plateau and East Down (Waller's supposed position), with Cheriton as the little village on Waller's left flank. Yet the documentary evidence suggests that the village was in fact Hinton Ampner (Harley, who knew the name of 'Cherrytowne' refers to it simply as 'a little village'). Captain Jones, who served in one of the City regiments, stated explicitly that 'we fought in East Down', *A Letter from Captain Jones; being a relation of the proceedings of Sir William Waller's Armie*, T.T. E. 40 (12). Lastly, there is local evidence to support the theory that the barrow on the western end of East Down is in fact a burial mound containing those who fell in battle. The location of two cannon balls found on the south of East Down (in the stream) also supports the site of the battle put forward in this chapter

17. *Military Memoir of Colonel Birch*, p. 9

18. H.M.C., *Portland* MSS, Vol. 3, pp. 106–10. Heselrige gave the number as 600 (notes on Heselrige's speech in the House of Commons, in 'Diary of Walter Yonge', B.M. Add. MS 18, 779, f. 87)

19. *C.S.P.D., 1644*, p. 172

20. *The Scottish Dove*, 19–26 April, T.T. E. 44 (2)

21. *Experiences*, ff. 19–20

22. *A Fuller Relation* . . ., T.T. E. 40 (1); *Mercurius Aulicus*, 31 March–6 Apr., T.T. E. 43 (18)

23. *A Letter of Captain Jones* . . ., T.T. E. 40 (12); H.M.C., *Portland* MSS, Vol. 3, pp. 106–10; Yonge, Add. MS 18, 779, f. 87; *A Fuller Relation* . . ., T.T. E. 40 (1); *C.S.P.D., 1644*, p. 99

24. 'Journal of Occurrences 1643–1646', B.M. Add. MS 24, 465, f. 11

25. *L.J.*, Vol. 6, p. 505

26. For Heselrige, see Yonge, Add. MS. 18, 779, f. 87

27. *C.S.P.D., 1644*, p. 69; *L.J.*, Vol. 6, p. 505; *Six Speeches spoken in the Guild-Hall, London*, T.T. E. 42 (18)

28. *Select Tracts Relating to the Civil War in England* . . ., ed. F. Maseres (1815), p. 206

29. *Sir William Balfore's Letter to the Earl of Essex*, T.T. E. 40 (13)

30. *C.S.P.D., 1644*, pp. 83–4. Cf. the adjacent entries 'The news of the great defeat at Newark. The news of Sir William Waller's victory near Winchester . . .' in

Notes and References

'The Diary of John Greene (1635–57)', ed. E. M. Symonds, *E.H.R.*, Vol. 43 (1928), p. 599

31. 'A true Relation of my Lord Ogel's Engagements before the battle of Edghill and after', B.M. Add. MS 27, 402, f. 94

32. Waller to Speaker (5 April, Ringwood), *C.J.*, Vol. 3, p. 455. (A report in the Commons on 8 April gave Waller's strength at Christchurch as 1,000 Horse and 1,000 dragoons, D'Ewes, B.M. Harl. MS 166, f. 47.)

33. Waller to Speaker (4 May, Farnham), reported in D'Ewes, Harl. 166, f. 56

34. *A Perfect Diurnall*, 6–13 May, T.T. E. 252 (32)

35. E. Walker, *Historical Discourses*, p. 7

CHAPTER TWENTY-ONE: TO OXFORD

1. *The Knyvett Letters (1620–1644)*, ed. B. Schofield (1949), p. 137

2. *The Kingdome's Weekly Intelligencer*, 10–16 Apr., T.T. E. 42 (28)

3. *L.J.*, Vol. 6, pp. 545, 548; Vol. 7, p. 364

4. *C.S.P.D., 1644*, pp. 137, 147, 150, 151; A.R. Bayley, *The Great Civil War in Dorset, 1642–1660* (1910), pp. 153–6

5. D'Ewes, Harl. MS 166, f. 61; *A Perfect Diurnall*, 13–20 May, T.T. E. 252 (33); *The Kingdome's Weekly Intelligencer*, 14–21 May, T.T. E. 49 (5)

6. *Mercurius Civicus*, 23–30 May, T.T. E. 49 (34); D'Ewes, Harl. MS 166, f. 61

7. *The Kingdome's Weekly Intelligencer*, 8–15 Apr., 1646, T.T. E. 278 (8)

8. *The Parliamentary Scout*, 9–16 May, T.T. E. 47 (26). Cf. H.M.C., *Portland* MSS Vol. 1, p. 148

9. *C.J.*, Vol. 3, pp. 493, 478; *A Perfect Diurnall*, 13–20 May, T.T. E. 252 (33); *The Declaration of Commissary-Generall Behre against divers slanders and lies spread abroad against him*, T.T. 669, f. 10(3); *Observations on the Declaration of Commissary General Behre: signed by Colonels John Middleton and James Holburne and Captaine Gilbert Carr and James Innes*, T.T. 669, f. 10(8). For the March 1643 quarrel, see Whitaker, Add. MS 31, 116, f. 66

10. R. Coe, *An Exact Diarie. Or a breife Relation of the progresse of Sir William Waller's Army since the joyning of the London Auxillaries*, T.T. E. 2 (20). Richard Coe served in the company of Capt. Gore of the Tower Hamlets regiment. The colonels of the brigade were James Houblon (Swk. White Aux.), James Prince (West. Aux.) and Wm. Willoughby (Tower Hamlets – until 17 May, then Francis Zachary), Kent R.O. Brabourne MSS, 'Military Papers 1644'. Many companies mustered for pay from mid-April to May in Surrey, P.R.O. S.P. 28/121A, Pt. 3, ff. 343–575; Pt. 5, ff. 577–655. Col. Willoughby mustered 15 officers and 90 men in his company, and reported 58 absentees (Pt. 3, f. 545)

11. Apsley, a Sussex gentleman, had served Waller as a staff officer at the siege of Arundel, see his account of it (from the Apsley MSS) in W. K. Blauw, 'Passages of the Civil War in Sussex, *Sussex Archaeological Collections*, Vol. 5 (1852). The origins of this regiment lay in the resolution of the Commons (30 Nov. 1643) directing the Committee of Sussex to raise the 850 Foot they had been assessed for, and ordering Waller to send officers to receive them. Waller issued commissions to Lt.-Col. George Davidson and Capt. John Duncan to raise companies in Apsley's regiment on 30 March, P.R.O. S.P. 28/40, Pt. 2, f. 153; 37/Pt. 3

12. For the establishment of the train, see 'A List of the Officers of the Trayne of Artillerie their Entertaynment per weeke', P.R.O. S.P. 28/145. The total pay for a week (excluding the Bluecoats) came to £84 15s 8d

13. Waller to Speaker (19 May, Bagshot), reported in D'Ewes, Harl. MS 166, f. 63

14. Waller to Speaker (21 May, Hartley Row), reported in D'Ewes, Harl. MS 166, ff. 65, 66

15. D'Ewes, B.M. Harl. MS 166, f. 67

16. 'A list of the several quarters of Sir William Waller's Army in his march towards the King's Army . . . from May to last of July', B.M. Harl. MS 378, f. 6. Beside each of the names of the 36 quarters listed, the author placed the county, number of nights spent there and whether the army was lodged in houses or the fields. By comparing his list with R. Coe's narrative it is probable that the document was written by an officer in Waller's cavalry

288

17. R. Coe, *An exact Diarie*, T.T. E. 2 (20). For the terror in Oxford, see A. Wood, *Life and Times*, Vol. 1, p. 107
18. E. Walker, *Historical Discourses*, p. 17. Walker's account may be described as the King's 'official war history' for 1644, providing the most detailed account of the campaign from the Royalist point of view. The other continuous Royalist narratives are the *Diary of the Marches of the Royal Army during the Great Civil War kept by Richard Symonds*, ed. C.E. Long, C. S. (1859) and Clarendon, *op. cit.*, Vol. 3
19. *Mercurius Aulicus*, 19–25 May, T.T. E. 51 (7)
20. R. Coe, *An exact Diarie*, T.T. E. 2 (20)
21. Waller and Heselrige to the Speaker (4 June, Newbridge), D'Ewes, B.M. Harl. MS 166, f. 83
22. Lord Digby to Prince Rupert (8 June), E. Warburton, *Memoirs of Prince Rupert* (1849), Vol. 2, p. 417; R. Symonds, *op. cit.*, p. 8; E. Walker, *op. cit.*, pp. 19, 20, and V. Thomas, *Account of the Night March of King Charles the First from Oxford* (1850)
23. Waller and Heselrige to C.B.K. (4 June, Witney), D'Ewes, Harl. MS 166, f. 84
24. *C.S.P.D., 1644*, p. 206

CHAPTER TWENTY-TWO: A DANCE IN THE MIDLANDS

1. *C.S.P.D., 1644*, pp. 181–2
2. *Ibid*, p. 198
3. *Ibid*, pp. 214–15
4. Waller to Denbigh (7 June, Stow-on-the-Wold), H.M.C., *4th Report*, p. 267
5. *C.S.P.D., 1644*, p. 249
6. Waller's proclamation to the inhabitants of Worcester (12 June, Evesham) can be found in Kent R.O. Brabourne MSS 'Military Papers 1644'. It emphasised the role of the King's 'evil counsellors' and called on the readers to repair to Waller's headquarters
7. 'Memorial of Denzil, Lord Holles', *Select Tracts Relating to the Civil Wars in England . . .*, ed. F. Maseres (1815), p. 204
8. *C.J.*, Vol. 3, p. 256. The debate was resumed on 12 June when A. Nicholl

produced a letter from Col. Pyndar in Essex's army (5 June, Chipping Norton), setting forth the council of war's decision to march into the West, D'Ewes, Harl. MS 166, f. 72. For further details of the debates in the Commons on the 11–17 June on the Lord General's strategy, see Whitaker, Add. MS 31, 116, ff. 144–7
9. *C.S.P.D., 1644*, pp. 237, 242. Essex had summoned a council of war. Sir William Brereton carried the council of war's supporting letter (15 June, Stourbridge) in person to London, and read it in the Lower House on 17 June, backing it with his own arguments, D'Ewes, Harl. MS 166, f. 74
10. *C.S.P.D., 1644*, p. 247; Waller to Earl of Leven, Earl of Manchester and Lord Fairfax, H.M.C. *9th Report*, II, p. 436
11. For a Parliamentarian assertion to the same effect, see 'Journall of Occurrences, 1643–1646', B.M. Add. MS 24, 465
12. E. Warburton, *Memoirs of Prince Rupert* (1849), Vol. 2, pp. 418–19
13. Waller to C.B.K. (19 June, Pershore), *C.S.P.D., 1644*, p. 252
14. On 17 June Essex's letter (12 June, Blandford) was read in the House. John Glyn suggested that Essex should be encouraged; D'Ewes pointed out that he had disobeyed the C.B.K., Harl. MS 166, f. 74. Cf. letters defending the decision from Essex and his officers, *Ibid.* ff. 84–6; *C.S.P.D., 1644*, pp. 240, 242
15. Waller to C.B.K. (21 July, Sandhurst, Glos.), *Ibid*, pp. 248, 253, 262, 267–8
16. E. Walker, *op. cit.*, p. 29
17. *C.S.P.D., 1644*, p. 279
18. *Perfect Occurrences*, 21–8 June, T.T. E. 252 (51)

CHAPTER TWENTY-THREE: A DISHONOURABLE LOSS AT CROPREDY BRIDGE

1. *C.S.P.D., 1644*, p. 288
2. *C.S.P.D., 1644*, p. 290. For R. accounts of Cropredy fight, see *Mercurius Aulicus*, 23–9 June, T.T. E. 2 (6); Lord Digby to the Queen (4 July, Williamscote), *C.S.P.D.,*

1644, p. 316; Lord Digby to Prince Rupert (12 July), E. Warburton, *Memoirs of Prince Rupert*, Vol. 2 (1849), p. 472. For local topographical details, see P. Young and M. Toynbee, *Cropredy Bridge 1644* (1970)

3.   *An exact and Full Relation of the last fight between the Kings Forces and Sir William Waller on 29 June*, T.T. E. 53 (18)

4.   Waller to C.B.K. (30 June), *C.S.P.D., 1644*, p. 293

5.   *Military Memoir of Colonel Birch*, p. 13

6.   Waller to Speaker (1 July, Bourton), D'Ewes, B.M. Harl. MS 166, f. 87

7.   *Mercurius Aulicus*, 23–9 June, T.T. E. 2 (6)

8.   *Experiences*, p. 107

9.   *C.S.P.D., 1644*, pp. 293–4, 298; *Perfect Occurrences*, 28 June–5 July, T.T. E. 252 (51)

10.   Experiences, ff. 63–4

11.   For casualties and prisoners on either side, see also *Mercurius Aulicus*, 23–9 June, T.T. E. 2 (6); *Perfect Occurrences*, 28 June–5 July, T.T. E. 252 (51). For Sleamaker's case, see Somerset Quarter Session Records

12.   *Experiences*, f. 7

13.   *Perfect Occurrences*, 28 June–5 July, T.T. E. 252 (51). Potley besieged Donnington Castle in the first week of August, the last mention of him in the field, *The True Informer*, 3–10 Aug, T.T. E. 4 (32)

14.   *C.S.P.D., 1644*, p. 301

15.   Kent R.O. Brabourne MSS, 'Military Papers, 1644'

16.   *C.S.P.D., 1644*, p. 326

17.   Lord Digby to Prince Rupert (12 July), E. Warburton, *op. cit.*, Vol. 2, p. 472. Cf. 'Sir William Waller followed the King who led his foot a long dance', 'Journal of Occurrences, 1643–1644', B.M. Add. MS 24, 465, f. 15

18.   Waller to Governor of Stafford (4 July), H.M.C., *4th Report*, Pt. 1, p. 275. In this letter Waller asked the Governor to find out where Lord Denbigh's forces were, and to ascertain the King's strength

19.   *C.J.*, Vol. 3, p. 554. A warrant from the Committee of Northampton (3 July) for raising 1,000 horses to mount a party of Waller's musketeers. The House resolved to send Waller 1,000 saddles and pistols

20.   H.M.C., *8th Report*, I, p. 3

21.   *Ibid.* Order of Beds. Committee to Sir Samuel Luke to raise horses; Waller to Beds. Committee (6 July); Beds. Committee to Waller (6 July); C.B.K. to Beds. Committee (15 July). Fifty-five musketeers in Weldon's foot had been mounted as early as 16 June and a second party of fifty-four N.C.O.s and men served as dragoons from 6–21 July, P.R.O. S.P. 28/130, ff. 133–53

22.   For Waller's correspondence, see *C.S.P.D., 1644*, pp. 307–57

CHAPTER TWENTY-FOUR:
FACING WESTWARDS

1.   *Letters of Lady Brilliana Harley*, ed. T. T. Lewis, C. S., 1853, p. 127

2.   *C.S.P.D., 1644*, p. 456. See *Mercurius Aulicus*, 1–7 Sept., T.T. E. 10 (20); 'Journal of Occurrences, 1643–1646', B.M. Add. MS 24, 465

3.   D'Ewes, Harl. MS 166, f. 123; *The Kingdome's Weekly Intelligencer*, 3–10 Sept., T.T. E. 8 (2)

4.   D'Ewes, Harl. MS 166, f. 179

5.   *The Parliament Scout*, 11–19 July, T.T. E. 2 (21)

6.   *C.S.P.D., 1644*, pp. 433, 436

7.   *C.S.P.D., 1644*, p. 420, 434–5. For Middleton's brief siege of Donnington Castle in late July, see *Mercurius Aulicus*, 28 July–3 Aug., T.T. E. 6 (10). For his subsequent actions in the West, see *The Weekly Account*, 21–7 Aug., T.T. E. 6 (13); *An exact [copy] of Lieut. General Middleton's Letter to Sir William Waller, wherein is set forth a victory obtained at Faringdon*, T.T. E. 7 (22); *Mercurius Aulicus*, 22–9 Aug., T.T. E. 7 (23); *Mercurius Aulicus*, 11–17 Aug., T.T. E. 8 (20); *Ibid*, 18–24 Aug., T.T. E. 9 (5); *C.J.*, Vol. 3, pp. 582, 605, 611

8.   P.R.O. S.P. 28/22, f. 130. The musters in question dated from 12 March 1644 to the reduction

9.   *C.S.P.D., 1644*, pp. 439–40

10.   *C.S.P.D., 1644*, p. 455

11.   *Ibid*, p. 450; *C.J.*, Vol. 3, p. 594; *L.J.*, Vol. 6, p. 629

12.   P.R.O. S.P. 28/135, f. 155: 'Col. Birch's Regiment raised by Ordinance of

Parliament, dated 12 July 1644'

13. See *C.S.P.D., 1644*, pp. 453–69, for Waller's correspondence with C.B.K. during these weeks. See also D'Ewes, B.M. Harl. MS 166, ff. 115–16

14. G.N. Godwin, *The Civil War in Hampshire 1642–45* (1904), pp. 248–9

15. *C.S.P.D., 1644*, pp. 476–7

16. *Memoirs*, Vol. 1, p. 97

17. *C.J.*, Vol. 3, p. 602, 21 August; *C.P.S.D., 1644*, p. 437

18. *C.S.P.D., 1644*, pp. 478–9

19. *C.S.P.D., 1644*, p. 482

20. *Ibid*, p. 484. Cf. *Court Mercurie*, 7–14 Sept., T.T. E. 9 (1), for a report of Royalist treatment of the prisoners

21. D'Ewes, B.M. Harl. MS 166, f. 109. See also *The Kingdome's Weekly Intelligencer*, 3–10 Sept., T.T. E. 8 (24), for Waller's denial of such accusations

22. *C.S.P.D., 1644*, pp. 489–95; Waller to C.B.K. (13 Sept., Blandford), D'Ewes, Harl. MS 166, f. 122

23. *C.S.P.D., 1644*, pp. 501–2

24. *Ibid*, pp. 502, 505–6, 516

25. 'Examination of Lt.Col. Nathaniel Rich', *C.S.P.D., 1644–1645*, p. 157

26. D'Ewes, B.M. Harl. MS 166, f. 128; Whitaker, Add. MS 31, 116, f. 165

27. *C.S.P.D., 1644*, p. 525. Cf. Waller and Heselrige to C.B.K. (20 Sept., Blandford), D'Ewes, Harl. MS 166, ff. 131–2

28. The Commons voted Waller £10,000 on 12 July; by 14 Aug. he had only received £1,900, *C.J.*, Vol. 4, pp. 163, 204

29. *C.S.P.D., 1644*, p. 532. Cf. Waller to Essex (24 Sept., Shaftesbury), H.M.C., *Portland* MSS, Vol. 1, p. 185

30. Jasper Clutterbuck (P.R.O. S.P. 28/22, f. 277). For details of the skirmish, see *The Parliament Scout*, 26 Sept.–3 Oct., T.T. E. 10 (31)

31. *C.S.P.D., 1644–1645*, pp. 12–13, 23. Dalbier to Waller (6 Oct., Blandford), D'Ewes, Harl. MS 166, f. 134

32. B.M. Whitaker, Add. MS 31, 116, f. 167

33. For the skirmish at Andover, see G.N. Godwin, *op. cit.*, pp. 270–1

34. Experiences, f. 20

35. *C.S.P.D., 1644–1645*, p. 60

Chapter Twenty-Five: The Second Battle of Newbury

1. Waller and Heselrige to Speaker (28 Oct., Blewbury), D'Ewes, Harl. MS 166, ff. 139–40

2. Simon Ashe, *A True Relation of the most chiefe occurrences at and since the Battell at Newbury until the disjunction of the three Armies*, T.T. E. 22 (10). Ashe was Manchester's chaplain. *A Letter wherein is related the Victory obtained by the Parliamentary Army near Newbury*, T.T. E. 14 (16). W. Money, *The First and Second Battles of Newbury and the Siege of Donnington Castle during the Civil War, 1643–6* (1881) gives much local topographical detail

3. R. Symonds, *op. cit.*, p. 145; *Mercurius Aulicus*, 28 Oct., printed in J. Rushworth, *Historical Collections*, Vol. 5, pp. 725–6

4. *The Memoirs of Edmund Ludlow*, ed. C.H. Firth (1894), Vol. 1, p. 103

5. Experiences, f. 20

6. For a list of Waller's Lifeguards see P.R.O. S.P. 28/135, f. 149 (17 names). Besides these gentlemen the Lifeguard served as a cadre of officers, and many reformado captains who had failed to raise troops or companies passed into it. Col. Edward Cooke was the captain of the troop 'commonly called the Lifeguard', S.P. 28/15, Pt. 1

7. R. Symonds, *op. cit.*, p. 145; R. Bulstrode, *Memoirs and Reflections* (1721), p. 118; Clarendon, Bk. VIII, paras. 156, 157

8. E. Walker, *op. cit.*, pp. 112–13. Cf. *Mercurius Aulicus*, 28 Oct., 'about four score' Parliamentarians had crossed through a gap in Speenhamfield before Goring charged

9. There were three Colonel Barclays in Essex's army: James, Alexander and Harry (P.R.O. S.P. 28/140, f. 157; 43, Pt. 5, f. 255; 15, Pt. 2, f. 226). This officer was probably Col. Harry Barclay (Cf. *L.J.*, Vol. 7, p. 106)

10. 'Narrative of the Earl of Manchester's Campaign', *The Quarrel between the Earl of Manchester and Oliver Cromwell*, ed. J. Bruce, C. S., (1875), pp. 63–4. Bruce believed that Maj.-Gen. Crawford wrote this narrative, with interpolations from Sir William Balfour (p. 70)

11. E. Walker, *op. cit.*, p. 114; 'Cromwell's Narrative', *op. cit.*, p. 86; D'Ewes, Harl. MS 166, ff. 139–40

12. R. Symonds, *op. cit.*, p. 146

Chapter Twenty-Six: Missed Opportunities

1. *C.S.P.D., 1644–1645*, pp. 83–4
2. 'Examination of Sir Arthur Heselrige'. *C.S.P.D., 1644–1645*, p. 156
3. *Ibid*, p. 157 'Examination of Sir William Waller'
4. Skippon to Essex (10 Nov., Newbury), J. Rushworth, *Historical Collections*, Vol. 5, pp. 730–1
5. 'Ordre of his Majesties Armee of 4200 Horse and 5000 Foote, and Battalie upon the plaine before Newbury, Commandett by his heighnisse Prince Rupert. the – October, 1644', B.M. Add. MS 16370, f. 61; Lord Byron to Marquis of Ormonde (15 Nov.), in T. Carte, *A Collection of Original Letters and Papers* (1739), Vol. 1, p. 71
6. *C.S.P.D., 1644–1645*, pp. 146–60; 'The Earl of Manchester's narrative to ye house of Peers in Parliament concerning Donnington Castle, & which was in November 9th, 1644', T.T. E. 903 (3)
7. 'Journal of Occurrences, 1643–1646', Add. MS 24, 465, ff. 24–5
8. *C.S.P.D., 1644–1645*, pp. 113, 155. For the military situation, see letter of Committee of Dorset (9 Nov., Blandford), printed in *L.J.*, Vol. 7, p. 68. The committee found Waller's foot soldiers 'very ready upon Duty, but necessited for Want of Pay'
9. D'Ewes, Harl. MS 166, f. 143
10. Waller to Prince Rupert (19 Nov.), Bodl. MS Eng.lett. c. 196, f. 5
11. 'Journal of Occurrences, 1643–1646', Add. MS 24, 465, ff. 24–5
12. *C.S.P.D., 1644–1645*, p. 161
13. 'Memorial of Denzil Lord Holles', *Select Tracts Relating to the Civil Wars in England . . .*, ed. J. Maseres (1815), p. 206; *C.J.*, Vol. 3, p. 696
14. *C.J.*, Vol. 3, p. 704; B.M. Add. MS 31, 116, f. 175
15. *C.J.*, Vol. 3, p. 704; *C.S.P.D., 1644–1645*,

pp. 146–60; 'Cromwell's Narrative', *op. cit.*, p. 79

16. 'Journal of Occurrences, 1643–1646', Add. MS 24, 465, f. 20
17. *Ibid*, f. 24
18. *C.J.*, Vol. 3, p. 703
19. *C.J.*, Vol. 4, p. 27
20. *C.J.*, Vol. 3, p. 718; 'Journal of Occurrences, 1643–1646', Add. MS 24, 465, f. 26
21. E. Ludlow, *op. cit.*, p. 115.
22. *Vindication*, p. 109. Cf. Clarendon's statement that Waller opposed the Self-Denying Ordinance, *op. cit.*, Bk. VIII, para. 260
23. *The True Informer*, 21–8 Dec., T.T. E. 22 (14). The countess had been captured after Second Newbury, see *The Kingdome's Weekly Intelligencer*, 8–15 April 1645, T.T. E. 278 (8); *Military Memoir of Colonel Birch*, p. 21
24. *Vindication*, p. 109; *The Weekly Account*, 19–25 Dec., T.T. E. 21 (12). This journal contains a list of members of both Houses holding commands

Chapter Twenty-Seven: Hopeless Employment Into The West

1. *C.J.*, Vol. 4, pp. 20–1
2. *C.J.*, Vol. 3, p. 734; Vol. 4, pp. 8, 15; *C.S.P.D., 1644–1645*, pp. 182–282, *passim*
3. *C.S.P.D., 1644–1645*, p. 282
4. *C.J.*, Vol. 4, p. 39; *L.J.*, Vol. 7, p. 192
5. *C.S.P.D., 1644–1645*, p. 282
6. *Ibid*, p. 291
7. *Mercurius Aulicus*, 27 Jan.–3 Feb., T.T. E. 33 (20)
8. B.M. Whitaker, Add. MS. 31, 116, f. 192
9. H.M.C., *Portland* MSS Vol. 1, pp. 208–9
10. *C.J.*, Vol. 4, p. 46
11. *C.S.P.D., 1644–1645*, pp. 303–4
12. 'Journal of Occurrences, 1643–1646', Add. MS 24, 465, f. 31; *Mercurius Civicus*, 13–20 Feb., T.T. E. 270 (9)
13. Whitaker, Add. MS 31, 116, ff. 192–3
14. *C.S.P.D., 1644–1645*, pp. 313–14
15. Add. MS 24, 465, f. 31

16. *C.S.P.D., 1644–1645*, p. 317

17. *Ibid*, p. 310; *C.J.*, Vol. 4, p. 47

18. *C.S.P.D., 1644–1645*, p. 318; Add. MS 24, 465; Whitaker, Add. MS 31, 116, ff. 195–6

19. *C.J.*, Vol. 4, p. 63

20. *C.S.P.D., 1644–1645*, p. 323

21. *C.J.*, Vol. 4, p. 66; *C.S.P.D., 1644–1645*, p. 334

22. *A Perfect Diurnall*, 3–10 March, T.T. E. 258 (33); *Perfect Passages*, 5–11 March, T.T. E. 258 (34)

23. Cooke to Luke (12 March, Lavington), *Letter Books of Sir Samuel Luke*, ed. H. G. Tibbutt (1963), p. 475. For the necessity of moving from Surrey, see *C.S.P.D., 1644–1645*, pp. 284, 320, 341

24. *A Copie of Sir William Waller's Letter &c. A Great Victorie obtained by Sir William Waller and Lieutenant-Generall Cromwell against Colonell Sir James Long, who was driven from the Devizes*, 12 March, T.T. E. 274 (4)

25. Waller to Speaker (13 March, West Lavington), in *The Weekly Account*, 12–19 March, T.T. E. 274 (23). According to this letter Cromwell 'fell in' between Devizes and the Lavingtons, Sir H. Waller at Trowbridge and Sir W. Waller at Lavington

26. *A Copie of Sir William Waller's Letter, &c.*, T.T. E. 274 (4)

27. *The Weekly Account*, 12–19 March, T.T. E. 274 (23)

28. *Experiences*, pp. 125–6. Lord Henry Percy was captured in the second week of March, *A Perfect Diurnall*, 10–17 March, T.T. E. 258 (36)

29. *C.S.P.D., 1644–1645*, p. 229

30. *Ibid*, p. 226.

31. Waller to C.B.K. (23 March, Marshfield), B.M. Sloane MS 1519, f. 66

32. According to the *Experiences*, f. 52, this was 'Major Bowles'. Richard Bolles was in fact the Lt.-Col. of Long's regiment, his major being one Lister. These officers, two captains, a lieutenant, a cornet and sixty troopers were captured on this occasion, T.T. E. 276 (7).

33. Copy of Sir William Waller's letter (26 March, Downton) *A Perfect Diurnall*, 24–31 March, T.T. E. 260 (5)

34. Waller to C.B.K. (27 March, Ringwood), Bodl. Tanner MS 60, ff. 15–16

35. *Perfect Passages*, 26 March–2 April, T.T. E. 260 (8)

36. For Goring's intentions and his movements between 27 March and 6 April, see his correspondence with Lord Culpeper, Bodl. Tanner MS 60, ff. 19–63, *passim*. For R. organisation in the West and dissensions among the generals, see Clarendon, Bk. IX, paras. 9–17; R. Granville, *The King's General in the West* (1908), p. 115; M. Coate, *Cornwall in the Great Civil War and Interregnum 1642–1660* (1963), Chap. 10

37. A Letter from Sir William Waller's quarters, in *Perfect Passages*, 16–23 April, T.T. E. 260 (20)

38. W.C. Abbott, *The Writings and Speeches of Oliver Cromwell* (1947), Vol. I, p. 336

39. Sir Richard Bulstrode, *Memoirs of the Reign and Government of King Charles I and King Charles II* (1721), p. 120. The letter is clearly a reply to an overture from Goring

40. *Ibid*, p. 122

41. W.C. Abbott, *op. cit.*, p. 337

42. Culpeper to Goring (Bristol, 6 April), Bodl. Tanner MS 60, ff. 62–3

43. *The Weekly Postmaster*, 8–15 April, T.T. E. 260 (15)

44. Whitaker, Add. MS 31, 116 ff. 205–6

45. *Perfect Occurrences*, 18–25 April, T.T. E. 260 (22)

46. *Vindication*, pp. 17–18

CHAPTER TWENTY-EIGHT: LAID ASIDE LIKE A BROKEN VESSEL

1. H.M.C., *Portland* MSS, Vol. 1, p. 215

2. The regiments included officers and men from Hardress Waller's Foot (P.R.O. S.P. 28/29, Pt. 5, f. 474) and Holborne's dragoons, S.P. 28/35, Pt. 5, f. 635. Captains Wm. Tatton, John Clarke and Thomas Clarke and their officers were reduced at Ockingham on 25 April. The former was of Holborne's dragoons; the others were also dragoon officers, *Ibid*, f. 635

3. *C.S.P.D., 1644–1645*, pp. 400, 415; *The Memoirs of Edmund Ludlow*, Vol. 1, p. 115

4. C.B.K. to Fairfax, B.M. Sloane MS

1519, f. 100

5. B.M. Sloane MS 1519, f. 108

6. Capt. John Long's troop was serving with his regiment in June 1645, H.M.C., *6th Report*, p. 63

7. *C.S.P.D., 1644–1645*, pp. 398, 459, 464, 598.

8. Ludlow's Horse, for example, deployed about Guildford in April to intercept Kentish runaways, either deserted with Major Francis Dowett or were disbanded by November, *C.S.P.D., 1644–1645*, p. 409; *The Memoirs of Edmund Ludlow*, Vol. 1, p. 116. Col. John Fiennes regiment of Horse disintegrated in the summer of 1645, H.M.C., *Portland* MSS, Vol. 1, p. 116

9. *C.S.P.D., 1644–1645*, pp. 402, 472, 601; *C.J.*, Vol. 4, p. 139; P.R.O. S.P. 28/31, Pt. 6, ff. 554–68; 30, Pt. 6, ff. 609–21. Thompson's Horse disbanded on 10 Nov. 1645, P.R.O. S.P. 28/38, Pt. 3, f. 245. The Bluecoats dispersed before the end of April, see 'The Officers that are reduced out of Collonell James Wemyes regiment' (Windsor, 26 April), and a similar list for Capt. Henry Hazzard's officers reduced at Ockingham on 25 April, Bodl. Tanner MS 60, ff. 130, 146

10. 'Sir William Waller's reduc't officers', Windsor, 26 April, P.R.O. S.P. 28/122, Pt. 2

11. *C.J.*, Vol. 4, p. 112; *C.S.P.D., 1644–1645*, p. 285; *Perfect Diurnall*, 14–21 April, T.T. E. 260 (18); Whitaker, Add. MS 31, 116, ff. 205–6

12. *Perfect Passages*, 16–23 April, T.T. E. 260 (20). Whitaker, Add. MS 31, 116, f. 312

13. *C.S.P. Venetian, 1643–1646*, p. 135

14. *Mercurius Aulicus*, 8–14 Sept., T.T. E. 12 (18). Quoting *Mercurius Britanicus*

15. *Ibid*, 11–17 Aug., T.T. E. 8 (20)

16. *Ibid*, 4–10 Aug., T.T. E. 8 (2)

17. *Ibid*, 18–24 Aug., T.T. E. 9 (5)

18. *Ibid*, 18–24 Aug., T.T. E. 9 (5). Cf. a report in October 1643 that she sent her own warrants to the court of guard at Tyburn to stop any horsemen who had listed under her husband

19. *Ibid*, 1–7 Oct., T.T. E. 74 (8)

20. *Ibid*, 28 July–3 Aug., T.T. E. 6 (10)

21. *The Spie*, 26 April–1 May, T.T. E. 44 (18)

22. *Mercurius Aulicus*, 8–14 Sept., T.T. E. 12 (18). She was 'the chief encourager' of her husband's rebellion

23. *Experiences*, p. 131, cf. Mercurius Britanicus, 8–15 July

24. Vindication, pp. 17–18, 207–8

25. *Experiences*, pp. 128–9

26. *C.S.P. Venetian, 1643–1646*, p. 236

27. *C.J.*, Vol. 3, p. 449

28. *Vindication*, p. 208

29. *Mercurius Aulicus*, 28 Jan.–3 Feb. 1644, T.T. E. 30 (20). Parliament renewed Waller's grant of butlerage on 12 July 1643, *L.J.*, Vol. 6, p. 130

30. *Vindication*, p. 207

31. *Ibid*, pp. 208–9

32. 'Memorial of Denzil Lord Holles', *Select Tracts*, ed. F. Maseres, Vol. 1 (1815), p. 269

33. *C.S.P.D., 1645–1647, passim*

34. B.M. Add. MS 24,860, f. 145. G.N. Godwin, *The Civil War in Hampshire 1642–1648* (1904), p. 336

35. *C.S.P. Venetian, 1643–1646*, pp. 216, 221–2, 236, 245

36. B. Whitelocke, *Memorials of the English Affairs from the Beginnings of the Reign of Charles the First to the Happy Restoration of King Charles the Second* (1732), p. 82

38. *Experiences*, p. 132

CHAPTER TWENTY-NINE: THE ROAD TO EXILE

1. *The True Manner and Forme of the Proceeding to the Funerall of the Right Honourable Robert Earle of Essex . . .* (1646)

2. *Vindication*, pp. 42–4

3. *L.J.*, Vol. 9, p. 122; *C.J.*, Vol. 5, pp. 131–2

4. H.M.C., *7th Report*, p. 237

5. *Vindication*, pp. 44–5

6. *Ibid*, pp. 46–50

7. *The Nicholas Papers*, ed. G.F. Warner, C. S. (1886), Vol. 1, p. 65; *Vindication*, p. 72

8. *Vindication*, pp. 22–3. For the work of the commissioners at Saffron Walden, see Bodl. Tanner MS 58, Pt. 1, f. 5; *C.S.P.D., 1645–1647*, p. 547; *L.J.*, Vol. 9, p. 152; J. Rushworth, *Historical Collections* (1721), Vol. 6, pp. 457, 460, 464; *The Clarke Papers*, ed. C.H. Firth, C.S., Vol. 1, (1891), pp. 5–15

9.   *Vindication*, pp. 63–97. *L.J.*, Vol. 9, p. 114. Cf. *The Clarke Papers*, Vol. 1, pp. 114–15
10.   For the charges against the Eleven Members, see B. Whitelocke, *op. cit.*, p. 253; cf. *The Araignment of Major Generall Massie, Sir William Waller, Col. Poyntz . . . and other citizens of the Presbyterian faction*, T.T. E. 404 (6).
11.   *Vindication*, pp. 187–9. The House of Commons voted him to command the Horse on 3 Aug., *C.J.*, Vol. 5, p. 26
12.   B. Whitelocke, *op. cit.*, p. 262. Besides Waller and Massey, Sydenham Poyntz also listed reformadoes on 30 July 1647, cf. *The Disconsolate Reformadoe, or the sad-look'd Presbyterian Jack*, T.T. E. 404 (4)
13.   Experiences, ff. 39–42. Southwark declined to join the City against the Army, J. Rushworth, *op. cit.*, Vol. 7, pp. 741–2. Cp. Holles' account of the movements of Waller and himself before and during the apprentices' riot, 'Memorial of Denzil Lord Holles', *Select Tracts*, ed. F. Maseres (1815), Vol. 1, p. 279
14.   Experiences, ff. 32–3. For the attitude of the City and its correspondence with the Army during these critical weeks, see 'Journals of the Court of Common Council', Vol. 40, ff. 217–48 (Guildhall R.O.)
15.   *The Letters of Lady Brilliana Harley*, ed. T.T. Lewis, C.S., (1854), p. 231
16.   Experiences, f. 37
17.   *Vindication*, pp. 201–2. For Sir William Batten, see *D.N.B.*
18.   *Experiences*, p. 108
19.   Experiences, ff. 37–8
20.   G. Thomas-Stanford, *Sussex in the Great Civil War and the Interregnum 1642–1660* (1910), p. 209
21.   *Vindication*, pp. 202–18
22.   *C.S.P. Ireland, 1647–1660*, p. 24; *C.J.*, Vol. 5, p. 584

CHAPTER THIRTY: THREE YEARS IN CAPTIVITY

1.   *C.J.*, Vol. 5, p. 986
2.   Experiences, f. 3. *The Parliamentary or Constitutional History of England* (1763), Vol. 18, pp. 447, 453
3.   *A Declaration of the taking away of Sir William Waller, Sir John Clotworthy, Major Generall Massie and Collonel Copley . . . from the Kings head in the Strand to St. James: Together with their Protestation at their removall*, T.T. 669, f. 13 (57). Printed in 1648
4.   *C.S.P.D., 1650*, p. 255
5.   *Experiences*, p. 118. For FitzJames, see P.R.O. S.P. 28/36, Pt. 4, f. 357.
6.   H.M.C., *Portland* MSS, Vol. 3, p. 168
7.   Experiences, f. 25
8.   *Ibid; C.S.P.D., 1651*, p. 151
9.   *Experiences*, pp. 104–5
10.   H.M.C., *Portland* MSS, Vol. 3, p. 196
11.   *Experiences*, p. 131
12.   *Vindication*, pp. 5–6
13.   *Experiences*, p. 131
14.   *Ibid*, p. 105

CHAPTER THIRTY-ONE: SO ENSNARING A TIME

1.   Experiences, ff. 59–60
2.   'Journal of Lady Anna Waller', *Harcourt Papers*, Vol. 1, pp. 170–3
3.   Waller referred to the birth of Thomas at his Aldersgate Street house in *Experiences*, p. 108, but the dates of birth of the three children are not known
4.   *Journal*, p. 173. See also pp. 179–81
5.   'L.K.' probably stands for 'my Lord Keeper'. Sir Richard Lane (the last holder before 1652) died in 1650 and no one else was appointed until 1653. Waller, however, is almost certainly referring to Sir John Finch (1584–1660) a relative of his second wife, appointed Lord Keeper in January 1640. Finch lived as an exile in The Hague after 1640 and Waller must have met him there in 1647 or 1648
6.   Experiences, ff. 67–71
7.   'Nordern's Survey' (1596), cited in D. Lysons, *The Environs of London* (1793), Vol. 3, p. 25
8.   Middlesex R.O., Acc. 436 Bundle 8(2). A Collection of indentures signed by Waller. He sold the ruin of Winchester Castle to the Corporation on 2 May 1656 for 203 sovereigns, G.N. Godwin, *The Civil War in Hampshire, 1642–1645* (1904), p. 377
9.   *Divine Meditations*, p. 203. Waller cited

Bacon's Essays in a footnote to this passage. He probably had 'On Dissimulation' in mind

10.   D. Underdown, *Royalist Conspiracy in England, 1649–1660* (1960), pp. 117, 136

11.   *A Collection of the State Papers of John Thurloe*, ed. T. Birch (1742), Vol. 1, p. 749

12.   *Experiences*, p. 120

13.   Journal, p. 175

14.   *Experiences*, p. 116

15.   *State Papers of John Thurloe*, Vol. 4, pp. 99–100; *Ibid*, Vol. 7, p. 20; W. C. Abbott, *The Writings and Speeches of Oliver Cromwell* (1947), Vol. 4, p. 768

16.   Journal, p. 183

17.   *C.S.P.D., 1654*, p. 128; *Ibid, 1656 –1657*, pp. 269–73; *Ibid, 1657–1658, passim*

18.   *C.S.P. Ireland, Adventures for Land, 1642–1659*, p. 344

CHAPTER THIRTY-TWO: THE RESTORATION

1.   See D. Underdown, *op. cit.*, chapter 11 and 12, *passim*

2.   *The Letter-Book of John Viscount Mordaunt 1658–1660*, ed. M. Coate, C.S. (1945), 'Introduction', *passim*. Mordaunt's first known contact with Waller was in 1656, D. Underdown, *op. cit.*, p. 209

3.   Waller to Lord Mordaunt (unsigned), *The Letter-Book of John Viscount Mordaunt*, p. 34. Cf. a letter from Hyde to Mordaunt (8 June 1659) in which he hoped that Waller will be persuaded not to aim at the chief command in Kent, *Ibid*, p. 22. Mordaunt had given Waller a commission to serve the King in May, *Ibid*, pp. 10, 12. By June he was fully involved in the plotting, H.M.C., *10th Report*, IV, pp. 205–7. General Monck noted in July 1659 that Waller had gone to Tonbridge 'where the first corruption is feared'. Later rumours made him Lt.-Gen. in the North, *The Clarke Papers*, ed. C.H. Firth, C.S. (1891–1901), Vol. 4, pp. 29, 39

4.   Journal, pp. 175–6

5.   *Experiences*, pp. 105–6

6.   Mordaunt to Waller (26 Nov., Calais), *The Letter-Book of John Viscount Mordaunt*, p. 114

7.   Hartgill Baron to Mordaunt (23 Dec., London), *Ibid*, p. 144

8.   Hartgill Baron to Mordaunt (29 Dec., London), *ibid*, p. 147; D. Underdown, *op. cit.*, pp. 307–8

9.   Hyde to Sir Henry Bennett (17 Jan. 1660), *Clarendon State Papers*, Vol. 3, p. 647. For published protests from the excluded members at this time, see *Catalogue of the Thomason Tracts, 1640–1661* (1908), Vol. 2, pp. 275–80. Waller was also active with Massey and Robert Harley in stirring up the soldiers in London, leading to a mutiny on 1 February 1660. D. Underdown, *op. cit.*, p. 309

10.   *The Diary of Samuel Pepys*, ed. H. B. Wheatley (1904), Vol. 1, p. 50

11.   J. Aubrey, *Letters written by Eminent Persons . . . and Lives of Eminent Men* (1813), Vol. 2, Pt. 2, p. 509

12.   *The Memoirs of Edmund Ludlow*, ed. C.H. Firth (1894), Vol. 2, p. 239. See also Sir Hardress Waller, *D.N.B.*

CHAPTER THIRTY-THREE: A CLEAR EVENING

1.   H.M.C., *Portland* MSS,. Vol. 3, pp. 240–1

2.   Journal, pp. 172, 194–5. According to the chapel register the wedding took place on 21 February

3.   Edmund Calamy, *The Happiness of those who Sleep in Jesus* (1662). Preached in New Church, Westminster on 31 October 1661. Calamy was a noted Presbyterian divine

4.   Walter was buried on 3 Dec. 1654, D. Lysons, *The Environs of London*, Vol. 5 (1800), p. 42

5.   Journal, pp. 170–82, *passim*

6.   *The Life and Times of Anthony Wood*, ed. A. Clarke (1892), Vol. 2, p. 19

7.   *C.S.P.D., 1663–1664*, p. 484

8.   *Divine Meditations*, p. 169. Two similar versions of the *Dayly Directory* were appended to each copy of the *Experiences* which make it of much earlier date than the *Divine Meditations*. Waller probably revised it for publication, however, in the 1660s

9. Strong internal evidence suggests that the Wadham MS of the *Experiences* was destined for Margaret Waller. Her mother's virtues, for example, are listed twice in this version, and her (dead) brother's name given. References to Waller's second wife are made more explicit by naming her. There is also the fact that the earliest known owner of this MS lived in Devon (see Bibliography). For a discussion of Waller's concept of Providence, see B. Donagan, 'Understanding Providence: The Difficulties of Sir William and Lady Waller', *J. of Ecclesiastical History*, Vol. 39, 1988

10. P.C.C. 78 Coke.

11. W.A. Waller, *Our Family Record* (1898), p. 17. Sir William's eldest son married Catherine, eldest daughter of Sir Edward Stradling of St Donat's Castle. Their only child, Katharine, married her first cousin, Richard Courtenay, fourth son of Sir William Courtenay and Margaret Waller, *Notes and Queries*, Seventh Series, Vol. 10, p. 437

12. Thomas Jekyll to A. Wood (22 Dec. 1694), Bodl. Wood MS 42, f. 303

13. *C.S.P.D., 1668–1669*, p. 2

Bibliography

A. WALLER'S WRITINGS

1. *Letters and Despatches*

A considerable number of Waller's official despatches written during the war have survived and these form the most important source for his military career. By contrast very few of Waller's private letters (none to any members of his family) are extant, a fact probably explained by the confiscation of his papers during the Protectorate.

The largest collection of his despatches may be found in the *Calendar of State Papers, Domestic Series, of the Reign of Charles I, 1644* (1888) and *1644–1645* (1890), both edited by W.D. Hamilton. The letters printed here are accurate transcripts from the Letter Books of the Committee of Both Kingdoms in the Public Records Office. Other despatches to the committee not to be found in these volumes, official letters to the Speaker and lord general, correspondence with other parliamentarian commanders and county committees, and with royalist generals concerning the exchange of prisoners, and lastly the few extant private letters are to be found in the following collections:

Manuscript
> Bodleian Library:
>> Tanner MSS 60–2
>> Clarendon MS 22
>> MS Eng. c. 196
> British Museum:
>> Harleian MSS 164–6
>> Sloane MS 1519
> Kent Record Office:
>> Earl de la Warr MSS U. 269 c. 290
> Folger Shakespeare Library:
>> Scudamore MSS
> Private collection:
>> MSS at Prideaux Place, Padstow

Printed
> *Journals of the House of Commons*
> *Journals of the House of Lords*
> J. Vicars, *Jehovah-Jireh, God in the Mount*, 1643
> R. Bulstrode, *Memoirs and Reflections upon the Reign and Government of King Charles Ist and K. Charles IInd*, 1721
> Historical Manuscripts Commission:
>> MSS of Earl of Denbigh, *4th Report*, Pt. 1
>> MSS of Duke of Marlborough, *8th Report*, Pt. 1
>> MSS of A. Morrison, *9th Report*, Pt. 2
>> MSS of Lord Braye, *10th Report*, Pt. 6
>> MSS of Duke of Portland, *13th Report*, App., Pt. 1–2

Military Memoir of Colonel John Birch . . . written by Roe, his secretary . . ., ed. J. Webb and T.W. Webb, C.S., New Series, Vol. 7, 1873

M. Coate, *Cornwall in the Great Civil War and Interregnum, 1642–1660*, (2nd edn, 1963)

The Letter-Book of John Viscount Mordaunt, 1658–1660, ed. M. Coate, 3rd Series, Vol. 69, 1945

Thomason Tracts, British Museum. As cited in the 'Notes and References'.

2. *Literary Works*

    (a) An autograph fair copy MS of Waller's *Vindication* is in the Bodleian (MS Don. d. 57). The work was published in 1793 by the then Lord Chancellor (MS notes by J. Mitford (1816) in front page of B.M. copy, 4406, ff. 20) and the printed copy corresponds with the Bodl. MS except in one or two minor details. There is another copy, signed by Waller, in Powderham Castle. Evidently this once belonged to Margaret.

    (b) Two versions of the *Experiences* are extant. The earliest survives only in print as an appendix to *The Poems of Anna Matilda* (1788). The MS was 'present in a family to which its editor is allied', but the name of the editor cannot be traced. The second version is an autograph fair copy in Wadham College Library. From internal evidence it was almost certainly intended for Waller's daughter, Margaret, who lived in Devon. The MS first came to light in that county, for it is endorsed 'Rd. Warner 1726. The gift of Mr. J. Howard, who had it from Sir John Lear of Devon. R.T. Warner, 1765 of Woodford Row, Essex.'

    (c) No MS of Waller's *Divine Meditations* exists. The author of the 1680 edition assured the reader 'thou hast this copy from his own hand without the addition or subtraction of one word, one syllable one letter'. A second edition appeared in 1839, printed directly from the first.

    (d) Lady Anna Waller's MS Journal was printed in the *Harcourt Papers* Vol. 1 (a limited edition of 50 copies). The original is in the Harcourt family archives at Stanton Harcourt.

B.   OTHER SOURCES FOR WALLER'S LIFE

1. *Manuscript Journals*

British Museum:

    Sir Simonds D'Ewes, 'A Journall of the Parliament begunne Nov. 3, Tuesday, Anno Domini, 1640'. Harl. MSS 162–6

    Laurence Whitaker, 'Diary of proceedings in the House of Commons, 8 Oct, 1642–8 July, 1647.' Add. MS 31116

    Walter Yonge, 'Journal of proceedings in the House of Commons, 19 Sept., 1642–10 Dec., 1645'. Add. MS 18777–8

    'Journal of Occurrences, 1643–1646', Add. MS 24465. An MS copy of an original, made in Aug. 1879. According to the antiquarian Revd J. Hunter (ff. 1, 85) the transcript was an accurate one. The only clue to the identity of the author is that he was married by Brother Bifield in St Giles-in-the-Fields, Shrove Tuesday, 1646. The parish register shows that John Skinner married Tabitha Morris on that day, but nothing is known about Skinner.

2. *Letters and Papers relative to Waller's Army*

The largest collection of papers connected with Waller's army are the 300 or more volumes in the Public Record Office which form the so-called 'Commonwealth Exchequer Papers (supplementary State Papers)', S.P. 28. These have only loosely been sorted out, and no full catalogue of them exists. Among other documents they contain the accounts probably submitted to the Committee of Accounts in London as a result of the ordinance of 22 Feb. 1644, directing that all receivers of sums of money and goods shall make a 'perfect Accompt' of them (Firth and Rait, *op. cit.*, Vol. 1, p. 387).

The MSS relating to Waller's army may be divided as follows:

(a) Accounts, receipts and warrants. S.P. 28

    1–46

        Accounts of Essex's army, warrants and claims for arrears

    121A, 121B, 122

        Muster rolls

    128–35, 177, 235, 244

        Accounts of County Committees in the Western and Southern Associations

    140–7, 228, 262, 298–9

        Miscellaneous accounts, receipts and vouchers, 1642–1650

(b) Train of Artillery

    P.R.O.

        S.P. 28/31, 147 Accounts of Waller's train

        W.O. 55/457–8, 460 Warrants and Entry Book relating to stores

    British Museum

        Add. MS 34, 315 Issue book

    Bodleian

        Tanner MS 60 'Bluecoat' musters

(c) Staff officer records

    Public Record Office

        S.P. 28/135 Two account books of Commissary General Cowling

    British Museum

        Harl. MS 378 'A list of the several quarters of Sir William Waller's Army . . . 23 May to last of July'

    Kent Record Office

        Braburne MSS 'Military Papers 1644'

        (The minutes of 22 court martials in Waller's army between 22 April and 20 Dec. 1644. This volume also contains proclamations issued in the army and some standing orders. These have been edited by the author and published in *J.S.A.H.R.*, Vol. 44 (1966) and in *Cheriton 1644* (1973)

C. OTHER MANUSCRIPTS

As cited in 'Notes and References'

Unpublished theses

    Bodleian

        G.H. Brown, 'The Place of Sir Arthur Heselrige in English Politics, 1659–1660', B. Litt. 1949

        I. Roy, 'The Royalist Army in the First Civil War', D. Phil. 1963

        C.M. Williams, 'The Political Career of Henry Marten, with particular reference to the origins of republicanism in the Long Parliament', D. Phil. 1954

    University of London Library

        D.S. Evans, 'The Career of Edward Massey', Ph.D. 1993

        A.M. Everitt, 'Kent and its Gentry, 1640–1660', Ph.D. 1957

        V. Rowe, 'The Political and Administrative Career of Sir Henry Vane the Younger, 1640 to April 1653', Ph.D. 1965

Bibliography

University of Manchester Library
M.D.G. Wanklyn, 'The King's Army in the West 1642–6', M.A. 1966

D. PRINTED WORKS

1. *Tracts and Periodical Literature*

It is not possible to list here the pamphlets and news journals consulted or cited in the text but the following catalogues and guides give further information about them:

Catalogue of the Pamphlets, Books, Newspapers, and Manuscripts Relating to the Civil War, the Commonwealth, and Restoration, collected by George Thomason, 1640–1661, I. W. Fortescue, 2 Vols, 1908

An Exact collection of All Remonstrances, Declarations, Votes, Orders, Ordinances, Proclamations, Petitions, Messages, Answers and other Remarkable Passages . . . December 1641 . . . until 21 March, 1643 (4). Printed for Edward Husbands, 1643/4

R.T. Milford and D.M. Sutherland, *A Catalogue of English Newspapers and Periodicals in the Bodleian Library, 1622–1800*, Oxford Bibliographical Society, 1936

The Somers Collections of Tracts, ed. W. Scott, 2nd edn, 13 Vols, 1809–13, Vols IV, V

F.J. Varley, *Mercurius Aulicus . . . summarized extracts from each weekly issue*, Oxford, 1948

2. *Official Records*

Acts and Ordinances of the Interregnum, 1642–1660, ed. C.H. Firth and R.S. Rait, 3 Vols, Vol. 1 (1642–1649), 1911

Register of the University of Oxford. Vol. 2. (1571–1622), ed. A. Clark, Oxford, 1887–9

Calendars of State Papers, Domestic Series

Calendars of State Papers, Ireland

Calendars of State Papers, Venetian

Calendar of the Clarendon State Papers, ed. O. Ogle, W.H. Bliss, W.D. Macray, F.J. Routledge, 4 Vols, Oxford, 1869

State Papers Collected by Edward, Earl of Clarendon, ed. R. Scrope and T. Monkhouse, 3 Vols, Oxford, 1767–86

Constitutional Documents of the Puritan Revolution 1625–1666, ed. S.R. Gardiner, 3rd edn, Oxford, 1906

Journals of the House of Commons

Journals of the House of Lords

The Army Lists of the Roundheads and Cavaliers, containing the Names of the officers in the Royal and Parliamentary Armies of 1642, ed. E. Peacock, 2nd edn, 1874

Journal of Sir Samuel Luke, ed. I.G. Philip, 3 Vols, Oxfordshire Record Society, Vols 29, 31, 33, 1947–53

The Letter Books of Sir Samuel Luke, 1644–45, ed. H. G. Tibbutt, Bedfordshire Historical Record Society, Bedford, Vol. 42, 1963

J. Rushworth, *Historical Collections*, 8 Vols, 1659–1700

A Collection of the State Papers of John Thurloe Esq. Secretary first to the council of State and afterwards to the two Protectors, ed. T. Birch, 7 Vols, 1742

The Visitations of the County of Devon, ed. J.L. Vivian, Exeter, 1895

The Visitation of Kent, 1619–21, ed. R. Hovenden, 1898

3. *Correspondence*

J. Aubrey, *Letters written by Eminent Persons . . . and Lives of Eminent Men*, 2 Vols, 1813

The Writings and Speeches of Oliver Cromwell, ed. W.C. Abbott, 4 Vols, Cambridge, Mass., 1937–47

The Letters and Journals of Robert Baillie, Principal of the University of Glasgow, 1637–1662, ed. D. Laing, 3 Vols, Edinburgh, 1841–2

T. Carte, *A Collection of Original Letters and Papers concerning the Affairs of England from the Year 1641 to 1660*, 2 Vols, 1739

Letters of Lady Brilliana Harley, ed. T.T. Lewis, C.S., Vol. 58, 1853

The Clarke Papers, ed. C.H. Firth, C.S., New Series, 4 Vols, 1891–1900

The Knyvett Letters (1620–1644), ed. B. Schofield, 1949

The Letter-Book of John Viscount Mordaunt, 1658–1660, ed. M. Coate, C.S., 3rd series, Vol. 69, 1945

The Nicholas Papers. Correspondence of Sir Edward Nicholas, Secretary of State, ed. G.F. Warner, 4 Vols, C.S., New Series, Vols 40 (1886), 50 (1892), 57 (1897), 3rd Series, Vol. 31 (1920)

Correspondence of the Scots Commissioners in London, 1644–1646, ed. H.W. Meikle, 1917

E.G.B. Warburton, *Memoirs of Prince Rupert and the Cavaliers, including their Private Correspondence*, 3 Vols, 1849

4. *Contemporary diaries, memoirs, histories and military manuals*
    'The Praying Captain' – 'A Cavalier's Memoirs', ed. P. Young, *J.S.A.H.R.*, Vol. 35, 1957

    An edited version of '*The Vindication of Richard Atkyns Esquire, as also A Relation of Severall Passages in the Western War*', 1669

    Colonel Joseph Bamfield's Apologie, written by himselfe and printed at his desire, [? The Hague] 1685

    Military Memoir of Colonel John Birch . . . written by Roe, his Secretary . . ., ed. J. Webb and T.W. Webb, C.S., New Series, Vol. 7, 1873

    R. Bulstrode, *Memoirs and Reflections upon the Reign and Government of King Charles the Ist and K. Charles the IInd . . .*, 1721

    J. Corbet, 'The Military Government of Gloucester', *Bibliotheca Gloucestrensis: A collection of scarce and curious Tracts Relating to the county and City of Gloucester: Illustrative of and Published during the Civil War*, ed. J. Washbourn, Gloucester, 1825

    'On a MS, List of Officers of the London Trained Bands in 1643', ed. H.A. Dillon, *Archaeologia*, Vol. 50, 1890

    The Autobiography and Correspondence of Sir Simonds D'Ewes, Bart . . . during the reigns of James I and Charles I, ed. J.O. Halliwell, 2 Vols, 1845

    The Life, Diary and Correspondence of Sir William Dugdale, Knight . . . with an Appendix . . ., ed. W. Hamper, 1827

    'The Diary of John Greene (1635–57)', ed. E.M. Symonds, *E.H.R.*, Vol. 43, 1928

    J. Heath, *A Brief Chronicle of the late Intestine Warr in the Three Kingdoms of England, Scotland & Ireland . . . From 1637 to 1663*

    The Memorial of Denzil, Lord Holles, Select Tracts Relating to the Civil Wars in England in the Reign of King Charles the First . . ., ed. F. Maseres, 2 Vols, 1815

    Bellum Civile. Hopton's Narrative of his Campaign in the West (1642–1644), and other papers, ed. C.E.H. Chadwyck Healy, Somerset Record Society, Vol. 18, 1902. (Includes Colonel Walter Slingsby's relation of the Western and Cheriton campaigns, 1643–4.)

    E. Hyde, Earl of Clarendon, *History of the Rebellion and Civil Wars in England*, ed. W.D. Macray, 6 Vols, Oxford, 1888

    The Life of Edward, Earl of Clarendon . . . A Continuation of the same, 2 Vols, Oxford, 1760

    D. Lloyd, *Memoires of the Lives, Actions, Sufferings and Deaths of those noble, reverend and excellent personages that suffered . . . in our late intestine wars . . .*, 1668

    D. Lloyd, *State Worthie, or the Statesmen and favourites of England, from the Reformation to the Revolution . . .*, 2 Vols, 1766

    The Memoirs of Edmund Ludlow . . . 1625–1672, ed. C.H. Firth, 2 Vols, Oxford, 1894

    G. Markham, *The Souldier's Exercise*, 1643

Bibliography

The Diary of Samuel Pepys, ed. H.B. Wheatley, 1964

Edward Reynell, *The Life and Death of the Religious and Virtuous Lady, the Lady Lucie Reynell, of Forde in Devon*, 1654. In Bibliothèque Nationale, Paris.

R. Symonds, *Diary of the Marches of the Royal Army during the Great Civil War*, ed. C.E. Long, C.S., Vol. 74, 1859

Diary of Henry Townshend of Elmley Lovett, 1640–1663, ed. J.W. Willis-Bund, 2 Vols, Worcestershire Historical Society, 1920

J. Vicars, *England's Parliamentarie Chronicle*, 3 Vols, 1643–6. Comprises: *Jehovah-Jireh, God in the mount* (1641–Oct. 1643); *God's arke overtopping the worlds waves* (July 1643–July 1644); *The Burning-bush not consumed* (Aug. 1644–July 1646)

J. Vicars, *England's Worthies, under whom all the bloudy warres since anno 1642 to anno 1647 are related*, 1647

E. Walker, *Historical Discourses upon Several Occasions . . .*, 1705

B. Whitelocke, *Memorials of the English Affaires from the beginnings of the Reign of Charles the First to King Charles the Second his Happy Restauration*, 1722

A. Wood, *Athenae Oxoniensis, An Exact History of all the Writers and Bishops who have had their Education in the University of Oxford. To which are added the Fasti, or the Annals of the said University*, ed. P. Bliss, 4 Vols., 1813–20

Diary of Walter Yonge, Justice of the Peace and M.P. for Honiton . . . from 1604–1628, ed. G. Roberts, C.S., Vol. 41, 1843

5. *Secondary authorities: books*
    (Place of publication, London, unless otherwise stated)
    H. Abell, *Kent and the Great Civil War*, Ashford, 1901
    J. Adair, *Cheriton 1644: The Campaign and the Battle*, Kineton, 1973
    R. Ashton, *The Counter Revolution*, Yale UP, 1994
    F.J. Baigent and J.E. Millard, *A History of the Ancient Town and Manor of Basingstoke . . . with a Brief Account of the Siege of Basing House, 1643–1645*, Basingstoke, 1889
    A.R. Bayley, *The Great Civil War in Dorset, 1642–1660*, Taunton, 1910
    D. Blackmore, *Arms and Armour of the English Civil War*, 1990
    D. Brunton and D.H. Pennington, *Members of the Long Parliament*, 1953
    J.W. Willis-Bund, *The Civil War in Worcestershire, 1642–1646; and the Scotch Invasion of 1651*, 1905
    The Quarrel between the Earl of Manchester and Oliver Cromwell: An Episode of the English Civil War, ed. J. Bruce and D. Masson, C.S., New Series, Vol. 12, 1875
    A.H. Burne and P. Young, *The Great Civil War. A Military History of the First Civil War, 1642–1646*, 1959
    J.T. Cliffe, *The Puritan Gentry: The Great Puritan Families of Early Stuart England*, 1984
    M. Coate, *Cornwall in the Great Civil War and Interregnum 1642–1660. A Social and Political Study*, Truro, 1933, 1963
    R.W. Cotton, *Barnstaple and the Northern Part of Devonshire during the Great Civil War, 1642–1646*, 1889
    W. Curtis, *History of Alton*, 1896
    W.B. Devereux, *Lives and Letters of the Devereux, Earls of Essex . . . 1540–1646*, 2 Vols, 1853
    F.T.R. Edgar, *Sir Ralph Hopton: The King's Man in the West (1642–1652)*, Oxford, 1968
    A.M. Everitt, *The County Committee of Kent in the Civil War*, Occasional Papers No. 9, Department of Local History, University College, Leicester, 1957: *The Community of Kent and the Great Rebellion*, Leicester, 1961
    C.H. Firth, *Cromwell's Army. A History of the English soldier during the Civil Wars, the Commonwealth and Protectorate*, 3rd edn (1921), reissued by Greenhill Books (1992)

with introduction by John Adair; *Oliver Cromwell and the Rule of the Puritans in England*, 1935

C.H. Firth and G. Davies, *The Regimental History of Cromwell's Army*, 2 Vols, Oxford, 1940

A. Fletcher, *A County Community in Peace and War: Sussex 1600–1660*, 1975

A. Fletcher, *The Outbreak of the Civil War*, 1981

J. Frank, *The Beginnings of the English Newspaper 1620–1660*, Cambridge, Mass., 1621

S.R. Gardiner, *History of England from the Accession of James I to the Outbreak of the Civil War, 1603–1642*, 10 Vols, 1883–4, edition of 1901–3; *History of the Great Civil War, 1642–1648*, 4 Vols, 1901

I. Gentles, *The New Model Army in England, Ireland and Scotland, 1645–1653*, 1991

M.A. Gibb, *The Lord General; A Life of Thomas Fairfax*, 1938

G.N. Godwin, *The Civil War in Hampshire, 1642–5, and the story of Basing House*, 1904

R. Granville, *History of the Granville Family*, Exeter, 1895; *The King's General in the West: The Life of Sir Richard Granville, Bart., 1600–1659*, 1908

P. Gregg, *King Charles I*, 1981

E. Hasted, *The History and Topographical Survey of the County of Kent*, 4 Vols, 1778–9

J. Hexter, *The Reign of King Pym*, Harvard Historical Studies, Vol. 48, Cambridge, Mass., 1941; *Puritanism and Revolution*, 1958

C. Hill, *Intellectual Origins of the English Revolution*, Oxford, 1965

J.H. Hillier, *The Sieges of Arundel Castle*, 1854

C. Holmes, *The Eastern Association and the English Civil War*, 1974

A. Hughes, *The Causes of the English Civil War*, 1991

R. Hutton, *The Royalist War Effort 1642–6*, 1982

M.F. Keeler, *The Long Parliament, 1640–1641. A Biographical Study of its Members.* Memoirs of the American Philosophical Society, Vol. 36, Philadelphia, 1954

J. Kenyon, *The Civil Wars of England*, 1988

A. Kingston, *Hertfordshire during the Great Civil War*, 1894

M. Kishlansky, *The Rise of the New Model Army*, 1979

W.M. Lamont, *Marginal Prynne 1600–1669*, 1963

J. Latimer, *The Annals of Bristol in the Seventeenth Century*, Bristol, 1900

D. Lysons, *The Environs of London*, 5 Vols, 1790–1800

P. McGrath, *Bristol and the Civil War*, Bristol, 1981

J.L. Malcolm, *Caesar's Due: Loyalty and King Charles 1642–6*, 1983

C.R. Markham, *The Fighting Veres*, 1888

W. Money, *The First and Second Battles of Newbury and the Siege of Donnington Castle during the Civil War, A.D. 1643–6*, 2nd edn., 1884

J. Morrill, *The Revolt of the Provinces*, 1976

J. Morrill, *Oliver Cromwell and the English Revolution*, 1990

M. O'Hagan, *A History of Forde House*, Teignmouth District Council, 1990

C. Oman, *Elizabeth of Bohemia*, 1938

V. Pearl, *London and the Outbreak of the Puritan Revolution, City Government and National Politics, 1625–43*, Oxford, 1961

C. Russell, *Unrevolutionary England, 1603–1642*, 1990

J.L. Sanford, *Studies and Illustrations of the Great Rebellion*, 1858

R.R. Sharpe, *London and the Kingdom*, 3 Vols, 1894–5

W.A. Shaw, *The Knights of England*, 2 Vols, 1906

W.F. Snow, *Essex the Rebel*, Lincoln (Nebraska), 1970

E. Straker, *Wealden Iron . . . a monograph on the former iron works in the counties of Sussex, Surrey and Kent . . .*, 1931

C. Thomas-Stanford, *Sussex in the Great Civil War and the Interregnum, 1642–1660*, 1910

M.A. Tierney, *The History of Arundel*, 1854

M. Toynbee and P. Young, *Cropredy Bridge 1644: The Campaign and the Battle*, Kineton, 1970

D. Underdown, *Royalist Conspiracy in England, 1649–1660*, Yale Historical Studies, No. 19, New Haven, 1960

D. Underdown, *Somerset in the Civil War and Interregnum*, 1973

F.J. Varley, *The Siege of Oxford . . . An Account of Oxford during the Civil War, 1642–1646 . . .*, Oxford, 1932, and Supplement, 1935

Victoria County Histories

C.V. Wedgwood, *The King's Peace*, 1955; *The King's War*, 1958

J.S. Wheeler, *English Army Finance and Logistics, 1642–1660*, 1980

A. Woolrych, *Soldiers and Statesmen: the General Council of the Army and its Debates, 1647–48*, 1987

J. Wroughton, *Community at War: The Civil War in Bath and North Somerset*, Bath, 1992

G. Yule, *The Independents in the English Civil War*, Cambridge, 1958

P. Young, *Edgehill 1642: The Campaign and the Battle*, Kineton, 1967

P. Young and J. Adair, *Hastings to Culloden*, Stroud, 1996

P. Young and R. Holmes, *The English Civil War 1642–51*, 1974

6. *Secondary authorities: articles*

Revd E.J. Bodington, *The Battle of Roundway Down*, Wiltshire Archaeological and Natural History Magazine, Vol. 37, 1912

L.H. Carlson, 'A History of the Presbyterian Party from Pride's purge to the Dissolution of the Long Parliament', *Church History*, Vol. 11, 1942

R.W. Cotton, 'Forde and its Associations', *Transactions of the Devonshire Association*, Vol. 33, 1901

G. Davies, 'The Army of the Eastern Association, 1644–5', *E.H.R.*, Vol. 46, 1931; 'The Parliament Army under the Earl of Essex', 1642–5, *E.H.R.*, Vol. 49, 1934

B. Donagan, 'Understanding Providence: The Difficulties of Sir William and Lady Waller', *J. of Ecclesiastical History*, Vol. 39, 1988

C.H. Firth, 'The Siege and Capture of Bristol by the Royalist Forces in 1643', *J.S.A.H.R.*, Vol. 4, 1925; 'The Raising of the Ironsides', *Transactions of the Royal Historical Society*, New Series, Vol. 13, 1899; 'The Later History of the Ironsides', *Ibid*, New Series, Vol. 15, 1901

L. Glow, 'Political Affiliations of the House of Commons after Pym's Death', *Bulletin of the Institute of Historical Research*, Vol. 38, No. 97, 1965; 'The Committee of Safety', *E.H.R.*, Vol. 80, 1965

E. Green, 'On the Civil War in Somerset', *Proceedings of the Somerset Archaeological and Natural History Society*, Vol. 14, 1867; 'The Siege and Defence of Taunton, 1644–5', *Ibid*, Vol. 25, 1879

S.G. Harris, 'Notes on the History of Newton Abbot', *Transactions of the Devonshire Association*, Vol. 31, 1899

J. Hexter, 'The Problem of the Presbyterian Independents', *American Historical Review*, Vol. 44, 1938

F.A. Hyett, 'The Civil War in the Forest of Dean', *Transactions of the Bristol and Gloucestershire Archaeological Society*, Vol. 18, 1893–4

'Extracts from the MSS of Samuel Jeake', *Sussex Archaeological Collections*, Vol. 18, 1878

J.R. Jones, 'Booth's Rising', *Bulletin of the John Rylands Library*, Vol. 39, 1956–7

P. Laslett, 'The Gentry of Kent in 1640', *Cambridge Historical Journal*, Vol. 9, 1948

F.G. Mellersh, 'The Civil War in the Hundred of Godalming', *Surrey Archaeological Collections*, Vol. 61, 1964–5

P.R. Newman, 'The Royalist Officer Corps', *Historical Journal*, 1990

W. Notestein, 'The Establishment of the Committee of Both Kingdoms', *American Historical Review*, Vol. 17, 1911–12

V. Pearl, 'Oliver St. John and the "Middle Group" in the Long Parliament: August 1643–May 1644', *E.H.R.*, Vol. 81, 1966; 'The "Royal Independents" in the English Civil War', *Transactions of the Royal Historical Society*, Vol. 18, 1968

J.M. Prest, 'The Campaign of Roundway Down', *The Wiltshire Archaeological and Natural History Magazine*, Vol. 53, 1949–50

W.G. Ross, 'Military Engineering during the Great Civil War, 1642–9', *Papers of Royal Engineers*, Vol. 13, 1887

W.O. Scroggs, 'English Finances under the Long Parliament', *Quarterly Journal of Economics*, Vol. 21, Harvard University, 1907

M. Toynbee and J. Leeming, 'Cropredy Bridge', *Oxoniensa*, Vol. 3, 1938

J.W. Webb, *Memorials of the Civil War . . . as it affected Herefordshire*, 2 Vols, 1877

P. Young, 'The Royalist Army at the Battle of Roundway Down, 13 July, 1643', *J.S.A.H.R.*, Vol. 31, 1953

Index

Adwalton Moor, battle of 97
Allen, Martha 273
Alton, capture of by Waller 142–6
Appleyard, Col. Matthew 162, 164
Apsley, Col. Edward 177, 200
Archer, Lt. Elias 128, 130, 135, 139, 143
Arundel, Lord 78
Arundel castle: capture of by Waller ix, 44, 46; recovery by Royalists 140, 141; recapture by Waller 147–50
Ashe, John 77
Ashe, Simeon 103, 219
Astley, Sir Bernard 191, 212
Atkyns, Richard 87, 90–1; accounts of fighting 63–4, 83, 84, 85, 94

Baillie, Robert 142
Baines, Lt. Col. Jeremy 128, 190, 193, 194
Baker, Lt. Col. 194, 202
Balfour, Sir William 111, 157, 207, 219, 226; at Cheriton 159–60, 166, 167, 169, 170; at Second Newbury 212, 213
Barclay, Col. Harry 215, 230
Bard, Col. Henry 165, 166
Barnham, Sir Robert 273
Barrington, Capt. 264
Barrington, Sir Thomas 25
Basing House 52, 128, 142, 169; siege of 130–5, 138; second siege of 203–4, 205, 207, 209, 219–20
Bath 19, 75, 81, 87; Abbey 18
Batten, Vice-Admiral 247, 248
Baynton, Sir Edward 53, 90
Beauchamp, Lady 88
Behre, Commissary-Gen. Hans 176–7, 207
Bennet, Sir Humphrey 167, 212
Berkeley, Sir John 138, 229
Birch, Lt. Col. John 116, 123–4, 203; at Alton 142, 144, 145; at Arundel 148; at Cheriton 164, 167, 168, 170; at Cropredy Bridge 193
Bishop, Sir Edward 152
Bishop's War 22
Blayney, Capt. Thomas 67
Boles, Col. Richard 144, 145
Booth, Sir George, and Booth's Rising 263, 264
Bower, Capt. Robert 67
Braddock Down, battle of 51
Brandon, Lucy see Reynell, Lucy, Lady
Brereton, Sir William 73, 154, 182
Brett, Col. Jerome 58–9
Bristol 56, 67–8; capture of by Waller 55, 70; fall of 106, 108, 111, 112
The British Mercury 154
Brown, Robert, and Brownism 119, 124
Browne, Maj. Gen. Richard 41, 187, 203, 236, 246, 267; at

Cheriton 157, 158, 159, 171; after Cropredy Bridge 195, 197, 198, 199; as commander of City forces 259–60; coup in London 263, 264
Buckingham, George Villiers, 1st Duke of 17, 185
Buckner, James 67
Bulstrode, Sir Richard 232
Burghill, Col. Robert 59, 67, 73, 80–1, 84, 116
Bushell, Capt. Browne 34, 36
Butler, Capt. John 166, 190, 227, 228, 234, 243
Byron, Sir John 95, 109, 154, 218–19; account of Roundway Down 95, 96

Calamy, Edmund (pastor) 269
Carey, Col. Horatio 38, 45, 77, 78
Carisbrooke Castle 248
Carnarvon, Earl of 74, 81, 84
Carr, Col. James 78, 116, 142, 168, 170, 175
Carr, Col. William 97, 116, 122, 210
Cave, Col. Sir Richard 68, 69
Cawley, William 47, 138
Chalgrove Field, battle of 97, 154
Charles I, King: visits to Forde House 16, 24; at odds with Parliament 17, 25–6, 29–30; granting of Winchester Castle to Waller 20; territorial power 29, 31, 51; at Edgehill 38, 39; march to London 40; mercy shown towards prisoner 41; jest about Heselrige 94; pursuit of by Waller 177–80, 181–2, 183–4, 187–8, 197–9; flight from Oxford 180; at Cropredy Bridge 189–94; victory at Lostwithiel 201, 206; at Second Newbury 211–13, 216, 218–19; seizure of by New Model Army 245; imprisonment 248; negotiations with Parliament 248–9, 250; execution 251, 255, 265
Charles II, King 266, 267
Chepstow, capture of Dragon of Bristol 62
Cheriton: maps of campaign 155, 162; battle of 160–72, 175
Chichester, capture of by Waller 44–8
Chudleigh, Maj. James 69
Cirencester, capture of by Prince Rupert 51, 53, 58
Civil War: Waller's successes ix, x, 146; soldiers 8, 20, 25, 60; maps of England during 13, 28, 88, 102; Waller's abhorrence of 30; weapons 129, 143, see also place-names of battles
Clarendon, Earl of, comments: on Waller's choice of loyalties 23–4; on Goring 32; on Heselrige and

his 'lobsters' 54, 75; on Prince Maurice 62; on Hopton 74; on Essex 101, 115; on Alton 146; on Lord Robartes 185; on Cropredy Bridge 200; on Cromwell 242
Cleveland, Earl of 191, 213, 215
Clinton, Capt. 132
Clotworthy, Sir John 25, 242, 243, 244, 247, 250
Coe, Lt. Richard, account of pursuit of the King 178, 180
Committee of Both Kingdoms, establishment of 154–7
Committee of Militia 103, 106, 113, 120, see also London trained bands
Cooke, Capt. Edward 59, 69, 77
Cooke, Col. Edward 97, 98, 116, 227, 234
Cooke, Sir Robert 58, 59, 67, 72–3
Corbet, John, account of withdrawal to Tewkesbury 66
Courtenay, Sir William 257, 269
Cowling, Nicholas 138, 150
Cox, Thomas 273
Craddock, David 67
Crawford, Earl of 144, 145–6
Crewe, John 117, 181
Cromwell, Henry 260
Cromwell, Oliver x, 20, 39, 104, 118, 156, 170, 199, 228, 244, 254, 269; comparisons with Waller 5, 25, 117; comment on Waller's defeat at Roundway Down 98; victory at Marston Moor 196; at Second Newbury and aftermath 212, 213, 215, 216, 219, 220; and the Self-Denying Ordinance 221; service with Waller 226–7, 230–2; Waller's impressions of 228–9, 260; opposition to Waller 242; victory at Preston 248; death 262
Cromwell, Richard 262, 263
Cropredy Bridge, battle of 189–95, 200; map 192
Culpeper, Lord 232

Dacres, Lord 244
Denbigh, Earl of 177, 182, 183, 185
Denbigh Castle, Waller's imprisonment in 252–5, 270
Denham, Sir John 40, 41, 98
Devereux, Robert see Essex, Robert Devereux, 2nd Earl of
Devizes, Waller's advance to 87–8, 91
D'Ewes, Sir Simonds 95, 104, 110, 201
Digby, Lord; letter to Prince Rupert 186–7
Divine Meditations (Waller) 270–3
Donnington castle 202, 216, 218, 219, 220–1
Dorset, Thomas Sackville, Earl of 4, 5
Dover Castle 3, 4

Dowett, Maj. Francis 80, 83, 91, 112, 116, 122
Dragon of Bristol 62
Dudley castle, siege of 182, 183
Dury, John (Puritan divine) 25
Dyves, Sir Lewis 224, 227

Edgehill, battle of 38–40, 103
Eliot, Sir John 17
Elizabeth of Bohemia, Queen 8, 9, 10, 23, 248, 262
Erle, Sir Walter 54, 71
Essex, Robert Devereux, 2nd Earl of 25, 27, 29, 43, 45, 51, 68, 91, 103, 107, 110, 123, 127; as volunteer in Palatinate 8, 10; appointment as lord general 27, 29; at Edgehill 38, 39; capture of Reading 66; misunderstandings with Waller 69, 110, 200; resentment of Waller 95, 107, 109–10, 115, 121, 141–2, 184; peace overtures 96, 101, 110; unpopularity 101, 108, 122; relief of Gloucester 114, 115, 119; and first battle of Newbury 120; *rapprochement* with Waller 121–2; conflict with Parliament 154–6; on Cheriton victory 169–70; campaign against Oxford 175, 177, 178–9, 180; relief of Lyme 181, 184; defeat at Lostwithiel 201, 206, 207; illness 211; death and funeral 241
Essex, Col. Thomas 55, 56
Evelyn, John (diarist) 37
Evesham, Epiphanius (sculptor) 18
Experiences (Waller) 3, 6, 22, 45, 93, 111, 194, 228–9, 270–1

Fairfax, family 97, 154, 197
Fairfax, Sir Thomas 20, 186, 269; and New Model Army 221, 234, 244, 246–7
Falkland, Viscount 30
Fane, Sir Thomas 4
Farnham Castle: capture of by Waller 40, 44; as Waller's base 127, 128, 138
Ferdinand of Austria, Archduke 7
Fiennes, Capt. John 56, 59–60, 68, 71–2
Fiennes, Col. Nathaniel 27, 55, 56, 62, 67–8, 71, 97–8; court martial and defence 98, 108, 112
Finch, Lord 22
Finch, Anne, Lady *see* Waller, Anne, Lady (second wife)
Finch, Heneage 273
Finch, John (Lord Keeper) 20
Fincher, QMG Richard 171, 235, 243
FitzJames, Col. 206, 232, 235, 251
Fitzwilliam, Lord 273
Fleming, Capt John 139, 166
Ford, Col. Sir Edward 44, 147, 151, 152
Forde House 11, 12, 19, 269; visits of Charles I 16, 24
Fortescue, Sir Faithful 38, 39
Forth, Countess of 222
Forth, Gen. Patrick Ruthven, Earl

of 158, 160, 161, 162, 165, 166, 168, 169
Frederick, Elector Palatine 8

Gell, Sir John 182
Gerrard, Col. Charles 127, 129
Gerrard, Sir Gilbert 32, 156, 265
Giles, Capt. 229
Gloucester, relief of by Essex 106, 114, 115, 119
Glynn, John 27, 114
Goodwin, Arthur 41
Goring, Col. George 223, 226; and siege of Portsmouth 31–2, 33–5, 36–7; at Second Newbury 215; pursuit by Waller in the west 229–31; letter from Waller 231–2
Grandison, Lord 41–3, 44, 62, 65
Greene, John, diary entry 101
Grenvile, Sir Bevil 14, 15–16, 23, 25, 84, 85, 91
Grenvile, Sir Richard 225, 231
Gresham, Sir Thomas 259
Gustavus Adolphus, King of Sweden 38, 39, 142, 219

Hakluyt, Capt. Francis 123
Hamilton, Sir James 80
Hammond, Lt. Gen. Thomas 243
Hampden, John 22, 27, 43, 97, 154
Harcourt, Lady Anna *see* Waller, Lady Anna (third wife)
Harcourt, Frederick 269
Harcourt, Sir Philip 268
Harcourt, Sir Simon 257
Harcourt, Simon (grandson) 274
Harley, Lady Brilliana 201
Harley, Capt. Edward: account of Roundway Down 94, 96; account of Cheriton 159, 160, 162, 164, 168, 169
Harley, Col. Edward 175, 234, 252, 253
Harley, Col. Robert 116, 141, 267–8
Harley, Sir Robert 120, 252
Harrington, Maj.-Gen. Sir James 128, 177, 197
Harvey, Col. Edmund 176, 261
Haynes, John 67
Henrietta Maria, Queen 31, 32, 97, 109
Henrietta Maria (Royalist pinnace), seizure of 34
Henry of Nassau, Count 7
Herbert, Lord 59, 62
Hereford, capture of by Waller 68–9
Hertford, Marquess of 34, 71, 74, 78, 87, 88, 108, 109
Heselrige, Sir Arthur 8, 26, 53–4, 75, 97, 117, 118, 122, 123–4, 207, 216, 220, 237, 238; as commander 41, 47, 52, 67, 77, 86; and capture of Malmesbury 57; at Roundway Down 94, 111, 157; on Committee of Both Kingdoms 156, 184, 198; at Cheriton 164, 165–6, 170; reports on campaigns 179–80, 181–2
Highnam House 56, 58–9
Hillersdon, Maj. John 116

Historical Collections (Rushworth) 17
Holbourne, Maj. Gen. James 176, 195, 203, 220, 231, 234
Holland, Waller's exile in 247–8
Holles, Col. Denzil 27, 111, 156, 170, 220, 238, 247
Hopton, Sir Ralph 8–9, 10, 14, 17, 55, 91, 127, 135–6; as friend of Waller 14, 23, 266; at Braddock Down 51; victory at Stratton 71; Clarendon's comments on 74, 146; letter from Waller 78–9, 248; at Lansdown 81, 83, 87; at Roundway Down 90, 93; recapture of Winchester 129–30; attack on by Waller near Farnham 138–40; at Alton 143–4, 146; letter to Waller after Alton 145; at Arundel 147, 150; at Cheriton 157, 158–9, 160, 161–4, 166, 168, 169; exile in Holland 248
Howard, Henry *see* Northampton, Henry Howard, Earl of
Hungerford, Sir Edward 53, 58, 71–2, 78; *Vindication* 60–1

Ireland and Irish rebels 26, 241–2, 243
Ireton, Henry 226, 243–4, 245, 250

Jackson, Sir John 22
James I, King 8, 11
Jones, Col. Samuel 128, 129
Joyce, George 244

Knyvett, Thomas 101

Lambert, Col. John 244
Lansdown, battle of 81–6, 87; maps **76, 82**
Laud, Archbishop William 22
Leighton, Col. 64, 162, 164
Lely, Sir Peter, portrait of Waller 267
Lennard, Margaret *see* Waller, Margaret (mother)
Lenthall, Speaker 119
Leven, Alexander Leslie, Earl of 154–6, 170
Lewis, Sir William 37, 247
Lilburne, Col. John 123, 233, 243
Lisle, Col. George 161, 168
Livesay, Sir Michael 138, 199, 203, 234
Lloyd, Sir Charles 228
'Lobsters' (cuirassiers) 75–7, 83, 84, 94, 124, 129, 234
London trained bands; Green Auxiliaries 128; Westminster Liberty (Red) Regiment 128, 134, 144; Yellow Auxiliaries 128; Southwark White Auxiliaries 177, 197; Tower Hamlets Regiment 177, 193; Westminster Auxiliaries 177, *see also* Committee of Militia
Long, Col. Sir James 227, 228
Long, Walter 247
Lostwithiel, battle of 201, 206
Ludlow, Capt. Edmund 54, 111, 221
Ludlow, Col. 205–6, 219

Index

Luke, Sir Samuel 108, 109–10
Lunsford, Lt. Col. Herbert 58, 78
Lyme Regis, relief of 175, 181, 184, 187

Malmesbury 53; capture of by Waller 56–8; reoccupation by Prince Rupert 60, 61
Manchester, Edward Montague, Earl of 103, 119, 123, 157, 186, 197, 267; at Second Newbury and aftermath 212, 213, 216, 218, 221
Mansfeldt, Count 8, 17
Marlborough 53, 208; capture of by Waller 41
Marshall, Capt. Thomas 195
Marston Moor; battle of 196–7
Marten, Col. Henry 27, 104, 113–14, 118, 235
Marvell, Andrew (poet) 241
Massey, Col. Edward 98, 106, 182, 206, 234, 244, 246, 267; in the western campaign 56, 58, 59, 64, 122; imprisonment 250
Maurice, Prince of Bohemia 10, 62–5, 71, 74, 154, 175, 198; at Ripple Field 65–6; at Lansdown 81, 84; at Roundway Down 90, 93; at Second Newbury 213
Meldrum, Sir John 34, 37
Mercurius Aulicus: on Waller and his army 52, 55, 56, 61, 124, 156, 203, 224; on Covenant with Scotland 118; publication of letter to London soldier 133; on Cheriton 162; on armoured vehicles 194; on Col. Wemyss 195; attacks on Waller and Lady Anne 235–6
Mercurius Britanicus 139
Merrick, Sir John 27, 178
Middleton, Lt. Gen. John 176, 190, 201, 207, 215, 226, 234
Milton, John (poet) 117
Mompesson, Sir Giles 8
Monck, Gen. George 265, 266
Montague, Edward *see* Manchester, Edward Montague, Earl of
Mordaunt, John 262–4, 264–5
Mosse, Mr 58

Naseby, battle of 241
New Model Army 221–2, 234–5, 241–2, 244–7
Newbury, battle of 16, 120, 127, 154
Newbury, second battle 175, 211–16, 217; map **214**; aftermath 218, 220–1
Newcastle, Earl of 29, 97
Newport, Treaty of 262
Newport Pagnell 123, 127
Nicholl, Anthony 113, 114
Northampton, Henry Howard, Earl of 4, 15
Norton, Col. Richard 33, 36, 166, 203

Ogle, Sir William 41, 42, 127
Onslow, Sir Richard 51, 265
Ormonde, Marquess of 260
Osterley Park 259, 272, 274
Oxford, Earl of 10

Oxford, Essex's campaign against 175–80
Oxford University 5, 6

Paddy, Sir William 6
Palatinate wars 8, 9–10
Parliament: in conflict with Charles I 17, 25–6, 29–30; the 'Long' 22–3, 54; the 'Short' 22; and the Grand Remonstrance 25–6; forming of Committee of Safety 29; Independents 101, 118, 119, 121, 122, 233; 'vehements' and 'moderates' 101, 114, 118; and Self-Denying Ordinance 221, 232; in conflict with army 232, 244–7; negotiations with Charles I 248–9, 250; restoration of Rump 262, 265
The Parliamentary Scout 176
Pennington, Isaac 101, 106
Penruddock's Rising 260
Pepys, Samuel 265–6
Percival, Sir Philip 242
Peyton, Sir Edward 7
Pierrepoint, William 27
Popham, Col. Alexander 71, 72, 74, 96, 97, 116
Portsmouth, siege of 32–7
Potley, Maj. Gen. Andrew 141, 180, 195
Powderham Castle 269
Presbyterians 118, 248–9, 250, 262–3
Preston, battle of 248
Pride, Col. Thomas 243, 250
Prynne, William 22, 112, 265–7
Puritanism 23, 25, 104
Pym, John 27, 54–5; as leader of opposition to the king 22, 25–6; as leader of 'vehements' 101, 104, 105–6, 113, 114, 118; death 154

Ramsey, Lt. Col. 116
Ramsey, Sir James 38
Rawdon, Col. Marmaduke 130–1
Reading 51, 211; surrender to Essex 66, 69
The Remonstrance 109, 110, 111–12, 250
Reynell, Edward; memoir of Lucy Reynell 11–12, 14, 19
Reynell, Jane *see* Waller, Jane (first wife)
Reynell, Lucy, Lady 11–14, 15, 19–20, 21, 253
Reynell, Sir Richard 11, 16, 19
Reynell, Sir Thomas 24
Rich, Sir Charles 17
Rich, Sir Nathaniel 25, 243
Ripple Field, battle of 65–6, 67, 83
Robartes, Lord 175, 184–5, 208, 225
Roe, Secretary: account of Arundel 148, 149; account of Cheriton 164, 168, 169
Rossiter, Sir Edward 244
Roundway Down, battle of 88–97, 154, 201; map **92**
Royalist conspiracies 259, 262, 263
Rupert, Prince 10, 52, 55, 98, 109, 182, 199, 218; at Edgehill 38, 39;

capture of Cirencester and raid on Alton 51; reoccupation of Malmesbury 60, 61; at Chalgrove Field 97; relief of Newark 161; defeat at Marston Moor 196, 198
Rushworth, John, *Historical Collections* 17
Ruthven, Gen. Patrick *see* Forth, Gen. Patrick Ruthven, Earl of

Sackville, Thomas *see* Dorset, Thomas Sackville, Earl of
St James's Palace, Waller's imprisonment in 251, 252, 255–6
St John, Oliver 25, 117, 156, 229
Salisbury 209; Waller's entry into 53
Salter, Lord 133
Salway, Richard 243
Sandys, Col. William 72
Scotland and Scots 22, 154, 248; support of moderates 101, 106; Waller's admiration for 116–17, *see also* Solemn League and Covenant
Scots Treaty 27
The Scottish Dove 166
Skippon, Maj. Gen. Philip 113, 176, 206, 212, 218, 219, 226
Slanning, Sir Nicholas 84
Sleamaker, James 195
Slingsby, Lt. Col., reports: of Lansdown 81, 83, 84, 85–6; of Roundway Down 91, 95; of Cheriton 158, 166, 167, 168
Smith, Maj.-Gen. Sir John 42, 159, 161, 168
Solemn League and Covenant 118, 121, 177
Somerset, Sir John 58
Sourton Down, battle of 69
Southsea Castle 31, 36–7
Stamford, Earl of 51, 55, 56, 71
Stapleton, Sir Philip 27, 43, 105, 156, 247
Stewart, Lord John 166, 168
Stowell, Sir Edward 139, 166
Strachan, Maj. Archibald 52, 120, 134, 168, 175
Strafford, Earl of 22, 23
Strangeways, Sir John 54
Sudeley castle, capture of 182–3
Symonds, Richard, accounts of battles 189, 215

Taunton, relief of 234
Tewkesbury 182; Waller's occupation of 59–60, 65, 66
Thurloe, John 259, 260, 263
Tilly, Count 9–10
Trenchard, John 119, 120
The True Informer 142–3
Twistleton, Col. George 253

Urry, Maj. Alexander 175
Urry, Sir. John 32, 33, 36, 37, 41, 43, 211

Vandruske, Commissary Gen. Jonas 97, 116, 139
Vane, Sir Henry (jr) 110, 117, 156
Vane, Sir Henry (sr) 43, 114, 156

Veale, Martha 273
Vere, Sir Horace 7, 8, 9
Vernon, Henry 23
Vicars, John 55
Vindication (Hungerford) 60–1
Vindication (Waller) 5, 15, 116, 237, 246, 253–5, 269, 271, 274

Walker, Clement 112
Walker, Sir Edward, accounts: of Cheriton 172; of march to Banbury 188; of Cropredy Bridge 190, 194, 198, 200; of Second Newbury 211–12, 213, 215
Walker, Robert; portrait of Waller ii, x
Waller, Alured de 3
Waller, Lady Anna (third wife) 257, 260, 264, 267, 268; death and funeral 269
Waller, Lady Anne (second wife) ix, 20, 21, 88, 108, 153, 251; satirical attacks on 235–6; exile in Holland 247–8; Waller's tribute to 252–3; death 256
Waller, Anne (daughter) 257, 268, 269
Waller, Dorothy (daughter) 257
Waller, Edmund (poet) 4, 18–19, 121, 175
Waller, Fenes (sister) 5, 6, 22
Waller, Sir George (uncle) 4
Waller, Sir Hardress (cousin) 4, 226, 227, 228, 234, 242, 250, 266
Waller, Jane (first wife) 11, 12, 18; death 18; tomb and effigy 18–19
Waller, Katherine (daughter) 269
Waller, Margaret (daughter) 18, 19, 20, 222, 257, 269, 271
Waller, Margaret (mother) 5
Waller, Moll (daughter) 257, 269
Waller, Sir Richard (of Kent) 3
Waller, Richard (son) 18, 19
Waller, Richard (grandson) 269
Waller, Sir Thomas (father) 3, 4–5, 5–6
Waller, Thomas (son) 257, 267–8, 274
Waller, Sir Walter (brother) 5, 17–18
Waller, Walter (son) 269
Waller, Sir William: analysis of career ix–x; appearance x; nicknames ix, 48, 70; portraits of ii, x, 267, 269; verses in praise of ix, 153; early life, education and travel 3, 5–8; comparisons with Cromwell 5, 25, 117; service in the Palatinate 8–10; knighthood of 11; marriages 11, 20, 257; residence in Devon 11–18; gift of Winchester Castle to 20–2; failure to enter Long Parliament 22–3; support for Parliamentarians 23–5; reasons for opposition to the King 24,

25; entry into Parliament 26; entry into Parliamentary army 27; election to Committee of Safety 29; abhorrence of Civil War 30; and siege of Portsmouth 32–7; and battle of Edgehill 38–40; capture of Farnham Castle 40; capture of Marl-borough 41; capture of Winchester 41–3; capture of Chichester 44–8; appointment as major general 51; advance to the west 52–3; entry into Salisbury 53; capture of Bristol 55; capture of Malmesbury 56–8; Severn Valley campaign 56–66; capture of Highnam House 58–9; attack on Prince Maurice 62–5; at battle of Ripple Field 65–6; capture of Hereford 68–9; misunderstandings with Essex 69, 118; attempt on Worcester 72–3; entry into Bath 74; letter to Hopton 78–9, 248; at battle of Lansdown 81–6; compassion towards prisoner 87; pursuit of Royalists to Devizes 87–8; defeat at Roundway Down 88–97; back in London 98, 104–15; effect of Roundway Down 103, 104, 108, 112–13, 124; commissions from Par-liament 104–6, 121, 124; promotion blocked by Essex 105; political struggle with Essex 108; commission from Essex 113–15, 121; opinion of Scots 116–17, 248; organisation of new army 116–18, 119–20, 122; placed under Essex's command 121; at Farnham Castle 127, 128; attempt on Basing House 130–5; attack on Hopton near Farnham 138–9; capture of Alton 142–6; recapture of Arundel castle 147–50; and Cheriton campaign 154–72; as member of Comm-ittee of Both Kingdoms 156–7, 238; and Essex's Oxford campaign 175–80; preventing of Edmund Waller's execution 175; pursuit of King's army 177–80, 181–2, 183–4, 187–8, 197–9; capture of Sudeley castle 182–3; defeat at Cropredy Bridge 189–95, 200; blame for Lostwithiel 201; joining with forces of Essex and Manchester 209, 210; at Second Newbury and aftermath 212–16, 217, 219, 220; as commander-in-chief of western forces 223–5; service with Cromwell 226–7, 230–2; capture of Royalist regiment 228; impressions of Cromwell 228–9, 260; pursuit of Goring in the west 229–32; letter to

Goring 231–2; obeys Self-Denying Ordinance 232; caricaturing of 236; shortage of money 237–8; made a baron 238; offer of service to Venice 238; at Essex's funeral 241; support for Parliament against army 244; exile in Holland 247–8; return to Parliament 249, 250; imprisonment 250–6, 264; letters from prison 252–3; tribute to Lady Anne 252–3; views on Church 253–4; writing of *Vindication* 253–5; views on monarchy 254–5; love for Parliament 255; spiritual dedication 255, 257–9; release from prison 256, 264; involvement in Royalist conspiracy 259; purchase of Osterley House 259; interr-ogation by Cromwell 260; commitment to the Restoration 262–3; letter to Col. Harley 267–8; retirement from public life 267; writing of *Divine Meditations* 270–3; last will and testament 273–4; death and burial 274
Waller, William (of Hampshire) 4, 21
Waller, William (son) 257, 267, 274
Wardour Castle 78, 111, 127
Warrenne, John de 257
Warwick, Earl of 25, 33, 244, 247
Weldon, Col. Ralph 207–8, 234
Weldon, Maj. Anthony 165
Wemyss, Col. James 116, 131, 142–3, 170, 193, 194, 195
Wemyss Castle 143
Wentworth, Lord 32, 34, 35
Whalley, Lt. Col. Edward 232
Wharton, Nathaniel 68
White Mountain, battle of 9–10
Willis, Sir Richard 42
Willoughby, Lord 259
Wilmot, Lord 91, 93, 95, 191
Winchester, Marquess of 130, 131
Winchester: Castle 20, 21, 42, 238; capture of by Waller 41–3, 44, 47; recapture by Royalists 127, 129–30; Waller's march to 129–30; storming of by Heselrige 171
Windebanke, Sir Francis 22
Windsor Castle, Waller's imprison-ment in 251–2, 269
Wither, Capt. George 40, 41
Wolborough (Devon), church 11, 19
Wood, Maj. Edward 196
Worcester, Marquess of 29, 59, 62
Worcester: Waller's attempt on 72–3; battle of 255
Wotton, Sir Henry; poem to Elizabeth of Bohemia 9